Ka Po'e Mo'o Akua

Ka Poʻe Moʻo Akua
Hawaiian Reptilian Water Deities

Marie Alohalani Brown

University of Hawaiʻi Press
Honolulu

27 26 25 24 23 22   6 5 4 3 2 1

Library of Congress Cataloging-in-Publication Data

Names: Brown, Marie Alohalani, author.
Title: Ka poʻe moʻo akua = Hawaiian reptilian water deities / Marie
  Alohalani Brown.
Other titles: Hawaiian reptilian water deities
Description: Honolulu : University of Hawaiʻi Press, 2022. I Includes
  bibliographical references and index.
Identifiers: LCCN 2021028039 I ISBN 9780824889944 (hardback) I ISBN
  9780824889951 (paperback) I ISBN 9780824891091 (adobe pdf) I ISBN
  9780824891107 (epub) I ISBN 9780824891114 (kindle edition)
Subjects: LCSH: Moʻo (Hawaiian deities)
Classification: LCC BL2620.H3 B76 2022 I DDC 299/.92420212—dc23
LC record available at https://lccn.loc.gov/2021028039

Cover art: *Moʻo Wahine,* by Jason Makaneʻole.

For ka po'e mo'o akua and their descendants.

For everyone who loves mo'o.

For everyone who has mo'o-like qualities—beautiful, brilliant, bold, sassy, seductive, kolohe.

E ola!

P.S. E ola nō ho'i Pele mā and their descendants, even though most of you can't stand mo'o—you're still family.

Figure 0.1. Moʻo wahine. Artwork by Jelena Clay.

Mo'o Wahine

Mirage of femininity,
Rain-darkened earth-colored skin
Covers 'alā stone muscles.
Hidden recesses beckon and promise,
A shadowy cave, moist dark-green moss,
Her scent stagnates and inundates the senses.
Beside a deep pool of dark water,
She combs her black waterfall hair that
Swirls in eddies around her breasts and
Ends in a whirlpool between her thighs.
From a throne of cold wet stone,
Obsidian eyes follow her prey.
A flickering tongue
Sibilates soul-deadening songs
Sucking men into a sensual abyss
From which they cannot escape.
Masculine essence morphs in her swollen belly.
Phrenic eunuchs, emasculated of their reason,
Decompose in watery depths.
Mo'o nurses the creature of her womb
Delights her she-lizard child
With the rattling of its human sire's bones.

—Marie Alohalani Brown

Contents

Preface

UNLESS INDICATED OTHERWISE, all translations are mine. Translations, no matter how persuasive, can never fully capture the cultural nuances, poetics, and beauty of the original Hawaiian-language texts. All too often, problematic English-language translations of Hawaiian source materials have been deemed adequate replacements or even superior to the originals. For this reason, I generally offer extended passages first in ʻōlelo Hawaiʻi (Hawaiian language) followed by translations to honor the language in which our ancestors composed their artistic-intellectual works and for those who can access ʻōlelo Hawaiʻi. This approach, while valuable, has greatly lengthened the book, and thus in some cases, I offer only my translation or translative summary.

When writing primarily in one language, it is customary to treat phrases and words from other languages as foreign even when the writer may be bilingual, trilingual, or polyglot. I do not follow this protocol for ʻōlelo Hawaiʻi. Although this book is primarily in English, it is about nā mea Hawaiʻi (things Hawaiian) and is written by an ʻŌiwi (Hawaiian). Consequently, I do not italicize Hawaiian words unless they are italicized in the quoted material (any emphasis I add is noted).

Modern Hawaiian-language diacritics include the kahakō (macron) and the ʻokina (glottal stop). Nineteenth- and twentieth-century Hawaiian-language newspaper contributors rarely used diacritics, but when they did, they used either a dash before a vowel to indicate a macron (e.g., Luhi–a for Luhiā) or an apostrophe to mark a glottal stop (e.g., ka'u for kaʻu). Tahitians, past and present, use an apostrophe to indicate a glottal stop, and therefore I do as well when I discuss their lizard deities. When quoting Hawaiian-language sources, I replicate their diacritics, and if there are none, I do not add them. However, I do add modern diacritics to my translations of those passages. That said, I add diacritics only when the intended meaning of a word or name is evident by the context in which it is being used. Hawaiian names have meanings, and the use of diacritics fixes a single meaning rather than allowing the possibility of several. In this case, I follow Noenoe K. Silva's example: "For names of persons, I conservatively avoid using marks, except in cases where such spelling has become standard (e.g., Kalākaua) or where the meaning of the name has been explained or is obvious."[1]

Although I may add diacritics to the names of newspaper contributors in my own discussion (e.g., Hoʻoulumāhiehie), when citing them I write their names as they originally appeared (e.g., Hooulumahiehie). When someone is known for not spelling their name with diacritics (e.g., Mary Kawena Pukui), I respect that decision. I rarely translate deities' names. In the case of deities with very long names, I may add hyphens for readability when I first cite them, as our kūpuna sometimes did.

Hawaiian Terms

WHEN HAWAIIAN TERMS are culturally dense, such as those referencing institutions and kinship connections, I prefer to use ʻōlelo Hawaiʻi for these reasons: because they do not have a direct correlation in English, because the closest English term has a negative connotation that is absent in the Hawaiian, or because they require a long explanation. That said, my explanations of these terms are by no means exhaustive.

ahupuaʻa. A land division that typically runs from the mountain to the sea and contains at least one significant water source.

akua. While "akua" is commonly translated into English as "deity" (which is how I use it), Western and Hawaiian ideas of what constitutes a "deity" differ greatly. The following fall under the category of "akua": a deity, a spirit, mana, strength, knowledge, things without a source, a ruling aliʻi, a corpse, a ghost, a kauā (outcast of the despised class), a devil.[1] While "akua" does denote "deity," it is important to note that not all akua were actively worshipped. The term has more to do with the more than human. Our akua are nature deities. They are the elements, natural phenomena, flora, fauna, and geographic features that characterize our island world: the sun is Kāne, the ocean is Kanaloa, the lava is Pele, the earth is Papa/Haumea, the sky's wide expanse is Wākea, and so on. Moreover, while some akua manifest as human, unlike the Christian God it is not their primary form.

aliʻi. Often translated in English using the male-gender-inflected "chief," this is a gender-neutral term referring to ʻŌiwi of the ruling class, whether they rule or not. Members of this class were further distinguished according to rank, which was ultimately based on genealogy. Noted nineteenth-century historians of nā mea Hawaiʻi Davida Malo and Samuel M. Kamakau offer their classifications, the former ten and the latter seven, and although they differ, both place the offspring of brother-sister unions at the top of the hierarchy.[2]

heiau. A large stone structure or enclosure where akua are worshipped.

Hoʻomana and mana. "Hoʻomana" is often glossed as "religion" or "to worship," and while these definitions are not technically incorrect, neither are they perfect equivalents. What contitutes "religion" and "worship" according to Hawaiian religious traditions differs substantially from Western ideas about the same, which are often Christian-centric. "Hoʻomana" means to generate, bestow, increase mana: "hoʻo" expresses causation, to make something happen or to bring something into being, while "mana" is broadly related to power, although "power" is inadequate to capture fully the nuances of this complex concept. To begin, mana has other-than-human origins; Pukui has variously described it as "supernatural," "spiritual," "divine," or "power."[3] Because everything in nature comes into existence with some degree of mana, it is reasonable to describe mana as an entity in its own right. By "entity," I mean "a thing with distinct and independent existence."[4] Mana is a capacity, a potential to effect positive or negative change; it can be spiritual, intellectual, or physical; it powers and empowers; it is intangible but has tangible manifestations; it can be embedded in or transferred to something else; it is intrinsic but can be increased or diminished; and it grants authority and defines status.[5]

Based on the core meaning of "hoʻomana," we can infer that worshipping a deity sustains, imparts, or increases the mana of said deity. Kamakau supports this inference in his 1870 series on Hawaiian history in which he explains that kahuna noticed that the spirits of the deceased whose bones were offered to akua gained mana from this ritual and, in turn, became akua in their own right.[6] Hoʻomana is a religious system in its own right, and thus I capitalize it to accord it the same respect granted to other "world religions," such as Hinduism, Catholicism, Buddhism, Shinto, and Voodoo—all of which are descriptors like Hoʻomana. In my past works, I added "Hawaiʻi" to "Hoʻomana," gave an in-depth explanation like the one I offer here, and then glossed it as "Hawaiian religion," which I now realize inadvertently eclipsed the points I argued. There are 15,459 instances of "hoomana" in the Papakilo Database newspapers. Contributors' use of lower or upper case differs; some use "hoomana," some use "Hoomana," and others alternate between the two depending on whether they use it as a verb (i.e., to worship) or as a noun, and in the latter case, they sometimes capitalize it. Approaches to capitalization in the body of articles (not titles) include: Hoomana

Kalawina (Calvinism), Hoomana (used as a collective noun to de-note religion), Hoomana Moremona (Mormonism), Hoomana Budisa Mongolia (Mongolian Buddhism), hoomana Kahiko (Ancient religion), hoomana Kakolika (Catholicism), hoomana Kalawina (Calvinism), hoomana Pegana o Hawaii (Pagan religion of Hawaiʻi), and hoomana kahiko (ancient religion). In short, it comes down to whether we understand "hoomana" to mean "religion" generally or a specific religious tradition belonging to Hawaiians—and the latter is how I understand it, in which case it makes sense to capitalize it. This is a decolonial approach to religious studies—one I also use to treat moʻo akua.

kahuna. An expert in a profession who performs religious rites for said profession.

kamaʻāina. This term translates as "child [of the] land" and is used for those who either grew up in a place or lived there for a long time—long enough to know it very well.

kāne and wahine. "Kāne" refers to a man, male, or male romantic partner. "Wahine" (plural, wāhine) refers to a woman, female, or female romantic partner. Because our ancestors did not have anything like the Western institution of marriage, the Western concepts of "husband" and "wife" do not accurately capture the many nuances of "kāne" and "wahine" according to a traditional understanding of the term in connection with the idea of "romantic" partner. Although the union known as "hoʻao" is often translated as "marriage," Pukui offers that it probably meant "to stay until daylight" since "ao" refers to "day" or "daylight."[7] Thus, we should understand "hoʻao" not as "marriage" but as an acknowledged union or a question of habit and intent. However, after the introduction of Christianity, ʻŌiwi did formalize unions through the Christian rite of marriage. That "hoʻao" was not a Hawaiian equivalent to the Christian marriage is clear by the use of "male" (ma-lay) or "mare" (ma-ray), a transliteration of "marry" or "married," in marriage announcements rather than "hoʻao" in Hawaiian-language newspapers.

kupua. Supernaturals; humans with extraordinary powers or abilities; things with special powers. "Kupua" is most often used for beings who can take different forms, some of whom may have a human mother but were born in a nonhuman form, such as Kamapuaʻa, who was born as a pig. Occasionally, the term is also used for entities usually referenced elsewhere as akua, such as moʻo and major akua like Uli, Haumea, Kāmehaʻikana, Pele, Kāne, and Kanaloa.[8]

luakini. A type of heiau primarily used for religious ceremonies connected to war and politics but that could also be used for agriculture-related rites.

muliwai. A river, a river mouth, a pool in a stream, or the place where a freshwater course pools before a sandbar. It is not always possible from the Hawaiian to know to which it refers.

ʻŌiwi. An identity marker or descriptor Hawaiians use for themselves, along with Kanaka, Kanaka Hawaiʻi, Kanaka Maoli, and Kanaka ʻŌiwi.[9]

ʻōlelo noʻeau. Poetic sayings that can be didactic and/or commemorative.

The Hawaiian Islands and Nā ʻĀina Akua

Hawaiian Islands. Because I continually reference different Hawaiian Islands, readers who are unfamiliar with them should know that there are eight main islands: Niʻihau, Kauaʻi, Oʻahu, Molokaʻi, Lānaʻi, Kahoʻolawe, Maui, and Hawaiʻi. "Hawaiʻi" refers both to the island of Hawaiʻi and the Hawaiian Islands. To avoid confusion, I use "Hawaiʻi" solely for "island of Hawaiʻi." Otherwise, I refer to the eight islands collectively as the "Hawaiian Islands" or "the islands." Islets, such as Kaʻula, Lehua and Nīhoa (Niʻihau), Mokoliʻi (Oʻahu), and Molokini (Maui and Kahoʻolawe), are found here and there near different islands. The Hawaiian Islands are part of a greater archipelago that includes the Northwestern Hawaiian Islands (NWHI). At twelve hundred nautical miles, a map of NWHI superimposed upon the continental United States "would cover a distance equal to that between New York City and Omaha, or Boston and the Florida Everglades."[10]

Nā ʻĀina Akua. Among the places that moʻo dwell are ʻāina akua, which include Kānehūnāmoku, Kuaihelani, Nuʻumealani, Kalānuike-ʻeakāne, and Paliuli. Explanations about these places vary greatly.[11] Hoʻoulumāhiehie notes, "O keia aina o Kanehunamoku ma keia moolelo, oia o Nuumealani. He mokupuni kakaa wale iho no keia iluna o ka ili o ke kai" (This land Kānehūnāmoku in this account is Nuʻumealani. This is an island that revolves on the surface of the sea). Hoʻoulumāhiehie adds, "Oia hoi o Kuaihelani, a o Ulu-kaa hoi ma kahi olelo ana" (which is Kuaihelani, and ʻUlukaʻa some say), and "o Kanehunamoku, oia hoi o Kuaihelani, a o Ualakaa hoi ma kekahi olelo ana. O kekahi inoa o keia aina o

Ulupa'upa'u, ka aina o ka A-ai-anuhe-nui-a-Kane." (Kānehūnāmoku is also Kuaihelani, and 'Ualaka'a too some say. Another name for this land is Ulupa'upa'u, the land of the 'A'ai'anuhenuiaKāne.)[12] For others, Kānehūnāmoku, Kuaihelani, and Nu'umealani exist together in the sky.[13] W. S. Lokai and J. S. Kamoe also understand Kuaihelani as an island in the sky: "O ka aina o Kuaihelani ko laua [Kane and Kanaloa] wahi noho, he aina oia i ka lewa o Tahiti" (The land of Kuaihelani is their [Kāne and Kanaloa] home, an island in the sky of Tahiti).[14]

Kamakau states that Kuaihelani is an actual place found in Kahiki (Tahiti or a foreign land) and that, according to one source, to sail there from the Hawaiian Islands "ma ke Komohana o Niihau ka holo ana i Kuaihelani" (go West of Ni'ihau to sail to Kuaihelani).[15] An editorial states that Kuaihelani and Nu'umealani are islands that are not very distant from Kaua'i:

O Kuaihelani ka mokupuni kokoke loa ia Kauai, no ka mea ua hoike mai keia mau moolelo kahiko, he ekolu la hele ma na auwaa ahiki i Kuaihelani mai Kauai aku. A mai Kuaihelani ahiki i Nuumealani, he ehiku la; a oia hoi he umi la mai Kauai aku.[16]

Kuaihelani is the island very close to Kaua'i, because these ancient accounts show that it takes a canoe fleet three days to reach Kuaihelani from Kaua'i. And from Kuaihelani to Nu'umealani, it takes seven days; which is ten days from Kaua'i.

Kalāke'enuiakāne is, according to Kaunamano, "o Asia ma ka olelo haole" (Asia in English).[17] Ho'oulumāhiehie gives a different explanation:

O Ka-Lakee-Nui-a-Kane, wahi a ka poe kahiko, a i hoomaopopoia hoi e lakou, e like me ka lakou ike, a pela hoi me ka ike a me ka hoomaopopo ana a na makua a me na kupuna o lakou, oia ka aina puni ole o Amerika i keia wa; e hele ana mai ka akau a i ka hema.[18]

Kalāke'enuiakāne, according to the people of old, as they understood and knew it, and as the parents and their grandparents also knew and understood, is the continent known as America at this time; going from the north to the south.

As for Paliuli, it "is a mythical place in the mountain region back of the Pana'ewa forest, Hawai'i" in the area known as 'Ōla'a in the district of Hilo.[19] In one version of the Hi'iakaikapoliopele tradition, Paliuli is poetically referred to as the hidden land of Kāne.[20]

PART I

'Ike no ka Po'e Mo'o Akua, Knowledge about Mo'o Deities

Introduction

K a Po'e Mo'o Akua: Hawaiian Reptilian Water Deities is about the fearsome and fascinating Hawaiian gods known as mo'o who embody the life-giving and death-dealing properties of water, the element with which they are associated. Mo'o are not ocean dwellers. Instead, they live primarily in or near bodies of fresh water. As a class of deities, they vary greatly in size—as huge as a mountain or as tiny as a house gecko. Many mo'o have alternate forms. Predominately female, those mo'o who masquerade as humans are often described as stunningly beautiful. Tradition holds that when you come across a body of fresh water in a secluded area and everything is eerily still, you should not linger for you have stumbled across the home of a mo'o. When the plants are yellowed and the water covered with a greenish-yellow froth, the mo'o is at home. If so, you should leave quickly lest the mo'o make itself known to you, to your detriment. It might eat ('ai) you or take you as a lover (ai, "to have sex")—either way, you are doomed because it will consume you completely.

World Religions and Reptiles: Placing Mo'o Akua into a Global Context

Reptiles are a global phenomenon—snakes, crocodiles, alligators, and lizards are found in most parts of the world. Revered or reviled, across place and time they have held and continue to hold a prominent place in the religions or cultures of many peoples. Whether land or water dwellers, or a bit of both, they have slithered, glided, crawled, and climbed their way through the human imagination and into many belief systems. Here, I offer a sampling of supernatural reptiles from around the world with the exception of those in Polynesia, which I treat in the next section. I do not exhaust the topic of reptilian entities around the world or in Polynesia nor do I attempt to give examples for every cultural group. The purpose of this partial overview is to provide the elementary context by which readers will be able to, after reading this book, recognize that mo'o akua are not a cultural anomaly and that although mo'o are uniquely Hawaiian, they share certain features with reptilian beings elsewhere in the world.

Collectively, supernatural reptiles may be entirely reptilian, humanoid, or composite creatures; may possess multiple forms; or may have been human before their reptilian transfiguration or born as a reptile from a human mother. Chinese mythology abounds with snake or snakelike dragon beings who might appear as human above and serpentine below.[1] Sobek of Shedet, who rose to prominence in the Egyptian pantheon as its premier crocodile deity, is depicted alternatively "as a crocodile or a man with the head of a crocodile wearing an *atef* crown."[2] Aapep, an Egyptian "moon-serpent," was variously depicted "as a snake with a human head, as a contorted crocodile, or in the more familiar form as the vast cosmic reptile."[3] Naga (snake beings), present in the cultural-religious traditions of Buddhism, Hinduism, and Jainism, appear as huge snakes, humans with a serpent lower body, or entirely human.[4] A recurring figure in Hindu mythology and temple iconography is the makara, whose "acknowledged prototype is the crocodile."[5] The Maya visualize their reptilian deity as a "creature that incorporates elements of the heads, bodies, and appendages of snakes, lizards, iguanas, and alligators and/or caimans."[6] Quetzalcoatl of the Aztecs takes the form of a human or a feathered serpent. The Bamana of Mali in Africa honor Faro, an androgynous reptilian water deity whose "physical characteristics include a white feminine face, long, smooth black hair, black eyes, no external ears, a body surface equally covered by skin and copper, and a webbed tail." He can manifest as a crocodile, as an iguana, and also as "beautiful women who enter villages for the purpose of seducing young boys."[7] In Trinidad and Tobago, the transnational African deity Mami Wata (Mother Water) has a beautiful human form but can appear "as an anaconda from the hips down."[8] The African rainbow serpent, Dañh-sio (also Dañhgbi), appears as a rainbow or a gigantic python.[9] An example of a snake spirit born of a human mother is Bunosi, whom the Solomon Islanders of Lavelai honor as a minor creation deity.[10]

Whether major or minor divinities, demigods, or monsters, supernatural reptiles have held diverse cultural-religious roles. As cosmic influences they may represent order or chaos, and their behavior or actions may create, preserve, or destroy the world. As creator deities they may be the origin of the sky, weather phenomena, the earth, geographic features, humans, animals, or plants. In Norse mythology, the colossal Midgard Serpent, Jörmungandr, lies curled around the earth in the ocean. A prophecy about the Norse gods' destiny, which concerns catastrophic events that will lead to some of their deaths, says Jörmungandr will emerge from the sea, flooding the land, and spew its venom about.[11] For the Petén Maya, the reptilian Itzamna are "supports for the sky," its "ceiling," and the earth's "floor."[12] For the Aztec, the sky and the earth are the upper and lower halves of Tlaltecuhtli, a "great earth monster" whom the gods Quetzalcoatl and Tezcatlipoca, in their serpent forms, tore in two. From the lower portion also derive the plants on which humans depend. Tlaltecuhtli is sometimes noted as "a great caiman whose spiny crocodilian back forms the mountain ridges of the world."[13] In Sumerian myths, the sky and the earth are the son and daughter of Nammu, "the great serpent goddess of the abyss."[14] Aboriginals of Australia honor the Rainbow Serpent, a creator deity who "creates water ways."[15] While creation myths about the Rainbow Serpent "differ slightly from one region to another ... all the stories share a common thread; the fundamental role of water in nature's cycle of growth and regeneration."[16] Solomon Islanders of Makira (San Cristobal) venerate Agunua, the supreme *figona* (spirit) embodied in the serpent, who "created all things—the sea, the land, men, and animals, thunder, lightning, rain, and storms, rivers, trees, and mountains."[17] For the Solomon Islanders of Lavetai, Bunosi "coughed up the first plants and pigs."[18] Fijians say humans owe their existence to Ndengei, depicted as a huge snake or with a snake's head and stone body.[19]

Like any other class of deities, reptilian beings' interactions with humans may be helpful or harmful, or both. As benevolent entities they may be creators, ancestors, protectors, healers, or the source of or associated with knowledge and arts. In Hinduism, serpents "represent divinity, eternity, materiality, life and death, and time as well as timelessness."[20] Itzamna are variously connected to creation, agriculture, healing, and "the estoteric knowledge of priests."[21] In Chinese mythology, Fu Xi, depicted as a human above the waist and a snake below, invented writing, divination, and hunting weapons.[22] The rainbow serpent Dañh-sio, "immortal, almighty, omniscient," could bestow wealth. The Baganda of Africa honor the python god Selwanga, who grants fertility to women who have difficulty conceiving children. Mwanga, a Bagheshu snake god, also has this power. Fijians sacrificed humans and hogs to Ndengei, who in exchange gave prophecies and relieved droughts.[23] Ratu-mai-Mbulu, a Fijian god whose form is a great serpent, is responsible for agricultural fertility.[24]

As malevolent beings, reptilian entities may be predators, may be the origin of diseases and afflictions, or may punish bad behavior. Ancient Egyptians feared Aapep, whom they associated with "all the dark features of existence such as storms, night, and death," because it might eat their souls when they journeyed into the afterlife. If this happened, "their fate was nonexistence, unless they were pitied and rescued by one of the gods."[25] In Hebraic and Christian traditions, the serpent and the dragon are agents of evil, and both are, to different degrees, associated with Satan, the former noted as the tempter of Eve.[26] The Mentawai of Siberut Island in Indonesia recognize a "water-dwelling spirit" they term "Sikaoinana," the word for "crocodile" in many Mentawai dialects. Gendered primarily as female, this spirit causes illness and attacks those who do not share their meat with others. Mentawai pay shamans to perform ceremonies to heal those whom Sikaoinana has stricken with illness.[27] The primary deity of Bioko Island (Fernando Po), who appears as a cobra, "can inflict disease or death" but also "give riches."[28] A malicious horned serpent is a cross-cultural Native American entity. Even in his human form, "certain aspects of his person and dress are reminiscent of a snake." In this guise, he "is a dangerous male who preys on naïve women."[29]

As elementals, supernatural and ordinary reptiles may be associated with fire, water, air, or earth and may control or protect them. Ndengei called forth in anger a flood that covered the entire Earth except for the top of one mountain.[30] Mami Wata "dwells in the waters of the forest she protects" but uses her beautiful human form "and promises of wealth to attract followers, and is not above sleeping with her devotees or taking them as spouses."[31] Makara water spirits are associated with life and death because "the waters engender and dissolve all of life."[32]

Moʻo Akua in the Polynesian Context

Discerning readers will notice the exclusion of certain island groups and a discrepancy between the ways included groups are treated. An exhaustive treatment of Polynesian moʻo would be a monograph on its own. Thus, I am obliged to curtail my discussion. There are more than twenty different Polynesian groups (including archipelagoes) and countless lizard-related accounts.

Sāmoa

Lizards, both divine and ordinary, occupy important roles in Samoan tradition in terms of the right to rule and wage war. Pili (lizard) is a lizard god who appears in a "considerable body of literature" and is notable in that he is the ancestor of Savea, the first mālietoa, a chiefly title for ruling families.[33] He is "credited with achievements in fishing and farming, with the transfer of prestige and power from Nauʻa to the western Samoan islands, and with the establishment of the political organization of ʻUpolu."[34] Certain villages worshipped Pili in connection with "war, famine, and pestilence," while others honored Lesā as a war god.[35] Warriors believed that the actions of ordinary lizards could predict the outcome of a battle. There were four ways in which this might occur. The first entailed watching for a lizard as warriors marched to battle: a lizard crossing their path meant a disastrous outcome, and they returned home; a lizard traveling ahead in the same direction signified victory, and they continued on. The second required weaving a coconut leaf mat around the central pole of the "great house, from the floor to the ridge pole," and waiting to see what direction a lizard would take as it descended: a zigzag path foretold defeat, which meant they should cease fighting; a straight path down indicated success and thus they continued.[36] The third concerned a bundle of spears: "If the lizard ran about the points of the spears and the outside of the bundle, it was a good omen; but if it rather worked its way into the centre for concealment, it was a bad sign."[37] The fourth regarded a lizard's descent from the rafters: if it ran down a post around which matting had been woven, it was a good sign, but if it ran down a bare pole, it was a bad sign.[38]

In 1839 Charles Wilkes, landing at Sāmoa during the course of an exploration expedition for the US, noted that in an area of ʻUpolu near Safata, people venerated a lizard whom they considered an *aitu* (spirit). From the description, Wilkes explains, it was about twelve feet long, its girth like that of a coconut tree, "with huge scales, and a mouth filled with sharp teeth." The people tossed meat frequently into the stream in which it lived. Wilkes adds, "Some of them declare that they have seen him, and that he has dwelt there upwards of fifty years."[39]

Samoan and Tongan history and legend merge in the account of Sanalālā, named after a lizard. Sanalālā was a high-ranking Samoan Tongan who established the *tafaʻifa*, "a political institution."[40] His father, Samoa-na-galo, declared that "having no guardian divinity himself . . . considered Le Sa, the Lizard, his only protector" and thus named his son Sanalālā to honor it.[41]

Tonga

As in Sāmoa, the royal family of Tonga has a reptilian progenitor. Heimoana, who has the form of a sea snake, is the ancestress of the Tui Tonga, the hereditary rulers of Tonga.[42] A Tongan god's progeny became the first rulers of several islands in the Pacific: Sinilau, who could appear as a lizard and whose first child from his human wife was born as "a fat lizard (piliopo)," made his sons the first kings of Tonga, Sāmoa, Uea (Rotuma) and Futuna (Wallis and Futuna), Niue, and Rarotonga (Cook Islands).[43] The origin of the Magellanic Clouds is linked to the twin sons of Tongan chief Ma'afu Tukuiaulahi and a supernatural lizard.[44] Tui Ha'afakafonua, who manifests as a lizard, was an important deity for the Maofango people and their chief, Fakafonua. Attracted to human females, this lizard god sometimes appeared in his sacred pool, and women who bathed there became either ill or pregnant.[45] Finau-tau-iku, who lived at "the eastern end of Tongatabu, near the chief residence of the Tui Tonga," was linked to the *pili*, a "pretty little blue and green lizard" that was sacred to him. He is termed the "god of carrying away, or who carries away," the significance of which is not explained.[46]

Aotearoa

Early scholarship on Māori *ngārara* (reptiles—supernatural and ordinary) and *mokomoko* (lizards) is primarily concerned with the negative beliefs about them and rarely bothers with the positive ones.[47] As with Sāmoa, Māori warriors looked to the lizard for omens regarding battle. For the Tūhoe tribes, a lizard is the *aria* (manifestation) of the war gods Te Hūkitā and Te Rehu-o-Tainui, and seeing a lizard "in the earth oven" as they are heading to battle is "an evil omen."[48] A lizard is part of a divination for its connection to Te Hūkitā.[49] The tohunga who acts as the medium for Te Hūkitā calls upon him to appear, "which he soon does in lizard form." The tohunga then passes the lizard from one warrior to the next until everyone has laid hands upon it. But if the lizard is not passed but crawls "on to another man's hand," it is considered "an aitua (omen of evil) and that man will not accompany the party, for he knows full well that death awaits him in the fray" and neither "will the other members of his *hapu* or sub-tribe lift the trail of Tu the Fierce-Eyed, inasmuch as the warning applies to them all."[50] Enemies could send a lizard to cause harm, "an act of witchcraft."[51] Whoever encounters a single lizard takes measures through rituals to counter the enemy's intention to harm. Meeting "two or three lizards in one day" signals imminent "disaster" for the individual and companions and probably means "that a fight looms in the immediate future."[52] "Te Purewa, a famous warrior of Tuhoe," consulted Peketahi, who had a lizard form (elsewhere a *taniwha* water spirit), about a battle's outcome.[53]

Today, certain *iwi* (people or a tribe) are drawing awareness to the *ngārara*'s cultural value. The Ruahine *iwi* of Taranaki recognizes that "for Māori, whilst lizards could be feared and seen as a bad omen—representing Whiro (darkness and death), they are often used as guardians, and released near the burial sites of loved ones, and used as a talisman and kaitiaki [guardian], as a means to offer protection for important whare/buildings. The placement of the lizard would inspire fear for prospective trespassers, and show that the protection of the atua (gods) has been placed on the tapu place."[54] For the Te Ātiawa ki Whakarongotai *iwi*, "Ngārara are valued as a source of energy, life and mauri that has sustained the people and the land of Te Ātiawa ki Whakarongotai. They are respected because of their whakapapa; their genealogical and ecological relationships with the environment and people. They are of ancient origin and we consider them our tuakana, or elder siblings."[55] These statements remind us that the study of reptilian deities needs to be contextualized within a larger cultural framework, which should also take into consideration that the "fearsome" can also be "sacred." Perhaps like mo'o akua, the *ngārara* embody the life-giving and death-dealing aspects of the natural and spiritual realms.

Reptilian deities abound in Māori mythology. In cosmic genealogies, Punga or his sons, Tū-te-wanawana and Tū-te-wehiwehi, are cited as the parent or origin of lizards.[56] Tū-te-wanawana's sons—Tū-tangata-kino, Uenuku, Tuātara, Moko-i-kuwharu, Kaweau, and Mokomoko—are also *ngārara* gods.[57] Moko-huku-waru, Tū-tangata-kino, and other *ngārara* dwell with the underworld goddess Miru.[58] Tū-tangata-kino causes illnesses, and Mokotiti "causes lung diseases."[59] Other supernatural *ngārara* include Hine-hua-rau (f), Hotu-Puku, Koronaki, Mārongorongo, Matipou, Mokoroa, Ngārara-huarau (f), Paoru, Paroroariki, Pouatehuri, Rehu, Rimurapa, Rinootakaka, Taungapiki, and Utai.[60] Supernatural *ngārara* tend to manifest entirely as huge reptiles. An exception is Ngārara-huarau (a.k.a. Te-karara-hu-ara), who is a woman above and a reptile below.[61] The war god Te-rehu-o-tainui began his existence as a human. Born prematurely, his "spirit entered into a green lizard, the *moko-kakariki*."[62] The deceased can be deified as *ngārara,* such as two Tūhoe *iwi* ancestors, Tamarau and Te Hukita.[63]

A *ngārara* might take a human as its partner. Te Mata-o-te-rangi
abducted Hine-te-kakara while she and another woman, Hine-te-
piripiri, were in "a grove of tarata trees."[64] When her friend ran to the
village to report it, someone asked, "What sort of ngarara?" She replied,
"He is a Te Mata-o-te-rangi; he is sixty feet long." After Hine-te-kakara
had lived with Te Mata-o-te-rangi "for a long time," she asked for and
received permission to visit her brothers. She told her family that she
wanted to bring them to meet her *ngārara* husband, but they insisted
that he come to them.[65] As it turns out, Hine-te-kakara wanted her
brothers to kill him. She told them to completely surround the house
with stacks of firewood.[66] When the *ngārara* arrived, the brothers called
him "fish" (*ika*) as they welcomed him, to which he took offense, but he
entered the house anyway. The story clarifies, "He was sixty feet long,
and so was the house; when he stretched out, he was exactly the same
length as the house." The *ngārara* ate the food provided for him, "a
thousand basketsful," and then fell asleep.[67] It was then that "they set
fire to the house," and although Te Mata-o-te-rangi rolled around trying
to extinguish it, "he was burnt to death."[68]

The cultural undertones of this story require commentary, which
the translator, Margaret Orbell, offers in footnotes. We learn that the
question about "what sort" of *ngārara* has cultural significance, as does
the reply:

> Williams' Dictionary defines the word kumi as (1) a measure of ten
> fathoms, (2) a huge fabulous reptile. When the woman is asked what
> kind of ngarara (or dragon) the creature is, she answers that he is a
> kumi. Later, we learn that this ngarara, or kumi, fits exactly inside a
> house which is a kumi in length (i.e. 10 fathoms or sixty feet; though if
> the word had this meaning in pre-European times, it could not have
> corresponded exactly to the European measure). So in this case, at any
> rate, the word kumi apparently means "a huge fabulous reptile some
> 60 feet in length."[69]

Here, I should note that "kiha" is a specific Hawaiian term for "supernatural lizard," as opposed to "mo'o," which refers to both supernatural
and ordinary lizards. While Hawaiian dictionaries do not say "kiha"
denotes "large mo'o," one cites three mo'o akua whose names bear the
prefix "kiha," including the gigantic Kihanuilūlūmoku (Great island-
shaking Kiha/supernatural lizard)—a mo'o akua so huge that the earth
quakes when it moves (see chapters 2, 3, and 4).[70] There is also the

curious comparison of a *ngārara* to a fish, which is left unexplained, as is Te Mata-o-te-rangi's negative reaction. But *ika* is a play on words that is lost in translation—it denotes "fish" but also "lizard," as in *ika-whenua* (land fish/lizard), as well as "victim" and "first person killed or captured in a fight."[71] Thus, Te Mata-o-te-rangi's negative reaction is no longer puzzling.

In regard to an account about a *ngārara* named Te Kaiwhakaruaki, Orbell notes, "As a rule they [*ngārara*] lived on land, while taniwha, or dragons, were usually to be found in water, but in this story, the ngarara lives in a stream. Te Kaiwhakaruaki is a name that is often given to nga-rara in such stories."[72] Here, I summarize the lengthy account of Te Kai-whakaruaki. His den was in the Te Paparara river, and he considered humans food. He ate anyone who passed by his den.[73] Te Kaiwhaka-ruaki ended up dying when a local man, Potoru, united over three hun-dred warriors to end him. One of these men was "a famous seal hunter" (unnamed), whose only weapons were his bare hands."[74] He told Po-toru, "One blow of my fist, and this ngarara dies! Is he of more conse-quence than the seals that I kill with a single blow of my fist?"[75] Needless to say, he ignored Pororu's plan, waded into the river, and threw a bas-ket of red ochre into the stream. Orbell explains the significance of this act: "Red ochre was considered to be a defence against supernatural creatures; for it was said that fairies were frightened of it. Here it is ap-parently a challenge to the ngarara, a declaration of the presence of a human being."[76] After throwing the red ochre, the seal hunter struck Te Kaiwhakaruaki on his snout, but as he attempted a second blow, the *ngārara* swallowed him, and "he disappeared into its belly."[77] The other men killed Te Kaiwhakaruaki. His struggles left "banks six feet high" in the river, which still exist.[78]

Like *ngārara, taniwha* may be benign or malevolent.[79] Stories abound about *taniwha,* some of which "are described as being water-dwelling creatures of saurian form, while a few are said to have inhab-ited caves; few were harmless, and most of them were man slayers and man eaters."[80] Urea, a *taniwha* of Paeroa, is said to manifest "in the form of a gigantic lizard" and, as such, satisfied his cravings for the flesh of "young maidens."[81] *Taniwha* may have shape-shifting abilities and are "apt to change their form in a most haphazard and perplexing manner."[82] According to the Ngāti Tamatera *iwi,* Tupe to Tauhai, who is their protector, is one such *taniwha.* To "warn the tribe of impending invasion, [he] would take the form of a dolphin and gambol in the river until its movements had been reported to all the chiefs." And in going to war, he "appeared as a blue cloud, and, in that form, led to the battle, and invariably (they claim) to victory."[83] The belief that a *taniwha* may appear to lead warriors is not relegated to the distant past: "During World War I," a *taniwha* manifested "as a small cloud of smoke" and led a "platoon out of danger."[84] Some *taniwha* have an important function as village guardians. Tipaera is one such lizard-like *taniwha*, whom the Māori near the Whanganui river consider "a kind of guardian" and whose appearance warned of imminent "misfortune."[85]

One *taniwha*, Tutaeporoporo, transformed from a shark to a dragon.[86] This was a pet shark who belonged to Tu-ariki. He quickly grew to the size of a whale, and then his body changed. His skin deepened in hue from grayish-silver to black and "became hard and spiky"; from his back emerged "wings like those of a bat" while "his tail changed to resemble that of a lizard." Where there were once fins, legs grew, along with webbed feet with "claws like those of a hawk." His head became that of a featherless bird but retained his shark teeth.[87] Although Tu-ariki's pet had become "a taniwha, a dragon," he "remained friendly towards his master" and caused no harm to others. But one day, Whanganui warriors killed Tu-ariki and took his corpse away "for food." Tutaeporporo searched for Tu-ariki and came to suspect what had happened. Eventually, he scented "the smell of human flesh being cooked in an oven." He followed it "to the mouth of the Whanganui River," which he entered. He then hid in a cave to "lay in wait for his enemies." Not long after, he carried out his revenge, swallowing a group of people "and their canoes as well."[88] After having eaten human flesh, he ate anyone who passed his cave.[89] He was eventually killed.[90]

This *taniwha* transformation story hints at a slippage between sharks and lizards, which is further evidenced by a pattern used in *tuku-tuku*, "lattice work," or woven panels. This design, noted as a common motif in weaving, is described as "teeth of the Taniwha (e.g. Mako), which was used as a threat to children when they misbehaved."[91] The mako is a species of shark. Another *taniwha* is also described as a shark.[92] Sharks and moʻo are connected in Hawaiian culture, albeit in ways that differ from those of the Māori (see chapter 5).

Earlier, I explained that Punga and his sons are credited with being either the parents or creators of ordinary lizards. There are also *taniwha*-related origin stories. One account states that Tu-te-hurutea is the origin of "*taniwha* and all *mokopeke* (lizards)."[93] Some *taniwha* began their existence as humans, but upon their death, became *taniwha*. After his death, Ngā Rangi-hangu came back as a *taniwha*, and the people of

Manawa in the Galatea district claim him as their ancestor. As a *taniwha*, Ngā Rangi-hangu never harmed humans, but he enjoyed "interfering with the activities of eel fishers."[94] A young woman, Haumapuia, became a *taniwha* after she drowned due to her angry father pushing her into "a river at Hopuruahine, near Ruatahuna." As she raced around, "looking for a way to reach the sea," she inadvertently created "lake Waikaremoana."[95] This tale is doubly an etiology in that it relates both the origin of this *taniwha* and the lake she makes her home. In addition to crediting *taniwha* with creating geological features, some features are said to be the remains of their petrified bodies. The remains of Hinehuarau, a "monster Saurian," are scattered stones in Wairarapa.[96] Hawai'i has many stories citing mo'o as sources of geological features, which I share throughout this book.

Metamorphosis from human to *taniwha* as a result of breaking a tapu and dwelling with *taniwha* is the backbone of a story about a woman named Parekawa. When Parekawa broke a tapu, "she became exposed to many dangers."[97] Before long, her appearance and behavior greatly changed, and "she became as one demented, and finally she fled to the forest." When her friends followed her, "she leaped into a river and disappeared." They assumed she had drowned, but they were mistaken. The *taniwha* Peketahi had taken her to dwell with "his kindred apparently in some subterranean region, for he conducted Parakawa through the water and through the earth until they emerged in the region where dwelt the strange *taniwha* folk." One day, Peketahi allowed her to return to the human realm, "guided by one of the *taniwha* folk."[98] He gave her detailed instructions on how to reach "the *tuahu* or sacred place of the village without being seen by her people." Her ability to live again in the village would depend on this point. In living with these *taniwha*, "Parekawa had lost some of her human attributes" and had begun to resemble a *taniwha*.[99] She was seen before she could reach the tuahu and returned to live with the *taniwha*. Petetahi then escorted her himself, and she was successful. Parekawa's father conducted "a certain rite over her," which "restored to her human form, appearance, and attributes."[100]

One female *taniwha*, Karitake, is never cited as a lizard, but because her appearance and actions recall certain Hawaiian mo'o women, I include her. Karitake lived at Patangata in Otane in "a spring off the lake around which was a covering of rusty quicksand, like mud."[101] She cared for eel weirs, "which were owned by a larger number of her 'uris' or relations." She had long *urukehu* (reddish) hair. She made Waikarepu river in Opoho her second home. When she traveled to and fro, she pushed aside the soil, thus creating a wide "drain or trench," which is still seen today. When "the sand bar was opened at Patangata in order to let the lake out to sea," she grieved "the loss of her waters and the food most of which was sent out to waste in the sea." The sign of her laments was "a low droning sound, followed immediately with a heavy down-pour of rain or the show of the rainbow."[102] When her relatives' quarrels over eel weirs angered her, she sent the eels elsewhere, the sign of which was "the showing of her red eyes in the water." The imminent death of her kin was foretold by her hair "strewn all over the water, and it is said today that instead of hair being seen, there are only feathers."[103]

At one point, a windmill was built beside Karitake's spring. When this account was published in 1957, it noted that "older Maoris believe she is still there today because the water turns a rusty color, and flows continuously. When this place dries up they say that Karitake has gone back to her other home in Opoho."[104] While in the past she had been destructive, having "burrowed through fields and ruined many lands," she seems less "wild" today, "behaving excellently, and has even re-formed with the hope that none of her relations would ill-treat the soil as she had done in the past."[105] Here, Karitake's relations seem to be humans.

The account of Karitake ends with a cautionary tale of sorts in which she punishes five relatives, all human children.[106] Three of them, Chum Munro, Darky Nohinohi, and William Raurty, "played foolishly on the banks of the Opoho drains. They took big spades and began dig-ging carelessly into the soil uprooting everything which had been treated as tapu by Karitake."[107] After they had created a cave, "they pretended it was a big house or shop." They asked their playmates, Molly and Charlotte, "to go in and buy their goods." But just then, Darky and another boy climbed atop the cave and stamped, sang, danced, and whistled. When these two boys joined the third in their cave and before Molly and Charlotte joined them, "Charlotte was put to sleep by a strange spell and after followed a rumbling noise," and the cave collapsed on the boys. Chum and Darky were revived, but William suffocated to death.[108]

As readers will see, there are notable similarities between this *tani-wha* and Hawaiian mo‘o, but I will note them here: (1) Karitake is a water spirit who has reddish hair, which in Hawaiian is termed *‘ehu*. While not all mo‘o have ‘ehu hair, it is associated with them, and more-over, it is said that they like humans with this hair color; (2) she cares for eels and will lead them elsewhere if angered, and moʻo are known to do the same with fish; (3) she protects her waters and the food it nurtures, also a moʻo trait; (4) certain signs and water colors are associated with her, and this is true for moʻo; (5) Karitake punishes her human kin for offending her, as do moʻo.

Male *taniwha* may kidnap women to take as wives. In one account, a woman bore six children to a *taniwha* (its appearance is unexplained), "three of whom were monsters like their father, while the other three were of human form."[109] Previously, I shared the story about the death of the water-dwelling *ngārara* Kaiwhakaruaki. Elsewhere, he is described as a *taniwha* who resembles a huge lizard and is called Te Whakaruaki.[110] He took a human female as his wife, and the child she birthed "was half lizard and half human in form." Eventually, the people killed Te Whakaruaki by trapping him in a house and burning him. However, his tail broke off, "wriggled out through the wall of fire, and sought refuge in the forest."[111] From this tail derived the species "*moko papa* (the tree lizard, *Dactylocnemus pacificus*)," who shed and regrow their tails.[112] Hawaiʻi has a similar story about the origin of ordinary lizards (see chapter 4).

Female *taniwha* also took human partners. Hinekorako is described as a "taniwha and goddess of the Ngati Hine Hika of Te Reinga" and Tane Kino as the "great ancestor of Ngati Hine Hika."[113] Hinekorako "originally inhabited Wahakapunaki, a hill in the vicinity and also Te Reinga itself." The story notes, "The first six generations from Iwhara to Hinekorako, were not quite men and women as we understand them, but a species of man-god, or water spirit." Here, the son's name is Taurenga. Before Taurenga's birth, however, Hinekorako extracted a promise from Tane Kino—namely, "that to break the spell of taniwha and god, cast over her through her ancestry, he would have to care for the child, and nurse it, until it was old enough to care for itself."[114] This promise proved easier to make than keep.

When Taurenga "was old enough to crawl," his parents took him with them "to attend a meeting of the tribe on the Marae."[115] The promise was broken when the child soiled himself at the meeting, and instead of cleaning the child himself, Tane Kino called for Hinekorako to do it. She "came, picked up her baby, and took him with her to the stream which now flows past the Te Reinga Marae. There she washed and fed him." When Tane Kino realized what he had done, he sought her out and "begged forgiveness for his thoughtless action, but there was no remedy." Rather than deny him his son after crying over the child, "she stood up and handed the babe to Tane Kino." She told him that because of his broken promise "she was doomed to go back to her watery home under Te Reinga Falls." There she remains until this day, "watching over the interests of her descendants whenever called upon."

Hinekorako later intervened to save the Ngāti Hine Hika when the rivers flooded, and people in canoes were being swept toward Te Reinga Falls, which was "now a raging cascade." Hearing the cry for help from an "old Tohunga" (kahuna) to save the people, she immediately stopped "the rush of the canoes towards the Falls."[116] This account stands in stark contrast to depictions of *taniwha* as inherently evil. For the Ngāti Hine Hika *iwi*, Hinekorako is a respected ancestor to whom they owe their existence, as she gave up her beloved child to live a human existence, and she continues to protect her descendants. Te Reinga Marae claims and honors her: "Ko Hinekorako te taniwha" (Hinekorako is the *taniwha*) of Te Reinga Marae.[117]

The *ngārara* is an element in Māori material culture. While the lizard is undeniably decorative from an aesthetic standpoint in terms of artistic rendering, its inclusion invariably serves an important symbolic purpose. Informing this symbolism are the collective beliefs and belief-related practices concerning supernatural and ordinary lizards in Māori culture, which I have presented throughout this section. As we have seen, *ngārara* are fierce entities. They are associated with death or the afterlife and are thus valued as guardians for the dead.

In 1902, two white men entered a cave as they were pig hunting and found a funerary *waka* (chest, canoe-shaped box) with a lizard carved into its cover.[118] According to Heremania Kauere, a descendant of those buried in that cave, this lizard was meant to protect human remains from harm and disrespect, and he related an event that happened to his grandfather, Kahu Makaka, in 1840.[119] This waka with the lizard carving was "stretched across the mouth inside" of the cave. Makaka, who had come to the cave with the remains of his relative Hui, "walked over the top of the lizard and placed the bones at the other end of the cave." Makaka, as Kauere remarks, "must have been confused; he did not go round the *waka* as was the custom. He stepped back again over the lizard, and was bitten by the spirit of the lizard. He felt sick when he got out; went home, and died." Kauere explains, "The lizard was endowed by the incantations of our forefathers with powers of evil. It was placed as a guard over the bones of the dead, to prevent interference."[120] When Te Rangihīroa (a.k.a. Sir Peter Henry Buck) passed away, among the motifs carved into his bier was "the tuatara (lizard), the almost universal symbol of death."[121]

As protective forces, lizards stand sentient over that which is entrusted to them. A gift presented to Queen Elizabeth II, "a *papahou,* or treasure box for a person of high rank," includes "two lizard figures on the lid." The symbolism is explained as follows: "The presence of a lizard on a carved object warns viewers of its sacredness, and in this concept has a protective role. The lizards are locked together at the mouth, as sentinels, to ensure that no evil enters the box and no harm befalls the owner."[122] Carved lizards sometimes appear in bas-relief on lintels, ridgepoles, and *koruru* (gable images), mirroring the habits of their living counterparts, and undoubtedly serve a sacred purpose.[123] A lizard may replace a "projecting tongue" in carvings.[124] Lizards are also carved or painted on cave walls.[125]

Cook Islands

The lizard's traditional significance in the Cook Islands is evidenced in a cosmogony for Aʻuaʻu (Mangaia), which attributes an illustrious lineage to a widely venerated lizard deity. At the dawn of creation, there was only Vari-ma-te-takere. Because she was alone but wanted children, she created them by tearing off bits of her sides. Vātea was her firstborn, a son.[126] From Vātea and Papa was born Tonga-iti, whose "visible form was white and black spotted lizards," also known as Matarau.[127] His older brothers are the twins Tangaroa and Rongo.[128] Tonga-iti's parentage and siblings are significant because they are major Polynesian gods. There may be a mythological link between fish and lizards given that Vātea, whose body was divided vertically between human and dolphin, was the father of a lizard god.[129]

William Wyatt Gill (1828–1896), who was a missionary at Mangaia for twenty-two years, claimed that Tongans are responsible for introducing "lizard-worship" to the Cook Islands. As evidence, he cites the example of a "large tree-lizard" found in Rarotonga forests, "formerly regarded as the incarnation of a Tongan deity, devouring solitary travellers."[130] This information overlaps with the Tongan myth about Sinilau, who could appear as a lizard and who sent his sons out to become the first kings of Tonga, Sāmoa, Uea, Futuna, Niue, and Rarotonga. Sinilau would be Tinirau in the Cook Islands—the name of Vari-ma-te-takere's second son, a fish entity.[131] The relationship between supernatural and ordinary lizards may be why the latter inspire dread in Mangaia. Gill recalls, "The fear of the lizard was intense. I have seen strong men tremble at the sudden approach of one."[132]

In addition to Tonga-iti, there is also "Moko, or Great Lizard, the king of all lizards."[133] He assists his grandson Ngaru with besting his enemies.[134] Moko is clearly on good terms with the great god Tangaroa, for he reached out to him to replace Ngaru's hair after he became bald in an effort to thwart his foes. Moko was unsatisfied with the first two types of hair Tangaroa sent: the first was frizzy, and the second was blond. He asked for the best hair, and Tangaroa gave him "a profusion of wavy, smooth raven locks."[135] At one point, Moko sent "his servants, i.e. all the little lizards" to spy on Miru, goddess of the underworld, Ngaru's enemy.[136] Then he sent them to spy on Amai-te-rangi, a human-eating "sky-demon" who dropped a basket down from the sky realm hoping to entice Ngaru to enter it. The lizards filled the basket, but when Amai-te-rangi saw them, he lowered the basket, and the lizards ran to Moko to tell him what they had seen.[137] Eight times Amai-te-rangi sent the basket, hoping to find Ngaru, and each time Moko filled it with lizards, but the last time Ngaru entered it, having decided to kill him.[138] As soon as Ngaru stepped out of the basket, the lizards "rushed up the legs of Amai-te-rangi, covering his face, neck, arms, and body," especially "clustering about the armpits," which "tickled the giant to such a degree that it was impossible for him to strike with precision." No matter how hard he tried, he was unable to "brush off these little fellows from his naked body" until, finally, he dropped his weapons, which Ngaru used to kill him.[139] Moko also sent two birds, the *karakerake,* which Ngaru recognized as "belonging to Moko."[140] From this story we learn that ordinary lizards, through their supernatural lizard master's power, are able to access the underworld and the sky, acting as messengers to a god, as does a bird species named karakerake.[141] Indeed, as Gill notes, "Birds, fish, reptiles, insects, and specially inspired priests, were reverenced as incarnations, mouth-pieces, or messengers of the gods."[142] This is a common theme in Polynesia.

French Polynesia
The importance of the lizard in Tahiti is exemplified in the account about why the island once called 'Aimeho is now known as Mo'orea:

> Quant à la substitution de Moorea à Aimeho, elle a pour origine le nom que se donna la famille régnante après que le grand-prête de l'un de ses marae, Nuurua, eut la vision d'un très beau lézard jaune (moorea) qui devint en quelque sorte l'emblème de la famille.[143]

As for Mo'orea replacing 'Aimeho, the royal family gave it its name after the high priest of one of its mārae, Nu'urua, had the vision of a very beautiful yellow lizard (mo'orea), which became a sort of emblem for the family.

According to Teuira Henry, "Lizards were gods to the royal Oropaa family," and when their children were born, a longevity ritual was performed in which "these lizards were presented and invoked before" them.[144] The last child for whom this ritual was carried out was Pomare II, who was born circa 1774—fewer than 250 years ago.[145]

An unspecified marae "was consecrated to a deity who appeared as a lizard; and here the god was represented by a stone figure carved in the form of a lizard."[146] This may have been the Taputuarai marae at Papara whose tutelary deity was Mo'o and manifested as a lizard.[147] Several deities are noted as having lizard forms. The 'Oropa'a worshipped Tipa, "who presided over sickness and healed diseases" and is incarnate in the "mo'oareva, a lizard with face erect and forked tail."[148] A sky deity, "Tū-o-te-ra'i–marama (Stability-of-the-moonlit-sky)" is embodied in the "mo'otea, a light-colored lizard."[149] Two lizards, "mo'ouri (dark-lizard) and mo'oarara (streaked-lizard)" are the forms of "Te-ohiu-maeva (The-victorious-dart)."[150] Te-ohiu-maeva emerges in a cosmogony with the lizard deity Mo'ouri, who bears the name of his lizard manifestation. Mo'ouri "showed himself in the lowering sky along the horizon; he guided those who sailed from the low islands."[151] Both of them "were the special deities of fools; they sometimes bewitched the priests and were very powerful gods when they possessed them; only after a little while would it be discovered that the gods of fools were possessing them."[152] Other lizard spirits are associated with a flower-dwelling lizard, "mo'opuapua (flower lizard)."[153]

Perhaps it was because Tahitians view lizards positively that accidentally harming one was an omen of impending war. An example of how this might occur is as follows: "If in trimming off the thatch of the eaves of a house a man cut a lizard in half, it was a sure sign of coming war, and he stopped his work to prepare for the emergency." Warriors are likened to lizards in a war chant: "Ei tao mato te nu'u / E mo'o pua-pua tini tei roto—Let the army be as a cleft in the rock / Issuing out innumerable lizards."[154]

Supernatural mo'o-human relations are a motif in Tahitian legends. An etiological account collected between 1844 and 1848 relates the origin of a mountain peak's ledge that resembles "the form of a gigantic lizard" about "fifty feet long."[155] This geographic feature is the petrified remains of a lizard born to a human female who had been abducted by a "demon." This so-called demon was probably a supernatural lizard, given the woman's lizard son, who was entirely reptilian. The woman escaped, leaving behind her lizard child, and returned home. There, she met a man, and a daughter was born. Within a short time, however, she experienced misfortune—the death of her parents and her husband.[156] While the cause of her misfortune was not indicated, it might have had to do with her abduction by this entity.

A few years passed, and "a huge lizard" appeared at the woman's home. They instinctively recognized their kinship, and the woman welcomed her lizard son into her home.[157] For a while, all went well. The lizard caught fish for them and played with and watched over the daughter. But one day, the woman asked him to watch his sister for three days so that she could absent herself to worship 'Oro at Atehuru. The lizard was patient with the child, who climbed over his body and "counted its teeth," and even bathed her and put her to sleep with a song. After a few days of constantly caring for his sister, however, the lizard was exhausted. As he napped, the child woke him, so he went to find a place to hide and sleep. But the child found him and woke him again.[158] Infuriated, he ate her "and made off to the bush."[159]

When the woman came home and found her child and the lizard gone, she imagined what had happened and hunted the lizard.[160] She pursued him relentlessly, and thus the lizard had no opportunity to eat or rest. Finally, at the top of a high peak on "the edge of the precipice," the lizard begged his mother for mercy, which she denied him. As she rushed at him, he tripped and fell to his death. His petrified body "remains to show that none can escape a mother's vengeance." From his blood grew the papaya tree, which "the good God gave . . . in mercy, for any woman that eats of it will be fruitful."[161]

In this next account, the daughter of a human couple is born as a lizard. Mo'otuaraha had no human form, but "she could act and speak like a human being."[162] She used her powers to convince Paiti'a, a chief of Papeno'o, to mate with her. She was with him for an hour, and after she left, he came to his senses and returned home. She bore a son, who closely resembled Paiti'a, and named the child after him. When the son came of age, he set out to meet his father, dressed in "a girdle made from smooth, glossy skin from the under side of his mother."[163] Because his mother was a lizard, the man rejected him. After her son told her about his father's reaction, Mo'otuaraha set out to change his mind. She learned that he had gone to Tetiaroa, so she headed there. As she was climbing up the reef, he ordered his men to kill her, which they did by hitting her head with a stone. Because they left her corpse on the reef, her bones were eventually exposed, and there they remained for a long time. Some Tahitians are her descendants, but their identity is unknown.[164] This account showcases the Tahitian belief that humans could birth supernatural lizards and that these lizards could bear human children. Furthermore, Mo'otuaraha had sex with Paiti'a in her lizard form. This story and the one that precedes it are instances of interspecies sexual intercourse. Another version, however, says Mo'otuaraha is also known as Maai a Ruahine and that she was a lizard during the day and a woman at night: "Cette déesse avait l'apparence d'une femme la nuit" (This goddess had the appearance of a woman at night), but as soon as the sun rose, "elle se métamorphosait en lézard" (she transformed into a lizard).[165] A deity with a similar name, Tuaraha te vahine pa'a mo'o (Tuaraha the scaly mo'o woman), is associated with a long stone near the Tuauru river in Mahina, which symbolizes her tail: "Tuaraha d'un grand coup de hanche envoya sa queue de lézard dans les airs et alla atterrir sur une des îles de Hawaii" (Tuaraha, in a great explosive hip movement, sent her lizard tail into the air, which landed on one of the Hawaiian Islands).[166]

John Francis Stimson's dictionary of Tuamotuan dialects notes that *moko* denotes "lizard" and "phallus," which invites speculation. The long bodies of eels and snakes make them phallic symbols in some cultures and perhaps finds a correlation in Pa'umotu with lizards.[167] Given that *moko* denotes "lizard," deities whose names includes *moko* are probably reptilian. Entities with *moko*-related names are Moko (lizard), "an evil supernatural being"; Mokongārara, a "monstrous lizard"; Mokotea (white lizard); and Mokouri (dark-colored lizard).[168] Puna, who is Punga in Māori lore, is also a Tuamotuan lizard god.[169]

At Ra'iātea, "a lizard goddess dwelt in a small gulch back of the settlement of Tevaitoa, who was regarded as the protector of the chief of that place." The great lizard Moovi, whose cave is in Maupiti, "was dreaded as an eater of men."[170] M. Firuu of Maupiti related a legend his father had told him regarding "lézards géants" (giant lizards) living in a cave at Vaipōiri, which had long necks ("un long cou") and were herbivores ("ils mangeaient beaucoup d'herbs").[171] Elsewhere, these lizards were carnivores ("étaient carnivores").[172] A Taha'a native once told missionary Elsdon Best about "a man-destroying monster named 'Aifa 'arua 'i," who "lived on a small islet called Motue'a, at Tahaa in ancient times."[173] And while this so-called monster was not indicated to be a lizard, there is good reason to believe it was. As Best points out, if we replace the glottal stops marking "missing consonants" with *k* and replace the *f* with *wh*, 'Aifa 'arua 'i then becomes Kaiwhakaruaki, the name of the Māori water-dwelling and human-eating *ngārara*, whose story I have shared. By this same method, Motue'a and Ta'a'a become Motueka and Takaka—Māori place names connected to Kaiwhakaruaki. Best supposes the Māori may have introduced Kaiwhakaruaki and "the place names connected with it, when they moved down from eastern Polynesia to New Zealand."[174]

Like elsewhere in Polynesia, in Te Henua 'Enana (Marquesas Islands) traditions, monstrous lizards lived alongside humans. *Moko,* ordinary and supernatural, are both honored and feared in these islands. In 1813, David Porter reported that the "common lizard" was the only reptile on these islands, and the natives feared them and their eggs.[175] That they believed in supernatural reptiles is evidenced in a statement given in 1895: Moko-Hae rules over "the lizard gods, hostile to mankind; producers of internal ailments and racking pains."[176] While this may be the case, it is also true that they frequently used *moko* as a motif in material arts, including wood carvings, tattoos, and textiles. Depictions of lizards and anthropomorphic lizards are also the topic of petroglyphs, but they are rare.[177] This suggests that *moko* also had a positive value, perhaps as fearsome entities who could ward off evil.

As with the reptilian deities in other areas, male and female *moko* in Te Henua 'Enana abduct humans and make them their romantic partners. In this first account, a lizard takes Hina-Te-Au-Ihi, the wife of the cultural hero Māui:

> 1. While Maui was planting *kawa,* the Nanaa-lizard came to his house,
> 2, and stole Maui's wife, Hina-Te-Au-Ihi. 3. In the evening Maui came
> to this house. 4. He saw his mother crying. 5. Maui asked his mother,
> "Why do you cry?" 6. "Your wife has been taken by Nanaa-Moe-Oho
> (The White Lizard)." 7. The mother said, "How will you find her? She
> has disappeared in the ravine." 8. Maui said, "This is an easy matter for
> me." 9. Maui then twisted ropes. 10. He did this for one, two and three
> days until he had enough rope; 200 yards of it. 11. Maui climbed up to
> the top of the ravine. 12. He fastened the carrying net to the rope.
> 13. He let himself down to Nanaa and the woman. 14. Maui approached the cave of Nanaa and the woman at noon. 15. There he

waited for night. 16. Maui jumped out of the carrying net at midnight. 17. He heard the snoring of Nanaa and the woman. 18. Maui came closer and saw Nanaa and the woman asleep with their heads together on the same spot. 19. The first hit with the club was weak. 20. Maui was afraid he would kill the woman. 21. When Maui had hit with the club the first time, Nanaa put his tail around Maui. 22. Maui hit with his left hand and broke Nanaa's tail. 23. After the third hit with the club, Nanaa died. 24. Maui threw Nanaa down into the ravine. 25. Maui said to the woman, "Mat of belly-cringing! You are the wife of a human and you are putting up with Nanaa." 26. He took the woman and went home with her.[178]

Here, a giant lizard abducts a human female, who seemingly accepts him. Whether they had sex is unknown, but since the lizard did not use her as food, we can imagine that he used her in other ways. Maui's comment to Hina-Te-Au-Ihi is a clear statement about the supremacy of a human husband to that of a lizard. Like other supernatural reptiles, this lizard uses its tail as a weapon. In Hawai'i, while there are many accounts of mo'o taking human lovers, stories of male mo'o doing so are less common.

In this next account from Atuona, a young man finds himself constrained to be the lover of Te-moo-nieve. Huuti is playing *teka* (a reed-throwing game) with other unmarried youths and boasts that his *teka* "is going right into the ear of Te-moo-nieve at Otua."[179] His *teka* does indeed enter her ear, and by her mana, she knows it belongs to him. He finds it in her cave and is "terrified."[180] She threatens to kill him, but he sweet-talks her, calling her "his woman" and asking why she is angry. Thus begins their living together, but he escapes and she comes looking for him.[181] She casts a spell over everyone in the house so they fall asleep, picks up Huuti, and carries him back to her cave. When she wakes him, he is horrified.[182] She threatens to eat him and changes her form, which has a long centipede-like tongue, pops her eyes out, and licks her jaws.[183] In the end, Huuti learns to care for her and takes her home with him, and from then on, she behaves. They have three children, two boys and a girl, and her descendants "still live in Taaoa valley, Hivaoa."[184] Although this account describes Te-moo-nieve as a *vehine hae* (wild woman)" and "ogress," her long tongue and her name hint at a reptilian nature.[185] Indeed, she is noted elsewhere as "la déesse des crustacée représentée par un lézard" (the goddess of crustaceans represented by a lizard).[186]

Lastly, petroglyphs depicting anthropomorphic lizards have been found in French Polynesia in Tīpaeru'i, Ra'iātea, Ha'akapa, Hatiheu, and Ra'ivavae.[187]

Te Pito o Te Fenua—Rapa Nui

According to a Te Pito o Te Fenua origin story, a moʻo was birthed by a mountain named Te Vahine at a place called Motu ʻUra. As the moʻo emerged from the mountain with its umbilical cord still attached, it leaped out into the Pacific. At one point, the umbilical cord fell into the ocean and became Te Pito o te Fenua (the umbilical cord of the earth), also known as Rapa Nui. As the moʻo walked across the Pacific, islands were formed with each step he took—the Moʻotū (moʻo steps) or Tuamotu—until he reached the island where he would make his home, Moʻorea Island in Tahiti. "Motu ʻUra" in Hawaiian is Moku ʻUla, and "Mauna Te Vahine" is Mauna Ka Wahine, a place and mountain in West Maui. Notably, a mountain named Āhia, which resembles a moʻo, is adjacent to Mauna Ka Wahine. Mauna Āhia is considered an ʻaumakua (ancestral guardian) of this area. Akoni Akana heard this origin story from a group of natives from Te Pito o Te Fenua in the late 1990s and explains that the name of this moʻo, which means "obscure" or "faded," refers to the moʻo as sometimes being there, sometimes not.[188]

In 1940, Alfred Métraux wrote, "The harmless little lizards (moko) may have been stowaways on Polynesian canoes. They have haunted the imagination of Easter Islanders, who have carved ceremonial objects in their shape."[189] An anthropomorphic lizard petroglyph is found at Ahu Nau Nau.[190] As part of the ceremony for a new house, "two wooden lizards were put formally on each side of the entrance to the porch."[191] Lizards made of toromiro wood with inlaid eyes of bone and obsidian served as house gods. Anthropomorphic lizard figurines, some of which were used as pendants, were carved out of wood, also with inlaid eyes.[192] Both types were used "during communal activities," and around "sixty specimens are known."[193] The handles of paoa (heavy wooden cudgels), the weapons of choice "for hand-to-hand fighting," were often carved in the shape of a lizard's head.[194] One such club is nearly twenty-one inches long, has a maximum width of four inches, and has inlaid bone and obsidian eyes.[195] The lizard serves a symbolic purpose, which is related to its habits. Catherine Orliac and Michel Orliac explain that the lizard's "visits to the underground world place them in permanent contact with beings of the next world, whose messages they transmit." For this reason carved lizards were "vigorously manipulated at the inauguration of houses" to ward off "malevolent spirits."[196]

Supernatural entities termed *akuaku* abound in Rapa Nui mythology. *Moko* denotes "lizard" in Rapa Nui, and there are several *akuaku moku*. Mokomoko-puapua (Beating lizard) and Moko-piki (Climbing lizard) are lizard *akuaku*.[197] Raraku, a famous figure in Rapa Nui, goes mad after biting the head of an octopus and runs around with "a rat in his mouth" and "a wooden lizard in his hand," which was probably a *paoa*.[198] He kills off spirits, one of whom is named Moko, presumably a lizard.[199]

In one tale, a young boy named Moko-arangi-roa (Face of the long lizard) is not specified as having a lizard form, but his name hints at it.[200] When his family leaves Anakara to live at Mataveri, they leave him behind. When his older sisters realize this, they cry out to their father, who states, "Leave him there. That is his country."[201] This cryptic comment is not explained. A spirit helps the boy to survive, speaking to him, but never reveals himself.[202] Years later, the sisters return and encounter him as they cook food over a fire, but he warns them to put the fire out lest the spirit kill them.[203] It is then that his sisters see "a lizard on his cheek." While this comment is not explained, we can imagine that given Moko-arangi-roa's name, the fact that his father left him behind, the helpful but invisible spirit, and the unexplained lizard on his cheek that these things are related. Perhaps Moko-arangi-roa's father left him behind because he is somehow connected to lizards, which would explain his name and the lizard on his cheek. The lizard on his cheek may also be the manifestation of the helpful spirit, although unbeknownst to Moko-arangi-roa. The story concludes with the three siblings going to Mataveri, where Moko-arangi-roa's father welcomes him.[204]

Two women, Vie-moko, who manifested as a lizard, and Vie-kena, who manifested as a gannet (white seabird), introduced tattooing to Rapa Nui.[205] Sometimes they are explained as mother and daughter, other times as sisters.[206] The former "is a popular character in the folkore of the island."[207] Perhaps the belief that a lizard woman introduced tattooing has its origins in the markings that characterize the skin of many lizard species. Vie-moku and Vie-kena "were tattooed on the thighs, the cheek bones, the throat, the lips, the fore arms, the jaws, and marked with circles on the buttocks."[208] They were from Hakarava and swam to Motu-nui. After taking two men as their partners, they each bore a son and tattooed them "on their legs and jaws."[209]

While the examples of beliefs related to lizards and lizard deities shared in this section overlap with those of ʻŌiwi, there are also important differences. To begin, the role of ordinary lizards as omens of war and politics in Sāmoa, in Aotearoa, and to a lesser extent in Tahiti is absent in Hawaiʻi, but the worship of supernatural moʻo in connection with war and politics is a shared tradition. While some ʻŌiwi, especially those related to the Pele clan, may dislike lizards, they do not fear them as harbingers of bad luck, as some Māori might. That said, a traditional fear of lizards for their association with moʻo akua is present is Hawaiʻi, Aotearoa, and French Polynesia. At the same time, however, the Māori attribute protective powers to the lizard, which is why the lizard sometimes appears as a motif in carvings, which is especially true for the people of Rapa Nui, where the lizard is a frequent motif. While the worship of moʻo was widespread in Hawaiʻi, there are fewer remaining examples of lizards as a motif in earlier material art, with the exception of a few kiʻi (images of deities) described in nineteenth-century treatises. In present-day Hawaiʻi, however, lizards are a frequent motif in tattoos, paintings, and carvings.

In Hawaiʻi, as with Aotearoa, the Cook Islands, and Tahiti, supernatural lizards (and lizard-like *taniwha*) may have offspring with humans, and some of them may protect their human descendants. Across Polynesia, beliefs about supernatural and ordinary lizards are preserved in traditions—accounts passed down from one generation to the next. The number of Hawaiian traditions primarily concerned with moʻo akua or in which moʻo akua appear is impressive.

The Politics and Poetics of Reconstructing ʻIke Kupuna from Moʻolelo and Kaʻao

Recovering and reconstructing ʻike kupuna (ancestral knowledge) about moʻo akua is the primary impetus for this book, and genre analysis is a critical component of my efforts in that regard. "Genre" refers to "a category of artistic, musical, or literary composition characterized by a particular style, form, or content."[210] From time immemorial, our kūpuna (plural of kupuna) preserved and disseminated their ʻike in diverse genres of ʻŌiwi artistic-intellectual production.[211] The descriptor "artistic-intellectual" for our genres is purposeful because it recognizes that ʻŌiwi aesthetics—the principles underlying composition, including ideas about what is pleasing and proper—guides their creation and that they are indeed intellectual products, as worthy of study as the great literatures of other nations. Most of what is known about moʻo akua—how our kūpuna understood and envisioned them and their cultural-religious-political-societal roles in our society—is preserved in two genres, moʻolelo and kaʻao, widely recognized as important archives of ʻike kupuna. Moʻolelo and kaʻao are rich examples of ʻŌiwi aesthetics because they share certain elements and often include yet other genres, which suggests that their structure is informed by a cultural sense of what they should contain.

Over countless generations, our ancestors' intimate relationship with and close observation of our island world helped form their understandings of genre. The genre termed "moʻolelo" is predicated on ʻŌiwi ways of knowing and being. Pukui's definition of "moʻolelo" showcases the way that it is culturally informed: moʻo and ʻōlelo combined denote "series of talks," a union reflecting a long history of oral tradition, as Pukui points out.[212] Although this genre is distinctly ʻŌiwi, it is capacious in that it encompasses and may incorporate and weave together elements from what in English would be termed story, history, myth, epic, legend, origin story, cautionary tale, folktale, and life writing, such as an autobiography, biography, or memoir.[213] "Moʻo" also denotes "moʻolelo." Indeed, "moʻo" has many meanings, including "lizard," "reptile," and "moʻo akua." As Kamakau states, the little lizard recalls the greater forms of moʻo akua.[214] As I show in chapter 5, Pukui provides an example of ʻŌiwi literary theory when she makes a significant connection between lizards and the idea of continuity implied in the concept of "series," another meaning of "moʻo," along with "succession, especially a genealogical line."[215]

While moʻolelo and kaʻao were originally oral traditions, many made the transition to literary genres in print with their publication in Hawaiian-language newspapers beginning in 1834. Oral traditions are generally understood as a community production. It is imperative, however, to know that individuals are a critical part of the process by which an account becomes a tradition. An "oral" tradition is called such because it is passed on by word of mouth. At some point in time, someone told a moʻolelo for the first time, and whoever heard it told it to someone else. A moʻolelo becomes a tradition when one generation passes it on to the next. Moreover, a moʻolelo may have several versions that owe their existence to individual storytellers—all of which clearly belong to the same discrete tradition. This is the case for the Hiʻiakaikapoliopele and ʻAukelenuiaʻīkū traditions, which have at least ten versions each in print. It is also true that distinct traditions sometimes overlap. A good example is the Haʻinākolo tradition, which has at least six versions in print and more if you count that of Keaniniʻulaokalani because they are essentially the same story told from two perspectives. Haʻinākolo and Keanini become a couple, have a child, and Keanini abandons her shortly thereafter.[216] Last, when someone puts to pen and paper and publishes an oral tradition, it goes on to exist both as a verbal and written product. Crucially, both are "traditions"—the written product is merely an oral tradition preserved in writing. Moreover, a written tradition can be the catalyst for other textual versions. Next, I discuss the genre termed "kaʻao" and its relationship to moʻolelo.

Theories and Methods for the Study of Moʻolelo and Kaʻao

During the nineteenth and twentieth centuries, a small group of scholars conducted systematic and sometimes comparative studies of moʻolelo and kaʻao, but their efforts barely scratched the surface, as there is much more work to be done. The comparative study of Hawaiian literature is in formation. While present-day scholars have published treatises on or translations of *specific* moʻolelo or kaʻao, very few have made the systematic study of these genres the backbone of their academic careers. What is lacking in past and present scholarship is a discussion on the theories and methods for the collection and investigation of these genres, and thus I take up this task. Theories and methods for the study of moʻolelo and kaʻao should take into account the extent to which our island world has shaped our ontology (ways of being) and epistemology (ways of knowing), which in turn influence our metadiscursive practices—genre specification, titles, subtitles, prefaces, introductions, greetings, authorial asides, caveats, closing remarks, and complimentary closings. Significantly, our metadiscursive practices can inform Ōiwi literary theory.

An analysis of metadiscourse can help us to comprehend how our kūpuna understood the connection between kaʻao and moʻolelo. On the one hand, kaʻao have been characterized as lacking the historicity of moʻolelo. On the other hand, they have also been explained as a narrative approach to relating history. In his dictionary, Lorrin Andrews (1865) explains "kaʻao" as "a legend; a tale of ancient times," a "traditional story; a fable," or a "history in the manner of a story." Henry H. Parker revised Andrews' dictionary (1922) and drastically edited his entry for "kaʻao": "To recite, to narrate; applicable only to fictitious and traditionary tales: I ua po nei e kaao ana oia ia makou; on that night he was telling us a story." Pukui (1986) defines "kaʻao" as a "legend, tale, novel, romance, usually fanciful; fiction." As we see, several Western genres are given as definitions for "ka'ao," which suggests that they, like mo'olelo, are a capacious genre.[217]

Hawaiian-language-newspaper contributors also offered their ideas about ka'ao. In 1862, in his critique of a foreign story published by a fellow Hawaiian, S. N. Hale'ole defined "ka'ao" as "he mea i hakuia" (something made up). Elsewhere, he offered a more nuanced understanding of ka'ao, which can be gleaned from the metadata of his works. For his serialized account about the heroine Lā'ieikawai in the newspaper *Ka Nupepa Kuokoa,* Hale'ole used the genre designation "mo'olelo," but when he republished it as a book, he changed the genre designation to "ka'ao."[218] However, the book's cover page notes, "Ka-kauia mailoko mai o na Moolelo Kahiko o Hawaii nei," which means that this story was inspired by or taken from traditional accounts. Lā'ieikawai, in fact, appears in several traditions other than the one that bears her name.[219]

P. W. Ka'awa, a Lahainaluna Seminary student who wrote about akua in his installments for the seminary's series on Ho'omana in 1865, offers his understanding of ka'ao:

He mea pili i ka noho hoonanea ana o na 'Lii, he mea lealea maoli no. He mea hoopau molowa paha. Malaila ka olu o kekahi poe ma ka paa o na kaao.[220]

It is a thing related to the leisure of Ali'i, something very entertaining. Perhaps a thing to end inactivity. Some people find pleasure there in memorizing ka'ao.

That people enjoy memorizing ka'ao to retell them underscores their status as traditional stories.

Kamakau dismisses ka'ao outright: "Pela ke ano o na Moolelo Kaao, aole oiaio, i haku wale ia no" (That is the nature of mo'olelo ka'ao, they are not true, just made up).[221] Here he uses *mo'olelo* as *narrative* in a general sense and *ka'ao* as a type of narrative, in this case fiction.

What these different definitions and commentary that I have thus shared do not provide is a theory to explain how ka'ao come into being. John E. Bush and Simeon Pa'aluhi are notable in that they offer a literary theory about ka'ao in their version of the Hi'iakaikapoliopele tradition, which they published in 1893. Here, before continuing, a summary of this tradition is helpful. Hi'iakaikapoliopele is the youngest and most-favored younger sister of Pele, the volcano deity whose name means "lava." After Pele meets Lohiʻau, the handsome ruler of Kauaʻi, in her spirit form as she is sleeping, Pele sends Hiʻiaka on a journey to re-trieve him. As Hiʻiaka travels across the Hawaiian Islands searching for Lohiʻau, whom two moʻo akua have abducted, she encounters and bat-tles adversaries, including many moʻo akua. In their introduction to the first installment of their account, Bush and Paʻaluhi call attention to the relationship between moʻolelo and kaʻao:

> E like me ke ano mau o na moolelo o ka wa kahiko, i haawi waha ia mai kahi hanauna mai a kekahi hanauna, ua lilo mau ke ano o ka moolelo, a ua hookikepakepa ia iho hoi i kela a me keia manawa o ka poe malama mookuauhau moolelo, a mai ia wa i kuakaao a ka moolelo io maoli o keia ohana a hiki i keia la, a lilo ai hoi na hana i hookuiia me ka huakai imi kane a Hiiaka i hele ai, he mau hana hookalakupua.[222]

> As always with moʻolelo belonging to the distant past, transmitted orally from one generation to another generation, the moʻolelo con-tinually evolves, altered each time [it is told] by the people who pre-serve the continuity of the moʻolelo, and from then on, the actual moʻolelo of that family transformed into a kaʻao, and the exploits of that man-seeking journey upon which Hiʻiaka embarked transformed into wondrous acts.

From this perspective, kaʻao are based on moʻolelo, which through mul-tiple retellings across generations transform historical figures into heroes (or even antiheroes) and their actions into fantastical exploits. In this sense, kaʻao resemble legends, which are accounts believed to contain the seeds of truth even if they cannot be fully authenticated.

There is yet another possibility to explain how kaʻao come into be-ing. Kaʻao based on traditional knowledge about gods, cultural heroes, or notable humans and that have abundant cultural references can also be the product of redaction. John Charlot, who uses form and redaction criticism to analyze the literatures of Hawaiʻi and Sāmoa, notes: "Just as historical subjects could be treated in story form, so such stories can be combined to form larger complexes.... A complex is constructed by combining redactionally a number of traditional pieces."[223] Although Charlot does not reference kaʻao specifically, his observations can apply to them. A redactor might create kaʻao by combining episodes or motifs from different moʻolelo, editing them, composing new data to join them, and then adding metadiscursive devices to this framework. In short, kaʻao can be "new" takes on "old" topics, but they are rooted in tradition. Those kaʻao that lack traditional figures and cultural references are the ʻŌiwi equivalent of Western fiction genres such as fairy tales, romances, or adventure stories, which perhaps inspired them. These kinds of kaʻao began to appear in Hawaiian-language newspapers in the 1860s.

An example of a kaʻao as a new composition based on traditional figures and themes is "Kaao Hooniua Puuwai no Ka-Miki" by John Wise and J. W. H. I. Kihe, which ran from 1914 to 1917.[224] Kepa Maly and Onaona Maly offer their cogent assessment of this account:

> The story of Ka-Miki is a long and complex account, that was recorded for the paper by Hawaiian historians John Wise and J.W.H.I. Kihe— with contributions by local informants. While "Ka-Miki" is not an ancient account, the authors used a mixture of local stories, tales, and family traditions in association with place names to tie together fragments of site specific history that had been handed down over the generations.

> The complete narratives include historical accounts for approximately 800 place names (many personified, commemorating particular individuals) of the island of Hawaiʻi. While the personification of all the identified individuals and their associated place names may not be entirely "ancient," the site documentation within the "story of Ka-Miki" is of significant cultural and historical value.[225]

As Maly and Maly's extensive analysis of Ka-Miki shows, kaʻao composed by informed individuals are valuable. Kaʻao, like moʻolelo, should be collected and studied as significant examples of ʻŌiwi artistic-intellectual production and important archives of ʻike kupuna.

Moʻolelo and kaʻao reflect a distinctly ʻŌiwi approach to narration. Their unfolding is rarely straightforward, unlike the common Western preference for linear explication with little embellishment. For this reason, readers new to this narrative approach may find them difficult to read. Like spiderwebs, moʻolelo and kaʻao are intricate creations, and how the spider creates its web can be read as an allegory for traditional ʻŌiwi narrative techniques. A spider weaves its web by releasing strands that it then carefully connects as it goes back and forth, up and down, and crosses here and there until the web is complete. And just as its method for constructing its web is informed by the countless spiders that existed before it, likewise moʻolelo and kaʻao reflect the countless generations of ʻŌiwi who have, collectively, contributed to the formation of a uniquely Hawaiian poetics, or literary aesthetic.

Poetical devices are a critical feature of ʻŌiwi aesthetics. Hiapokeikikāne Kitchie Perreira identifies twenty-four poetical devices in ʻŌiwi genres, which include metadiscursive practices, some of which I listed at the beginning of this section. Perreira terms these poetical devices "meiwi moʻokalaleo" (ethnoliterary devices).[226] His neologism calls attention to the way that meiwi are the iwi (bones) that provide the structure for ʻŌiwi artistic-intellectual products. The ʻōlelo noʻeau "ola nā iwi" (the bones live) refers to descendants who uphold their responsibility to care for their elders just as their elders cared for them, forming a chain of respect and reciprocity between generations. When we use meiwi to structure or analyze narratives, we ensure that ola nā meiwi (the meiwi live), which perpetuates the culture that birthed them.

All cultures are dynamic and evolve over time, but when it comes to Indigenous cultures, including that of Hawaiʻi, there has been a problematic tendency to view "precontact" cultures as somehow more authentic and "postcontact" cultures as less so.[227] It bears saying that everything we consider a tradition—whether a moʻolelo or a kaʻao, a practice or a custom—was once an innovation. As I have previously stressed, an artistic-intellectual practice or process becomes a tradition when the community finds it useful or important enough to replicate, teach, and transmit from one generation to another.[228] It is imperative to understand, however, that innovations are generally rooted in tradition: small differences in traditional processes or practices lead to improved or new ways of doing things. Should an innovation or a tradition stray too far from what is considered acceptable, the community may refuse it. ʻŌiwi should be the judge of what is significant in our culture, what should be conserved for posterity and prosperity, and when innovation is desired, needed, or unwanted.

Researching the Hawaiian-Language Newspapers for Knowledge about Moʻo Akua

Much of what we know about the beliefs and practices concerning moʻo akua comes from the writings of nineteenth- and twentieth-century ʻŌiwi who came of age, or whose near relatives did, during the period in which moʻo held a prominent place in Hawaiian religion and culture. This does not mean that what today's ʻŌiwi have to say about our cultural practices and mo'o akua is less significant but that it is essential to nānā i ke kumu (look to the origin or source)—in other words, attend to the beliefs and practices surrounding this class of deities when they were widely and openly worshipped, as they are the foundation for today's beliefs and practices.

The Hawaiian-language archive of 'Ōiwi self-representation during those centuries is impressive for the amount of works that were produced and for the variety of topics they covered. Yet, as M. Puakea Nogelmeier notes, "For generations, knowledge about Hawai'i has been limited at every level by scholarship that accepts a fraction of the available sources as being sufficient to represent the huge collection of material that actually exists. Over a century of documentation by Hawaiian writers has been ignored or dismissed through this mindset of acceptance, and perceptions about Hawai'i, past and present, are seriously affected." Nogelmeier terms this phenomemon a "discourse of sufficiency."[229] The largest archive of 'Ōiwi artistic-intellectual production is the corpus of Hawaiian-language newspapers. Approximately one hundred newspapers were published between 1834 and 1948. Their publication frequency ranged from daily, semiweekly, weekly, to monthly, and, depending on their content and format, fall into these categories: evangelical organs, government press, independent and nationalist gazettes, literary periodicals, bulletins, newsletters, or magazines.[230] Many but not all of these newspapers have been microfilmed. It has been calculated that more than one hundred thousand pages were produced, but the dimensions and font sizes of these pages vary greatly, so this number does not fully capture the magnitude of this resource.[231] It has been estimated that were these pages reformatted into word documents, they would exceed one million pages.[232]

The largest collection of these newspapers is the electronic archive Papakilo Database, which also incorporates Ulukau, another electronic repository that includes books.

Attending to the politics of recovering 'ike kupuna includes drawing attention to the nature of knowledge production about nā mea Hawai'i. A great many newspapers and their issues were microfilmed, but only forty-eight newspapers have so far been digitized and uploaded to the Papakilo Database and to Ulukau. A good number of these pages have also undergone optical character recognition (OCR). According to the Papakilo Database, its "collection contains 11,934 issues comprising 58,612 pages, and 379,918 articles."[233] Despite these valuable technological advances, researching these newspapers is still challenging: a systematic investigation of them is a time-consuming and painstaking process and thus requires patience, determination, and attention to detail. Here are ten things everyone should know about this process:

1. To declare that being able to access the Hawaiian language is a prerequisite for researching 'ike kupuna might seem obvious and thus unnecessary, but this is still a critical declaration given the ongoing production of knowledge on nā mea Hawai'i by scholars who rely on translations, many of which are often problematic. Moreover, non-Hawaiian scholars have often treated knowledgeable 'Ōiwi as informants rather than recognizing them as the experts, many of whom go on to establish a reputation as an authority on nā mea Hawai'i. While it is possible to search for and collect mo'olelo and ka'ao without proficiency in 'ōlelo Hawai'i, that lack of proficiency makes it difficult to investigate and understand them. That said, ma ka hana ka 'ike—you gain 'ike (knowledge and experience) when you do the work. Our ability to read Hawaiian-language newspapers increases as we read them, but reading them will always be time-consuming for reasons beyond language proficiency.

2. Many mo'olelo and ka'ao were published as serials, which presents its own particular challenges. While some lasted only a few installments, others ran for several months or even years, such as "Ka-Miki," which ran from January 8, 1914, to December 6, 1917, and has 210 installments.[234] I first download the series installments as PDFs, rename them in a way that facilitates research and citation, and then save them in the correct order. This method allows me to read them off-line and share them with colleagues and students.

3. Some scholars, myself included, transcribe these PDFs, which is incredibly time-consuming. The advantages of doing so, however, include creating a searchable document, recording anything of note, and facilitating translation.

4. Researching and collecting mo'olelo includes hunting down missing installments. Not everyone knows about *Hawai'i Newspapers: A Union List,* which records existing issues and their location, some issues of which have never been microfilmed.[235] In short, if an issue is not found in Papakilo or on microfilm, this does not mean that it does not exist.

5. Not every archive where hard copies of newspapers are kept is easily accessible. For example, the Kawaiaha'o Church Archive has unmicrofilmed copies of *Ka Na'i Aupuni*. To access this archive, you must send a letter explaining who you are and why you want to access it, which is submitted to the board for approval. Notably, this archive is not included in the *Hawai'i Newspapers Union List*, and while its newspaper holdings are noted in the *Directory of Historical Records Repositories in Hawai'i,* the name of its newspapers are not given.[236]

6. In the case of unmicrofilmed issues, or illegible microfilmed issues, I need to photograph them—if this is allowed. If not, I must transcribe them. In 2012 I collected Ho'oulumāhiehie's version of the Kamaakamahi'ai mo'olelo in *Ke Aloha Aina* from 1909 to 1912 online, but many issues were either illegible or missing. In the summer of 2016, Noenoe K. Silva and I photographed these pages at the Hawaiian Historical Society, which gave us permission to do so. We took extra photos where they were bound to capture the portion of the page not visible in the overhead photos. Next, I resaved several hundred photos with the paper's name, date, and page number. This method is critical because I must place these hundreds of photos in chronological order before I tranform them into PDFs. I have finished this portion of the work, and we have nearly completed transcribing this account.

7. Research on nā mea Hawai'i also entails searching the newspapers for specific information, such as a name, concept, or practice that appears in a mo'olelo or in a ka'ao. This logistical challenge concerns going through a great number of results. For example, for this book I looked up "moo," which had 8,140 results. While not every result concerned mo'o akua, a great number of them did. Also, because I am interested in what our kūpuna had to say about mo'olelo and ka'ao, how they understood them, and which information therein engendered debates, I searched for "mo'olelo" and "ka'ao." There are 48,956 results for the term "moolelo" and 9,234 for "kaao." I have finished the latter but am still going through the former.

8. To better understand the context of whatever I search for, I may need to read more of the mo'olelo and ka'ao than just the installment containing the data. I usually read the entire account. Furthermore, it is also important to consider the political and religious orientation of the newspaper in which a mo'olelo was published

because it may be relevant in terms of understanding why a moʻolelo was selected.[237]

9. In any examination of nā mea Hawaiʻi, especially traditions, practices, and akua, it is important to acknowledge that many perspectives exist on any given topic, each of which should be honored rather than dimissed in a mistaken belief that there is only one "truth" or "correct" viewpoint. The Hawaiian-language newspapers and other Hawaiʻi archives offer us access to the multiplicity of Hawaiian intellectuality. A discourse of sufficiency is the antithesis to these recorded multiple genealogies of knowledge and practices. This rich worldview is memorialized in an ʻōlelo noʻeau "'Aʻohe pau ka ʻike i ka hālau hoʻokahi," which Pukui translates as "All knowledge is not taught in the same school." She offers this interpretation: "One can learn from many sources." We are best served in the study of nā mea Hawaiʻi by adopting this saying as a method of inquiry. Indeed, this ʻōlelo noʻeau appears in newspapers in debates over variants of and variations in moʻolelo.[238] In short, when a moʻolelo has different versions, they should all be studied. This method yields important findings because each version contains ʻike that the others do not. The most impressive comparative work belongs to kuʻualoha hoʻomanawanui. For her six-hundred-page dissertation on Pele and Hiʻiaka literature, she gathered and analyzed every version, of which there are more than ten and several that are epic-length. She created several charts to show her findings: one offers publication data; another lists 843 chants that appear in these versions; yet another records the episodes, of which there are 356.[239]

10. Comparative moʻolelo research cannot be limited to the written word. Papakilo and Ulukau are not the only archives of moʻolelo ʻŌiwi. Not all traditions were published in newspapers or even written down. Individuals and families were and continue to be important repositories of moʻolelo. For example, Pukui interviewed kūpuna across the islands beginning in the early 1950s, and her taped interviews are priceless archives of ʻike kupuna and an important reminder that not all stories are widely available to the public. These recordings are found in the Bishop Museum Archives. Larry Lindsey Kauanoe Kimura also interviewed kūpuna for his radio broadcast *Ka Leo Hawaiʻi,* which has recently been made available in Ulukau.[240] Some of what I learned about moʻo akua from their interviews I have not found anywhere else. Although many moʻolelo and kaʻao have been preserved, we can imagine that countless

others, for whatever reason, were not. Fortunately, the oral and written record of information about moʻo that is widely available to the public is substantial. What is not widely available are the oral histories that were never published in the newspapers; stories known only to certain families or communities. Interviews with Hawaiians from diverse communities over the decades raise our awareness about the rich oral history that remains unknown to most people. This holds true for my own research on moʻo akua. While I have systematically researched all available archives for more than a decade, I know that people have moʻo-related ʻike that I cannot access.

The Value of Moʻolelo and Kaʻao

Moʻolelo and kaʻao have a broad intellectual value. It is helpful to understand that this value can be intrinsic or instrumental. "Intrinsic value" refers to that which is valuable in its own right. "Instrumental value" refers to something's value as a means to an end. Moʻolelo and kaʻao have an intrinsic value in that they exist and were told, which signifies that our kūpuna considered them important. Studying moʻolelo and kaʻao for ʻike assigns them an instrumental value. Reading or listening to them for pleasure speaks to their intrinsic value as modes of entertainment. But even then, their value can be inadvertently instrumental because as we enjoy them, we also absorb the ʻike they contain. First and foremost, moʻolelo and kaʻao are important archives of ʻike kupuna, which includes not only ancestral knowledge but also ancestral ways of knowing and being.

Archives of ʻŌiwi philosophical thought. By philosophical, I mean that our kūpuna theorized about the fundamental nature of knowledge, reality, and existence in connection with our island world. Examples of philosophical questions embedded in moʻolelo or for which they offer answers include the origins of the cosmos, our akua, our islands, and ourselves as well as the relationship or kinship between the same and also what happens to us after death. Some of these philosophical questions are also religion related.

Records of ʻŌiwi religion and spirituality across place and time. In religion studies, religion is generally understood as an organized or structured system of beliefs and belief-related practices, whether personal or institutionalized, in relation to a transcendent power or powers. Spirituality refers to a person's recognition of and relationship with a transcendent power or powers whether this person practices an organized religion or not. Hoʻomana, as our moʻolelo and kaʻao show, is both organized and personal.

Critical carriers of our language. A perusal of the works cited in Pukui and Elbert's Hawaiian dictionary shows that many of the words contained therein were taken from moʻolelo, kaʻao, and other ʻŌiwi genres.[241] As any avid reader knows, moʻolelo and kaʻao often contain words and place names not found in any of our Hawaiian-language dictionaries or reference books. Moreover, because our worldview is encapsulated in our language, moʻolelo and kaʻao are significant records of the same. In a sense, reading them allows us to travel back in time to access a worldview belonging to the near and distant past and discover which aspects of that worldview have survived into the present.

Political value. Politics, in its most basic sense, refers to the ways that we engage with each other in small and large communities in order to organize ourselves. An important element in the study of politics is power relations, or relationships of power. Our moʻolelo and kaʻao record ʻŌiwi political history, which includes individual actions and larger political movements, regime changes, and power relations between aliʻi, between aliʻi and makaʻāinana, between makaʻāinana, between akua, and between akua and humans. There is also a political dimension to telling moʻolelo and kaʻao, which includes what and which versions were told. There is yet another political aspect, which is telling them for political purposes. When J. W. H. Kauwahi established *Ka Hoku of ka Pakipika,* the first newspaper published by ʻŌiwi, the first issue's front page was entirely dedicated to the moʻolelo of Kawelo, which I interpret as a clear declaration about the value of moʻolelo and an instance of what hoʻomanawanui terms "literary activism" and "literary nationalism," which she discusses extensively in her work on the political nature of Pele and Hiʻiaka literature.[242] We can put moʻolelo and kaʻao to use to further our poltical and cultural aims as we struggle to recover from historical trauma.

Archives of culture. "Culture" is an umbrella term that covers everything pertaining to humans and human activities. Moʻolelo and kaʻao contain information about our culture across place and time. They preserve cultural knowledge and impart important lessons. Because they contain information about many topics, our cultural literacy increases with each one that we read. The more we build up our knowledge base about nā mea Hawaiʻi, the better we can understand and contextualize the other information we acquire as we read moʻolelo, kaʻao, and other Ōiwi genres. Significantly, our culture informs our identity, and studying mo'olelo and ka'ao is an important part of our journey as we celebrate being 'Ōiwi. As we become more knowledgeable about our culture, we also strengthen our identity. Research on mo'olelo and ka'ao often has an emotional aspect, and we must understand that this is a result of the historical trauma that we have experienced and from which we are still recovering. (I return to this topic in the epilogue.)

Literary value. Literary studies are an important part of what, in Western academic institutions, is termed the "humanities," or "the study of how people process and document the human experience."[243] The creation and study of literary theories are an essential aspect of literary studies, which includes the study of genres and their development, the author, and the historical and cultural context in which literature is produced. Literary theory, in its most basic sense, refers to the set of ideas and methods used to study literature—the tools we use to investigate its underlying principles. Theories and methods for the study of mo'olelo and ka'ao are embedded in the mo'olelo and ka'ao themselves—in their content, in their poetical devices, and in their metadiscursive features.[244] But mo'olelo and ka'ao themselves have a matrix—the 'āina.

Expression of Aloha 'Āina. Mo'olelo and ka'ao express aloha 'āina—our visceral aloha for our 'āina—and reflect the countless ways that our identity and culture are grounded in our island world.[245] Nearly two thousand years ago, our seafaring Polynesian ancestors left their homeland, navigating the ocean until they reached the islands known today as Hawai'i. As centuries passed, our culture and language evolved to the point that we became a distinct people—the 'Ōiwi. Our islands shaped us physically, intellectually, and spiritually. Our 'ike is grounded in the realities of our island world existence. For countless generations, our kūpuna lived in close connection to the 'āina and observed it. Not only did we observe the 'āina, we claim/ed kinship with it. We are part of a complex web of relationality in which all—land, sea, sky, and everything therein—are kin. This relationality is also spiritual, for we are the human relatives of the other-than-human entities of our island world, many of whom we consider akua.

Reclaiming ancestral knowledge includes recovering knowledge that was once common but that, for whatever reason, became obscure and drawing attention to the ways that knowledge was preserved and the methods by which it was disseminated. This perspective guides my approach to organizing this book. Each chapter begins with a general statement about its main topic and its subtopics, for which I give examples. While this is standard practice, my approach is informed by helu (listing and enumeration), which is crucial to this reclamation project. Helu entails an introduction followed by a list of categories and examples. For each section, I instance a wide range of moʻo who fall into a particular category. Here, I should note that some examples require more explanation than others, and while I do offer insights when needed, I reserve any major conclusions for the end of each chapter. These lists are an inventory of moʻo who fit into a given category and introduce readers to many moʻo, the ʻike of which is not easily found. The wide range of examples are the critical foundation from which it is possible to draw a conclusion on the basis of evidence and reasoning.

Our intellectuals used and continue to use helu as a principle to guide their treatises on nā mea Hawaiʻi, whether they discuss deities, aliʻi ranking, or types of flora and fauna. John Charlot, in his phenomenal monograph *Classical Hawaiian Education,* treats helu extensively.[246] Charlot observes, "The prevalence of lists in Hawaiian literature is ample evidence of the extensiveness and variety of the practice of classifying and categorizing."[247] Helu is an important tool for dealing with discrete traditions and their respective versions. As Charlot notes, "The practice of reclassifying influences thinking, supporting the ability to view an object from different perspectives and to shift one's perspective rapidly," which "is supportive of the Hawaiian capacity to tolerate a variety of traditions with contradictory positions as more or less self-contained universes of discourse."[248] In other words, helu helps us to theorize about and make sense of large quantities of data. In their translation of Davida Malo's *Moʻolelo Hawaiʻi,* Charles Langlas and Jeffrey Lyon explain that Malo's extensive use of helu is a common approach to learning and a common practice in composition and note, "The first-time reader often finds this listing procedure tedious because it is foreign to those educated in the Western system."[249] While that may be true, the use of helu in reclamation projects like this book on moʻo is imperative.

This introduction contextualizes moʻo akua within a larger tradition to demonstrate that supernatural reptiles were and continue to be significant in the different religions and respective cultures of which they are part. It also raises awareness about the politics and poetics of recovering ʻike kupuna about moʻo akua. Another contribution it makes is to draw attention to the vast ʻŌiwi scholarly production of the past, which in turn shows that ʻŌiwi have an incredible artistic-intellectual heritage. It discusses what researching nā mea Hawaiʻi entails and its challenges and illuminates the value of moʻolelo. Chapter 1 explores why moʻo akua are considered water deities and determines the kind of water deities they are. This investigation provides the necessary foundation for better understanding the social, familial, political, economic, and religious roles that moʻo held in earlier Hawaiian history. Chapter 2 offers an overview of the kino lau system and the ways it undergirds Hawaiian religion, which is paramount for grasping the significance of the kino lau associated with all moʻo: the lizard, the brindled dog, the goby fish, and the spider. To foster deeper insights into this class of deities, I analyze the term "moʻo" and its many definitions, one of which is "lizard," and discuss lizard species indigenous to Hawaiʻi. Chapter 3 concerns moʻo-specific kino lau, forms associated only with certain moʻo. An exploration of moʻo-specific kino lau raises compelling questions about the nature of Hawaiian knowledge and the kino lau system. Chapter 4 examines the kinship and antagonism between the moʻo and Pele clans by exploring the ways in which their genealogies and kino lau overlap across moʻolelo. Chapter 5 focuses on the roles and functions of moʻo akua in an earlier time in Hawaiian history. In the epilogue, I consider the cultural relevance of moʻo for ʻŌiwi, past and present. The second half of this book is a catalog of nearly three hundred moʻo, which includes name, gender, characteristics, and source information.

Chapter 1
Mo'o Akua and Water

Life as we know it would be impossible without water. We can survive weeks without food but only a few days without water. We are composed largely of water. It is the base element of our reproductive fluids, and our offspring begin their existence surrounded by water in the form of amniotic fluid in their mother's womb. Everything we need to survive, in one way or another, also depends on water. Given that water is, as Mircea Eliade puts it, the "fons et origo, the source of all possible existence," it is unsurprising that peoples across place and time have ascribed religious significance to water and developed water symbolism.[1] But there is more to water symbolism than the fact that water is the source and origin of all life. Water's material attributes are fascinating, so we should also consider its many different qualities.

Water is a shape-shifter. In its pure state, water is "a colorless, transparent, odorless, tasteless liquid."[2] It is a substance that has no fixed shape, a liquid that occupies space and has weight but is not easily grasped. Water affects nearly everything it touches. Water "is able to dissolve many other substances."[3] A drop of water quickly disappears, either by evaporation or absorption, but the constant drip of individual water drops can wear a hole in stone. With the passage of time, streams and rivers can carve paths through soil and hew deep valleys out of mountains. When water evaporates, it loses moisture and becomes vapor. When water vapor condenses, it forms clouds, rain, fog, mist, and dew. In the right conditions, rain refracts and disperses sunlight to create rainbows. Frozen water vapor and rain become snow and hail. Water not only affects nearly everything with which it comes into contact but is also affected in turn. Water's environment influences its attributes, including its taste, color, and shape and whether it is fresh, salty, or brackish.

Up until this point, I have spoken of water in the most general sense—H_2O—and discussed its many "distinctive physical and chemical" properties.[4] In English, the word "water" has a broad application; it can apply to fresh, brackish, or salt water. In contrast, such a term does not exist in Hawaiian. "Wai" is our word for water "of any kind other than sea water," whereas "kai" is used for seawater and "wai kai" for brackish water. Thus, when writing in English about Hawaiian "water"-related topics such as water deities, the potential for misunderstanding increases. In other words, given that the Hawaiian Islands are located in the Pacific Ocean, when I speak of mo'o akua as "water deities," readers might immediately think of ocean gods. However, mo'o are akua wai—not akua kai. Here, I continue with my discussion on "water," which is narrowly focused on wai and bodies of wai.

With its aesthetic qualities that delight our senses, wai is seductive. It is a rare person indeed who does not love rivers, streams, waterfalls, lakes, ponds, and pools. They call to us, especially when they are in secluded areas where we can momentarily find respite from the noise and bustle of cities. Such places abound in the Hawaiian Islands. Still, wai can also be destructive. The bodies of fresh water we find so alluring can be treacherous. Swift river currents can drag us under, trap us beneath an underwater ledge, or, in Hawai'i, pull us into submerged lava tubes, caves, or deep holes. It might happen that several miles away, unbeknown to us, a heavy rainfall occurs that can suddenly transform our excursion to an idyllic location into a deadly encounter. The pretty stream flowing amid moss-covered boulders near which we are picnicking can unexpectedly become a raging torrent, pummeling us with debris as it sweeps us away. Prolonged rainfall has disastrous effects on the countryside and neighborhoods. It can erode the ground beneath or around boulders, making them unstable to the point that gravity takes over—and they crush anything in their path. Heavy floods and mudslides can make roads impassible and destroy homes. Last, too much or too little rain can lead to famine and, consequently, death.

Because mo'o akua are akua wai, when investigating them we should keep the life-giving and death-dealing properties of wai in mind because as a collective they embody most if not all of its attributes. Mo'o, also like wai, are shape-shifters. They can, in a limited capacity, change their forms to suit their moods or aims. They can be beneficent or malevolent: protect us, nourish us, seduce us, or destroy us. Mo'o, also like wai, are powerful, unpredictable, and awe-inspiring. Moreover, if we consider the ways that wai, including water flow and the water cycle—ocean, evaporation, cloud formation, rainfall, water returning to the ocean as rain or runoff—can be understood as a metaphor for continuity, then we can also see how moʻo, as personifications of wai, can also symbolize the same. As Eliade explains, "Because it [water] incorporates in itself all potentiality, water becomes a symbol of life (living water)."[5] That early Hawaiians engaged in water symbolism, making a connection between water and regeneration, is clear. For example, the tradition of ʻAukelenuiaʻīkū notes the belief that the wai ola loa o Kāne (Kāne's water of eternal life) could bring the dead back to life (see chapter 4). As reptilian deities, moʻo also represent continuity and regeneration in the sense of an unbroken lineage, and thus moʻo are important symbols of moʻokūʻauhau (genealogy), a foundational and organizational concept in Hawaiian religion and the culture of which it is part (see chapter 5).

Moʻo Akua and Their Watery Abodes

Notwithstanding the fact that moʻo akua are akua wai, there is no evidence in the extensive archive of Hawaiian belief narratives and historical treatises to support the idea that the majority of our ancestors believed that this class of deities, *as a whole,* could transform into water. That said, a few moʻo do have a water-related form such as fog, mist, a rainbow, a kind of rain, or the power to control clouds or water. As a rule, their relationship with water is most evident in terms of where they live. Significantly, moʻo akua are generally associated with specific bodies of water or damp places and attributed with distinct dispositions that tend to parallel these locations. Thus, to better understand the ways that moʻo embody water, we should consider the physical attributes and cultural significance of their watery abodes.

A case in point is the Wailuku River on the island of Hawaiʻi, the largest and longest river in the islands at twenty-six miles long from its source on the slopes of Mauna Kea to its mouth at Hilo Bay.[6] That it is a dangerous river is implicit in its name, which means "destroying or destructive water." In 1920, Hilo resident Charlotte Hapai explained, "In olden times before there were bridges and other safeguards the river wrought considerable damage to property and during the rainy season it took its toll of human lives. Legends connected with Wailuku tend to confirm the belief that it was named for its violent habits."[7] Three well-known moʻo are associated with the lower portion of this river in Hilo: Kuna, Piliamoʻo, and Nohoamoʻo/Kuaua.

One of the Wailuku River's most famous features is Waiānuenue (Rainbow water). This eighty-foot waterfall, also known as "Rainbow Falls," takes its name from the large "rainbow formed from its mists many mornings."[8] This waterfall's pretty name is misleading. Even during prolonged dry weather when the waterfall subsides, swimming in this area is still dangerous.

The enormous Kuna once lived above Waiānuenue. When the deities Hina and Māui, mother and son, came to live in Hilo, Hina made her home in the cave beneath Waiānuenue.[9] In her account of Kuna, Hapai notes that he repeatedly tormented Hina but does not explain why. Perhaps the issue arose from the fact that Hina was an accomplished kapa (bark cloth) maker, and it is supposed that she would have passed several hours each day at this task. The cave would have greatly amplified the noise Hina made with her wooden kapa beater as she pounded the kapa against a wooden anvil. Whatever the reason, Kuna did all he could to annoy her, "sending over great torrents of water or by rolling logs and boulders down the stream. Quite often he would block the stream below the falls with sediment sent down by freshets during the rainy season."[10] Because Hina was well protected in the cave, she never worried about Kuna's efforts to drown her, and this indifference infuriated him. Māui, however, decided to kill him. In his efforts to escape Māui, Kuna fled from one hiding place to another in the river, and the hole that Māui's spear made when he threw it at Kuna as he hid is called PukaoMāui (Hole of Māui).[11] Finally, Kuna dove into one of the Wailuku River's deep pools. There, Māui bombarded Kuna with "hot stones and molten lava" that he had requested of Pele after cornering him. In the end, the boiling water killed Kuna. Today those deep pools are known as Boiling Pots. Kuna's corpse can still be seen, "a long, black-rock island known as Moo Kuna, between the rapids" in the Wailuku River below Waiānuenue.[12]

The story of Kuna exemplifies how mo'o become part of the 'āina (land), memorialized in topographical features and their names. Unsurprisingly, Kuna's great size and antagonistic nature mirror the perilous features of this portion of the Wailuku River. The same can be said for the other mo'o associated with this river.

Piliamo'o and a mo'o companion, sometimes identified as Nohoamo'o, sometimes as Kuaua, are two hostile, people-hating mo'o who control an important crossing point in the Wailuku River, a makeshift bridge called Papa Kāhulihuli o Wailuku (Unsteady Plank of Wailuku). Papa Kāhulihuli o Wailuku was located at a shallow place just above the Pāheʻeheʻe and Kaluakanaka cascades near the river's mouth and "was kept in a little cave near the falls on the Hamakua side, or in wet weather in a little cave up on the side of the bank a little farther upstream."[13] The names of these cascades record the dangers people faced when they crossed the river at this point. "Pāheʻeheʻe" means "to make slip," which can refer to the slippery river rocks and to the unsteady log that served as a bridge. "Kaluakanaka" means "the man/person pit or cave" and may refer to the fact that a person or persons once lived there. But given that this area is associated with Piliamoʻo and Nohoamoʻo/ Kuaua, we can easily imagine that this name refers to where these moʻo kept their food (humans). In *Place Names of Hawaii*, Mary Kawena Pukui, Samuel H. Elbert, and Esther Mookini record "Kaluakanaka" as "Kāluakanaka" (oven-baking man) and make no mention of a cascade. Instead, they note that Kāluakanaka was "a balancing stone" in the Wailuku River "believed connected by a tunnel to Coconut Island, and that persons falling over the stone into the stream would drown."[14] There is no entry for Pāheʻeheʻe in Hilo in *Place Names of Hawaii* or in John Clark's *Hawaiʻi Place Names*.

Piliamoʻo and Nohoamoʻo/Kuaua appear in the traditions of Hiʻiakaikapoliopele, while Piliamoʻo appears in those of Laukaʻieʻie, Keaomelemele, and Keaniniʻulaokalani.[15] Depending on the account, they are either both female or both male. Piliamoʻo, the smaller moʻo, "stayed under a big rock near the top of the bank just to the left of the old trail down to the river." From its cave "in the bank over which the falls drop and to the left of them," Nohoamoʻo kept watch over the pass on the Hāmākua side of this ford. They demanded a toll from those who needed to cross the log. According to one account, they accepted "food, or fish, or kapa."[16] When people neared the bridge, Piliamoʻo called out, "Kāhulihuli ka papa o Wailuku, he ʻole ke kaha kūʻai ai, hō mai ana he ʻai" (The plank of Wailuku is unsteady, the toll for crossing is not great, give me food) while Nohoamoʻo would demand, "Hō mai ana he iʻa" (Give me fish).[17] Moses Manu describes them as "moo pepehi kanaka" (moʻo who kill people), and for good reason.[18] If travelers fell from the bridge or tried to avoid paying the toll by swimming across the river, the moʻo ate them.[19] In Kaili's version of Hiʻiakaikapoliopele, Piliamoʻo uses her tail as a bridge for Hiʻiaka (figure 1.1). Because she shows respect, Hiʻiaka spares her life, and her "descendants are said to still occupy the Wailuku, and on special occasions will show themselves to a favored few."[20]

Figure 1.1. Hiʻiakaikapoliopele encounters Piliamoʻo at Wailuku River.
Artwork by Hinahina Gray.

For the unwary, even shallow ponds can be perilous if they are as-sociated with moʻo. An ʻŌiwi of Molokai, David Wallace, shared a strange incident that took place in the 1970s when he was a police officer in Molokai. Wallace had a friend who was an employee of Molokai Wa-ter Works, and part of his job entailed inspecting water reservoirs in the valleys. One day, the man's family called the police station to report him missing. Thinking that perhaps his car had broken down, Wallace and the other police officers each went to check out the different reservoirs to search for him. One officer went to Meyer's Pond (traditionally known as Keālia), and that is where the officer found the man's car, but he was not in or near it. Next to the car were his clothes, which he had neatly folded in a pile, and his shoes, into which he had tucked his socks. The officer found him floating face down in the middle of the pond. An au-topsy was performed to ascertain the cause of death. It was not a heart attack, as some had initially expected. The man had drowned. The post-mortem also revealed something puzzling. Around the man's body were marks resembling rope burns, but no ropes were found at the scene.

When Wallace and the others learned that the cause of death was drowning, they were astonished. Their friend had been six feet tall, and Meyer's Pond, which was about the size of a football field, was three or four feet deep at the very most. Given the strange circumstances of their friend's death—the fact that he had taken off all of his clothes and folded them neatly in a pile and walked straight to the middle of the pond, that he had died by drowning and not by a heart attack or something similar that would have prevented him from making his way back to dry ground, that he had strange marks like rope burns on his body but no rope was seen—there was really only one explanation. Wallace said there was a moʻo wahine (female moʻo) associated with that pond, and they wondered if she had used her power to draw him into the pond, where she then drowned him by wrapping her ropelike tail around his body to trap him beneath the water.[21]

Not all moʻo are evil, however, and ʻŌiwi often frequent bodies of fresh water associated with moʻo. Moʻo can also make their homes in geographical features caused by lava flows, which later fill with water. For example, when the upper portion of a lava flow hardens it can cre-ate a tube through which lava continues to course. Once the eruption ends, the lava tube remains, and in some cases a portion of its roof might collapse, leaving a channel or, eventually, a sinkhole. The pool known as ka wai ʻauʻau o Punaluʻu (the bathing pool of Punaluʻu), and alternatively as Queen's Bath, was a spring-fed pool in a collapsed lava conduit in Kapa'ahu in Punalu'u on Hawai'i. Emma Kapūnohu'ulaokalani Kauhi reminisced about swimming there as a child with other members of her community. Its water was fresh at the bottom and brackish near the surface, and she noted that a white mo'o (unidentified) was its kia'i (guardian). In 1988 a lava flow from Pu'u 'Ō'ō covered this pool.[22] The fact that people bathed there without concern suggests that this mo'o was benevolent.

Mountaintops are considered sacred places because they are areas where gods and spirits dwell. One of the Hawaiian Islands' sacred summits belongs to Mauna Kea on the island of Hawai'i, the tallest volcano in the world at nearly fourteen thousand feet in height from its base beneath the ocean to its summit.[23] Mo'oinanea (a.k.a. Kamo'oinanea), who appears in many traditions, is linked to Waiau, a sacred lake located at the top of Mauna Kea, in two different traditions, one related by Emma Ahu'ena Taylor about Kūkahau'ula and Poli'ahu and the other by Ho'oulumāhiehie about Ha'inākolo.[24] In Taylor's account, Mo'oinanea, who is gendered as male and described as a "merman," is ordered by the god Kāne to guard his daughter, the snow goddess Poli'ahu, and her sacred bathing place, Waiau.[25] In Ho'oulumāhiehie's account, Mo'oinanea is also male but is described as a mo'o. Here, it is Mo'oinanea's descendant Kū'aikāuakama, who will one day father Ha'inākolo, who orders the mo'o to go and live in Lilinoe's (another noted Mauna Kea goddess) sacred pool near Mauna Kea's summit.[26] Although Mo'oinanea is gendered as male in Taylor's and Ho'oulumāhiehie's accounts, she is identified as female elsewhere, where she is described as the highest-ranking mo'o and the origin of all other mo'o (see chapters 3 and 4).

Another powerful mo'o, Kalanamainu'u, in the tradition of Kamaakamahi'ai by Ho'oulumāhiehie, lives in a cave near the top of Mauna Loa, "the largest active volcano on Earth" that "dominates the Island of Hawai'i, covering just over half the island."[27] In this tradition she seems to be on good terms with Pele as she apparently visits her regularly: "Me he mea la, i kauoha ia mai nei oia e ka luahine (oia o Pele—Mea Kakau) e iho aku i Halema'uma'u, a o ka iho aku nei no ia" (It was as if she was ordered by the old woman (that is Pele—Writer) to come down to Halema'uma'u, and so she did).[28]

In Hawaiian culture, the lani (sky, heavens, firmament) is a space that belongs to the gods. For this reason, "ka lani" (heaven, or heavenly one) is an epithet traditionally used for high-ranking ali'i who had kept the purity of their lineage—descendants of akua—intact by intermarriage with close relatives and were therefore considered divine humans.²⁹ Moʻoinanea is also associated with the ʻāina akua of Kānehūnāmoku, Nuʻumealani, and Kuaihelani. In the Keaomelemele tradition, Moʻoinanea is sister to Kāne and Kanaloa, and she and Kāne are indicated as nā mākua (parents) of the moʻo clan and their large family:

> I keia manawa a Kamooinanea e noho pu nei me Kane ma ma Waolani, ua lilo keia kuahiwi i wahi makemake loa na ua makua nei o na moo a me kona ohana nui a pau, ua noho loihi lakou malaila a hiki wale i ka manawa i hele aku ai ka nui o na moo a noho ma keia pae aina.³⁰

> During this period that Kamoʻoinanea lived with Kāne and the others at Waolani, this mountain became a cherished place for the parent of the moʻo and all of her large family, and they lived there for a long time until most of the moʻo left to populate this archipelago.

In ʻŌiwi culture, Kāne and Kanaloa are brothers. Kāne, the elder, is associated with the sun and fresh water, without which life as we know it would not exist, and for this reason he is considered the god of procreation. Kanaloa is the primary ocean deity. Together, they represent the water cycle. In the Keaomelemele tradition, Moʻoinanea has power over clouds (masses of condensed water vapor), as she commands and places them where it pleases her. This mana makes sense given her status as the highest-ranking reptilian water deity and her close kinship with Kāne.³¹

As reptilian deities, moʻo have no trouble climbing steep rock faces, and thus many of them make their homes on cliffs near bodies of water. In one account, Moʻoinanea lives at the Kalalau cliffs on Kauaʻi. Because she lives there, Kalalau and its pali nihohiho (jagged cliffs) were noa (free) to supernatural beings and kapu (off-limits) to humans.³² Hiʻilawe Falls in Waipiʻo Valley in Hāmākua on Hawaiʻi is celebrated in songs, hula, ʻōlelo noʻeau, and moʻolelo. It "is the highest free-fall waterfall in Hawaiʻi and one of the highest in the world, with a vertical drop of about 1,000 feet."³³ Hiʻilawe is the home of a beautiful aliʻi wahine who is also a moʻo. This moʻo lives in Waiakealoha, a pool at the top of Hiʻilawe.³⁴ She is the caretaker of the kupua dog Pūpūlenalena (a.k.a. Puapualenalena), the same dog that stole the conch shell from the aliʻi ʻUmialīloa. When this aliʻi met this beautiful moʻo, his attraction to her was such that he attempted to make her his wahine.³⁵ ʻUmialīloa is an important historical figure, a famous ruling ali'i of Hawai'i about whom many stories are told. Another mo'o (unidentified) lived at Kīpū cliff on Kaua'i. She stopped up a stream, which caused all the streams seaward of it to turn yellow.[36] Kē'ē and Kalalau cliffs in Kaua'i are renown for the mo'o who live there, including Kilioe (a.k.a. Kilioeikapua), Kalanamainu'u, Aka, Kē'ē, Walinu'u, and Walimānoanoa. Kāmeha'ikana, a form of Haumea, is a mo'o in both versions of the Kamaakamahi'ai tradition who lives in Kaualehu Cave in 'Ioleka'a cliff in He'eia, O'ahu.[37]

I previously noted that Kalamainu'u is associated with a cave at the summit of Mauna Loa, but elsewhere, depending on the tradition, she lives in an upland cave somewhere in Molokai, an upland cave in Mokulē'ia on O'ahu, or a cliff-face cave at Waimānalo on O'ahu. Ahiki asserts that Kalamainu'u is Waka. He notes that Puahia cliff in Waimānalo has several caves, and "Ma kekahi o keia mau lua, kahi i noho ai o Waka me Punaaikoae, a holo ai o Punaaikoae i Hawaii, i o Pele la, a pakele i ka make ia Kalamainuu (o Waka no ia)." (Waka and Puna'aikoa'e lived in one of these caves. Puna'aikoa'e fled to Hawai'i to Pele to escape being killed by Kalamainu'u (who is Waka). Seaward is the cave of Hīnale, Kalamainu'u's brother, who helped Puna'aikoa'e to escape.)[38] Another mo'o (unidentified) lives in a cave near Kulaokaiwi'ula in Kalihi Kai on O'ahu. This cave has two subterranean/subocean paths: one goes to Kaua'i, and the other leads to Kahana in the Ko'olauloa district on O'ahu. The mo'o guards the subterranean path to Kahana.[39]

Mo'o also live in rain forests. The island of Hawai'i is famous for its 'ōhi'a lehua trees (*Metrosideros polymorpha*) with their characteristic lehua—the bright-red pom-pom-like clusters of flower stamens whence the tree takes its name. 'Ōhia lehua, also known as just lehua, figure prominently in Hawai'i's rain forests and are second only to the koa (*Acacia koa*) in terms of height: the former reaches fifty or more feet, and the latter, in the right conditions, can exceed one hundred. With their great height and massive trunks, old lehua trees are majestic.[40] Pana'ewa is the name of a celebrated rain forest in the Hilo district, famous for its lehua groves, that takes its name from the mo'o guardian of that forest.[41] At first, Pana'ewa may seem like an anomaly because this mo'o is associated with a rain forest and not with a specific body of water, as are most mo'o, but Pana'ewa's kino lau and status as guardian of the Pana'ewa lehua forest offer further insights into the complex ways that mo'o akua embody water (see chapter 3).

Kihanuilūlūmoku guards Paliuli on Hawai'i. This mo'o lives in a river named Muliwai-'ōlena, upland of Paliuli:

O na aoao o keia muliwai, oia kona mau kapa, ua paehumuia me na
pohaku a me na iliili onionio o na waihoolulu i like loa me ko ke anue-
nue. Aia hoi maloko o ka ponahawai, e moe ai ua Kihanuilulumoku
nei, he mau pohaku anapanapa a oaoaka, elike me na kukuna olinoo-
lino malamalama o ka La ke hulali.[42]

The borders of this river, which are its banks, are a sacred enclosure
made of stones and variegated pebbles of colors just like the rainbow.
In the pool where Kihanuilūlūmoku sleeps are also stones that shine
and shimmer like the sparkle of sunbeams.

Notably, this river's name includes "'ōlena," the word for "yellow," which
is associated with mo'o, and "turmeric," which produces a yellow dye.

Several mo'o frequent or live near the seashore. One mo'o (unidentified) lives at Ko'iahi, a gorge in Mākua Valley. A stream there,
also called Ko'iahi, runs into the ocean. This mo'o wahine will sometimes sit where the stream meets the seashore by the coral outcropping
known as Kūla'ila'i (figure 1.2). There, she waits for her lover, the shark
god Nanaue.[43]

Figure 1.2. Kūla'ila'i coral outcropping. Photograph by Jan Beckett.

Another mo'o associated with Mākua is Kilikilipua, who lives in an underground spring.[44] Pu'u'anuhe, a "hideous red-headed lizard-woman" infamous for hiding Māui's kite in the hills behind Hīlea, lived along the seashore of Ka'ū at Ka Lae (a.k.a. South Point). Because she would not tell him where she had hid it and because she "lured many a poor fisherman to death on the rocky coast of Kau," Māui killed her. He found his kite and named the spot after her.[45] Also at Ka Lae is Palahemo, who lives in a brackish pool about several hundred feet from the ocean. In the account of Ka-Miki, she is a luahine (old woman) kia'i of Ka Lae, where souls leap into the afterlife. Her favorite hānai (informally adopted) son is Puhi Oilo, an eel kupua, and she is one of Ka-Miki's kūpuna.[46] The people of Ka'ū believed that the pool continued underground to the sea.[47] An exploration confirmed that this anchialine pool leads to a lava tube one hundred feet beneath the ground and about one thousand feet long.[48] Palahemo is memorialized in an 'ōlelo no'eau, "I puni iā 'oe i Ka'ū a 'ike 'ole 'oe iā Palahemo, 'aohe nō 'oe i 'ike iā Ka'ū."[49] "'Ike" denotes "to see" and "to know," and when I searched in vain for Palahemo, a kama'āina of Ka'ū took pity on me and drove me there, and I had an epiphany. This 'ōlelo no'eau also speaks to the fact that Palahemo is not only worthy of visiting but nearly impossible to find if you do not know Ka'ū well. Thus, I translate this 'ōlelo no'eau as "If you have traveled around Ka'ū and you failed to see Palahemo, then you really do not know Ka'ū." Also on Hawai'i, female mo'o twins are associated with Keawehala Pond near the Mākole'ā Heiau (a women's heiau named after ali'i wahine Mākole'ā) at Keauhou.[50] Yet another Hawai'i mo'o, Mo'okini, lives near the sea of Kapakai at Maliu. Some mo'o are also associated with coastal loko i'a (fishponds). I discuss several of them in connection with different topics throughout the rest of this chapter.

A few mo'o live in sea caves. In the 'Aukelenuia'īkū tradition, Mo'oinanea lives at Kuaihelani in a subterranean cave with two entrances. The smaller one is inland, apparently just big enough for a person to enter, which her descendants cover with a rock. The other entrance is a cavern on the shore. There, she enters with the rising tide to eat the humans whom her descendants toss down through the other entrance. Below the cliffs of Kaumālapa'u Bay on Lāna'i is a sea cave known as Puhioka'ala (Blowhole of Ka'ala) whose entrance is beneath the water. Mo'oali'i lived there until the shark god Ukanipō sent its servants to oust him. They harassed him and threatened "to imprison him within [the cave] by piling a mountain of rocks against the opening." He left the cave and found a new one near Kalaupapa at Molokai. There, fishermen built many kuahu (rock altars) to honor him.[51] These kuahu speak to the belief that mo'o have the power to attract fish, a topic to which I will return.

Walewale and 'A'amo'o

In addition to dwelling near bodies of fresh water or damp places like rain forests, another indication that mo'o are water spirits is evident in the belief that they produce, similar to many fish species, a watery, slime-like substance termed "walewale." Samuel Keko'owai describes Hauwahine's mo'o form as having "ilipakika" (slippery skin) and being "pahee" (slippery) to the touch.[52] Hauwahine guards Kawainui fishpond in Kailua on O'ahu, but she also frequents Ka'elepulu fishpond and stream and Paeo fishpond upland of the bridge at Kahuku in Lā'ie.[53]

Even when a mo'o adopts a human form, its skin may continue to exude walewale. In the account of Kamiki, Kamiki goes hand-to-hand with the mo'o Waiākea (a.k.a. Waiaea), who lives in Hilo Hanakahi, Hawai'i. At first, Kamiki has trouble getting a good grip on her body because it is slippery, but he soon realizes that if he grabs her back, which is "kalakala" (spiny, knotty, or lumpy), he can put her in a firm hold.[54]

A mo'o's walewale also affects its human lovers. In the summer of 1935, during an ethnological study carried out in Ka'ū on Hawai'i, E. S. Craighill Handy and Mary Kawena Pukui, the latter a member of that same community, collected an account of a woman who acquired a mo'o lover during her visit with relatives on O'ahu. This mo'o would only visit her after sunset, and the woman's "right side, which came in contact with his body during the night, was said to have become slimy and pale like a fish's."[55] As the Puna'aikoa'e tradition suggests, this walewale could transform a human lover's physiognomy in more drastic ways.

Puna'aikoa'e, in the version by John Papa 'Ī'ī published in 1869, is a ruling ali'i of O'ahu who encountered the mo'o Kalamainu'u in her human form as he and his companions were surfing off the shores of Waimānalo on O'ahu.[56] The entire group was struck by her incredible beauty, but Kalamainu'u only had eyes for Puna'aikoa'e. With the excuse of showing him a better surfing site, she led him out to sea on their surfboards, all the way to Molokai—a voyage of more than thirty miles. There, she took him to her cave in a secluded upland area. She met his every need but kept him somewhat like a prisoner. One day, after he had been living with her for some time, the voices of people who seemed to be cheering reached him from a distance, and he requested permission from Kalamainu'u to join the festivities, which she granted. During the course of his excursion, he encountered Hīnale, who, unbeknownst to him, was Kalamainu'u's brother. 'Ī'ī explains, "Ua haohao wale no oia ma ke ano e o kona au hiohiona" (He was astonished at the strangeness of Puna'aikoa'e's features). Hīnale invited him to his house to eat a meal and relax. During their time together, Hīnale asked him about where he was from, where he currently resided, and how he had come to be there. After listening to Puna'aikoa'e's response, Hīnale informed him that his wahine was not really human but a kupua and that were he to sneak up on her when he went home, he would see her true form.[57]

Although not explicitly stated in the above passage about Hīnale's encounter with Puna'aikoa'e, the belief that prolonged contact with a mo'o's walewale can affect human physiognomy is clearly behind his reaction. Hīnale's response to Puna'aikoa'e's features suggests that there was something not quite human about them. Moreover, Hīnale's invitation to Puna'aikoa'e and subsequent questions hint that he suspected his sister of being the cause of Puna'aikoa'e's strange appearance, presumably because of her walewale.

As the tradition of Puna'aikoa'e also reveals, mo'o could emit copious amounts of walewale and use it as a weapon. During Puna'aikoa'e's meeting with Hīnale, Hīnale advised him on how to escape Kalamainu'u. Eventually, he escaped and traveled to Hawai'i, where he made his way to Halema'uma'u Crater in the Kīlauea volcano to seek refuge with the volcano deity Pele and her family. As it happens, in this version Puna'aikoa'e's first wife, Walinu'u, is Pele's eldest sister. When Kalamainu'u discovered that Puna'aikoa'e escaped, she was furious. Here, I share my translation of the battle in which the mo'o use their walewale as a weapon:

She [Kalamainu'u] called together all the mo'o of Molokai, Lāna'i, Maui, Kaho'olawe, and Hawai'i because she knew her kāne was with Pele and the others at Kīlauea.

After the mo'o gathered, they departed for Kukuilau'ānia and climbed Kīlauea. When she stood at the crater's rim, she demanded the crater dwellers to release her kāne, but they refused. They asked her, "Do you have a kāne here? This is our older sister's kāne. You will get nothing at all because you are a vile woman." This speech by Pele and her clan made Kalamainuʻu furious. She said, "If you do not release my kāne, I will command my people to fill this lava crater, and your fiery nature will soon be extinguished." Just as she had threatened, the moʻo filled the lava crater with their slime, and the Pele clan barely avoided catastrophe.

The craters of the Pele clan were nearly extinguished; only Kamohoaliʻi's crater remained. From there, the fire reignited until it was immense, and the moʻo slime became inconsequential. Kalamainuʻu and her legion of moʻo were unable to remain in the vicinity. The fire's heat came forth so aggressively everywhere that most of the moʻo were killed. They perished in the crevices that opened as they fled. As for Kalamainuʻu, she dove in the pond named after the moʻo Aka (Loko Aka). She was defeated, kāne-less, and barely escaped with her life.[58]

Whether the moʻo emitted walewale from their bodies or mouths, or both, is not explained.

In 1960 Josephine Medeiros related the following oral history about the moʻo at ʻOheʻo, in Kīpahulu on Maui. If you fell into one of the seven pools, you would end up sucked out into the ocean through the lava tube. A man named ʻŌpiopio was once pulled down into a pool by a moʻo when he was a child. He had been swimming with a group of children, and when they noticed he was gone, they thought he was hiding from them. As the sun was setting, they finally ran home to tell their parents, who then searched for him, unsuccessfully. The boy returned the next day, covered in slime and speechless from fright. After a few days, he was finally able to speak. He said that a half-woman-and-half-fish being had pulled him down into the pool. This experience left him half bald. Medeiros said that he had been pulled down into the lava tube.[59] This description speaks to the fishlike nature of moʻo. "Moʻo" is a suffix for "ʻaʻamoʻo" (lizard slime). ʻAʻamoʻo also refers to the slime on the surface of stagnant water. ʻAʻa, in this case, denotes a thin film or coating. There is cause to believe that a connection exists between the walewale of ka poʻe moʻo akua and the ʻaʻamoʻo that appears when they are present. Pukui explains, "Their homes were in ponds and streams and it is said that their presence was recognisable by the yellowing of the trees and shrubbery surrounding the ponds; in the accumulation of yellowish foam on the surface of the water; and in the peculiar yellow-green hue of the water itself."[60] The foam that Pukui describes is no doubt ʻaʻamoʻo, which may cause the water to turn yellow-green.

Oral histories link Hauwahine with 'a'amo'o. Archaeologist J. Gilbert McAllister, who conducted a nine-month study of sites on O'ahu in 1930, reported that if Hauwahine was away from Paeo fishpond, "famous for the size of its fish," its water was clear, but if she was present, "a blanket of leaves and other refuse (*aamoo*) covered the water."[61] McAllister notes, "On the Kahuku bank is a chalice-shaped stone about 3 feet high, where Hauwahine, the goddess (moo) of the pond is said to have been frequently seen combing her long black hair. This was a very sacred stone and could not be approached."[62] Another description of Hauwahine and her mo'o companion in Ho'oulumāhiehie's version of the Hi'iakaikapoliopele tradition mirrors Pukui's statements about mo'o:

Ina hoi mai kela wahine i kai o ia wahi mai uka aku nei o Kawainui, e pala ana ka lau o ka hala o kela wahi. A ua hoi mai nei laua a uka nei o Kawainui, ke ike aku la oe i ka olena mai o ka lau o ke uki a me ke naku o loko o ka wai. O ka hoailona ihola no keia o ka moo. He lena na mea a pau e pili aku ai lakou.[63]

If that woman heads seaward from the upland area of Kawainui, the hala leaves of that place will turn yellow. And now that they have returned upland of Kawainui, you can see that the leaves of the 'uki grass and naku bulrush turn yellow. This was the sign of the mo'o. Everything near them yellows.

Ho'oulumāhiehie does not name Hauwahine's companion, but she is indicated as Kahalakea in Joseph Moku'ōhai Poepoe's version of this tradition. In Kapihenui's version, Hauwahine is alone.[64] Poepoe also notes the ways the presence of mo'o affects plant growth:

Ina e nana aku oe i kela uluhala, e ike ana oe i ka uliuli maikai o ka lau o ka hala, elike no me ka kaua e ike aku nei. Aka, ina e hoi aku kela wahine ilaila, oia ka wa e pala ai ka lau o ka hala, a ua like me ka lau-i pala ke nana aku.[65]

If you look at that hala grove, you will see that the leaves are a healthy green, like those we have just seen. But, if that woman returns there, that is when the hala leaves turn yellow, like yellowed ti-leaves.

In other words, the presence of Hauwahine and Kahalakea affects the plants that grow in or near the bodies of water they occupy. Kīhei de

Silva explains that the yellowing vegetation signifying Hauwahine's presence means that Hauwahine has "returned with fish and fertility."[66] This is yet another instance of the belief in the power of moʻo to attract fish and make fishponds thrive.

In Hauʻula on Oʻahu, the flowers of hau trees (*Hibiscus tiliaceus*) indicate the presence or absence of the moʻo (unidentified) associated with Kaluakauā pond. When the hau flowers are red, the moʻo and her mullet are there. When the trees stop flowering, they have left.[67] By this reasoning, the moʻo leaves the pond in the morning and returns at night. The color of hau flowers changes throughout the day: pale yellow in the morning, muted orange in the afternoon, and subdued red in the evening.

Blossoming hau flowers, instead, mark the presence of Meheanu, who is the guardian of Heʻeia fishpond in Heʻeia Uli in Kāneʻohe on Oʻahu but lives in a nearby place called Luamoʻo beneath a hau grove. According to a kamaʻāina of that place, when the hau trees were not blossoming "she was more likely to be somewhere else in the form of an eel."[68] Ānuenue Punua, former project manager for Heʻeia fishpond, offers more details. Meheanu's presence or absence is indicated by the colors of hau tree flower buds—when they are green she is upland in Luamoʻo, but when they are in "full bloom and yellow, that's when we know she is in the pond."[69] L. L. Henry reports the belief that Meheanu's urine causes this yellowing.[70] Research at Heʻeia fishpond on the connection between oral history and natural phenomena such as the yellowing of hau is showcased in a video about Meheanu and the nitrogen cycle:

> Nitrogen is a very important nutrient in the fishpond. The forms of nitrogen in the environment are nitrogen gas (NO_2), ammonia (NH_4), nitrate (NO_3), and nitrite (NO_2). It is cycled by both biological and chemical processes: nitrogen reduction, nitrogen fixation, denitrification, and nitrification. The amount of nitrogen in the fishpond influences the rate of limu [seaweed] growth as well as decomposition. When Meheanu visits in moʻo form, her urine causes the hau to turn yellow because of increasing ammonia concentrations. This increase in nitrogen causes a bloom in the phytoplankton that the baby pua ʻaʻama [mullet] like to eat. The fish are then well taken care of and guarded by kiaʻi [guardian] Meheanu resulting in a thriving loko iʻa [fishpond]. The story of Meheanu portrays the nitrogen cycle of Heʻeia fishpond.[71]

A place known specifically for its 'a'amo'o is the wet cave Kapala'e at Hā'ena in the Hanalei district of Kaua'i.[72] In 1914, a visitor to Kapala'e recounted:

O ka wai o Kapalae ua kamaaina i ka poe apau i ike ia wai, wahi a ka oleloia he wai aamoo, ua like ka me ke ano o ka moo, a ina e nou aku oe i ka pohaku, a ma kahi e haule iho ai oia wale no kahi o ka wai i maweheia ae a hoi hou ae no nae a pili elike me mamua.[73]

Everyone who has seen the water of Kapala'e [knows the nature of] that water. According to what is said, it is 'a'amo'o water, which is mo'o-like. If you were to throw a stone in it, the water would open where it fell, only to close behind it as it was before.

The description of the tossed stone is a clear reference to the water's surface being covered with 'a'amo'o, which in this case seems to be an algae layer.

Saltwater and freshwater seaweeds are a type of algae, and the water-spirit nature of these reptilian deities is captured perfectly in the belief about a mo'o associated with 'Auwaiolimu at Pauoa in Honolulu on O'ahu. This mo'o, who some call Kahalaopuna, frequents this 'auwai (water course) and has long limu-like (moss or seaweed) hair, hence Auwaiolimu's name.[74]

Nothing I have shared so far gives the impression that 'a'amo'o is perceived as anything more than a sign indicating the presence of a mo'o. Yet the notion of 'a'amo'o as a noxious mo'o-related phenomenon could be linked to 'a'amo'o in the sense of pond slime, which is often found in stagnant water and caused by algae. A stagnant pond is an unhealthy pond. This possibility is evidenced in a story about the mo'o of Ka'apīpā Pond, which is near Kīpahulu, Maui. According to Julie Naone, a mo'o made her home in this pond. If people caught fish there when 'a'amo'o covered it, the fish were unfit to eat. Furthermore, some believed that such fish could come back to life and thus should be put back in the pond.[75] At first glance, this view seemingly contrasts with the belief in mo'o as beneficial fishpond guardians, but we can interpret it as an indication that a mo'o is unhappy. Perhaps someone offended it, and it caused an increase in 'a'amo'o to show its displeasure. 'Ōiwi value the presence of mo'o in fishponds because fish thrive when there is a mo'o kia'i. As for the fish coming back to life, there are several stories about this, a topic I cover in chapter 2.

Another perspective, one in which moʻo are perceived as malevolent entities, is evident in the belief that certain forest-dwelling moʻo may be harmful to rain forests because they cause an overabundance of water that leads plants to yellow, represent dense understory growth that strangles a rain forest, or induce the ʻōhiʻa tree blight known as Rapid ʻŌhiʻa Death (ROD).[76] ROD is new to Hawaiʻi and is caused by the *Ceratocystis* fungus, which kills healthy trees within mere days or weeks.[77] Notably, the moʻo Kakana was said to have caused a taro blight at Lāʻiewai on Oʻahu in late 1921 and early 1922, and some believed that the blight itself was one of its kino lau.[78] The belief in malicious moʻo who cause blights correlates with the view that moʻo could cause diseases affecting the skin, which has less to do with their water-spirit status and more to do with their reptilian nature (see chapter 5).

Moʻo and Red Water

Oral histories report that the water of Kaloko fishpond in Honokōhau, Kona District, on Hawaiʻi turned red whenever the moʻo of Kaloko had her menses. During those times, it was best not to enter the water.[79] An observation about Kaloko's waters turning red is found elsewhere, but the change is not linked to menses. (I discuss this point later in connection with fishponds.)

Accounts from Kauaʻi seem to link Kihawahine to the color red. According to J. K. Farley, Kihawahine lived in Maulili Pool in the Waikomo stream.[80] Frederich Wichman reports that whenever Kihawahine "was in residence, the water turned red and no one dared to swim there."[81] Wichman's source is Ethel Damon, who cites Farley, but Wichman adds information not found in either source. This added information might reflect Kauaʻi beliefs with which Wichman was familiar as he was a Kauaʻi kamaʻāina and a descendant of William Hyde Rice, who collected oral histories. Wichman cites Theodore Kelsey as his source for another account about Kihawahine:

> Wai-a-ula, "water becoming red," is a pond near the mouth of Kāhili Stream. Waiaʻula was a *lua-moʻo* (a dragon hole) belonging to Kihawahine, a dreaded man-killing goddess. The place was taboo to all except the chiefs who went there to swim. At certain times, the water gushed up in the spring so that part of the water was red, and part remained dark as before. When the water became red, it was the sign of the

return of Kihawahine, who, like other mo'o, could transform her body in different colors and shapes. The red water was the body of Kihawahine.[82]

It is unclear which part of the quote is Wichman's and which is Kelsey's.

There is one point that I would like to address—namely, the idea of all mo'o being able to change the color of their bodies. This generalization is not supported by the vast archive of 'Ōiwi artistic-intellectual production that mentions these deities. This is not to say that a tradition upholding this belief is somehow invalid—merely that it is an outlier, perhaps one specific to Kaua'i. Here, I share an anecdote to show that some generalizations about mo'o are the result of someone having read a problematic secondary source. I have heard or read assertations made in the present time that all mo'o are female, but my research proves this incorrect.

Water-Related Mana

Mo'o embody water in other significant ways. Some have the power to control or influence water, while others manifest as some configuration of water. The water source called Punahou (New spring), which still exists, is ultimately attributed to the mo'o Kākea, who guards and controls the waters of Mānoa and Makiki. To help his descendants, a brother and a sister who live on arid land and are therefore required to travel far to get water, he agrees to "divide the water supply of the neighboring Wailele spring, and let it run into the watercourse that the boy would make, thus insuring its permanence."[83]

The "rain rock" known as Manaua is also the name of the mo'o wahine who frequents it. This large monolith sits in a grassy area near the parking lot of the Jacaranda Inn in Waimea on Hawai'i. Along its top, the contour of a large lizard in repose is clearly discernable. Pua Case, a Waimea kama'āina, took me to visit Manaua and told me the story of this rain rock and the mo'o wahine with whom it is associated. Manaua and her family (her kāne and two children, all mo'o) live upland of the monolith near Kohākōhau stream. Case shared that whenever there was a drought, offerings were made to Manaua to bring rain. Indeed, "Manaua" refers to the power (mana) to cause rain (ua). When we visited the rain rock, we found lei and other floral offerings on it. I had brought rainwater from my land, and after greeting Manaua, I poured it over the monolith. Wai is a suitable offering for mo'o. A year

later, I visited Manaua on my own, and there were many new offerings.
A treatise on the history of the Parker Ranch notes that many generations of kamaʻāina have honored the rain rock they call "Manaua."[84]
Over the years, people have shared their moʻo stories with me. In a few
instances, they shared their knowledge to deepen my own understanding of these deities and asked that I not retell those stories, and I have
kept my promise. That said, I can share that there are others who call
upon moʻo when a water source dries up, who then calls forth water.
People turn to these moʻo just as generations of Waimea kamaʻāina have
and continue to turn to Manaua for help during a drought.

Here, I turn my attention to Hauwahine and Kahalakea. That these
moʻo can either control water or become water is suggested in Poepoe's
version of the Hiʻiakaikapoliopele tradition. After Hiʻiaka reveals to
Hauwahine and Kahalakea that she knows they are moʻo, they vanish.
After they disappear, Hiʻiaka's human companion, Wahineʻōmaʻo, feels
a chill around her ankles. Hiʻiaka tells her that it is the spray of Kawainui.
She adds, "He li ka mai me ke anu, aia i ka wai ka make" (Chills and
coldness are the illness, death is in the water).[85] Because both of
Wahineʻōmaʻo's legs are cold, Hiʻiaka takes that as a sign that there are
two moʻo. To combat the moʻo, Hiʻiaka chants. Hiʻiaka is famed for the
power of her chants because her utterances have the power to effect
change—whatever she declares will come to pass. Interspersed with her
descriptions of the moʻo are two declarations of victory:

> E ka moo pane[e] ke alo, e ka moo noʻu ka ai; e ka moo, ohua ka opu;
> e ka moo, konini ka huelo; e ka moo, popolo-hua na maka; e ka moo,
> omaomao ka waha; e ka moo, moe wai-e. He anu. He anu kau, he me-
> hana kaʻu. Na Hauwahine, ua anu, wahine moo o Kawainui.[86]

> O the moʻo who moves along on its front, oh the moʻo, the destruction
> is mine; O moʻo, stomach-slider; O moʻo, moving the tail to and fro;
> O moʻo with black pōpolo-berry eyes; O moʻo with a green mouth;
> O moʻo, water dweller—O. A coldness. Cold is yours, but warmth is
> mine. Hauwahine causes that coldness, moʻo woman of Kawainui.

Despite Hiʻiaka's chant, the cold continues to creep up from
Wahineʻōmaʻo's legs to the rest of her body. Hiʻiaka observes, "Ua
haalele na moo i ou mau wawae, a ua kolo aku la i ko kua. He kaua
holo wale ka laua." (The moʻo has left your legs and crawled up your
back. They do battle quickly.) Hiʻiaka chants once more, and the cold

leaves Wahine'ōma'o's body.[87] From this passage, it is clear that the mo'o became invisible as they attacked Wahine'ōma'o, and we can interpret their efforts to harm her in two ways. The imagery suggests that they either transformed into the invisible, illness-causing coldness or controlled it.

Mo'o and Fish

Yet another way that mo'o embody water is evidenced by their power over fish. As Kamakau explained in his 1870 treatise on mo'o, like shark deities they have the ability to attract fish and lead them elsewhere.[88] For this reason, mo'o are prized fishpond guardians (see chapter 5). Kāmeha'ikana, although more well known as the breadfruit tree goddess and as a form of Haumea, has a mo'o form in one tradition (see chapter 4). McAllister reports that an "akua stone" named Kāmeha'ikana was located at Hanapēpē "near the first bridge on the Kahuku side of Laie" and was considered "a female fish god" that people "worshipped," leaving the first catch of fish as an offering.[89]

Significantly, there is a record of Hawaiians who think of mo'o as fishlike. In Pukui's interview with Josephine Medeiros in 1960, Medeiros notes that the fish of Punahoa pond, near the beach of Pueokahi at Hāna Bay, Maui, are strange: one side has flesh and the other only bone. Pukui says this is a mo'o and that these strange fish might have the head of a weke (goatfish) and the body of a mullet. When a fish is unusual like that, Pukui explains, it is a mo'o.[90] Medeiros adds that mo'o are half fish.[91] Fins are generally associated with fish, including long dorsal fins like those of certain eel species, and none of the gecko or skinks our ancestors knew had finlike dorsal ridges. Yet the idea of fishlike mo'o is hinted at in the name of a Kāne'ohe stream, Kamo'olāli'i, which Pukui translates as "the mo'o [with a] small fin."[92]

Last, Pukui indicates that mermaids "belonged to the great mo'o family," which further underscores the fishlike nature of these reptilian water deities.[93] In Western folklore, a mermaid (water maid) is a composite water spirit whose upper half is human and whose lower half is that of a fish. But what constitutes that which in English is termed a "mermaid" varies according to a given culture. For example, in Trinidad and Tobago, stories abound not only of mermaids with fish tails but also of a mermaid whose lower body is that of an anaconda.[94] In Hawai'i we have the usual mermaid—accounts of which, incidentally, are rare—but mo'o have also been referred to as such, perhaps incorrectly. We can understand such descriptions as a blend of the old and the new. The Hawaiian mermaid may not necessarily have a fish tail—perhaps the lower half of its body could be reptilian, as in the case of Kihawahine and her companions, or eellike. Joseph Emerson, in his discussion of Hawaiian gods, notes in connection with Kihawahine, "She is represented as a mermaid, a woman above with long flowing tresses, while below the waist she is a *moo*." Emerson adds, "Her mermaid companions are said to assume also the form of an imaginary water-lizard of a light color, called *moo inanea*, rarely appearing on land." Emerson, although not Hawaiian, grew up in Hawai'i and mined his 'Ōiwi acquaintances for information about nā mea Hawai'i, as he points out in the rest of his treatise.[95] Notably, "moo inanea" is similar to "Mo'oinanea." It comes naturally to wonder whether mo'o inanea describes the color of Mo'oinanea's body.

In this chapter I shared examples of the various kinds of bodies of fresh water linked to mo'o and also the diverse geographical areas and features with which they are associated, including localities not known for an abundance of water. Mo'o generally live in or near bodies of fresh water, such as rivers, streams, springs, waterfalls, lakes, ponds, pools, and swamps. They are also associated with damp areas where heavy rainfall is frequent, such as rain forests. Several mo'o are associated with plains. Others live in upland or seaside caves or cliffs. Some live in fresh or brackish water sources near the sea, including marshes, estuaries, and fishponds.

A comparative analysis of the data on nearly three hundred mo'o suggests that if a mo'o is associated with a given area, we can assume that there is or once existed a water source in the vicinity. Stories about changes in the vegetation or water bodies where mo'o dwell are important records of natural phenomena affecting those localities. Accounts about seashore-dwelling mo'o are valuable archives of 'ike 'Ōiwi about brackish water sources and their origins and reflect views about the relationship between the land and sea and all therein. This chapter is the first step toward understanding mo'o akua as a class of water deities. The second step, the topic of chapter 2, entails gaining insights into their reptilian nature, which is obtained by examining the kino lau associated with all mo'o.

Chapter 2

The Mo'o Akua Form and the Kino Lau Associated with All Mo'o

According to our ancestors, our island world—from the sky and its celestial bodies to the islands and the ocean that surround them, along with the myriad natural phenomena, features, flora, and fauna of sky, land, and sea—is the modality by which our akua make themselves known. Over countless generations, our ancestors have closely interacted with and scrutinized their island environment, accumulating extensive knowledge about the similarities between natural phenomena, features, flora, and fauna in terms of form, markings, color, and habit.[1] Based on these observations and their understanding of their akua, they devised the kino lau system. "Kino" (form, body) "lau" (many, multiple) refers to the forms that akua—greater and lesser—assume or with which they are symbolically associated and may reflect an akua's function, realm, or name.

By way of illustration, Pele is our volcanic deity. Her function is to create land, her realm is the volcano, and lava is one of her kino lau. "Pele" means "lava"—Pele *is* the lava, and she also controls it. Pele's youngest sister is Hiʻiakaikapoliopele, and her function is to revegetate the land after Pele's lava flows, which heals it. This new vegetation emerges from the cracks in the lava. Hiʻiakaikapoliopele's name reflects her function and her relationship to her sister—the embryo cradled in the lava: Hiʻi (to hold)—aka (embryo)—i (in)—ka (the)—poli (bosom)—o (of)—pele (lava). Given that lava/destruction precedes revegetation/healing, it makes sense that Pele is the elder sister, and Hiʻiakaikapoliopele is the younger sister.

Significantly, the concept of kino lau is a product and record of Hawaiian philosophy.[2] Studying kino lau, seeking to uncover the rationale behind them, allows us to access, to some degree, the philosophical thoughts of Hawaiians who lived in the very distant past. We are fortunate to have a written record of kino lau theory from our literary ancestors who did not limit themselves to merely reproducing a narrative but also included explanations for their readers. Such asides give us further insights into the principles undergirding kino lau theory. These revelations help us to map and reconstruct ancestral ways of knowing and, equally important, to continue, like our kūpuna, to theorize kino lau and find new applications for kino lau theory.

Far from being a relic of the past, the concept of kino lau continues to inform Hawaiian cultural practices. Hula, a uniquely Hawaiian practice with which many people around the world are familiar, is an example of how ancient kino lau–related practices are still carried out today. Traditionally, kumu hula (hula masters) and hula students drape the hula kuahu (altar) with the plant kino lau of Laka, who, as Pualani Kanaka'ole Kanahele notes, "is the primary deity of hula kuahu," and hula practitioners consider these kino lau, which include "'ie'ie, pua lehua, halapepe, and maile," sacred. Kanahele explains, "Laka is the plants and the plants are Laka. Inspiration for hula is received when the plants are present and when the dancer wears the plants for hula. The honor of 'master of hula' is given to Laka, and the patrons and devotees of the hula recognize this fact."[3] As Kanahele reveals, people connected to a deity through a practice will consider its kino lau sacred, and this holds true for those linked in some way to mo'o akua.

Mo'o kino lau can be grouped into two main categories: those associated with all mo'o, which I term "general" kino lau, and those identified with only certain mo'o, which I term "mo'o-specific" kino lau. There are four general kino lau: the mo'o (lizard), the 'īlio mo'o (brindled dog), the 'o'opu (goby fish), and the nananana/lanalana (spider). These kino lau are sacred to all mo'o. In order to better comprehend mo'o akua, we must grasp their relationships with their kino lau, which inform the beliefs and belief-related practices surrounding them. Descriptions of Hawaiian reptilian deities' bodies—size, skin color, and other physical features—provide the necessary context for investigating the rationale behind the kino lau associated with all mo'o. In this next section on the mo'o akua form, I offer an overview of the depth and breadth of 'Ōiwi representations of mo'o. I continue this discussion in the sections on the lizard, brindled dog, goby, and spider kino lau as I trace the rationale behind these forms.

The Mo'o Akua Form

Certain mo'o either seem to be able to change the size of their mo'o form, or their size varies according to different traditions. Mo'oinanea is a case in point. In the 'Aukelenuia'īkū tradition, she is large enough to eat two men one after the other. Soon after, she vomits the chunky contents of her stomach and uses them to create a map to teach her grandson, 'Aukelenuia'īkū, how to navigate certain islands to reach Nāmakaokaha'i, the akua destined to become his wahine.[4] In a version of the Ha'inākolo tradition, it is clear that Mo'oinanea is able to increase the size of her body when she stretches it from Waolani (Nu'uanu, O'ahu) to Kuaihelani.[5]

Another enormous mo'o is Kihanuilūlūmoku (Great Island-Shaking Lizard), who appears in several traditions. Its name marks its great size and fierce nature, both of which are evidenced in the Lā'ieikawai tradition. Kihanuilūlūmoku (gender unspecified) protects Lā'ieikawai and guards Paliuli in 'Ōla'a, Hawai'i. Kaua'i ali'i 'Aiwohikupua asks his sisters Maileha'iwale, Mailekaluhea, Mailelauli'i, Mailepākaha, and Kahalaomapuana (the "Maile sisters") to woo Lā'ieikawai for him. When they are unsuccessful, 'Aiwohikupua abandons them, and they become her companions. When he discovers this, he demands again that they help him to woo her, but they refuse. He sends ten warriors one night to destroy his sisters.[6]

As dawn is breaking, the warriors arrive within sight of Paliuli. Just then, the sound of wind roaring through the forest reaches them, a wind created by the tongue of the great mo'o, Kihanuilūlūmoku, who is coming to attack them. But they cannot see it, so they continue onward. Not much later, they see the mo'o's upper jaw closing down upon them—they were in the middle of the mo'o's mouth, standing on its tongue! The mo'o snaps its jaws shut. No one survives.[7] From this passage, we get an idea of Kihanuilūlūmoku's great size from its mouth, seemingly a large cave into which the ten warriors mistakenly wander. Here, a question arises: How did the men fail to see this gigantic mo'o? Perhaps this episode mythologizes the fact that lizards' markings enable them to blend in with their surroundings so they are difficult to spot. Kalei Nu'uhiwa wonders if this passage refers to an opening in the lava tube known today as Kazumura Cave, which is nearly forty miles long and has many openings, including in 'Ōla'a where Paliuli is said to be located.[8]

In the Kekalukaluokēwā tradition, Kihanuilūlūmoku (gender unspecified) has the power to hide itself and its passengers from view.[9] When it carries Lā'ieikawai and the Maile sisters on its tongue from

Paliuli to Keaʻau, its body remains at Paliuli while its tongue stretches all the way to Keaʻau. They are apparently invisible except for Kihanuilūlūmoku's tongue, which appears to people as a pūnohu ua koko (a low-lying rainbow).[10]

The anonymous contributor also offers a detailed description of Kihanuilūlūmoku's skin and its bearing:

> O na unahi opakapaka e uhi ana i kona kino a puni, ua like ko lakou mau hulali me ko ke dala, ke gula a me ke daimana, ke olelo ae ma ka olelo o keia au. A ina paha ma ka hoohalike ana ae me ko ua wai-hooluu nani maa i ka ikeia ma ka olelo Hawaii, ua hiki no ke hooma-ikeike wale ia ae penei:
>> O ke aiai hulali o kekahi wai hooluu o kona mau unahi, ua like me ke aliali maikai o na kulu hau maluna o na pua mauu i ka malu oluolu a huʻihuʻi o na eheu o ke kakahiaka laʻilaʻi maikai. O ka memele halelolelo o kekahi waihooluu o ua moo nei, ua like me ka memele o ka hulu mamo, a o ka a hulali o kekahi waihooluu o kona mau unahi, ua like me ka a o ka mea i oleloia i kekahi wa, he ʻmaka-ihu-waa.'
>> E hoopuni ana he mau anuenue nani maluna iho o ke kino o ua moo nei, a o kona mau ano a pau ke ike aku, he ku no i ka nani, ka maikai, ka hano a me ka ihiihi o ke kulana.[11]

The scales covering its entire body were shiny like silver, gold, and diamonds in the parlance of this time. If we were to compare the coloration with the beautiful colors we are used to seeing in the Hawaiian language, we could describe it in this way:
> The sparkling shine of its scales were like the beautiful crystal-clear dew drops on flowers in the pleasant and cool wings of a beautiful, still morning. The hues of yellow in that moʻo's coloration were like the yellow of the mamo bird's feathers, and the brightness of certain colors of its scales were similar to that which is sometimes termed a "sharp point at the bow of a canoe."
> Beautiful rainbows surrounded the top of this moʻo's body, and everything about it was exquisitely beautiful, and its bearing was stately and majestic.

As we have seen, the contributor first describes the moʻo using precious stones not naturally found in the islands but then acknowledges this poetic conceit and offers a description more in keeping with the colors of things intrinsic to the Hawaiian Islands. Notably, Kihanuilūlūmoku has extremely shiny, varigated yellow skin, a color linked to mo'o. Pukui asserts that mo'o were fond of this color, and I have also noted that it is associated with their watery abodes.[12] Their fondness of and association with the color yellow are why 'Ōiwi used kapa 'ōlena (tumeric-colored bark cloth) in mo'o-related rituals.[13] The name of a heaiu dedicated to Kihawahine, Hālauakalena ('ōlena shed), on Kaua'i attests to this practice.[14]

Mo'o akua come in many colors. Mo'omomi is a mo'o of Molokai whose body is covered in shiny pearly-white scales. She lives in a cave below Kaiehu Point. Whenever "she suns on the rocks, she can be seen as a pearly white mo'o."[15] Her appearance undoubtedly accounts for her name, because "momi" denotes "pearl." An unspecified number of different-colored mo'o akua—red, black, shades of yellow, and shades of white—live in Kuaihelani, and the light their bodies emit illuminates it.[16] On the topic of mo'o who can produce light, Hoahoaiku has huge eyes that can radiate an intense red light. We can imagine the great size of her body and eyes by the fact that when she lit up her eyes on Hawai'i, they could be seen on Maui.[17]

A fascinating aspect of mo'o akua is that certain body parts may be special in ways that the rest of their body is not. In his human form, Luhiā could use the eyes of his mo'o body as stones in his ma'a (slingshot) when he fought someone.[18] Lanihuli lives in a cave high up in Nu'uanu Pali (cliff) on O'ahu. The scales above his right eye are red and those above his left are black. When placed on someone else's eye, the red scales allow that person to see what is far away; the black ones allow one to see what is near.[19] A scale from Mo'oinanea's body could help someone best adversaries. She can also remove her tail, which transforms into a weapon, and then gift it to someone (see chapter 4). Kalamainu'u is a mo'o who surfs in her human form, and her surfboard is the long tongue of her mo'o body. She would lend it to Puna'aikoa'e, who had no idea this surfboard was her tongue.[20]

J. K. Mokumaia, in his 1922 treatise on Moanalua (O'ahu), told this story about a blind luahine who was a mo'o and used her eyes to fish:

Ua hoopuka aku au i kela mau helu aku nei, e pili ana i keia puu o Kekuawailele, ua oleloia he luahine ka mea e noho ana ma keia kahawai, a e pili pu ana me keia puu, aia iwaena konu o keia puu he ana, kahi e noho ai keia wahine; ua oleloia i kekahi manawa he kino moo kona, a he ano kino papalua paha ke ano, i ka manawa e iho mai ai o kanaka, e noho ana i ka Manaiki, o ia kela oawa pali a na luawai o Waiapuka, e waiho nei, a maalo ae la ma kahi o ua luahine nei, alaila, olelo mai la kela: "Ke naue ae nei oukou i kai?" Ae aku la no hoi lakou. "E hele ae ana hoi i kahi lawai'a limu no hoi ame kahi hee, o i noho mai nei a ono i kahi mea pili kai, o ia keia kaoo nui au e ike ae la."

"Ae nui io no oukou," ua oleloia, aole kolohe o keia luahine, aka, he mau hana mana kana, pela ia mai ana hoi e ke poe i kamaaina, oiai ka oo nui e iho ana, aia oia e noho ana iluna o kekahi pohaku loihi, iwaenakonu o ke kahawai, ua ike kou meakakau nei, oiai oia e noho ana malaila, a hala ka huakai hope o kona emi no ia nalowale, a puka aku la i kai o ke Auau, a ua oleloia ia wahi, o ke ana pukalua.

. . .

Aia malaila he ana, a i ka puka ana ae o ua luahine nei, a okuu iluna o ua ana nei alaila o ka hoouna aku la no ia i na onohi maka ona e hele e lawai'a nana, a noho makapo iho la ua luahine nei a ke ike mai la no hoi kekahi poe i keia wahine makapo i ka noho aku, aole i manaoia, ua hele na onohi maka o ua wahine nei i ka lawai'a, no ka mea i ka hoi ana mai o ka lehulehu ua hoi mua mai keia, a e noke ana i ka unaunahi i ka i'a a he mea ha'oha'o no hoi keia i ka manao o kekahi poe, a he nune nui ia mawaena o lakou pela aku ana ia manawa hele no a ono ka i'a o kana hana no, o ka iho i keia wahi o ke ala ame kahi e hiki koke ai, o ia ka mea kupaianaha nui.

. . .

O kekahi o na hana kupaianaha a keia luahine, o ia kona hoolilo ana iaia i moo, a he nui aku na hana ana e hoololi mau ai, a o kahi i maikai loa ai, o ia kona kolohe ole ia ha'i, no ka mea, o kahi ana e noho ana, o ke alanui hele ia o na Ewa, ke pii, a pela no hoi me kahi e waiho la o ka pa iwi o na alii kolohe nui wale o kela awawa o Kamanaiki.[21]

Several installments ago, I wrote about this hill Kekuawailele. It was said that an old woman lived close to this stream near this hill. There in the middle of this hill was a cave where this woman lived. It was said that sometimes she had a mo'o form, a supernatural being. When people came down who lived at Kamanaiki, which is a ravine where the pools of Wai'āpuka are located, and passed that luahine, she would ask, "Are you going to the sea?" They said, "Yes, we are going somewhere to pick limu and fish for octopus, as we were craving seafood." The old woman replied, "So that's this large group I see."

"Go right ahead, you folks," she said. This old woman wasn't troublesome, but she often used her mana, which was what people who knew her said. As the big group traveled down, she sat on a long stone in the middle of the stream, which your writer has seen. Meanwhile, she sat there until after the last traveler had passed, and then she moved backward until she disappeared, and came out seaward of Auau, which was said to be a cave with two entrances.

There was a cave, and when the old woman exited it, she would squat above that cave and then send her eyeballs to fish for her, and then sit there blind. Anyone passing would see this blind woman and have no idea that she had sent her eyes to go fishing because when the crowd came back, she had returned before them, and would be scaling her fish. It was something that astonished some people and they wondered greatly about it among themselves. That's what she would do whenever she craved fish. She went down via the shortcut, that was the most astonishing thing.

. . .

Other strange things this old woman did included changing herself into a moʻo, and there were many bodies into which she would transform. What was outstanding was that she did not trouble anyone, because where she lived was the path the people of ʻEwa took to go up, and also where the bones of the aliʻi of Kamanaiki valley who had been tyrants were interred.[22]

Here we see that some people realized that this luahine was strange, while others knew she was a moʻo wahine, but they let her be because she never harmed anyone.

Lizard Kino Lau

Take a moment to visualize a gecko. In the islands, geckos share our homes. We see these little lizards clinging to the walls or windowpanes and hear their characteristic chirping-clicking sounds at night. Every so often, they shoot out their long tongues to snatch up an unsuspecting moth, which they crunch up with their one hundred tiny teeth. Geckos are cute. Cartoon versions of smiling geckos appear on a great variety of items for sale here in the islands. Now imagine a dinosaur-sized gecko with a twenty-foot-long tongue in a cavernous mouth with one hundred teeth the size of your hand. A gecko that size is no longer cute—it is horrifying.

Because little lizards bring to mind the great, terrifying reptilian forms of moʻo akua, they are the primary kino lau of these Hawaiian reptilian water deities. For this reason, lizards are especially sacred to moʻo akua, and they do not take kindly to people who mistreat these creatures that resemble them in miniature. An ʻōlelo noʻeau attests to this belief: "Mai kolohe i ka moʻo o lele i ka pali" (do not harm lizards lest you jump off a cliff). Pukui explains that this is "a warning not to bother lizards lest someday the moʻo cause a madness that makes one leap off a cliff."[23] In 1870, ʻĪʻī shared an anecdote from his childhood about an aliʻi named Kahiko—he was beset by troubles because he killed lizards.[24]

Kamakau dedicated two installments of his long-running series on Hawaiian history to moʻo akua in 1870, which is the only sustained and systematic discussion on these deities in the paper. Kamakau offers a clear statement about the difference between the ordinary lizard and moʻo akua. He notes that the little lizards Hawaiians saw were not moʻo akua, but their bodies recalled the long and frightening forms of these gods.[25] Kamakau's statement is a reminder that there is a difference between the ordinary lizard and the lizard deity. His declaration suggests that there might have been some confusion about this point, which he felt should be cleared up. His point is crucial, and it needs to be reiterated.

The ordinary lizard is a symbolic kino lau of moʻo akua. It is symbolic because it recalls the great reptilian form of moʻo akua and not because these deities turn into an ordinary gecko or skink. This point holds true for the other general kino lau even if there are a few moʻo who can change into a goby, a brindled dog, or a spider. There are exceptions to the general rule about kino lau—namely, that kino lau are the forms a deity can assume. As Pukui explains, "Kino lau nearly always refers to the many forms or bodies both the *akuas* (impersonal gods) and the *aumākua* (personalized ancestor gods) were thought to take."[26] The qualificatory word "nearly" in Pukui's statement refers to kino lau that are more symbolic associations than physical manifestations. That said, a few moʻo akua are reported to have assumed the form of a very small lizard, which may account for the misconception that the ordinary lizard is a moʻo akua.

Two accounts of moʻo who turn into little lizards are found in the Hiʻiakaikapoliopele tradition. Hiʻiaka's journey to retrieve Pele's lover

Lohiʻau took her to different Hawaiian Islands. When Hiʻiaka and Wahineʻōmaʻo reach the shores of Waialua on Oʻahu, Hiʻiaka spies the moʻo Piliʻaʻama in his human form in the distance. They continue and find him sitting near the trail, having just caught an ʻoʻopu. When Wahineʻōmaʻo sees the fish in his hands, she is overwhelmed with a craving for it. Hiʻiaka offers a chant in which she requests the fish. Piliʻaʻama responds rudely and runs away toward an outcrop of boulders. There, still in his human form, he steps up on a stone, then transforms into a little lizard and hides in a crevice. The last step he took in his human form remains to this day as an imprint on the stone.[27] Later, as Hiʻiaka traverses the ʻEwa plains on Oʻahu, she sees two moʻo women stringing ʻilima (*Sida fallax*) lei. One of them recognizes her and tells the other, "Peʻe kāua" (Let's hide). Because Hiʻiaka has the power to kill them, they fear her, so they run to a large stone where they transform into small lizards and slip into cracks to hide. Thus, the stone is named Peʻekāua.[28]

In one version of the Haʻinākolo tradition, Moʻoinanea not only has the usual moʻo form but is able to divide its large body into a horde of small lizards. The horde chases a butterfly swarm in unison, moving as if it were a single entity.[29] Manu reports Waka changing into a "Mookaala onionio ulaula" (a snake-eyed skink mottled with red) and then again into "kekahi ano kino Mookaula" (a form resembling a mourning gecko).[30] I will discuss these lizard species shortly. Whether these forms were small like the actual species or much larger versions is unclear. Because Waka is a deity, however, it is clear she did not turn into ordinary lizards but took divine forms that resembled them.

These are the only instances I have found of moʻo akua whose moʻo kino is tiny like that of an ordinary lizard, or in the case of Waka, possibly small. Generally, their moʻo bodies are enormous. Kamakau asserts that moʻo akua were about two to three anana long. An anana refers to an arm span: the distance between the middle fingertips of both hands with the arms held perpendicular to the body. A person's arm span is usually the same as a person's height. So a person who is six feet tall would have a six-foot anana. In this case, two to three anana would equal twelve to fifteen feet. But, as I have shown, moʻo akua could be much larger. The difference between moʻo akua and ordinary lizards is a matter of mana. The ability of moʻo akua to shape-shift derives from their mana akua. Ordinary lizards are just that—ordinary. They have no mana akua, and thus they cannot transform into gigantic lizards.

Here, I continue discussing the rationale behind the ordinary lizard's status as a general kino lau for mo'o akua. The most obvious connection between them is that they are both termed "mo'o." Given the visual and linguistic links between lizards and mo'o akua, it comes naturally to wonder about the lizards with which our ancestors were familiar. It is vitally important to establish which lizards have been in the islands long enough to inspire kino lau–related beliefs because of their forms, markings, characteristics, habits, or habitats. It is impossible to ascertain with surety all the lizard species in the Hawaiian Islands across place and time. However, we can identify those that existed when the islands first became a common port of call for European and American ships and a destination for scientific expeditions in the early nineteenth century. Lizard species catalogued at that time had probably been around for much longer.

Matching lizard species with their Hawaiian counterparts is tricky. No one has ever tried to discover exactly which species, according to scientific nomenclature, correspond to the Hawaiian names. Hawaiian-language dictionaries record only three types of lizard. The first is the mo'o kāula (seer or prophet lizard), also known as the mo'o makāula (seer or prophet lizard), and mo'o ali'i (royal lizard), which Pukui describes as "a variety of gray lizard." The second is the mo'o 'alā ('alā-stone lizard), also known as the mo'o ka'alā and mo'o kā, which Pukui describes as "a black lizard." The third is the mo'o kā lā'au (tree-smiting lizard).[31] A search for mo'o in the electronic archives Papakilo Database and Ulukau to find other kinds of lizards proved unfruitful. If they exist, their names are not found in these archives' substantial holdings.

Reports from the Charles Wilkes expedition (1838–1842) to gather data on Polynesian flora and fauna are a valuable source of information on lizards found in the Hawaiian Islands, but they do not note the Hawaiian names. In 1899, Leonhard Stejneger, curator of the Division of Reptiles and Batrachians for the Smithsonian Institution, published the first treatise on land reptiles of the Hawaiian Islands, which gathered together "scattered literature" on the topic.[32] He notes, "There are no true land reptiles in Hawai'i other than geckoes and skinks," which are as follows:

Family Gekkonidae:

1. *Lepidodactylus lugubris:* mourning gecko
2. *Hemidactylus garnotii:* Indo-Pacific gecko

3. *Peropus mutilatus:* stump-toed gecko
4. *Hemiphyllodactylus leucostictus:* Indo-Pacific tree gecko

Family Scincidae:

5. *Leiolopisma noctua:* moth skink
6. *Emoia cyanura:* copper-tailed skink
7. *Ablepharus boutonii poecilopleurus:* snake-eyed skink[33]

None of these species are endemic to the Hawaiian Islands: "All three skinks and three of the four species of geckoes belong to species widely distributed over the Indo-Polynesian island world, and, finally, that the remaining gecko has close relatives in New Caledonia, Java, Sumatra, and Ceylon."[34]

After Stejneger precludes the possibility of these species arriving to the Hawaiian Islands via ocean currents or wind, he offers this hypothesis:

> It is a well-known fact, however, that these small lizards are easily transported in vessels and among household goods over great distances, and when looking for the means by which these animals may have reached the Hawaiian Islands it is not possible to escape the conclusion that they have been introduced by man's agency. From the circumstances that the true home of these lizards is to the south and west of Hawai'i; that nearly all the species were collected there as early as the visit of the United States Exploring Expedition under Wilkes; and that the species are more or less common on the principal islands of the Hawaiian group; from these circumstances it is permissible to conclude that the lizards immigrated to the islands with the ancestors of the Hawaiians.[35]

If we accept Stejneger's hypothesis, then those early seafaring Polynesians who first arrived at the group of islands known today as the Hawaiian Islands were already familiar with these lizard species, which had inavertently accompanied them on their canoes. Countless generations would have observed these species, which they grouped under the descriptors mo'o 'alā, mo'o kā lā'au, and mo'o kāula, and about which they theorized, making a connection between them and mo'o akua. But which of these Hawaiian lizards correlate with these six species? Under "gecko" in the English portion of their dictionary,

Pukui and Elbert list "moʻo ʻalā"; "moʻokā" (another name for "moʻo kaʻalā"); "moʻo kaʻalā"; and "ʻanaka" (the transliteration of "gecko"). None of the Hawaiian-language dictionaries have an entry for "skink" in their English sections. Fortunately, during a broadcast of the Hawaiian-language radio program *Ka Leo Hawaiʻi* (1972–1988), Iokepa Makaʻai spoke about moʻo, and his explanations helped me to bridge this linguistic divide.

According to Makaʻai, there were three kinds of lizard in the islands: moʻo ʻalā, moʻo kāula, and moʻo kīauwahine, and he is the only source of information on the latter.[36] Makaʻai explained that the moʻo ʻalā was rather large, about eleven inches, and could be found nibbling seaweed on the shore. When it saw humans, it changed its color to black to merge with the ʻalā stones. Here, I should point out that ʻalā are "dense, waterworn volcanic stone"[37]—they are gray when dry and shiny black when wet. As stated earlier, Pukui characterized the moʻo ʻalā as a "black lizard." Clearly, this lizard derives its name from the ʻalā stones, which it resembles and frequents (figure 2.1). The other name by which it is known, moʻo kaʻalā, might be a shortened version of moʻo kaʻa ʻalā (moʻo that moves along or is found among the ʻalā stones).

In terms of habit and coloring, the moʻo ʻalā matches *Ablepharus boutonii poecilopleurus,* the snake-eyed skink. Herpetologist Sean McKeown notes that these skinks habitually frequent "rocky shoreline areas," and while their dorsal color may vary, they tend to be mottled brown or gray, and "the entire ventral area is pale yellow."[38] Photos from a reptile database of specimens in the Hawaiian Islands show examples with blackish-gray or black-copper skin speckled with rows of barely discernable white scales.[39] This species's skin is extremely shiny. Moʻo ʻalā abound on my three-acre property in a lehua rain forest (twenty-one hundred feet elevation) in one of the wettest areas of upper Puna, less than fifteen miles from Halemaʻumaʻu Crater at Kīlauea. It rains more often than not. Thus, these moʻo thrive in wet areas. They are quite snakelike with their narrow, streamlined bodies, but they are fewer than five inches long.

The moʻo kīauwahine, Makaʻai explains, is nearly a foot in length and can be found in coconut trees, where it gnaws coconuts. It is black with yellow eyes, and it can alter its color to fit in with the coconut tree. Significantly, both the moʻo kīauwahine and the moʻo ʻalā, in terms of coloring, match Kamakau's description of moʻo akua, which he asserts were black.

Figure 2.1. Snake-eyed skink, or moʻo ʻalā.
Photograph by Kai Markell.

Kihawahine is a black-colored moʻo. An account of the aliʻi Kihapiʻilani published in 1870 describes her: "He puhi U-ha la ke ano o ka ili, aka, he oi aku nae ka eleele o ka ili me ka hinuhinu launaole" (The skin was like that of an ūhā eel, but much blacker and very shiny).[40] The puhi ūhā (*Conger cinereus,* mustache conger) "has a white ventral side and darker dorsal side."[41] Another version gives a similar description: "Eleele hinuhinu . . . me he ili la no ka puhi uha la ke ano ke nana aku" (Shiny black . . . with skin like that of a puhi ūhā).[42] It seems that her body is also rather eellike in terms of flexibility: "Ke kino moo o ua Kihawahine nei, ua wili ae la kona kino a poepoe, me he pokaakaula la ke ano" (The body of Kihawahine was curled up in a circle like a coil of rope).[43] Such detailed descriptions of Kihawahine are rare.

The moʻo kāula, Makaʻai states, lives in peoples' homes and is pale or whitish in color. This description fits the habits and coloring of the mourning gecko, the stump-toed gecko, and the Indo-Pacific gecko (figure 2.2).

Figure 2.2. Mourning gecko, or mo'o kāula. Photograph by Kai Markell.

Having grown up in the islands, I can confirm that at night, the first two species' skin becomes noticeably paler, nearly transparent. Descriptions of mo'o akua having white, pearly, or nearly transparent skin match these geckos' appearance. The Indo-Pacific gecko is found in trees and is thus a match for the mo'o kā-lā'au (tree-smiting lizard).

Significantly, the six species of geckos and skinks I have discussed are, to differing degrees, brindled, the word for which is "mo'o." Brindled, from a Hawaiian perspective, does not refer only to darker streaks of color against a lighter background but also that which is streaked and speckled. This point is significant because the lizard is the nexus for the connections between mo'o akua and their 'o'opu and 'īlio mo'o kino lau.

Goby Kino Lau

'O'opu bear a remarkable resemblance to lizards. To begin, most 'o'opu are brindled (figure 2.3). Moreover, certain species possess fused pelvic fins that act like suction cups, which allow them to climb vertical surfaces like lizards. Alamo'o are known to climb three-hundred-foot waterfalls.[44] Nōpili can also climb, but their skills do not compare to

those of the alamo'o.[45] Furthermore, many 'o'opu species use their
sturdy pectoral fins to raise themselves on rocks, a pose that is quite lizard-like. They also use their pelvic and pectoral fins to hop from rock to
rock in streams and tidal pools in a manner that recalls a lizard's short
bursts of movement.

Several accounts stress the connection between 'o'opu, lizards,
and mo'o akua. 'Ai'ai is the son of the ocean deities Kū'ula and
Hinapukui'a, both associated with fish. 'Ai'ai punishes the people of
Wailau on Molokai because they are catching too many 'o'opu and not
leaving any to ensure the viability of the species. He turns the 'o'opu
that people have placed in gourds into lizards.[46] Elsewhere, a woman
named Kahīnano catches 'o'opu for dinner in a stream near her home.
She guts and salts the fish by the water, puts them in a wooden bowl,
carries them to her home, and then leaves to do other errands. Near
sunset, Kahīnano makes her way home. She sees a woman with 'ehu
hair searching here and there around her house and hears her call out
the names of different species of 'o'opu. As each species answers, it
jumps out of the wooden bowl, and runs back to the stream on its lizard-like limbs.[47] This next account has never been translated into English, and so I offer my translation:

Figure 2.3. Nākea goby. Artwork by Kalei Nu'uhiwa.

A man named Luhiā lived just below where Henry Cobb Adams is now living [in Kāneʻohe, Oʻahu]. Seaward of his makeshift hut, he farmed sweet potatoes, and upland of it and below, he farmed taro along with everyone who also lived in those places down to Kalokoloa.

There was a large, very flat stone in the front of a house of some men. There were other stones standing there nearby when I left, but after 1908, I never saw them again; perhaps they were broken to bits, perhaps not? I never saw them again!

Every morning that this Luhiā saw houses that had lit a cooking fire, on which lāwalu (ti-leaf bundles of fish or meat) were placed, he would go to that house and spy as the people prepared their lāwalu, which they would return later to eat. However, while the people of those homes looked on with regret, he would release the cooked lāwalu, or bundles of goby fish. Furthermore, to get revenge, he would go straight to that flat rock, step on it, and say, "Through the handle of the food bundle is life, oh younger siblings."

As soon as Luhiā would call out, the goby-fish lāwalu would open up, and everyone there jumped in shock and surprise when they saw with their own eyes the hundreds and hundreds of moʻo-kā-lāʻau (black lizards) jumping out from inside the various cooked bundles through the handles (where they were knotted) and fled from atop the flat rock where Luhiā stood.

When this Luhiā turned around, the people realized that he was not a real man, but a moʻo. His cave is about fifteen or twenty yards seaward of the Kauwa Bridge.[48]

According to Ahiki, the place where Luhiā called out to the gobies is near the mouth of Puha River at Waimānalo.[49] Kāneʻohe and Waimānalo are in the Koʻolaupoko district of Oʻahu.

All three accounts are cautionary tales. The first warns about the consequences of not caring properly for resources. In this case, people were punished for overfishing. Here, a god associated with fishing, ʻAiʻai, turns the ʻoʻopu into lizards—something inedible that resembles them. The other narratives speak to the belief that ʻoʻopu are sacred to moʻo, and the punishment is similar to the first account. A moʻo resurrects ʻoʻopu, which then either run like lizards back to the creek or have been transformed into lizards.

At least one moʻo is known to transform into an ʻoʻopu. That said, while ʻoʻopu are a general kino lau for moʻo akua, this does not signify that every moʻo can therefore become an ʻoʻopu. The moʻo in question is

Waka, who has a nu'ukole form (a.k.a. hi'ukole, hi'u'ula, and alamo'o).[50] This freshwater 'o'opu has a pinkish or reddish tail. Pukui notes, "It is a sign of bad luck to find one in a net when fishing for other fish for it keeps other fish away and must be thrown out of the net with an exclamation of disgust if one expects to be successful with the catch."[51] Pukui shared a story about alamo'o, which she had heard in Hilo in 1930:

> A woman was fishing for 'o'opu. She called out, "O Alamo'o, come and fill my basket until your tails stand upright." Her friends with her were surprised and disgusted to hear her calling out to a "mo'o" (lizard), an animal regarded with fear by Hawaiians because of its powers of evil. Her basket was filled, her friends were not as lucky. But when she emptied it at home a pinkish lizard ran out from among the fish. The woman screamed and dropped the basket. (This fish is kapu to many Hawaiians because of their belief that it is related to the mo'o gods.)[52]

Undoubtedly, a mo'o akua was watching and transformed one of the alamo'o into a lizard to warn the woman from eating this fish that is kin to them. Hawaiians did not eat this lizard-like fish for the same reason they did not harm lizards—lest a mo'o akua punish them.

Brindled-Dog Kino Lau

An 'īlio mo'o is called such because it is a dog ('īlio) that is brindled (mo'o). Thus, the status of an 'īlio mo'o as a general kino lau is informed by the similarity between the markings of lizards and this kind of dog. Just as mo'o are fond of 'o'opu, they seem to have a similar attachment to 'īlio mo'o, at least according to some traditions. Yet, among the different kinds of dogs sacrificed to mo'o akua, the 'īlio mo'o was the preferred offering. Another dog specifically linked to mo'o is the 'apowai, which Pukui describes as a "type of Hawaiian dog with solid grayish-brown body and nose tip and eyes of the same color, believed to love water and consequently offered as a sacrifice to *mo'o* water spirits."[53]

An account about the transfiguration of a young woman named Hauwahine into a deity mentions five kinds of dogs, each differentiated according to the markings or color of its fur. Although this story does not link the human Hauwahine to the mo'o Hauwahine, I believe they are one and the same. Pukui apparently made the same connection.

Luhiā and Hauwahine are famous moʻo in the Koʻolaupoko District on
Oʻahu. In the account, Luhiā tells Hauwahine that after she transfigures,
she will go on to help heal the sick. Pukui, who had read and translated
this account for the Bishop Museum, would later explain elsewhere,
"Hauwahine, the moʻo (water creature) goddess, warded off sickness."[54]
Here below, I share my summary of this story.

The moʻo Luhiā, while in his human form, comes across Hauwahine, who was paralyzed from birth. He informs her parents that she is
an akua trapped in human form. He explains the ritual that will transfigure her into a deity. During the five nights it takes for her to transform, five dogs will appear: "I ka po mua, he ilio moo; po elua, he ilio
ehu; po ekolu, kalakoa; po eha, he ilio hahai [hahei]; po elima, he ilio
keokeo" (The first night, a brindled dog; the second night, a reddish-
brown dog; the third night, a dog with mottled fur; the fourth night, a
dog with striped shoulders; the fifth night, a white dog). The significance
of the ʻīlio moʻo is clear. The reddish-brown dog speaks to the belief that
moʻo akua sometimes have reddish-brown hair. The third dog's mottled
coat recalls brindled fur, as does the fourth dog's striped shoulders. As
for the fifth, Kihawahine can appear as a large white dog.[55]

Two moʻo of Hawaiʻi enjoy exploring in their ʻīlio moʻo form: one
is named Paʻe, and the other's name is not mentioned.[56] They also have
a human form. At one point, Paʻe lets an elderly couple take her home,
not realizing they intend to eat her. Because Paʻe is too skinny to be
worth eating, the couple spend several weeks fattening her up. On the
day Paʻe is slated to be cooked in the imu (underground oven), her moʻo
companion arrives in her ʻīlio form. She compliments Paʻe on her attractive plumpness. Paʻe laments that the elderly couple whom she had "allowed to become" her keepers intend to eat her that very day. They kill
the couple and then travel to Oʻahu, where they make their home in
Nuʻuanu Valley, which traverses the Koʻolau mountain range. Thereafter, Paʻe is called "the dog of Koʻolau."[57] According to Pukui and Laura
C. Green, who published this account, these are the same moʻo in the
story about the Koʻolau moʻo who brings an ʻīlio moʻo back to life.

There are two other versions of this tale. In the first, an ʻīlio moʻo
named Paʻe is killed and cooked in an imu as a meal for an aliʻi. Paʻe's
moʻo companion is sitting in her human form, a beautiful woman with
ʻehu hair, next to a pool when she spots two men carrying the calabash. By
virtue of her mana, she knows it contains Paʻe and calls out to her. Paʻe,
who has resurrected herself, answers. The men, terrified, drop the calabash
and run away.[58] In the second version, an ʻīlio moʻo (unidentified) is killed

and cooked as a meal for Queen Ka'ahumanu. This dog also resurrects itself and answers a mo'o (unidentified) who asks where she is headed.[59] Like the stories about mo'o bringing 'o'opu back to life or transforming them into lizards, these accounts about 'īlio mo'o and mo'o are also cautionary tales.

In addition to the mo'o already mentioned, there are two others who appear as dogs: Lanihuli as an 'īlio 'ōlohe (hairless dog) and Waka as an 'īlio mo'o.[60] As I have stressed in my discussions on lizard and goby kino lau, however, it is a mistake to assume that because the 'īlio mo'o is a general kino lau for all mo'o, every mo'o can therefore transform into a dog.

Spider Kino Lau

I include spiders as general kino lau rather than identify them as a mo'o-specific kino lau because Pukui upheld, "Spiders, too, are said to be akin to the mo'o."[61] With the exception of Pukui, I have never found a clear statement anywhere, in written or oral sources, that spiders are a kino lau for all mo'o akua. Nor are there cautionary tales about harming spiders like those about 'o'opu and lizards, which would confirm her statement. She either arrived at this conclusion or learned it from someone else. In any case, the logic behind this kino lau is easy to imagine, and once again the lizard is the nexus, just as it is for the 'o'opu and 'īlio mo'o.

Like lizards, spiders crawl with their stomachs close to the ground, cling to vertical surfaces, and can jump. Some species are brindled; others are partially yellow or entirely yellow. Significantly, some Hawaiian spider species physically resemble lizards. We have many endemic spiders. By 1900, R. C. L. Perkins had identified more than one hundred Arachnida species, seventy-seven of which are found nowhere else.[62] Among these are jumping spiders, which Eugène Simon classified under the genus *Sandalodes* but later transferred to the genus *Havaika*.[63] Many *Havaika* are brindled, and the *Havaika jamiesoni* has a yellow sternum and coxae and a whitish-yellow abdomen.[64] Predominately yellow spiders include *Theridion grallator*, also known as the "happy-face spider."[65] There are six species of the genus *Ariamnes* with an elongated abdomen that resembles a lizard's body or tail.[66] These species "have been observed to catch their spider prey with a net held in their back legs."[67] This last fact overlaps with spiderlike mo'o in Hawaiian traditions.

In Manu's account about the battle between Pele and Waka, the link between spiders and mo'o is clear. During the battle, "Ua hookuu iho la o Kamooinanea he wahi upena pu-na-welewele mai ka lewa iho; aole i kana mai a ka hihipea i ka pu-na-welewele, a—na ia mea i ume ae i ua poe moo nei" (Kamoʻoinanea released a spiderweb net from the sky; the spiderweb was incredibly entangling, and it was the means by which those moʻo people were drawn up).[68] As each web dropped, the moʻo were tangled in its threads and brought to Punaluʻu on Hawaiʻi to help Waka fight Pele.[69] However, Manu never identifies Moʻoinanea as adopting the form of a spider in this or any other traditions he published in which he mentions her. A spider accompanies Waka to Punaluʻu, described as "he makua ia no ka moo; mailoko mai no a Kamooinanea a me Kihawahine ka moo Aliiaimoku o na Hono a Piilani o Maui" (a parent for the moʻo; through Kamoʻoinanea and Kihawahine the ruling aliʻi moʻo of the bays belonging to Piʻilani of Maui).[70] Waka has a spider form with a white stomach.[71] Notably, Kihawahine appears as a spider with a white stomach in a ritual to call her forth (see chapter 5). Lanihuli has a spider kino lau, the kind that spins webs, and he can also command spiders to do his bidding.[72]

───────────

The lizard, goby, brindled dog, and spider are symbolic kino lau for the entire class of water deities known as moʻo. The rationale for their connection to moʻo akua as general kino lau can be summarized in this way. The little lizard recalls in miniature the greater reptilian form of the moʻo akua. In turn, ʻoʻopu are similar to lizards in terms of markings, form, abilities, and habits. The ʻilio moʻo resembles lizards in terms of markings. The spider recalls lizards in terms of physicality, markings, and abilities but may also be yellow, a color linked to moʻo akua. These four kino lau illustrate the ways that moʻo akua are interesting anomalies in terms of the kino lau system: generally, kino lau are the forms a given deity can take, which is why they are sacred to that deity. To reiterate, all moʻo have a lizard form, but this divine form should not be confused with ordinary lizards, and while not all of them transform into a goby, brindled dog, or spider, all four are sacred to moʻo because they are symbolic kino lau in that they are associated with them.

Chapter 3 examines moʻo-specific kino lau (excluding the goby, brindled dog, and spider, as I have already discussed them here), which offer further insights into Hawaiian understandings of moʻo as a class of water deities, specific moʻo, the relationship between moʻo and the areas with which they are associated, and the kino lau system itself.

Chapter 3

Moʻo-Specific Kino Lau

Although most (possibly all) moʻo are technically "shape-shifters" given that they can shift between their respective kino lau, the substantial oral and written records of Hawaiian beliefs about moʻo suggest that this ability is limited. When sources speak of moʻo with many bodies, they mean the forms associated with those moʻo. In other words, moʻo are not able to change themselves into anything they please. This is an important distinction for reasons that will become clearer in the course of this chapter. My reasoning is based on two premises.

First, if our ancestors believed that moʻo had this remarkable ability, they would have incorporated it into their traditions. Given the great number of surviving traditions, it is reasonable to assume that at least a few of these would have noted that the moʻo's ability to shape-shift is boundless. Such an ability would be convenient, for example, when moʻo battle the Pele clan. Yet we never see moʻo turning into Pele clan–related forms such as tsunamis, lava flows, or lightning—sharks being the only exception (see chapter 4). Nor is a moʻo ever shown to have a pig form—a kino of the pig god Kamapuaʻa (Pig-Child) and Lono. This seems to be a general rule for shape-shifting akua. For example, Kamapuaʻa has many kino lau: human, pig, piglike fish, and several plants that in one way or another recall a pig. He has a love-hate relationship with Pele. In one instance he escapes her lava by jumping into the ocean and changing into his pig-fish form, Humuhumunukunuku-apuaʻa (Pig-snout Humuhumu), to swim to safety.[1] He never changes into a Pele clan–related form to fight "fire with fire." Conversely, Pele is never a moʻo or a pig. Second, if moʻo's shape-shifting abilities were unlimited, the kino lau system upon which beliefs about akua—not just moʻo akua—are based would not exist.

So how do we explain variation in a given deity's forms across traditions—meaning that some forms are noted in some moʻolelo but not in others? To begin, variations in a familial or localized tradition (i.e., specific to a family or a community) or across discrete "national" traditions in which mo'o figure prominently (e.g., Hi'iakaikapoliopele, Keaomelemele, Lā'ieikawai, Kihapi'ilani, Kamaakamahi'ai) suggest that perceptions of a given mo'o vary according to place and time, including ideas about the forms it might take. Such variation, however, is generally grounded in a deeply rooted cultural understanding of these deities.

By way of illustration, certain mo'o, Kilioeikapua, Kalamainu'u, and Waka, have human forms in all the traditions in which they appear, but the other kino lau with which they are associated vary according to the tradition. Furthermore, not all mo'o are attributed a human form. For example, Kihanuilūlūmoku is only ever depicted in reptilian form in the six different traditions in which it appears (Lā'ieikawai, Kepaka'ili'ula, Keaomelemele, Kekalukaluokēwā, Pele and Waka, and Puaka'ōhelo, including their respective variations), and furthermore, its gender is never specified.[2] That said, what seems to be a remnant (a single statement) from an O'ahu tradition holds that Kihanuilūlūmoku (if this is the same mo'o) is female and that in addition to her mo'o form she can assume those of a human and an eel.[3]

Because the kino lau system is founded on a fundamental principle, which I call "kino lau logic," it is possible to formulate plausible hypotheses to account for kino lau variation. This core principle is that kino lau always "make sense" because there is a rationale for their being linked to a deity. It may happen that we come across a kino lau that perplexes us, but this is only because we cannot grasp the principles behind it. For example, when I first read Pukui's assertion that the yellow chicken is one of Kihawahine's kino lau, for which she did not offer an explanation, I was puzzled. Despite my best efforts, I never made the connection. When I found the answer in two versions of the Kihapi'ilani tradition, which I share in this chapter, I was amazed at our ancestors' powers of observation and the subtleness of kino lau logic.

I offer three hypotheses for variation in kino lau. First, given that the entire kino lau system arises out of countless generations of close interaction with and observation of the environment and the various relationships between natural phenomena, fauna, and flora, the most obvious reason for variation in mo'o kino lau is that at one point someone noticed something that someone else did not. Second, perhaps there were other traditions that attributed a certain kino lau to a mo'o, but these accounts were lost, which is why this one instance may seem an anomaly to us today. Third, notable exceptions could also be attributed to the artistic license of storytellers who were intimately familiar with the depth and breadth of mo'o lore. Even in this instance, however, such a kino lau, no matter how unusual, would make sense if we knew how to make the connections. In this chapter, I discuss mo'o-specific kino lau and explicate the logic behind them.

Mo'o with Demihuman or Human Kino Lau

In some instances, mo'o who appear in demihuman or human form present a conundrum in terms of kino lau logic. By demihuman, I intend those mo'o who have both mo'o and human attributes at once, perhaps even a human upper half and a reptilian lower half. In the case of mo'o who have a human parent or mo'o who were once human but were then transformed into mo'o, the fact that they have a demihuman or human form makes sense. They either inherited it or they retained the use of it after they became mo'o. But what about mo'o whose status as such is firmly established mai ka pō mai (from the time of the pō, deep darkness, when akua first appeared, and thus from time immemorial) such as Mo'oinanea, the supreme mo'o and the origin of all other mo'o?

The great cosmogonic chant Kumulipo, which has sixteen wā (eras) and two thousand plus lines, references her in the fourth wā, when crawling creatures first appear in the world, under variants of her name— Mo'onanea, Milimilinanea, Milinanea. In the many traditions in which she appears, only two show her in human form; otherwise, she is depicted as a reptile, and no mention is made of her having a human form. I offer two hypotheses to account for this kino lau logic conundrum.

Taking a secular (not faith-based) approach, we might propose that like many other peoples across place and time 'Ōiwi engaged in anthropomorphism because it is human nature to attribute a human form, behavior, and emotions to other-than-human entities such as deities. Conversely, from a faith-based perspective, we might argue that because Hawaiians descend from akua, as many origin stories explain, all akua then, potentially, have human forms. Perhaps our human form mirrors theirs (as Christians claim about their God). Either way, this is a philosophical question that can only be debated and never truly answered, although I imagine that some will have very strong opinions about this point.

Here, I turn my attention to the demihuman mo'o form. While gigantic mo'o the size of small mountains with huge, gaping jaws are undeniably terrifying, the rare mo'o who appears as a demi-mo'o is singularly disturbing because it merges the human with the nonhuman, and the result is monstrous. Kamō'ili'ili is one such mo'o. After Hi'iaka and Wahina'ōma'o find Pele's lover Lohi'au, and while they are making their way back to Hawai'i, they encounter this mo'o on O'ahu in Mō'ili'ili, the area named after her. As she launches herself toward them:

> Wehe ke a o luna, wehe ke a o lalo o ua moo nei, a pulelo nohoi kona lauoho i hope, aa na maka, a ke-ke no hoi na niho. . . . Ke kokolo ala ka lia makau a weliweli iloko o Lohiau, oiai a kahi [akahi] no oia a ike maoli i nei mea he kino moowahine. O kaua [kana] e ike nei i kino o keia moowahine ia Kamoiliili, he kino wahine kanaka maoli kona, mai ke poo iho a hala iho malalo o na waiu, a ua ike pu aku nohoi o Lohiau i ka opu o ua wahine moo nei he opu maoli no ke kanaka. He ano hooluu olena o mua o ke aloma [alo ma] kekahi wahi a mai ke poo iho a hoea i ka umauma he ano kakeakea ka hooluu. He mau wawae nohoi o ka moo ame ka huelo. O luna iho o ke kua he ano okala a ooi a ua like paha ia me ke kokala o ke kua o ka moo moewai ai [a i] ike ia hoi ma ka inoa o ke korokodila o ua [na] aina e.[4]

The mo'o's upper and lower jaws opened, her hair flew behind her, [her] eyes blazing and teeth bared. . . . Shuddery terror slithered within Lohi'au, this being the first time he truly saw a mo'o wahine's form. We see that the form of this mo'owahine, Kamō'ili'ili, was a real human woman's body from the head to just below the breasts, and Lohi'au saw that the stomach of that female mo'o was like that of humans. Her front was yellowish in some places and from the head to the chest was whitish. Her legs and tail were reptilian. The surface of her back was rather rough with sharp protuberances, like the spiny ridges of the water-dwelling reptile known as the "crocodile" in other lands.

We can better appreciate Lohi'au's horror if we consider this fact: as we will see, Kilioeikapua and Kalanamainu'u, in their beautiful human forms, attempted to seduce him earlier in this account, and had it not been for Pele, they might have been successful. Imagine going to bed with a beautiful woman but waking up to an entity like Kamō'ili'ili (figure 3.1). After the two mo'o failed to seduce Lohi'au, they eventually kidnapped and killed him, but Hi'iaka brought him back to life.

Even mo'o who appear as humans may be unable to completely hide their true form.

Figure 3.1. Mo'o wahine in demi-mo'o form. Artwork
by Hinahina Gray.

Another mo'o that Hi'iaka encounters is Mo'olau (a.k.a. Mo'olauwahine),
who dwells at Kaho'oleiwai at Kahuā in South Kohala, Hawai'i. Re-
puted to be the angriest of all people-despising mo'o akua, when she
meets someone she dislikes or who angers her, she falls in a fit to the
ground in her mo'o form and thrashes around, which creates a dust
cloud.[5] In Poepoe's version of this account, Hi'iaka encounters Mo'olau
as she is seated in the middle of the road posing as a human. Poepoe
notes that her human form is beautiful, but he offers few details other
than that her skin is the color of "pala-lau-memele" (yellowed leaves)

and that she is wearing a red-and-white-colored pāʻū (skirt or sarong), which she has spread out over the road to block it. Hidden beneath her pāʻū are "na kino moo liilii o ua Moolau nei" (small moʻo features or many little moʻo bodies of Moʻolau).[6] Moʻolau knows that Hiʻiaka is coming. She waits as a human because she thinks that Hiʻiaka will not realize that she is a moʻo and then she can turn into a moʻo and kill her. When Hiʻiaka sees her, she chants: "O oe ia Moolau wahine/Hookohu-kohu ana me he wahine iʻo la/O Moolau wahine na o Waimea/He moo, a he moo no—e" (It is you Moʻolau wahine/Trying to resemble a real woman/O Moʻolau wahine of Waimea/A moʻo, a moʻo indeed—oh).[7]

Like Moʻolau, Alanapo appears human, but a closer look reveals that she retains certain reptilian features. This moʻo lives upland of Keʻei on Hawaiʻi and sleeps in a stream in her moʻo form. Alanapo is famed for her fighting skills. While she is acting as her brother's (Naulu-o-Wehi) second in his battle against Ka-Miki, Ka-Miki's brother, Ma-Kaʻiole (a rat kupua), who is Ka-Miki's second, recognizes her as a moʻo when he glimpses her legs as she is about to enter the fray. The thick folds of her pāʻū hide a moʻo body.[8]

There are, however, moʻo who manifest completely as humans, meaning they do not hide reptilian features beneath their clothing. But even then, they cannot hide their true nature from deities and humans with certain powers. In this case, ordinary humans to whom moʻo are attracted do not stand a chance. As we have seen, Punaʻaikoaʻe had no inkling that the stunningly beautiful Kalamainuʻu was a moʻo. At least she was more interested in consuming his body metaphorically rather than literally. There are moʻo wahine who have a taste for human flesh and use their human bodies to lure unsuspecting men to their death. In these stories of seduction, there are no happy endings for these humans. Waiākea is one such moʻo. She has a beautiful human form she uses to deceive travelers along the mountain ridge. She has killed many people this way. She combs her hair as she sits at the edge of a pool in front of her house. When the travelers accept her offer to enter her home, she changes into a moʻo and eats them.[9] But what about moʻo who have a taste for human flesh but have long lost their last vestiges of youthful beauty and thus cannot use themselves as bait? In that case, the moʻo might send her attractive granddaughter to lure someone back to the cave for her meal. This was Kaualehu's approach. At her cave in a cliff above Punaluʻu in Kaʻū, she would eat men, scooping out their eyeballs for appetizers.[10] Kaikapu was another old moʻo who used her grand-daughter Nīnole to lure men to her cave at Kaʻū so she could eat them.[11]

A few mo'o are known to kidnap young boys, and some of these mo'o eventually let them go. In these instances, companionship and not seduction seems to be the reason for the abduction. Annie Ka'aukai shared a story about the mo'o of Wai'ākōlea pond in Kalapana on Hawai'i. People sometimes see her in her human form combing her hair. She once took a boy from Ka'ū who had 'ehu hair. The people called "Lady" Konanui, who lived upland of that pond, to help. When Konanui called to the boy in Hawaiian, he finally appeared but he was "already growing scales." Ka'aukai added, "They say the mo'o like those with 'ehu hair."[12] On August 9, 1968, Carrie Ka'aelani Kenui told a story about a large mo'o associated with Nu'u, Kenui's birthplace, in Maui. The mo'o lived in a pond near a hau tree grove formerly used by ali'i. This area was called Pūpuka. Kenui says she was nearly taken by this mo'o. It later took a young boy to her cave and kept him for a week before finally releasing him.[13]

Male mo'o also kidnap humans. A mo'o of Kāne'ohe on O'ahu, Kamo'oali'i, grabbed an ali'i wahine visiting from Maui who happened to pass by his stream and dove with her into the water.[14] What happened after that remains unknown. Moanalihaikawaokele, while fighting in his human form, tells his opponent, Kū'aikauakama, that he will go in his mo'o body to take Kū'aikauakama's love interest, Hina'ai'ulunui, and make her his wahine. Whether she is willing is clearly irrelevant.[15] In one instance it is not a mo'o who kidnaps a woman but his servant who thinks he is acting in his master's best interests. Kalama'ula, who has a human form, is a ruling ali'i of Kawaihae, Hawai'i. His messenger, an 'elepaio bird kupua, sees a beautiful woman in a forest. Using trickery, he brings her to Kalama'ula.[16]

The inability of ordinary humans to perceive the true nature of mo'o wahine posing as humans is a common theme in Hawaiian mo'olelo. Kilioeikapua, Kalanamainu'u, Hauwahine, Kahalakea, and Kaluanou are notable examples.

Kilioeikapua and Kalanamainu'u are infamous mo'o, poetically termed the "wahine kiai pali o Haena nei" (women who guard the cliff of Hā'ena). They appear in several traditions, most famously that of Hi'iakaikapoliopele. When Pele first meets Lohi'au, a ruling ali'i of Kaua'i famed for his good looks and for his ability to dance hula, they are captivated with each other. Shortly after they meet, they retire and engage in lovemaking for three days and three nights. Pele, being a deity, has no real need to eat, but her human lover is finally in need of food, and so she accompanies him to the eating house.[17] As they sit there, they hear exclamations of surprise. Two beautiful women wearing mokihana lei entwined with the pahapaha limu of Polihale, Kaua'i, have entered the eating house. They are Kilioeikapua and Kalanamainu'u:

> O ka ui o keia mau wahine hapa moo e ike ia aku nei e na kamaaina, he ui no i like aku me ko Pele, a koe wale no ke ano nanana-kea o ko laua ili, aole hoi i loaa aku ka ui enaena o ka ui o Puna paia aala i ka hala me ka hinano.[18]

> The beauty of these half mo'o women the kama'āina saw was equal to Pele's beauty, except for their skin's paleness, which lacked the glowing attractiveness of the beauty of Puna, where the walls of the homes are perfumed with hala keys and hīnano flowers.

Kilioeikapua and Kalanamainu'u sit near Lohi'au and proceed to flirt with him. Such were their beauty and charm that he is soon mesmerized by them. The only thing holding him back from acting on his desire is the prohibition that Pele has placed upon his body. He is hers and hers alone under the pain of death. Meanwhile, Pele, by virtue of her mana, has shielded her presence so that the mo'o cannot see her. After everyone finishes eating, they all leave for the house set aside for dancing hula. There, Pele makes herself visible, using her mana to appear even more beautiful than before. Kilioe and Kalanamainu'u admire and envy Pele's beauty, unaware that they are in the presence of the fierce volcanic deity. Pele, however, knows exactly who they are and, moreover, resents their behavior with Lohi'au. Pele begins to level veiled insults at the mo'o, who then take offense and insult her in turn. Pele announces their true nature to everyone, but the mo'o deny it. Pele continues to berate them and finally intones a denigrating chant, which is the passage from the Kumulipo that chronicles the period when mo'o first appear in the world. When Kilioe and Kalanamainu'u vanish in front of the assembly, only then does everyone finally realize that these beauties were actually mo'o. Only Pele knew beforehand.

As for Hauwahine and Kahalakea, when Hi'iaka and Wahine'ōma'o encounter them, Wahine'ōma'o exclaims at their loveliness. She has difficulty believing Hi'iaka when she tells her that they are not real women but mo'o. Several versions of this tradition describe this encounter. In Ho'oulumāhiehie's version, the mo'o are sunning themselves in their human forms on the bank of Kawainui after having swum in its water (this version does not identify Hauwahine's companion by name). Their skin is golden like the 'ilima lei they are wearing, a deep yellow like hala

keys.[19] In Poepoe's version, they are in their moʻo forms. When they notice Hiʻiaka, Hauwahine turns to Kahalakea and suggests they dive into
the water to change into humans, hoping that she will mistake them as
such and not harm them: "Luu iho la ua mau moo nei iloko o ka wai, a
hooponopono iho la no ka wehe ana ae i ko laua mau alualu moo, a
lawe ae hoi i na kino kanaka maoli o laua" (The moʻo dove into the
water, made adjustments to remove their moʻo skins, and then took up
their real human bodies).[20]

Here an intriguing translation question arises. While "alualu"
(ʻaluʻalu) has several meanings, the only one that really fits here is "skin"
given the phrase "mau alualu moʻo" (moʻo skins). If these moʻo are indeed removing their moʻo skins to slip on their "kino kanaka maoli"
(forms like real humans), then what do they look like between one and
the other? While there is no answer, the imaginative possibilities are de-
lightfully gruesome to contemplate. If "mau alualu moʻo" (moʻo skins) is
intended as "moʻo bodies," then they dove into the water to carry out
their transformation in secret so that Hiʻiaka would not see it. Then
again, if "kino kanaka maoli" means their "actual human forms," then
this would imply that their primary form is human. But this translation
choice is not persuasive, as we shall see. Not long after the moʻo disguise
themselves as humans, Wahineʻōmaʻo notices them. When she exclaims
about the beautiful women wearing ʻilima lei on their heads, Hiʻiaka explains that they are not humans but moʻo, and the lei ʻilima they wear are
actually their moʻo tails, which they have twined into lei. Hiʻiaka tells
Wahineʻōmaʻo that she has mistaken the color of the upper part of their
tails, which is palai-lenalena (yellow palai fern or palai that has yellowed), for the color of ʻilima, which is a true yellow.[21] Significantly, lei
ʻilima are termed "lei ʻāpiki," or lei that attract mischievous spirits. Perhaps this is why moʻo wahine are sometimes depicted wearing or making
these lei. Elsewhere, Kihawahine appears as a beautiful young woman
wearing a lei ʻilima, which the account notes is also called a lei ʻāpiki.[22]

In the Hamanalau tradition, a young seer named Kaukanapōkiʻi
and his friend Kāʻili join a festive gathering at Hālawa on Molokai.
Kamoku and Kaluanou, a young couple, initiate a round of hula. Kāʻili
suggests that he and Kaukanapōkiʻi go to watch. Kaukanapōkiʻi senses
Kaluanou's moʻo nature. He asks Kāʻili about the attractive, long-
haired woman (Kaluanou). Kāʻili tells him, "Yes, that is a beautiful
woman. Her kāne (Kamoku) is sitting with her. They are kamaʻāina of
this area." Kaukanapōkiʻi replies, "Yes, a woman, but also a kupua,
unseen by those who are not seers." Kāʻili asks him, "How do you

know that woman is a kupua?" Kaukanapōki'i tells him, "Look at her features. They are not like those of a human, but like those who belong to the family of Kilioe and her ilk, which are like the features of the woman sitting there." He then uses his powers to make Kaluanou ill, and so she and Kamoku leave the gathering to return home.[23] I discuss this scene later in connection with mo'o and geographical features, but suffice it to say, Kamoku was unaware that his wahine was a mo'o. The exchange between Kaukanapōki'i and Kā'ili reveals a belief about mo'o masquerading as humans: their features are peculiar in some way but not enough for ordinary humans to notice. As the episode also shows, Kaukanapōki'i likens Kaluanou's features to Kilioe and her ilk (other mo'o). The mo'o's strange features in human form has to do with their being water deities.

In the Lauka'ie'ie tradition, the god Makanikeoe sees two women sitting in 'Ālele stream on O'ahu, who flee when they see him. After he reassures them, they reveal themselves to be the mo'o wahine Lauhuki and Kilioe and say that the waters of Kalena and all the springs and pools of Makawao are theirs.[24] Makanikeoe notes that their features resemble those of the akua wahine (female deities) Hinaulu'ōhi'a (Hina who makes the 'ōhi'a grow, or 'Ōhi'a-forest Hina). This is a significant observation. Hinaulu'ōhi'a is not a mo'o but a forest deity. She is also known as Laea (a.k.a. Lea, La'e), and her brothers are Kūka'ōhi'alaka (Kū the 'ōhi'a [of] Laka), Kūmokuhāli'i (Kū who spreads across islands), Kūpulupulukanahele (Ku of the undergrowth), and Kūpā'aike'e (Kū crookedness-eating adze)—all of whom are associated with canoe construction.[25] In this same account, Hinaulu'ōhi'a rises up in her 'ōhi'a lehua form from beneath the water of a pond near a large stream in Waipi'o, Hawai'i.[26] Her rising from within the pond marks her as a water deity of some sort, and indeed, she is noted as such in Hukilani's 1864 treatise on akua.

Hukilani divides akua wahine into three main groups: "na akua wahine i ka lua" (volcano crater-dwelling akua wahine); "na akua wahine i ka wai" (wai-dwelling akua wahine); and "na akua wahine noho mauna" (mountain-dwelling akua wahine). They are called such, he explains, because they live in the volcano crater, in bodies of fresh water, or in the mountains.[27] As examples of akua wahine who live in the lua, Hukilani lists Pele, Hi'iakaikapoliopele, Hi'iakaikapua'ena'ena, and Haumea. For akua wahine who live in the water, he names Kihawahine and Laniwahine, Hinaulu'ōhi'a, Lā'ieikawai, and Lā'ielohelohe. The first two are mo'o; the last two are the twin sisters of the Lā'ieikawai tradition. For akua wahine who dwell in the mountains, he lists Poliʻahu, Līlīnoe, Lanihuli, Hāpuʻu, and Kalaʻiohauola.²⁸ The first two live at Mauna Kea, the third in the Koʻolau mountain range, and the last two at upper Nuʻuanu.

From the traditions of Hamanalau and Laukaʻieʻie, together with Hukilani's treatise, we learn something important about akua wahine wai. A water deity's features, whether moʻo or forest deities, share something in common. Their intimate relationship with water—the fact that they embody water—shapes their features in some way.

Some moʻo with human forms are only ever depicted as elderly. In the tradition of Keamalu, Hapaimemeue warns Keamalu that as she travels to the land of Makaliʻi, she will encounter two luahine. When they see her, they will dive in the water. As she nears, she will see them in their moʻo forms. Although they will try to frighten her by winding their tails around her body, she should not show fear. If she succeeds, they will allow her to continue her travels.²⁹

Moʻoinanea is notable in that she is rarely shown to take human form, but when she does she only appears as a luahine. Only two traditions depict her thusly: Kepakaʻiliʻula and Haʻinākolo. Kepakaʻiliʻula is one of Moʻoinanea's descendants, although he does not know this when he first meets her. In this passage, he has just landed at Kuaihelani:

> I ko ia nei wa i pae aku ai, aohe mea e ae i halawai mai me ia nei, hoo-kahi wale no he luahine kuilena, ua hele a alualu, ua hele ke oho a pala (poohina), makau keia, hoolana mai la keia i ka waa mawaho iki mai, no ko ia nei makau i ua luahine la, no ka mea, he luahine ano e loa keia. O keia luahine he moo, oia ke kupunawahine o Aukelenuiaiku oia i oleloia e J. Kaunamano ma ka Pakipika, a no ko ia nei makau loa, hoohina malie no keia i ka waa. Alaila, hea mai la ua luahine la ia ia nei, "E! e Kalani, e kuu Haku, kuu Pulapula, e pae iuka." Alaila, pae aku la keia i ke one maloo.

When he landed, there was no one to meet him, only an old, yellow-toothed, wrinkled woman, whose hair had yellowed (gray hair). He was afraid and so he floated his canoe just offshore. This old woman scared him because she was such an incredibly strange old woman. This old woman was a moʻo, the grandmother of ʻAukelenuiaʻīkū, the one J. Kaunamano mentioned in [his account of ʻAukelenuiaʻīkū in the *Hoku o*] *ka Pakipika*. Because he was terrified, [his body trembled, which] made the canoe gently rock from side to side. Then, the old

woman called to him, "Oh! Oh Heavenly-One, my Lord, my Descendant, come ashore." So he came ashore to the dry sand.[30]

What is remarkable about this episode is that Kepakaili'ula is a re-
nowned warrior, yet when he sees this luahine, whom he instinctively
recognizes as eerie, he begins to tremble in fright.

In Mary Pa'ahana Kanaka'ole Wiggin's version of the Ha'inākolo
tradition, Mo'oinanea leaves her home at Waolani in Nu'uanu Valley on
O'ahu to come to Waipi'o on Hawai'i to take her mo'opuna (grandchild, descendant) Ha'inākolo to Kuaihelani. Just as Ha'inākolo is about
to eat a bundle of fish into which her evil sister Lu'ukia had inserted a
bit of Pacific golden plover, a form of their 'aumakua and therefore for-
bidden, "the old kupua snatched it from her." Shortly thereafter,
"Mo'oinanea assumed her animal body and stretched it out so that her
tail rested at Waipio and her nose lay on the beach at Kuaihelani, and
Hainakolo walked across her back while all about her hung rainbows as
signs of a divine chiefess. As soon as she stepped upon the beach the
mo'o woman resumed her human form, and led her to the home of
Keanini."[31] Notably, the backs of akua and akua-like ali'i are sacred.
Yet, this supreme mo'o akua allows her mo'opuna to walk upon her
sacred back—a bridge between realms and generations. Here, the cultural significance is mo'okū'auhau: Ha'inākolo can only conceive a
child, and thus help continue Mo'oinanea's lineage, if she is reunited
with her kāne.

A mere handful of male mo'o are shown to have a human form,
and only two of these are described as elderly, and both are found in accounts published by the same contributor. The first is the male
Mo'oinanea in Ho'oulumāhiehie's version of Ha'inākolo, and the other
is Lanihuli in Ho'oulumāhiehie's version of the Kamaakamahi'ai
tradition.

Initially, Mo'oinanea, during his battle with Kū'aikauakama, who
will one day father Ha'inākolo, is unaware he is fighting one of his descendants. As soon as he realizes this, he informs Kū'aikauakama, and
they end the battle.[32] In this account, Mo'oinanea alternates between his
great mo'o body and his human form, which is described as a "kanaka
poohina" (gray-haired man) and an "elemakule poohina" (old gray-
haired man).[33]

It comes naturally to wonder if this male Mo'oinanea is an instance of a mo'o whose gender varies according to a given version of a
tradition or if this is an entirely different mo'o who happens to be named

Moʻoinanea. I have collected data on 288 moʻo; however, because several entries are for groups of an unspecified number of moʻo, the number is actually much higher. These groups' gender is either not specified or indicated as female. Data from my list suggest that gender variation is uncommon. Gender-wise, 137 are identified as female, 53 as male, 93 as unspecified, and only 5 as either male, female, or gender unspecified depending on the account. These five moʻo are Piliamoʻo, Nohoamoʻo/Kuaua, Kamōʻiliʻili, Pāhoa, and Kamalō. There is, however, a sixth moʻo who, like Moʻoinanea, has been overwhelmingly recognized as female across traditions with one notable exception—Kihawahine. This deviation from the norm is found in Beni Kaulainamoku's 1874 account about Hiku:

> He ano lehulehu na kino o keia moo e like me ke ano o ka poe kupua, o kona mau kino maoli he wahine ui opiopio, o kekahi moo ua like me kekahi kuahiwi nui, o kekahi kino he luahine, a he elemakule, a kamalii kane opiopio, oia na kino lau o keia moo e hoomana ia e kekahi poe.

> This moʻo had numerous bodies as is the nature of kupua. A young, beautiful woman is her real form, another is that of a moʻo as large as a mountain, an old woman, an old man, a young man, and those are the many forms of this moʻo worshipped by some people.[34]

Given the substantial body of ʻŌiwi commentary on Kihawahine, which identify her as an akua wahine who was worshipped in a solemn ceremony that specifically honors female deities (see chapter 5), we can understand Kaulainamoku's perspective as an "outlier"—meaning that it is highly unusual. Because of this, although I note this discrepancy, I do not include Kihawahine among the moʻo who appear either as male or female. I use the same reasoning for Moʻoinanea.

Moʻoinanea appears in several distinct traditions and many of their variants. With the exception of two accounts, Moʻoinanea is gendered as female. The first is a three-page English-language account of Kūkahauʻula and Poliʻahu related by Emma Ahuʻena Taylor, which was published in *Paradise of the Pacific* in July 1931. The second is Hoʻoulumāhiehie's version of the Haʻinākolo tradition. I consider these two accounts outliers. Taylor's account is somewhat suspect "tradition-wise" in terms of certain details, and this departure from tradition might be because she adapted it for Western tastes or because the *Paradise of the Pacific* editors did. However, these hypotheses are difficult to prove because I have yet to find the Hawaiian-language version of Taylor's story. Taylor describes Moʻoinanea as a "merman" who guards Lake Waiau, Poliʻahu's sacred bathing place. I concede that variation in beliefs is the rule and not the exception in Hawaiian culture, but the portrayal of Moʻoinanea as a merman rings odd because variations tend to be slight deviations and not major departures from tradition.

As I have shown in chapter 1, accounts of Western-style mermaids are rare in Hawaiian culture. Some people have sometimes used the term "mermaid" to describe moʻo, but the distinctions that our ancestors made between them are clear in traditions told or written in Hawaiian, their mother tongue. While it is true that only a handful of moʻo are described as having a human upper half and a reptilian lower half, these entities are clearly reptilian. In other words, the distinction between reptile and fish is clear in these descriptions. In short, "moʻo" is not a synonym for "mermaid." Such descriptions can be explained as a blend of the old and new. It is more probable that Taylor's Moʻoinanea is actually a moʻo who, for whatever reason, is described as a merman. There are too many accounts about a moʻo named Moʻoinanea that share a certain cultural continuity—she is female and the highest-ranking moʻo—to accept without question a male merman named Moʻoinanea. That said, some might argue that Taylor's Moʻoinanea is a distinct entity. Although this is possible, certain details in Hoʻoulumāhiehie's and Wiggin's versions of Haʻinākolo, together with those from the many other traditions that feature Moʻoinanea, lead me to believe otherwise. Moreover, because of these same details, I am convinced that the Moʻoinanea in these two versions of the Haʻinākolo tradition is the same entity. The issue of this moʻo's gender being different in these two versions is merely a question of variation, just as it is for other famous moʻo such as Piliamoʻo and Nohoamoʻo/Kuaua.

Taylor's and Hoʻoulumāhiehie's accounts share the motif of a male entity named Moʻoinanea who is ordered to protect an akua wahine's sacred bathing place at Mauna Kea's summit. Hoʻoulumāhiehie's account differs in that it describes Moʻoinanea as a moʻo, and the akua wahine in question is Līlīnoe and not Poliʻahu. In Hoʻoulumāhiehie's account, Moʻoinanea is Haʻinākolo's male ancestor. This point overlaps with Wiggin's version: Moʻoinanea is a female moʻo and Haʻinākolo's female ancestor. (The motif of Moʻoinanea guarding a goddess' sacred bathing pool in the accounts by Taylor and Hoʻoulumāhiehie is absent here.)

Here, I return to my discussion of male mo'o with elderly human forms. Lanihuli is described as

he kanaka ilikou loihi poohina a umiumi hina hoi. He malo ninikea ma kona puhaka, he laau palau ma kona lima akau a he peahi launiu ma kona lima hema a he ahuula kona kapa e aahu ana.

a dark-skinned man with long gray hair and a gray beard too. Around his hips is a fine white loincloth, a wooden club in his right hand and a coconut fan in his left, and he wears a feathered cloak.[35]

If we did not already know Lanihuli was a high-ranking mo'o akua, his regalia would make it clear, as these are items ali'i typically wear.

Although many examples exist of mo'o who manifest as humans, not all of them use that form to wreak havoc. Mo'oinanea, as we have seen, helps her/his relatives. Kamo'oloa is an ali'i mo'o wahine with a human form who lives with her people on Kaho'olawe, and both are described as "na wahine ili-kalakala o Kanaloa" (the rough-skinned women of Kanaloa)—Kanaloa being another name for Kaho'olawe. They are beautiful. The cultural hero Mo'ikeha and his companions enjoy a pleasant stay with them, and he grants his brother Ka'alehāko'iko'i's request to remain with them.[36] I discuss other examples in chapter 5.

Mo'o with Caterpillar Kino Lau

The logic behind this form is easy to grasp. Like mo'o, caterpillars crawl and some have stripes, which recall the lizard's brindled skin. To date, I have found only two mo'o who have caterpillar kino lau, Lanihuli and Kūahailo. During the protracted battle between Lanihuli and Keakaokū, one of the forms Lanihuli adopted was that of a caterpillar, which is described as an "enuhe panio hookaa lepo" (streaked dirt-rolling caterpillar).[37]

Kūahailo transforms into a caterpillar during a lengthy passage in the Keanini'ulaokalani tradition, which describes his efforts to frighten the woman, Hi'ilei, destined to become his wahine and the mother of his child. This episode is worth sharing in its entirety. Kūahailo (a.k.a. Kūwahailo) is a fearsome war deity belonging to the Kū class of gods whom ruling ali'i worshipped in formal ceremonies. He also appears in several traditions, but he is not usually depicted as a mo'o. (As I show in chapter 4, he is a member of the Pele clan.) Kūahailo tries to frighten Hi'ilei, but her grandmother Kahele has forseen this encounter and warns her not to be afraid of him no matter what terrifying form he takes. Instead, she must praise him to appear unafraid. If she shows fear, he will kill her.[38]

First, Kūahailo appears as many mo'o, which twist here and there around Hi'ilei until her body is completely covered as she stands there watching them. After she praises them, they vanish. A huge caterpillar takes their place and begins to crawl up and down her body. After Hi'ilei compliments the caterpillar, it, too, vanishes. Kūahailo then appears as a stream of blood that sweeps her off her feet and takes her here and there. Hi'ilei calls out to her grandfather Kahuli to help her, and he intones a chant that calls up rain and disperses the blood. At that point Kūahailo appears before her as a horrific face with blazing eyes and a gaping mouth. Hi'ilei watches as his forked tongue swells. His eyes are like great lava craters and the pupils like a full moon. He seems to have been in his mo'o form because the next passage mentions his tail. After she speaks to him, showing no fear, his mouth grows smaller and his tail rolls up. Moments later, his body disintegrates into little pieces that disperse and then completely disappear. Finally, Kūahailo appears before her as an extremely handsome man. Kūahailo tells Hi'ilei her grandmother's prophecy, and eventually she agrees to be his wahine. The child born to them is a boy whom Kūahailo names Keanini'ulaokalani.[39] He is Ha'inākolo's future kāne.

The connection between lizards and mo'o kolokolo (creatures that crawl—e.g., insects), is implied in an English-language account about Pu'ukamo'o and the origin of wormlike lizards. A mo'o paid nightly visits to a Molokai woman. Unable to discover his identity, she "slowly wasted away." Her parents asked a kahuna (expert) to discern the cause.[40] It turns out that this mo'o could only appear as a man at night. The kahuna tracked the mo'o to Pu'u ka Mo'o (mo'o hill). As the huge mo'o slept, people laid wood around it and lit the wood. The fire caused the mo'o to explode, hurling countless little mo'o into the air, which then ran into the undergrowth. Thus is the origin of "little worm-like lizards" in the islands.[41] This story may be an etiology for mo'o 'alā (skinks), as they are quite wormlike. Also, here is yet another example of the belief that a kupua only visited its human lover at night, a topic I discussed in chapter 1.

Moʻo with Fish Kino Lau

Moʻo-specific fish kino lau include the shark, eel, mullet, kūmū (goatfish), and goby. Because sharks are closely connected to the Pele clan, I save their examination for chapter 4, which traces the kinship between the moʻo and Pele clans by looking at their shared "family" forms and genealogies. Regarding sharks and moʻo, however, I will note that they are considered apex predators: sharks were the threat in the ocean, and moʻo were the menace on the land.[42]

Eel

Although eel deities have a strong presence in Hawaiian culture, the record for moʻo with eel kino lau is scant. The three moʻo with an eel form, Meheanu, Kihanuilūlūmoku, and an unidentified moʻo, present different opportunities for an interpretive analysis of the connection between moʻo akua and eels.

Meheanu is the guardian of Heʻeia fishpond. The logic behind her eel kino lau is straightforward. To begin, eels are among the varieties of fish cultivated in fishponds.[43] Given this custom, it is unsurprising that a moʻo who guarded them might have an eel form. Meheanu "could change herself into many forms, as a frog or a lizard, but she was particularly fond of being an eel."[44] When the flowers of the hau trees surrounding Meheanu's dwelling at Luamoʻo were just green buds, "then she was more likely to be somewhere else in the form of an eel."[45] Her eel form is white, which is the kino lau she adopts whenever she is at Heʻeia fishpond.[46] As explained in chapter 2, Kihawahine's moʻo form resembles that of the puhi ūhā in terms of coloration and markings but is much darker and shinier. "White eel" is another name for this eel. During the day, its skin is white with a pale, mottled grayish-brown pattern. At night, the mottled colors appear as distinct bands. This eel's color and markings resemble those of other kino lau associated with moʻo, such as the lizard, the goby, and the brindled dog.

Before turning my attention to Kihanuilūlūmoku, I want to discuss Meheanu's frog kino lau. This kino lau is noteworthy because frogs were introduced to Hawaiʻi in 1857 to eat the mosquitoes, cockroaches, and centipedes that plagued the islands.[47] Frogs were either directly introduced to the Heʻeia fishpond or arrived there after spreading out from wherever they were first introduced. There are two important points about this kino lau. First, it speaks to the ways that the kino lau system is dynamic. Although the frog was a late introduction to the islands, a sufficient number of Hawaiians accepted the idea of it being her kino lau and passed this belief from one generation to the next, which solidified it. Second, the frog was introduced in 1857, and the fact that it eventually became Meheanu's kino lau implies that at least some kama'āina were still honoring her at that time and that they continued to do so well into the 1930s, when McAllister interviewed them about Meheanu and He'eia fishpond. They still honor her today.

The logic behind Kihanuilūlūmoku's eel kino lau is less clear than that of Meheanu's. In the many traditions that mention this mo'o, none of them associate it with a fishpond. Only one tradition, which is better described as a remnant because it consists of a single statement, upholds that Kihanuilūlūmoku has an eel kino lau: "The famous female *mo'o* Kihanui-lūlū-moku (great-island-shaking *mo'o*) lived here; she had an eel, lizard, and woman forms. She made plants thrive in Wa'a-loa ravine."[48] This ravine is located in upper Mānoa, O'ahu. Two possibilities come to mind as to why this mo'o has an eel form: either because the eel resembles her mo'o form in some way or because of her prowess in battle. Manu states that Kihanuilūlūmoku "was the lizard that possessed the greatest strength in fighting its enemies and none could make it captive. Its usual residence was in Olaa and it sometimes sat on the tall ohia trees, whenever it chose, to watch for enemies anywhere in Hilo and Puna."[49] The link between eels and warriors is implicit in Pukui's explanation of the phrase "Puhi niho wakawaka," or "sharp-toothed eel," which is a metaphor for "fierce warriors."[50] Eels are considered ferocious because once they bite, they do not release their prey, as incautious fishers and swimmers know.

As for the unidentified mo'o with an eel kino lau, it appears in Kamakau's story about Kawa'aokekupua (The canoe of the kupua). This account concerns a canoe intended for the ali'i Kahānaiakeakua and takes place on O'ahu.[51] A group of men were transporting this canoe, which they had carved in the forest, down to the shore. When they reach Kaho'okāne, a mo'o battled them for possession of the canoe. After calling this kupua a mo'o, Kamakau clarifies, "He kuna ka mea i paa ai o ka waa. (Ua oleloia he kuna ka mea nana i pani ka wai o Honolulu)."[52] Pukui translates this passage as: "When they reached Kaho'okāne they fought with the mo'o, which was a freshwater eel, a kuna. It caused the canoe to stick fast. (It is said that it was the eel that shut off the water of Honolulu)."[53] The slippage between mo'o and eel here is evident. Whether this mo'o was eellike or changed from mo'o to eel as it fought for the canoe is unclear.

Because "kuna" is the Hawaiian word for "a variety of freshwater eel," we can imagine the word refers to an eel that exists or once existed in the islands. Despite my best efforts, the only information I have found on the kuna is in moʻolelo and Hawaiian dictionaries. In other words, there are no freshwater eel species in Hawaiʻi at this time, but there are eels that live in brackish water. Elsewhere in the Pacific, one of the names for "eel" is "tuna" or "kuna." Tuna is the name of an infamous eel kupua in other Pacific Island cultures. It comes naturally to wonder if the Hawaiian kuna is a holdover from when our ancestors came from elsewhere in the Pacific to Hawaiʻi. This eel is mentioned in the genealogy Kamakau gives for the aliʻi Nanaulu: "O ke kuna ka ia a Moikeha i lawe pu ia e Olopana."[54] Pukui translates this passage as: "The freshwater eel, the kuna, was the 'fish' of Moʻikeha that was taken along by ʻOlopana."[55] Whether this was an actual eel or metaphor for a warrior is unclear. In the Kekalukaluokēwā tradition, Moʻikeha arrives to Hawaiʻi from Tahiti with two male warriors—Maulili, a moʻo with a human form, and Laʻalua, a human-eating dog kupua.[56]

As I noted in chapter 1, a moʻo akua named Kuna lived at Waiānuenue in the Wailuku River in the section that runs through Hilo. According to W. D. Westervelt, his informants called this water being "Moʻo Kuna." This name has two translative possibilities: "Moʻo named Kuna" or "Moʻo [who is a] freshwater eel."[57] None of the stories about Māui's battle with Kuna, however, say that this moʻo has an eel kino lau. Perhaps in earlier times, Kuna was not a moʻo but an eel, and his original eel form was replaced by that of a moʻo in our moʻolelo as the worship of moʻo akua gained importance.

Mullet

Two versions of the Kihapiʻilani tradition explain that the mullet is Kihawahine's kino lau because its head resembles the head of her moʻo form. Of all the moʻo species with which Hawaiians of the distant past were familiar, the moʻo ʻalā is the one that most closely resembles this fish whose head and body are streamlined.[58] Waka also has a mullet kino lau.[59]

Kūmū (Parupeneus porphyreus, or White Saddle Goatfish)

As I shared in chapter 2, according to Josephine Medeiros, a moʻo wahine of Hāna, Maui would sit on a rock adjacent to the ocean to groom her long, white hair. The logic behind this kino lau is one of association. Because her presence attracts many kūmū, the kamaʻāina of

Hāna considered them her kino lau. As this account and others confirm, the belief in, encounters with, and sightings of mo'o are not limited to the distant past nor to Hawaiians. Medeiros, who told this story in 1960, recalls that a Portuguese boy once saw this mo'o as he was preparing eel for bait at that rock to go 'ulua fishing.[60]

Mo'o with Multiple Sea Creature Forms

During a battle with Kekalukaluokēwā, Maulili, previously mentioned, assumes several kino lau and calls upon others to help him fight. After being bested in his human form, he continues the battle as a mo'o. Kekalukaluokēwā twists the mo'o's head off its body and throws it up into the sky. As Maulili's head flies up, it speaks and calls to its spirit to reenter it, which allows it to regenerate.[61] When Kekalukaluokēwā kills him for the second time, Maulili's spirit leaps into the sea and becomes a gigantic he'e (octopus).

As Kekalukaluokēwā stands on the sand telling Maulili that he will kill him again, he is blinded by sand. That sand thrown at Kekalukaluokēwā's face was the work of one of Maulili's forms, namely, the Long-eyed-Sand-Crab, because when Maulili's spirit jumped into the ocean, it called upon his many kino lau: the Long-eyed-Sand-Crabs (*Ocypode ceratophthalmus*); the milo-leaf eels; the spiny sea urchins; the large yellow-foot limpets; the top shells (*Turbo sandwicensis*); the cowry shells, the naka (*Ischnochiton petaloides*);[62] the sea cucumbers; the barracudas; the leaping swordfishes of the sea; the great, powerful sea turtle; the 'alamihi crab (*Metopograpsus thukuhar*); pokipoki crab (*Calappa hepatica*); 'a'ama crab (*Grapsus grapsus tenuicrustatus*); paiea crab (similar to the 'a'ama but with a harder shell); "ula niho wakawaka" (sharp-toothed lobster); "na i'a ili akoakoa a pau" (all the rough-skinned fishes); pioeoe (*Mytilus crebristriatus*); pipipi (*Theodoxus neglectus*); "pu ole-ole" (small conch shell), which is the "pu puhi" (blowing conch shell); and hā'uke'uke (*Colobocentrotus atratus*).[63] Unlike Hawaiian mo'o, Maulili has myriad sea-related kino lau—clearly a Tahitian tradition as no Hawaiian mo'o has such a large number of sea-related forms. Previously, I noted that the Tahitian mo'o Te-moo-nieve is the goddess of crustaceans.

Like Lanihuli in his battle with Keakaokū, Maulili can call upon his kino lau to help him fight. The examples of Lanihuli and Maulili provide insights into ancestral understandings of the kino lau system. Clearly, some akua, in addition to being able to manifest as the forms with which they are associated, are also able to command them. Other akua besides mo'o who are known to do this are Pele and Kamapua'a.

Pele can manifest as lava but also command it to go where she wills, such as when she sends lava to kill Waka and Puna'aikoa'e.[64] Kamapua'a directs his plant kino lau to immobilize Lonoka'eho, a kupua with eight stone foreheads, and then orders pigs to kill and eat him. He kills the dog kupua Kū'īlioloa in the same way, but here, he commands the pigs to enter Kū'īlioloa's mouth and devour him from the inside out.[65]

Mo'o with Bird Kino Lau

In one version of the Ha'inākolo tradition, Mo'oinanea has a gigantic bird form (species unspecified) that he (in this version, Mo'oinanea is male) uses to transport Ha'inākolo and her five "Maile" sisters.[66]

Owl

Hawaiian owls are brindled like lizards, gobies, and brindled dogs, and thus the logic behind this kino lau is clear—a similarity in markings. Three mo'o take the form of an owl: Waka, Lanihuli, and KawailoaikapolioLokoea. Waka becomes an owl as she flees from Pele who wants to kill her.[67] Lanihuli becomes an owl during his fight with Keakaokū. KawailoaikapolioLokoea changes into an owl when he sees Niuloahiki, a kupua from Tahiti, spying on him. Niuloahiki snares him with his wondrous net. When Kawailoa realizes that he has been caught, he tries unsuccessfully to rip it apart by changing from one form to another.[68]

Chicken

Kihawahine has a yellow chicken kino lau for the same reasons as her mullet form: the chicken's ischium, in profile, resembles the head of Kihawahine's lizard form.[69] The ischium, when viewed from this angle, does indeed recall a sleek mo'o head, like the mo'o 'alā. That the chicken kino lau is specifically yellow clearly speaks to this color's association with mo'o.

Mo'o with Plant Kino Lau

Limu Kala (Sargassum echinocarpum)

Limu kala is one of Kihawahine's kino lau.[70] If we consider the link between Kihawahine and Kalamainu'u and how the latter's name incorporates the word "kala," we can understand the logic behind

Kihawahine's limu kala kino lau as deriving from word association. More-over, this limu is a dull gold-yellow, and so the logic also pertains to color.

Kaioʻe

An entry in the *Hawaiian Dictionary* for "kaioʻe" notes that "a lizard god of the same name is associated with this plant." I cannot offer an explanation about the logic behind this kino lau because I could not find information on this plant other than the dictionary entry and men-tions of kaioʻe in chants, which do not, however, describe it.

Uluhe Fern

Anyone familiar with uluhe (*Dicranopteris linearis,* false staghorn fern) can understand why it might be a moʻo kino lau if we view moʻo as troublesome entities. The uluhe "spreads in impenetrable thickets, growing over its own dead branches and engulfing other plants, and becoming, with its brittle undergrowth, a source of devastating fires."[71] Like a lizard, uluhe can climb lehua trees, which smothers them and the hāpuʻu ferns that grow at their base. Moreover, dead uluhe is sharp, which makes it painful to grasp without leather gloves. Yet its bright green fronds are beautiful and its thickets thwart invasive species. Lani-huli has an uluhe kino lau.[72]

ʻŌhiʻa lehua, ʻAmaʻu, and Kukui

Panaʻewa has ʻōhiʻa lehua, ʻamaʻu, and kukui kino lau, as do its many moʻo servants.[73] Panaʻewa embodies both the frequent, substantial rain that characterizes rain forests and the damp lehua rain forest itself. That Panaʻewa the moʻo symbolizes the Panaʻewa rain forest is suggested by its kino lau and the fact that it guards it. The logic behind this moʻo's kino lau is easy to follow. ʻŌhiʻa play critical roles in Hawaiʻi's rain for-est ecosystem. Their great height attracts rain while their boughs and leaves break the rainfall, which allows the land time to absorb it so that some of the rain can enter our aquifers, important repositories of water. The ʻamaʻu tree fern (juvenile ʻamaʻu are called ʻamaʻumaʻu) is another important plant in ʻōhiʻa forests. A symbiotic relationship exists between the ʻōhiʻa lehua and the ʻamaʻu fern. ʻAmaʻu are plentiful in lehua forests, and as Pukui explains, lehua seeds often fall into these ferns, which pro-vide a good place for them to grow.[74] Like ʻōhiʻa, ʻamaʻu help break rain-fall and thus preserve the integrity of the land and its aquifers.

Mahiki appears mainly in versions of the Hiʻiakaikapoliopele tradition.[75] Generally, he is identified primarily as a forest deity, and the fact that he has a moʻo kino lau is secondary. In these cases he only transforms into a moʻo after Hiʻiaka has destroyed his many plant kino lau (unidentified).[76] In Kapihenui's version, Mahiki makes a brief appearance as a entity that stirs up dirt, which suggests that it is a moʻo, as this is something that they do in several traditions.[77] Nathaniel Emerson describes Mahiki as "a ferocious horde of moʻo called mahiki from their power to leap and spring like grasshoppers" who lived in a region that comprises a watershed known as Mahiki-waena (middle Mahiki), but he does not show them as having plant kino lau.[78] Manu describes Mahiki solely as a moʻo and does not mention plant kino lau.[79]

Meteorological Kino Lau

Given that moʻo are water deities, it stands to reason that some moʻo have water-related meteorological kino lau such as clouds, fog, mist, rain, rainbows, winds associated with stormy weather or heavy rainfall, and even snow or ice. Such kino lau are often connected to the locality with which these moʻo are associated.

Cloud

The logic behind cloud kino lau is clear: Clouds are masses of condensed water vapor. In Hoʻoulumāhiehie's version of Kamaakamahiʻai, Kalanamainuʻu has an ao ʻōpua (puffy cloud, cloud bank) kino lau, and she travels in this form.[80] In Manu's account of Keaomelemele, Moʻoinanea has the power to control clouds, but Manu does not show that she is able to manifest as one.[81]

Fog and Mist

Fog and mist are masses of water vapor, the difference between the two being the degree of density. Rain forests are often shrouded in fog and mist, and thus it is logical that rain forest moʻo might have them as kino lau. In Poepoe's version of the Hiʻiakaikapoliopele tradition, as Hiʻiaka and Wahineʻōmaʻo enter the Panaʻewa forest a dark fog suddenly covers their path: "O ke kino ohu keia o Panaewa e poipu nei mai o a o o ua ulu lehua nei" (This is the fog form of Panaʻewa spreading over the lehua forest from one end to the other).[82] In this same account, Pāʻieʻie and her moʻo call up fog to block the sun and darken the forest as they battle Hiʻiaka. While it is evident they control this fog, it is unclear as to whether they can also assume this form.[83]

Rainbow

In Hoʻoulumāhiehie's version of the Kamaakamahiʻai tradition, Kalanamainuʻu has a pūnohu ʻula (a low-lying rainbow or red mist) kino lau.[84] In the tradition of Kekalukaluokēwā, Kihanuilūlūmoku's tongue appears to people as a pūnohu ua koko (low-lying rainbow or rainbow-colored cloud), which we can understand as its kino lau or its mana appear as such, at least in part.

Snow or Ice

In Hoʻoulumāhiehie's version of the Kamaakamahiʻai tradition, Kalanamainuʻu lives in a cave near Mauna Loa's summit. She has a cloak called the ʻaʻahu kapa hau o Mauna Loa (snow/ice cloak of Mauna Loa), which affects the weather, causing extreme cold. She uses it as a weapon during her battle with Kāmehaʻikana and Kahelekūlani.[85] The cloak's provenance is not noted. The fact that she owns this ʻaʻahu kapa hau o Mauna Loa, lives near Mauna Loa's summit, which is occasionally covered in snow, and is able to wield this cloak suggests that it is something like a kino lau for her. If we accept this snow cloak as her kino lau, the logic is as follows: she is an akua wai who lives where it sometimes snows, and snow is frozen water vapor.

Whirlwind, Dust Cloud, Dust Devil, Wind, and Stormy Wind

Puahiohio (whirlwind), ʻeʻa lepo (dust cloud), and puahiohio ʻeʻa lepo (dust devil) are common phenomena in Hawaiʻi. A whirlwind is "a small-diameter columnar vortex of rapidly swirling air," which includes dust devils.[86] The logic behind these wind-related kino lau may have to do with the locality with which these moʻo are associated. Dust clouds and dust devils occur in dry areas. In the Pīkoiakaʻalalā tradition, while Pīkoi and his friends are in their canoe off the coast of Puakō in Kohala, Hawaiʻi, Pīkoi sees "ka wili mai a ka ea o ka lepo" (a twisting dirt cloud) in the distance at Puʻupā in Waimea. He knows it is the moʻo Kinilau. He tells his friends, "Ae, he moo nui o Kinilau, o kona kino maoli nae, ua make, a o ke kino lau ia ona e hoike mai la ia oe" (Yes, Kinilau is a large moʻo, but her real body died, and this is her kino lau she shows you). Kinilau's many children, their tails entwined, surround her form.[87]

In Hoʻoulumāhiehie's version of the Kamaakamahiʻai tradition, Kalanamainuʻu has a wind form. She uses it to accompany her hānai son Waikūmailani, whispering to him about the things she sees. Her wind form also becomes a puahiohio, which she wields as a weapon.[88] She also has a leleiaka (leap-in-shadow) kino lau—the shadow of her body that she can send elsewhere, which resembles a waipu'ilani (waterspout): "O ka ia nei make o ka hoolele ia ana mai nei, oia ka hooliloia ana ia oe i pupule i hehena e hooulaia ana hoi i kou mau noonoo a pau" (It kills by causing things to fly into it; it will make you crazy until insane, and also derange all of your thoughts).[89] I include her shadow form here because it is also a whirlwind.

Kākea controls the water sources of Mānoa and Makiki on O'ahu. A stormy Mānoa wind is called Kākea. Although not specified as such, it is probably his kino lau.[90] Other mo'o with wind kino lau include the brothers Hawai'iloa and KawailoaikapolioLokoea, who are associated with Loko Ea, a coastal fishpond in Kawailoa at Waialua, O'ahu.[91]

Mo'o as Geographical Features

A number of geographical features are indicated as the remnants of mo'o, and thus these mo'o are memorialized in the 'āina. Many places are also named after mo'o. Ancestral knowledge and wisdom about the 'āina are encoded in such features, places, and names. These wahi pana (a geographical feature or place celebrated in mele, 'ōlelo no'eau, and mo'olelo) are important archives of ancestral experiences, beliefs, and practices.

Riverbed and Coral Shoal

The seer Kaukanapōki'i used his powers to make the mo'o Kaluanou ill at a gathering of youth at Hālawa in Molokai. She left the party with her kāne, the ali'i Kamoku, to return home:

When she arrived there, she began to twist in pain. Her stomach distended until it became enormous. Kamoku, disturbed, asked her what was wrong. Kaluanou responded that the newcomer cursed her. When Kaluanou went outside to vomit, hoping to ease her discomfort, she spewed an incredible amount of water. There were many different kinds of sea creatures in that water, which terrified Kamoku. The place where Kaluanou vomited remains until this day. The force of her vomit carved a deep area near the Hālawa River, and because of its force, the river deepened and flowed to the ocean. There, her vomit created a coral shoal at Kauhuhu cape and Hālaumo'o cape. The debris from her vomit blocked the cave of the shark god Kauhuhu. When he returned to find it blocked, the children of the sea and those they bring from the Pillars of Kahiki cleared it. If that place was closed up, then there would be no channel for canoes to enter. As for Kaluanou, she became very thin, and an illness befell her from which she died.[92]

It was only because of this event that Kamoku realized that Kaluanou was not a normal woman.

Blowhole
Lehu and his two sisters (names unspecified) left Tahiti to travel to Hawai'i. When they reached Ni'ihau, the sisters decided to remain there, but Lehu wanted to continue. When he reached Kaua'i, he entered a blowhole at Lāwa'i and became stuck. You can hear him roar to this day.[93]

Cape, Islet, Hill, Land, Mountain Ridge, and Stone
Laniloa is a cape in Lā'ie in Ko'olauloa on O'ahu and the name of a people-killing mo'o. This cape is the remnants of its body after Kana killed him. Kana chopped Laniloa's head into five pieces, which became the five islets in front of Mālaekahana: Malualai (a.k.a. Mokuālai), Keauakaluapa'a, Pulemoku, Mokuaniwa (a.k.a. Moku'auia), and Kihewamoku (a.k.a. Kukuiho'olua).[94] According to W. H. Rice, "At the spot where Kana severed the head of the mo-o is a deep hole which even to this day has never been fathomed."[95] When Pu'uoinaina took Pele's lover, Lohi'au, as her own, Pele was furious. One day, while Pu'uoinaina was sleeping in her mo'o form, which stretched from Kaho'olawe to Makena Point on Maui, Pele cut her in half. The hill known as Pu'uōla'i at Mākena Point is the remnant of her tail, and the islet Mo'okini is her head.[96] Mokoli'i (gender unspecified) lived near the mountain whose peak is called Kānehoalani. This mountain divides the Ko'olaupoko and Ko'olauloa districts on O'ahu. In Poepoe's version of the Hi'iakaikapoliopele tradition, when Mokoli'i was alive, there was no way to go around the Kānehoalani pali other than by sea. When Hi'iaka killed Mokoli'i, its head and body became the land in front of the pali, and its tail became the islet known as Mokoli'i (figure 3.2).[97] From then on, people were able to go by land around this point. In the Kila and Mo'ikeha tradition, the kupua Mahinui kills the mo'o Wai'auia while it is in its human form, tearing it into two. The larger piece becomes the Popo-i'a Islet offshore of Kailua on O'ahu while the other becomes a "moopohaku" (stone mo'o). However, Wai'auia's mo'o form was still alive, so Mahinui shoved his spear in its throat and killed it.[98]

Figure 3.2. Mokoliʻi Islet. Photograph by Kai
Markell.

Koʻiahi and Kahanaiki are two ridges in Mākua Valley said to be
female moʻo. The first is deeper in the valley, and the other is closer to
the sea, but both are in an area unaccessible to the public unless part of
a military-sanctioned access. The moʻo associated with Koʻiahi ridge
and valley is the lover of the shark god Nanaue.[99]

There are several accounts about Kamalō, a male moʻo of Molokai
who is memorialized as a mountain ridge. In one version of this tradition, a shark god steals fish from nets, so the kamaʻāina ask Kamalō to
help them. In this version, Kamalō defeats the shark and becomes part
of the ridge, where he continues to be a warning for the shark.[100] In another version, the shark's name is Kainalu, and he challenges the moʻo
Kamalō, who is female in this account. Kamalō loses the battle and
crawls up the mountain. There, "she stretched herself out length-wise,
facing due north and died, becoming a permanent part of the landscape,

the ridge between the ahupuaʻa of Kamaloʻo and Kapualei. This is the ridge called Kaʻapahu or the Moʻo. Thus the moʻo indeed became the aumakua of the area forever, solidly implanted as a part of the land, where no-one could ever displace her."[101] Yet another version states that these two akua are constantly fighting, struggling for control over the land. The moʻo's blood can be discerned in parts of the ridge.[102] A similar version states that this moʻo is named Kapualei, and the shark god is named Kauhuhū.[103]

Accounts of moʻo immortalized as stones or rocks are numerous. I have already shared stories about the stone forms of Kuna and Waiʻauia. The other examples I share here illustrate the range of reasons for these lithic transformations. Hiʻiaka uses her lightning skirt to kill Piliamoʻo and Kuaua at the Wailuku River, Hawaiʻi, turning them to stones.[104] At Kaimukī, Oʻahu, Hiʻiaka turns a moʻo to stone and traps her voice in it. Before being turned into stone, she was known variously as Ua Līlīlehua, Līlīlehua, and Ka-ua-līlī-lehua-o-pālolo. After her transformation she was known as Pōhaku Kīkēkē, a well-known bellstone.[105] After Hiʻiaka left Kaimukī, she encountered Kamōʻiliʻili, whose terrifying demi-moʻo form I discussed earlier. When Hiʻiaka struck Kamōʻiliʻili with her lightning skirt, her body exploded. The remains of her body are the piles of stones found upland of that area and around Kamōʻiliʻili Church.[106] This area, named after Kamōʻiliʻili, means "The pebble moʻo." Pohakalani and her brother Pohakeola destroyed the ʻauwai (canal for wet-taro farming) that the aliʻi Ola had asked the menehune to build. Pohakalani was turned into a stone in a stream near Kīkīaola in Waimea, Kauaʻi. No rocks pass in front of this stone even when the water flows swiftly. In 1914, Kamahele, who told this story, visited this stone and confirmed that no rocks were in front it.[107] Kanimoe and Kanikū, associated with Wainānāliʻi (pond and fishpond, North Kona, Hawaiʻi), were turned into stones during a lava flow.[108] A kupua (unidentified) turned ʻAwapuhikeʻokeʻo and ʻAwapuhimele into stones as they fought.[109] At Kawainui Marsh, the domain of Hauwahine, stands a monolith named after her, which bears a remarkable resemblance to the profile of a moʻo's head as it sleeps (figure 3.3). This huge stone can be understood as her kino lau and not the result of some misdeed.

The nearly three hundred moʻo akua whose kino lau I have studied reveal that, as a collective, moʻo akua—who have been largely ignored and minimized compared to other akua such as Pele, Haumea, and

In the first half of her hypothesis, Beckwith suggests that the oppositional dyads of water and fire as well as heat and cold, as represented by
the elemental deities she listed, stand for competing schools of sorcery.
She acknowledges Nāmakaokaha'i's duality as an elemental with water-
and fire-related powers and supposes that it is explained by the deity's
diachronic transformation from water to fire deity but does not pursue
this line of reasoning. In the second half, she mentions the Puna'aikoa'e
tradition: Kamakau's version and those of Thrum and Westervelt. 'Ī'ī's
version is their unacknowledged source. I discuss it and the Haumea-
Walinu'u link later.[4]

In ho'omanawanui's analysis of Manu's account about the battle
between Pele and Waka, she identifies dualism as "an important aspect
of Hawaiian religious thought" and agrees with Beckwith that the antagonism between the two clans speaks to the juxtaposition of opposing
elements (water/fire) and their qualities (cold/heat). Another dyad in
Pele and Hi'iaka traditions that she identifies is 'anā'anā, in its "healing
(ho'ōla) and death dealing (ho'omake) forms." When Beckwith spoke of
competing schools of sorcery, she probably had 'anā'anā in mind, as it is
often (and problematically) translated as "sorcery."[5]

Additionally, ho'omanawanui offers a three-part hypothesis regarding the ambiguous relationship between these two clans. First, she
notes, "Manu not only explains the origins of the mo'o, but also claims
that they are related to the Pele 'ohana, as they are two different branches
of a larger family."[6] Second, drawing upon other traditions, she explains
that enmity between siblings is a theme in another migration story—
namely, the rift between the brothers Lonopele and Pā'ao: "While not
explained, perhaps there was a rift in the Pele family prior to their arrival in Hawai'i, which then carried over?"[7] Third, she recognizes
Nāmakaokaha'i as a link between the two clans: "Nāmakaokaha'i is
often portrayed as a sister who presided over water; here we see an opposition that makes sense: fire versus water," and furthermore, she "appears to be a part of the mo'o lineage, which is evident in her kinolau."[8]
Thus, ho'omanawanui extends Beckwith's inchoate considerations
about the mo'o and Pele clans, anchoring them in a larger tradition in
which they might be two branches of a larger family that split after a
violent disagreement between siblings or cousins, prompting one
branch's migration to Hawai'i.

The answers to the questions about the kinship and antagonism
between these two powerful clans are preserved in the many discrete
traditions that constitute the larger corpus of 'Ōiwi artistic-intellectual

production across place and time. We need only be aware of and read these traditions to retrieve this information. The moʻo and Pele clans' common ancestry is clearest in the genealogy Manu gives in his account of Pele and Waka, but their family ties are also evidenced elsewhere. Nāmakaokahaʻi is the means by which we can trace their kinship in the ʻAukelenuiaʻīkū tradition. The Lāʻiehau tradition is notable in that it shows Haumea and Moʻoinanea are close relatives belonging to the same generation. Even the Hiʻiakaikapoliopele tradition, which notoriously depicts moʻo unfavorably, reveals the kinship between their clans.

Origin, Kinship, Mana, and Kino Lau Connections

Haumea and Moʻoinanea

In the larger corpus of Hawaiian traditions, Haumea and Moʻoinanea have several attributes in common. Haumea's forms include other akua wahine. Papa (a.k.a. Papahānaumoku) and Kāmehaʻikana are two of her well-known manifestations.[9] As Haumea, she is the mother of Pele and her siblings, or their kupuna (a relative two or more generations remote).[10] Because she births her children via her head, eyes, ears, mouth, chest, palms, fingers, knuckles, knees, feet, and toes, she is called the akua of wondrous births.[11]

Moʻoinanea heads the moʻo clan. She is the origin of moʻo akua in three traditions contributed by Manu: Keaomelemele, Pele and Waka, and Laukaʻieʻie.[12] In Keaomelemele:

> O Mooinanea ke kupua nana i mahele iho iaia ma ka mana i loaa iaia ma kona ano i elima mau mahele, oia hoi keia: Ka mua, ka moo alii, ka lua, ka moo akua, ke kolu, ka moo kaula, ka ha, ka moo kahuna, ka lima hoi, oia ka moo o na makaainana.

> Moʻoinanea is the kupua who divided herself into five divisions, namely: the first, the royal class of moʻo; the second, the divine moʻo; the third, the seer moʻo; the fourth, the expert moʻo; and the fifth, those were the moʻo of the makaʻainana class.[13]

Thus, Moʻoinanea is to moʻo what Haumea is to the Pele clan.

In the Pele and Waka account, the Pele and moʻo clans have a common lineage. Here, Haumea and Moʻoinanea are punalua (sharing the same partner) because they share a kāne, Kāneilūhonua

(Earth-shaking Kāne). His other names, Manu explains, are Kūwahailo (Maggot-mouthed Kū), Hīkāpōloa (Spreading of the long night), Kapōkinikini (The myriad nights), Kapōmanomano (The great night), and Hoʻokumukalani (Establishing the heavens). Moʻoinanea is also known as Hoʻokumukahonua (Establishing the earth). From the union between Kāneilūhonua as Hoʻokumukalani and Moʻoinanea as Hoʻokumukahonua are born five divisions of moʻo: moʻo akua (deities), moʻo aliʻi (ruling class), moʻo kāula (seers), moʻo kahuna (experts), and moʻo kānaka (moʻo who had human forms or nonroyal moʻo).[14] The Hoʻokumukalani and Hoʻokumukahonua pairing mirrors the Sky Father (Wākea) and Earth Mother pairing (Papa, who is Haumea), another attribute that Haumea and Moʻoinanea share.

From one of these moʻo lineages (unspecified), Haumea is reborn when Moʻoinanea, as Hoʻokumukahonua, either gives birth to Haumea-niho-ʻoi (Sharp-toothed Haumea) or her children do. Thus, this new transformation of Haumea, Haumeanihoʻoi, is Moʻoinanea's descendant, either a daughter or granddaughter. Manu explains that Haumeanihoʻoi is also known as Haumea-niho-wakawaka (Serrated-toothed Haumea), Ka-naka-o-ke-ahi (The fissure-opening fire), and Ka-ʻowaka-o-ka-lani (The lightning flash of heaven). Here, Manu implies that Pele is a form of Haumea: "O keia ko Haumea inoa oi kelakela loa i kapaia he Pele" (This is Haumea's greatest name by which she was called, Pele).[15]

Haumeanihoʻoi then sleeps with Kāneilūhonua, and from this union are born the many sons and daughters commonly referred to collectively as the Pele clan. Their firstborn is a son, Ka-uila-nui-mākēhā-i-ka-lani (The flashing lightning in the heavens). Because he was born from her eyes and not from her vagina, he was called Ka-huila [uila]-o-ka-lani-ka-maka-o-ke-akua (The lightning of the heavens the eye of the deity). Their second son is Kamohoaliʻi. These two were Haumea's highest-ranking children. Pele was their firstborn daughter: "Oia ka i puka mai mai kawaha [ka waha] mai o Haumea he kino ahi, oia ka mea i hooholo loa ia aku ai kona inoa o Pele-Honuamea" (She was the one that came forth from Haumea's mouth in the form of fire, which is why they decided to call her Pele of the reddish-brown earth). Their second daughter is Kapōʻulakīnaʻu (The red-streaked night). From among the many sisters that followed, Pele became most attached to Hiʻiakaikapoliopele, who would hold her in her arms close to her chest.[16] Nāmakaokahaʻi is not mentioned in this account. Thus, this genealogy in Manu's account of Pele and Waka establishes a double kinship between Haumea and Moʻoinanea. They are not only punalua;

Haumea is also Moʻoinanea's descendant (figure 4.1). Thus, Moʻoinanea is the kupuna of the Pele clan. To reiterate, the moʻo and Pele clan kinship in Manu's account is as follows:

Punalua: Haumea (f) and Moʻoinanea (f) share Kāneilūhonua as their kāne.
Parent pairing: Kāneilūhonua and Moʻoinanea.
  Children: Ranks of moʻo akua, moʻo aliʻi, moʻo kāula, moʻo kahuna, moʻo kanaka. Haumeanihoʻoi (a form of Haumea) is born in or from one of these moʻo ranks.
Parent pairing: Haumeanihoʻoi and Kāneilūhonua.
  Children: Pele and her siblings.

The moʻo and Pele clans clearly have a common ancestry in the Lāʻiehau tradition. The details of their genealogy, however, are not found in any of the installments in the issues of this newspaper that remain. Here, Haumea-nui-owaka-o-ka-lani (Great Haumea lightning flash of the firmament) and Kū-nui-ʻāhua-ka-hoʻāno-lani (Great Kū filling the sacred firmament) are the parents of Nāmakaokahaʻi and Pele.[17] They live with their moʻo relatives at Kuaihelani, which is part of three lands arranged one above the other:

O Kanehunamoku, oia ka honua ponoi oluna hookahi no kiai o laila, o waena iho o Nuumealani, o lalo lilo loa o Hanaiakamalama ka makia hoonee ia Kuaihelani, e holo imua holo ihope a iho i na papaku olalo a pela aku na hana kupua o na ano like ole o keia aina.[18]

Kānehūnāmoku is the uppermost land, which has one guardian; Nuʻumealani is in the middle; and Hānaiakamalama [the moon] is at the very bottom, the mechanism that moves Kuaihelani forward, backward, and downward to the lower foundations [Earth?], and those are the different extraordinary features of this land.

Kuaihelani teems with moʻo:

He ku a hewa ka maka ina malamalama like ole o loko o kela aina hookalakupua, nui na moo o na ano like ole oloko, e laa ka ulaula, eleele, olenalena, keokeo, melemele, aliali, a o keia poe ka mea nana e hoʻomalamalama ia loko o Kuaihelani.[19]

The eyes are struck by the different lights in that wondrous land. There are many kinds of moʻo: red, black, pale yellow, white, yellow, transparent. They are the source of light in Kuaihelani.

Moʻoinana appears in this account as "Mōinanea." "Mō" is an abbreviated form of "moʻo." Nāmakaokahaʻi relies on Mōinanea for transportation: "O Moinanea na kiki hoonee ina wahi apau e like me ka makemake o ke alii o Namakaokahai, a o na lahui o keia Akua aliiwahine o ka aina lewa i ka moana" (Mōinanea is the swift means by which the aliʻi Nāmakaokahaʻi moves wherever she desires, and the subjects of

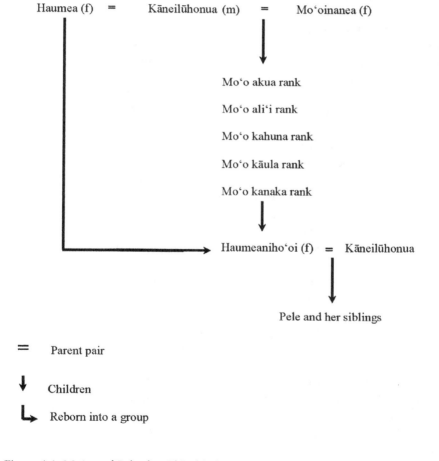

Figure 4.1. Moʻo and Pele clans' kinship in Mose Manu's account.

this Akua aliʻiwahine, of the floating land above the ocean). Pele has a respectful relationship with Mōinanea and the other moʻo, which is evident in this passage: "Oia ko Pele wa i huli ae ai a hoi aku la no kahi o Haumea ma na makua, a malaila aku iho e ike ia Moinanea ma na makua moo. Haawi ke aloha, a ninau koke ia mai la no keia kumu o kona hiki ana aku." (That is when Pele turned and went to where Haumea and the mākua were, and there she saw Mōinanea and the other moʻo, the moʻo mākua [parents/aunts/uncles]. They greeted her, and quickly asked why she had come.)[20] I revisit this scene when I discuss Pele's migration to Hawaiʻi.

Moʻoinanea and Nāmakaokahaʻi

Nāmakaokahaʻi is a nexus between the moʻo and Pele clans in the ʻAukelenuiaʻīkū tradition, of which there are nine versions.[21] ʻAukelenuiaʻīkū is Moʻoinanea's human grandson through her daughter, Kapapaiakea. Nāmakaokahaʻi's parentage is not given, but she is Moʻoinanea's moʻopuna (grandchild or descendant), ʻAukelenuiaʻīkū's kaikuahine (male's sister or female cousin), and the kaikuaʻana (elder same-sex sibling or near cousin) of Pele and Hiʻiaka. Moʻoinanea informs ʻAukelenuiaʻīkū that Nāmakaokahaʻi is destined to become his wahine, so he must voyage to Kalākeʻenuiakāne, the land she rules. To prepare him for this perilous journey, Moʻoinanea imparts the knowledge necessary to his survival. She instructs him on how to navigate to Kalākeʻenuiakāne, she warns him about the dangerous lands to avoid, and because Nāmakaokahaʻi will try to kill him, she tells him what he must do to remain alive.

She then severs her tail and gives it to him. She explains that it is her kino maoli (true form) and the weapon by which he will defeat his enemies.[22] Here, she is bestowing upon him certain aspects of her mana. She transforms her tail into a kapa lehu (cloak that turns things to ashes) for ʻAukelenuiaʻīkū to use. This battle cloak is the physical manifestation of her tail when it is detached from her body. It instantly reduces to ashes anything it touches.[23] Ashes are what remain after something is incinerated—whether by fire, lightning, or lava. In other words, Moʻoinanea has a fire-related kino lau because her tail, her kino maoli, gives this battle cloak its ability to reduce to ashes anything it touches. The immensity of her mana is suggested by the power of this weapon. Even Kūwahailo is thwarted when he sends his lightning bolt to strike ʻAukelenuiaʻīkū. The instant his bolt strikes the cloak, it is destroyed. Only Nāmakaokahaʻi can touch the cloak and remain unharmed.

Although the reason for this immunity is not given, I imagine it is because Moʻoinanea has given her the same kind of power.

Moʻoinanea tells ʻAukelenuiaʻīkū that she has given her battle kāhili (feather standard) and her battle pāʻū (skirt or sarong) to Nāmakaokahaʻi. If Nāmakaokahaʻi wears the pāʻū and strikes the kāhili on the ground, her enemies will be reduced to ashes. It is not clear if Moʻoinanea's tail is the origin of these weapons, but it seems likely as she used her tail to make a similar weapon for ʻAukelenuiaʻīkū. Given Moʻoinanea's mana and her reptilian nature, she may have regrown or manifested another tail to replace it. As I have shown in previous chapters, moʻo akua can regrow parts of their bodies or even reanimate themselves after being killed.

In some versions of the Hiʻiakaikapoliopele tradition, Pele gives Hiʻiaka a pāʻū imbued with lightning, which Hiʻiaka uses to destroy her enemies.[24] This pāʻū, like the one belonging to Nāmakaokahaʻi, and like ʻAukelenuiaʻīkū's kapa lehu, incinerates anything it touches. Strictly speaking, Hiʻiaka's and Nāmakaokahaʻi's pāʻū and ʻAukelenuiaʻīkū's kapa lehu are not kino lau; however, they owe their existence to the fire-related mana that the Pele clan and Moʻoinanea possess. Pele is a volcanic deity, and lava is her kino, but volcanic lightning is also a power belonging to her family. While the origin of Moʻoinanea's fire-related mana is not explained, the fact remains that this power is hers—her tail is her kino maoli, or true form.

It is extremely significant that Nāmakaokahaʻi has inherited her moʻo kupuna's battle pāʻū and kāhili. Clothing absorbs the mana of the person who wears it, and thus they are kapu. Pukui offers insights into clothing-related kapu: "In the matter of clothing, a general rule was that it was not right to wear clothing of anyone other than kin. But between generations, there were strict rules affecting this. A daughter's clothes might be worn by the mother, but not the mother's by the daughter, and the same rule applied as between aunts and nieces."[25] Taupōuri Tangarō refers to this kapu as the kapuʻili (skin law), which "prohibited the use of other people's clothing." Tangarō clarifies, "To wear someone else's clothing could adversely affect personal chemistry."[26] John Charlot, in his work on the feather pāʻū of Nāhiʻenaʻena, explains, "In Hawaiian thinking, the powers of a woman's genitals are transferred to her pāʻū. The apotropaic can be seen in skirts so powerful that they can be used as weapons in battle, such as the famous pāʻū o Hiʻiaka, 'skirt of Hiʻiaka.'"[27] The observations by Pukui, Tangarō, and Charlot inform my interpretation of Moʻoinanea's decision to give Nāmakaokahaʻi her pāʻū as an intentional intergenerational transference of generative mana.

The immense power of Nāmakaokahaʻi's genitals is evidenced in a moʻolelo that Kamakau offers, which brings together the ʻAukelenuiaʻīkū and Pāʻao traditions. He refers to ʻAukelenuiaʻīkū by a variant of his name, Waikelenuiaʻīkū. When Pāʻao migrated to Hawaiʻi, he brought new religious practice, Kamakau explains: "O Lonopele ke kaikuaana o Paao; oia ke Kahuna Nui; a he malama akua o Paao; o Kukailimoku ke akua, he akua hulu" (Lonopele was Pāʻao's elder brother, he was the Head Kahuna; and Pāʻao was the god-keeper, Kūkāʻilimoku [Island-snatching Kū] being the god, a feathered god).[28] Pāʻao introduced the practice of human sacrifice in this god's name. According to Kamakau, Kūkāʻilimoku's origin is as follows:

He mau hulu hinawenawe makalii no ka lae o Kiwaa. Ua pepehiia o Kiwaa e Waikelenuiaiku mahope o kona lawepio ia ana e ka manu; he mau hulu kapu hoi na hulu i ka lae, o Hinawaikolii, ua lele hoi ua mau hulu nei a ke alo o na uha a Namakaokahai: Ua lilo ua hulu nei i mea mana; oia o Kukailimoku.

Kīwaʻa had soft, tiny feathers on its forehead. When Waikelenuiaīkū killed Kīwaʻa after being captured by him, these sacred forehead feathers, which were called Hinawaikōliʻi, flew to Nāmakaokahaʻi and landed upon her thighs; there these feathers accumulated mana and became Kūkāʻilimoku.[29]

The feathers landed near Nāmakaokahaʻi's genitals, the source of her procreative mana, which is what brought this god into being. Although Kīwaʻa (a.k.a. Kīwaha) is present in the other versions of this tradition, this episode is absent. This bird kupua guarded Kalākeʻenuiakāne.[30]

That an akua wahine is the origin of Kūkāʻilimoku is significant because he was one of Kamehameha I's most important war deities and the principal war god honored in the luakini heiau to whom human sacrifices were made. Although Kamehameha I had female war akua, their rituals took place in the Hale o Papa heiau just outside the luakini compound. With the exception of a few powerful ruling aliʻi wahine, women could not enter the luakini.

The transference of Moʻoinanea's generative mana to Nāmakaokahaʻi can also be understood as the former's bestowing upon the latter an aspect of her reptilian nature. When Moʻoinanea severs her tail, she is manifesting the ability of lizards—geckos and skinks whom mo'o akua are said to resemble—to regenerate that part of their body. Nāmakaokaha'i has the power to re-form her body, which can be likened to the lizard's ability to regenerate its tail. Her lizard-like ability is worked into a rather macabre passage in which she desires to know what valuable gifts or powers 'Aukelenuia'īkū, who is both her kāne and her kaikūnane (brother or male cousin), brings to their union, and which their son will inherit.[31]

Among the gifts that Mo'oinanea gives 'Aukelenuia'īkū are an adze and a knife, which can cut instantly through anything they touch (he used these to kill Kīwa'a). Nāmakaokaha'i wants him to demonstrate their power, so she commands him to sever her limbs from her body. He is horrified at her request. She insists and so he does as she asks. As he cuts her limbs off one by one, she laughs, delighted with the gifts her son will inherit from his father. She then reassembles her body and draws back into it the blood she lost. Nāmakaokaha'i also has other powers that reflect her double lineage. For example, she has a tidal-wave kino lau.[32] Kaikahinaali'i (also Kaiakahinali'i), sometimes reported as the Pele clan's mother, is associated with tsunamis.[33] Pele, too, can raise tsunamis, another manifestation of volcanic activity.

Nāmakaokaha'i's wai- and kai-related mana is evidenced in a passage about an akua who is kin to both Mo'oinanea and Nāmakaokaha'i. Depending on the version, he is named Kahoali'i or Kamohoali'i. He lives in a deep pit in the sky and guards the "wai ola loa o Kāne" (Kāne's water of long-lasting life), which brings the dead back to life.[34] 'Aukelenuia'īkū steals the wai ola loa in order to bring back to life his brothers and his nephew whom Nāmakaokaha'i killed when they first arrived to her land.[35] 'Aukelenuia'īkū's efforts to resuscitate them are unsuccessful until Nāmakaokaha'i slaps the water in the palm of his hand and then sprinkles it on the ocean.[36] Hers is the power of water to resuscitate (by striking the wai ola loa) and destroy (tidal waves), and thus she embodies the life-giving and death-dealing properties of water in its broadest sense. She also possesses the destructive aspect of fire through her battle pā'ū and kāhili that she inherited from Mo'oinanea. Hence, on many levels she exemplifies 'Ōiwi understandings of dyads, oppositional and complementary, and the importance attributed to them as regulating forces in the universe.

Here, I draw attention to the ways that discrete mo'olelo connect larger histories and religious practices. In S. W. B. Kaulainamoku's version of the Kepaka'ili'ula tradition, the ali'i Kepaka'ili'ula is related to 'Aukelenuia'īkū (his cousin) and Mo'oinanea (kupuna). Like

'Aukelenuia'īkū, Kepaka'ili'ula's family god is Mo'oinanea's brother, Lonoika'ouali'i (Lono of sovereign ascendancy). Mo'oinanea gifts Kepaka'ili'ula with a bird kupua kia'i (guardian) and scales from her body.[37] These scales will give him the strength he needs to best his enemies.[38] He takes Pele and Hi'iaka, who live with their brother Kahoali'i (another name for Kamohoali'i) in Kuaihelani, as his platonic wāhine.[39] Later, he takes the ali'i Mākole'ā as his real wahine. Mākole'ā is a historical figure to whom a heiau is dedicated at Kahalu'u, Hawai'i. Henry E. P. Kekahuna's detailed map of this site notes that women who wished to conceive visited Mākole'ā heiau and that its sacred spring is called Kahoali'i. Adjacent to the heiau is Keawehala Pond, where twin mo'o wahine, "beings from deified fetuses," dwell.[40] Thus, in the overlapping traditions of Kepaka'ili'ula and 'Aukelenuia'īkū, beliefs about mo'o and heroic figures intertwine with histories of ruling ali'i, heiau, and religious practices.

Haumea, Kāmeha'ikana, Papa, Walinu'u

Another significant link between the mo'o and Pele clans is that Haumea's forms, Kāmeha'ikana and Walinu'u, have kino mo'o. In two versions of the Kamaakamahi'ai tradition contributed by J. W. K. Kaualilinoe (1870–1871) and Ho'oulumāhiehie (1909–1912), Kāmeha'ikana, therein acknowledged as a form of Haumea, spends most of the account in her human form but occasionally appears as a mo'o.[41] Her status as a mo'o akua is further evidenced when she transforms her hānai daughter Kahelekūlani into a mo'o akua upon her death. In her mo'o form, Kahelekūlani is known as Nāwāhineikawai (Women in the water).[42] Earlier in this chapter, I shared Beckwith's observation that Walinu'u is Haumea's human form. Establishing Walinu'u as Haumea's mo'o form is rather convoluted because it must be traced through Haumea's other forms, Papa and Kāmeha'ikana, and involves a two-step analytical sequence that first considers disparate beliefs and then brings them together.

First step. An origin chant about the Hawaiian Islands establishes the relationship between Papa and Walinu'u: "O Papa o Walinu'u ka wahine" (Papa is the woman Walinu'u).[43] Papa is credited with birthing several Hawaiian Islands through her unions with Wākea (Hawai'i, Maui, Kaho'olawe, Kaua'i, and Ni'ihau) and Lua (O'ahu). The remaining islands were a result of Wākea's unions with Kāulawahine (Lāna'i) and Hina (Molokai).[44] Kamakau, familiar with this genealogy, states, "No Papa, oia no o Walinu'u, a o Haumea i kapaia e kekahi poe" (As for Papa, she is Walinuʻu, and called Haumea by some people).[45] Walinuʻu is a well-known moʻo, although not identified as such in this genealogical chant. And, although Kamakau did not name her as a moʻo here, he does so later in his treatise on moʻo akua. There, he explains that Walinuʻu is one of the moʻo that ruling aliʻi honored in connection with war and politics.[46]

Second step. The next link between Haumea and Walinuʻu is the tradition about an akua wahine who enters a breadfruit tree. Depending on the version, she is either Haumea, Papa, or Kāmehaʻikana. The notable exception is ʻĪʻī's version, which he shares in his lengthy and detailed treatise on the Kapu Loulu ritual that honored akua wahine associated with war and politics. At one point he links Haumea to Kāmehaʻikana and notes their association with the breadfruit tree:

> He mau kii ano wahine elua a ekolu paha, e ku ana ma kahi kupono ia ano kii a me na kii ua uhiia na kino i na kapa olena, a ua kapaia hoi o Kalamainuu (Kihawahine) he moo ke ano. A o Haumea (Kamehai-kana) no kona komo kino ana iloko o ka uhi [sic: ulu] ma kona ano akua paha, a ua oleloia, ua pepehiia kana kane o Makea, a ua kauia kona kino make i luna o ka ulu, oia hoi, ua ulu la ana i komo kino okoa ai.[47]

> Two or three female kiʻi draped in turmeric-dyed kapa stood in the places designated for them. One was called Kalamainuʻu (Kihawa-hine). She was a moʻo. And Haumea (Kāmehaʻikana) because of her physically entering a breadfruit tree, perhaps by means of her akua nature. It was said that her kāne Makea had been killed and his corpse hung on a breadfruit tree, the same breadfruit tree she physically entered.

Makea is the name of Haumea's kāne in the Kumulipo, which also identifies her as the breadfruit tree deity.[48] However, according to the tradition that ʻĪʻī learned, "Aohe o Makea ka inoa o ua mea la i make, aka, o Punaai-koae, he alii no ka mokupuni o Oahu" (Makea was not the name of that person who died, but Punaʻaikoaʻe, an aliʻi of Oʻahu Island). ʻĪʻī then tells his readers that by way of explanation, he will share the moʻolelo about Punaʻaikoaʻe (Makea) and then continue with description of the ritual.[49] (I will explain the link between Kalamainuʻu and Kihawahine in chapter 5.)

In ʻĪʻī's version of this tradition, Kalamainuʻu seduces Punaʻaikoaʻe (Makea) away from his first wahine, Walinuʻu, who is Pele's elder sister.

Puna'aikoa'e escapes and seeks refuge with the Pele clan. Kalamainu'u calls her mo'o kin to battle with the Pele clan to get him back. The mo'o lose the battle, and Puna'aikoa'e and Walinu'u are reunited. This is the first half of the account, and when it ends, 'Ī'ī switches from talking about the ki'i of Kalamainu'u (Kihawahine) and Haumea (Kāmeha'ikana) to discussing those of Kalamainu'u (Kihawahine) and Walinu'u:

> Ua oleloia no hoi, ua hakaka kino a kanaka maoli ua poe wahine nei, oia hoi o Walinuu, ka wahine mua a Punaaikoae, me Kalamainuu (Kihawahine) a me Haumea (Kamehaikana) hoi. No ua kane nei no a lakou ke kumu o ia hakaka ana, mamuli paha o ke ano lili ia hakaka nui ana. Ma ia hakaka ana nae, ua makapaa o Kalamainuu, a ua mene hoi ko Walinuu ihu; a pela i hoikeia mai ma ko laua mau kii, i ka wa e ku ana ma Hale o Papa. O Papa wahine paha ia a Wakea.[50]

> It was said those women fought in their human forms, namely, Walinu'u, the first wahine of Puna'aikoa'e, with Kalamainu'u (Kihawahine) and Haumea (Kāmeha'ikana) too. Their kāne is the reason for fighting, maybe jealousy caused that big fight. In the fight however, Kalamainu'u lost an eye, and Walinu'u's nose was flattened; and so their ki'i reflect this when they stand in Hale o Papa. Papa being perhaps the wahine of Wākea.

The second half of 'Ī'ī's account, which relates what happened after Walinu'u and Puna'aikoa'e are united, is his version of the breadfruit tree deity tradition. One day, while Walinu'u is out gathering seafood, Puna'aikoa'e (Makea) takes a nap in a banana grove. An ali'i's men mistake him for a banana thief. They kill him and hang his corpse on the branch of a breadfruit tree. Walinu'u learns about his death and runs to where she has heard his corpse is being displayed. She grabs his body and slaps the breadfruit tree's trunk, which opens. She enters it with his corpse, and it closes behind her.[51]

There are two analytical challenges that need to be addressed here. First, 'Ī'ī never names Walinu'u as a mo'o. Second, neither does he identify her as Haumea or Kāmeha'ikana. Thus, the question arises as to whether he understands Walinu'u to be a mo'o and one of Haumea's manifestations. I believe, however, that he did. He begins by discussing the ki'i (carved images or statues) of Kalamainu'u (Kihawahine) and Haumea (Kāmeha'ikana) that are part of the Kapu Loulu ceremony, notes the latter is a breadfruit tree deity, tells the story behind the peculiar appearance of their kiʻi, and then describes those of Kalamainuʻu (Kihawahine) and Walinuʻu instead of Haumea (Kāmehaʻikana)—the kiʻi he intially described before he offered the account of Punaʻaikoaʻe. Here, it is crucial to note that ʻĪʻī was once Kihawahine's caretaker, one of Kamehameha I's most important war akua. As such, he would have received a general education about her and the other akua wahine that Kamehameha I worshipped in his quest to conquer all the islands and unite them under his rule. As her caretaker, ʻĪʻī would have participated in the ritual he described, which is why he knew so much about it. Perhaps his failure to cite Walinuʻu more clearly as Haumea (Kāmehaʻikana) is because the stories he shared were his way of drawing readers' attention to the connection. ʻĪʻī is notable in that he seems to assume his readers are generally informed about the topics he discusses in his various series, so he tends to skip certain details. By comparison, Kamakau, ʻĪʻī's contemporary, treats his readers as if they know very little, so his writing style is long-winded.

To summarize this section, Walinuʻu is a form of Haumea, who is a moʻo. Walinuʻu is equated with Papa, a well-known form of Haumea, in a genealogy. ʻĪʻī implicitly links Walinuʻu to Kāmehaʻikana in his description of the Haumea (Kāmehaʻikana) kiʻi. Walinuʻu, Papa, Kāmehaʻikana, and Haumea are all noted as akua wahine who entered the breadfruit tree, and the breadfruit tree deity Walinuʻu is also the moʻo akua honored in the Kapu Loulu ceremony.

Akua Kai and Akua Wai, Sharks and Moʻo

Given that shark akua are closely associated with the Pele clan, how do we account for akua who have both shark and moʻo forms? Kamohoaliʻi, the supreme shark akua and Pele's elder brother, is one such entity. In two versions of the Hiʻiakaikapoliopele tradition, Kamohoaliʻi also has a "kino kanaka maoli a moo no hoi" (an actual human form and a moʻo one too). In his shark, human, and moʻo forms, he led the Pele migration to Hawaiʻi.[52] Thus, although this akua is better known as a shark god, he is technically also a moʻo, even if only in these two versions.

In addition to Kamohoaliʻi, at least four, perhaps five, other deities have shark and moʻo forms: KawailoaikapolioLokoea (Waialua, Oʻahu), Hawaiʻiloa (Waialua, Oʻahu), ʻAlekoko (Nāwiliwili or Anahola, Kauaʻi), Māmala (Waikīkī), and possibly ʻOua (also ʻOuha; Waikīkī and Maunalua, Oʻahu). The first two are brothers, but their genealogy is unknown, so I cannot account for their having shark and moʻo forms and likewise for 'Alekoko and Māmala.[53] We can, however, account for 'Oua's lineage, but whether he has a mo'o form is uncertain. According to Pukui, "Oua was the offspring of a manō [shark] and a mo'o. He was the sweetheart of Mamala. When she left him for Hon[o]-ka-'upu, he went home to Kuapā."[54] She does not specify his form. Because Kuapā (also Keahupua-o-Maunalua) was an important fishpond, it comes naturally to wonder if he was its kia'i and, if so, whether he could transform into a mo'o. His parentage makes this possible. Elsewhere, Pukui indicates 'Oua as a shark god. Although she credits Westervelt as her reference, he is not her source for 'Oua's parentage because he never mentions it.[55] I include 'Oua in this section despite being unable to confirm him as a mo'o for two reasons. First, his parents belong to two clans famous for their enmity; however, as I have shown, and as his parentage confirms, these clans are not always at odds. Second, unions between shark and mo'o akua may have a symbolic environmental significance.

Emma Nakuina gave an account of Nanaue, son of Kamohoali'i and Kalei, a human.[56] The only sign of his shark nature was the shark mouth between his shoulder blades. One tradition holds that Nanaue made his home in the Kāneana cave in 'Ōhikilolo, Wai'anae, O'ahu. His wahine was a mo'o who frequented a stream near the coral outcropping called Pōhaku Kūla'ila'i.[57] I grew up in Wai'anae, and our family would spend a week in the summer camping next to this place. As a child, I knew a mo'o was associated with this area but had forgotten the particulars. A plaque was eventually placed near Pōhaku Kūla'ila'i, which relates the story of this mo'o and the significance of her union with Nanaue:

> This sacred coral outcrop projecting out from the sea was the meeting place for Nanaue, shark man of Kaneana and the mo'o, lizard goddess of Ko'iahi Valley. Nanaue arose from the ocean through papaloa (long reef) and the mo'o from the Makua stream. Their meeting marked the spawning season and signified the unity of land and sea. Kula'ila'i (to dash into pieces) describes the mana (power) of waves crashing on to the coral's surface.[58]

Thus, another way we can understand the unions between mo'o (akua wai) and sharks (akua kai) and the akua who possess both forms is that they symbolize the wai-kai water dyad. This dyad is at once oppositional and complementary: wai is potable, kai is not, but both sustain life and when united form the ideal conditions in which certain kinds of fish and seaweed flourish. The relationships between moʻo and sharks play out this multilayered duality. Furthermore, while moʻo are often referred to as freshwater dwellers, as I have shown, some moʻo are associated with wai kai or live near the sea. Morever, their fish kino lau, the ʻoʻopu, lives out its life cycle migrating between wai, wai kai, and kai.[59]

The Pele and Moʻo Clans and Geological Phenomena

These clans' kinship and antagonism have an additional symbolic significance if we consider their respective associations with volcanos, fresh water, mountains, cliffs, earthquakes, and the ocean. The combined activity of volcanic phenomena, fresh water, and the ocean's waves is the process by which the Hawaiian Islands were born and shaped. Hawaiʻi's mountains were created by the continuous upheaval of molten basaltic lava welling up from the mantle, but its pali were formed by stream or ocean erosion and faulting, which produce nearly vertical cliffs. This cycle is ongoing via Kīlauea and Mauna Loa's eruptions, which are "generally preceded by earthquake swarms consisting of thousands of individual earthquakes."[60]

The kinship between these clans who represent opposing elements acknowledges the critical role they collectively play in this cycle. Moʻo embody different forms or sources of fresh water, while the Pele clan is associated with volcanic-related phenomena: lava, earthquakes, and tidal waves. Haumea, the mother of the Pele clan, is an earth deity who belongs to the Palikū (Steep cliff) lineage in the Kumulipo. As we have seen in Manu's account of Pele and Waka, these two supposed clans are actually one large family: Haumea and Moʻoinanea's kāne, Kāneilūhonua, is an earthquake deity and the father of their children. Nāmakaokahaʻi, in the ʻAukelenuiaʻīkū tradition, is related to both clans and has pali and tsunami kino lau but also a wai-related power.[61] A link between moʻo and seismic activity, perhaps because of their great size, is implied in ʻĪʻī's account of Punaʻaikoaʻe. In the battle over Punaʻaikoaʻe: "Pau iho la ka hapa nui o na moo i ka make mawaena o na mawae i hoowaia ae, ma kahi a na moo e naholo ana" (Most of the moʻo were destroyed, dying in the crevices that opened in the places where moʻo were fleeing along the ground).[62] Their antagonism may equally represent this cycle if we view it as a metaphorical conflict in which opposing elements and forces battle for supremacy.

Beckwith offers another interpretation. Their enmity may symbolize conflicts between different groups who migrated to Hawaiʻi. In her analysis of the Lāʻieikawai tradition in 1918, Beckwith ties volcanic and earthquake activity to the creation of pali and then to the Palikū genealogy in the Kumulipo. She hypothesizes that moʻo are earthquake deities. As an example, she cites Kihanuilūlūmoku who guards Paliuli in ʻŌlaʻa, Hilo, in the Lāʻieikawai tradition.[63] But, she does not address the kinship between Haumea of the Palikū genealogy/Pele clan and the moʻo family in the larger corpus of Hawaiian traditions, which is a critical error. Based on her reading of Liliʻuokalani's translation of the Kumulipo and Davida Malo's comments about the Kumulipo and Palikū lineage, Beckwith asserts that moʻo "seem to have been connected to the coming of the Pali family to Hawaiʻi." She concludes, "By a plausible analogy, then, the earthquake which rends the earth is attributed to the god who clothes himself in the form of a lizard; still further, such a convulsion of nature may have been used to figure the arrival of some warlike band who peopled Hawaii, perhaps settling in this very Hilo region and forcing their cult upon the older form of worship."[64] Beckwith has it partially right.

Beckwith analyzed the Kumulipo, which she began researching in 1938 and published in 1951.[65] She relied on several informed Hawaiians for assistance. Regarding the fourth wā (era), she notes, "Kupihea believes we should relate the series to specific families of settlers belonging to the migration period." She adds, "In general I have followed Kupihea's fairly coherent interpretation because it seems to hang together, although this is not essential to Hawaiian poetic art, and to leave to each reader his own evaluation of the symbolism involved. If actually intended as a portrayal of conditions under a historic migration, it makes a pretty sorry indictment of the past."[66] What she means by "pretty sorry indictment of the past" is unclear, but she obviously finds Kupihea's migration hypothesis deficient. Her quick dismissal of it is surprising given her hypothesis that moʻo are earthquake deities and symbolize upheaval caused by the introduction of new forms of worship to Hawaiʻi. Kupihea's interpretation supports her theories because Moʻoinanea, the leader of the moʻo migration, appears in the fourth wā when moʻo emerge, and I believe that Moʻoinanea was once widely worshipped, as I will show.

Elsewhere, Beckwith revisits her hypothesis about moʻo as earthquake deities: "The *moʻo* seems to be regarded as an earthquake deity and to be for this reason connected with the goddess of the volcano. Pools of water formed in earthquake cracks are believed to be inhabited by *moʻo*, and two pools, one at Kalapana in Puna district, and the other some miles distant, are supposed to contain the head and tail of a gigantic *moʻo* whose body stretches between them."[67] This moʻo is quite possibly Moʻoinanea. There was once a huge heiau in Kalapana known by two names, Punalua and Kamoʻoinanea (figure 4.2).[68] Punalua can refer to two springs of water and to someone who shares a partner, and both meanings are a good fit for Moʻoinanea. Within the heiau compound was a spring called ʻAukelenuiaʻīkū, which is significant because she is ʻAukelenuiaʻīkū's grandmother. A lava flow covered the heiau sometime after 1951.

This heiau's existence suggests that a ruling aliʻi once worshipped Moʻoinanea, as only ruling aliʻi had the right to build heiau. We can also suppose that perhaps others worshipped her. If we take into account the fact that the ʻAukelenuiaʻīkū tradition explains the Pele migration and that moʻo appear in the fourth wā of the Kumulipo, long before the Palikū family is mentioned, it is reasonable to imagine that moʻo worship preceded Pele worship. The migration accounts of the Pele clan coming to Hawaiʻi may symbolize the arrival of a group who worshipped the Pele clan. As Pele worship gained popularity, Moʻoinanea may have been supplanted as a major akua, which would also account for why the Hiʻiakaikapoliopele tradition depicts moʻo negatively.

In a few versions of the Hiʻiakaikapoliopele tradition, Pele chants a kūamuamu (denigrating chant) taken from the fourth wā of the Kumulipo. This kūamuamu insults Kilioeikapua and Kalanamainuʻu, who were posing as humans, and unmasks their true identity. Pele taunts them as those who "cling to rocks, cling to trees, and cling to the dirt."[69] She calls them children of Moʻomilinanea, the mother of all crawlers, a clear reference to Moʻoinanea. Given the similarity of the names by which Moʻoinanea is known across traditions (Moʻoinanea, Kamoʻoinanea, Kamoʻoianea, Mōinanea, Mōʻīnanea, and Mōʻīnānea[70]) and the names (Milimilinanea, Milinanea, and Moʻonanea) and information found in the fourth wā of the Kumulipo, I believe that Moʻomilinanea and Moʻoinanea are different names for the same deity.

Premigration and Postmigration Conflicts

Migration accounts of these two clans could represent the arrival of separate schools bringing new religious practices or, when they migrated together, a larger school that later split off and vied for power. Conflicts between the clans fall into two main categories: before Pele came to Hawaiʻi and after she arrived. Premigration conflicts arise from destruction or seduction, but mainly the latter. Postmigration conflicts can be divided up into four subcategories: destruction, seduction, resentment born of perceived injustices, and unexplained clan-related enmity.

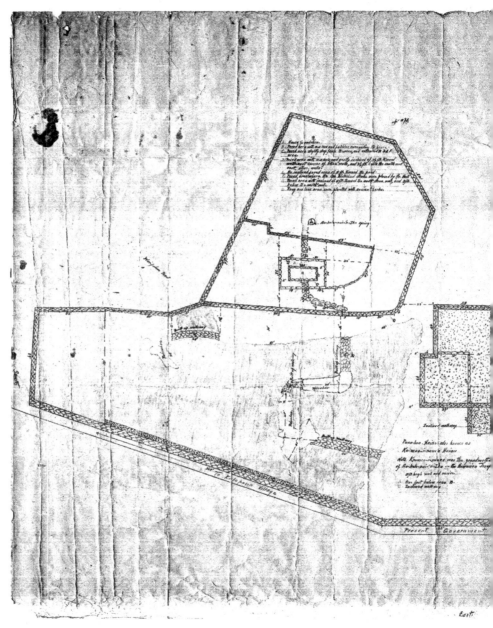

Figure 4.2. Henry E. P. Kekahuna's sketch *Punalua Heiau Also Known as Kamoo-inanea*. Courtesy of the Bishop Museum Archive (www.bishopmuseum.org).

Park Pavilion 43½' x 20½' w.

North

Waiololee Park
Kalapana, Hawaii
Hawaii, T.H.
July 10, 1903.

To Kaimu

Premigration Destruction

In the Lā'iehau tradition, as previously recounted, when Pele visits Haumea and the mo'o, they ask her about the reason for her visit. Pele confesses that she damaged part of the lands where they all dwell. A mo'o relative exclaims, "E huhu hou ia mai ana oe i ko kolohe i ka aina!" (You have once again offended because you trouble the land!).[71] Eventually, Nāmakaokaha'i banishes Pele from Kuaihelani because she is unable or unwilling to control her fire kino lau, so Pele migrates to Hawai'i.[72] This account's conclusion remains unknown because the newspaper issues in which its closing installments were published are missing. After Pele was exiled, she would have, imaginably, harbored a grudge against her sister and her mo'o relatives. A few mo'o loyal to Pele may have left with her, as happens elsewhere.

Premigration Seduction

In Emma Nakuina's English-language account of Pele's migration to Hawai'i, Nāmakaokaha'i, her kāne (unnamed), Pele, and their parents, Kāne and "Fire," lived in a volcano in a land called Ilao [Lalo]-o-Mehani. She hypothesizes that this land was "somewhere about the setting sun from here and about in a line with Java or the Philippines, probably Krakatoa."[73] Because Nāmakaokaha'i's kāne fell in love with Pele, she demanded that her parents banish Pele, so they did. To assuage his guilt, Kāne "gave Pele especial powers" so that she could rule over the siblings who decided to follow her.[74] Nakuina notes: "Pele was at the head of the expedition that left the mother country to seek a new home beyond the sea. Dragons, gnomes, serpents and sharks were ordered to go in Pele's train as servants and messengers or couriers."[75] Given that Nakuina is writing for a Western readership, dragons and serpents undoubtedly refer to mo'o. In "Hiiaka," which she published as "Kaili," she also calls them "water serpents" or "serpent."[76] Here, too, mo'o are relatives of the Pele clan and migrated with them to Hawai'i.[77]

In Poepoe's version of the Hi'iakaikapoliopele tradition, Pele'aihonuamea (Pele who eats the reddish-brown earth) steals Puna'aikoa'e from her sister Pelekumukalani (Pele who establishes the firmament), who then, in revenge, takes Wahieloa, Pele'aihonuamea's kāne.[78] Pele'aihonumea migrated to Hawai'i after she lost Wahieloa to her younger sister. According to some people, Poepoe explains, Pelekumukalani is Nāmakaokaha'i. Poepoe adds that in the Hawai'i Island version of this tradition, Pelekumukalani/Nāmakaokaha'i banishes Pele for sleeping with her kāne, so Pele migrates to Hawai'i.[79]

In the 'Aukelenuia'īkū tradition, Nāmakaokaha'i banishes Pele and Hi'iaka after they sleep with 'Aukelenuia'īkū. When she discovers that they have slept with her kāne, she attacks them with the intent to kill them. The sisters' brothers fear for their lives, and they attempt to intervene, but Nāmakaokaha'i tries to kill them too. None of them, even together, are able to overpower her. Pele and Hi'iaka flee, but Nāmakaokaha'i follows them. Pele and Hi'iaka arrive first to Kaua'i. Nāmakaokaha'i goes to Nu'umealani because it is a high place and thus a good vantage point from where she can see Kalāke'enuiakāne and Kaua'i. As she is sitting atop Nu'umealani, she sees Pele's fire and heads there to kill Pele and Hi'iaka. She manages to kill Pele and then returns to Nu'umealani. Although Pele's physical form is dead, her spirit survives. Pele and Hi'iaka then go from island to island trying to find the right home. O'ahu and Molokai are not suitable as there is no place deep enough to dig their crater home, but the enormous Haleakalā on Maui suits Pele and so they stay there. Meanwhile, Nāmakaokaha'i notices Pele's fire at Haleakalā and is surprised because she killed her. She goes to Maui and kills Pele and then returns to Nu'umealani. Pele, however, comes back to life again and goes to Hawai'i, where she makes her home at Mauna Loa. Once again, Nāmakaokaha'i spies Pele's fire but decides to leave her be and returns to Kalāke'enuiakāne to live with her kāne 'Aukelenuia'īkū.[80]

Postmigration Seduction

After Pele settles on Hawai'i, the situation is reversed—a mo'o seduces the kāne of a Pele clan member. I have already related the account of Kalamainu'u, who seduces Walinu'u's kāne, who in that account is Pele's eldest sister. Elsewhere, Puna'aikoa'e is Pele's kāne, whom she loses to Waka. Because Pele respects Waka, she asks her nicely to return him but Waka refuses. Pele sets out to kill them. The two lovers flee to Ka'ū and hide in Kaualehu's cave (Waka's mo'o relative) near the sea. Waka calls upon Mo'oinanea to help her. Mo'oinanea gathers mo'o from across the islands, but when she discovers that Waka is at fault, she forbids them to help her. Pele kills Waka and Puna'aikoa'e. Before Pele waged war against them with lava, earthquakes, and tsunamis, Ka'ū was a verdant area.[81] Today it is an immense lava plain. Lohi'au is Pele's lover in the Hi'iakaikapoliopele tradition. Kilioe and Kalanamainu'u flirt with Lohi'au, but Pele thwarts their efforts to seduce him. They eventually capture and kill him. Hi'iaka kills them and brings Lohi'au back to life.[82] Pele's kāne is also Lohi'au in an account about the origins

Table 4.1. Pre- and postmigration cycle of seduction

Tradition	Conflict	Victim and clan (clan in parentheses)	Perpetrator and clan (clan in parentheses)
Premigration conflicts			
Hiʻiakaikapoliopele	Seduction	Nāmakaokahaʻi (Pele)	Pele (Pele)
Hiʻiakaikapoliopele	Seduction	Peleʻaihonuamea (Pele)	Pelekumukalani (Pele)
Hiʻiakaikapoliopele	Seduction	Pelekumukalani (Pele)	Peleʻaihonuamea (Pele)
ʻAukelenuiaʻīkū	Seduction	Nāmakaokahaʻi (Pele and Moʻo)	Pele and Hiʻiaka (Pele)
Postmigration conflicts			
Punaʻaikoaʻe	Seduction	Walinuʻu (Pele)	Kalamainuʻu (Moʻo)
Pele and Waka	Seduction	Pele (Pele)	Waka (Moʻo)
Hiʻiakaikapoliopele	Seduction and murder	Pele (Pele)	Kilioe and Kalanamainuʻu (Moʻo)
Origin of Molokini	Seduction	Pele (Pele)	Puʻuoinaina (Moʻo)

of Molokini islet. Pele cuts the moʻo Puʻuoinaina in half for having slept with him. Her head becomes Molokini islet, and her tail becomes Puʻuōlaʻi Hill at Mākena on Maui.[83]

Table 4.1 summarizing the pre- and postmigration cycle of seduction across traditions is helpful. While kāne are also complicit in this cycle, the primary aim of this table is to show which clan members lost their kāne and which ones seduced them.

Postmigration Destruction

When Hiʻiaka begins her journey to retrieve Lohiʻau for Pele, as she and Wahineʻōmaʻo near Panaʻewa forest, Wahineʻōmaʻo warns her that it is the path of death because the dreaded moʻo Panaʻewa guards it.[84] When Hiʻiaka asks Panaʻewa to let them pass through its forest, Panaʻewa refuses and a battle ensues.[85] Panaʻewa's hostility toward Hiʻiaka stems from her belonging to the Pele clan. This is evident when it calls them "stone-eating, land-eating, lehua-grove-eating women"—an apt description of what occurs during a lava flow.[86] Panaʻewa's forest is located near Kīlauea where Pele resides, and her lava flows are a threat to its home. Thus, Panaʻewa has good reason to dislike the Pele clan. Given the many ʻōlelo noʻeau, chants, and moʻolelo that celebrate Panaʻewa's lehua groves, we can surmise that it is an ancient rain forest, one that has undoubtedly experienced many cycles of destruction and regeneration. Thus, the battle between Panaʻewa and Hiʻiaka may mythologize ancestral experiences of natural catastrophes.

Panaʻewa is both the Panaʻewa rain forest and its water cycle. This akua wai's function is to protect the rain forest, which is largely composed of its kino lau, the ʻōhiʻa and the ʻamaʻu. Together, these kino lau attract rain and break heavy rainfall, which preserves the integrity of the land and its aquifers. Protecting the forest includes safeguarding the viability of the rain forest's water cycle. Pele's function is to create land, but inevitably, her lava flows destroy everything in their path. Hiʻiaka is complicit in this process. Her function is to regenerate the land via revegetation. Not long after a lava flow hardens, ʻōhiʻa and fern shoots emerge from between its cracks. Thus begins the transformation of bleak lava plains into verdant forests. Kalei Nuʻuhiwa offers an interpretation: Panaʻewa, along with the moʻo who serve it, represent old forest growth, and thus Hiʻiaka heals the forest by killing them. From this viewpoint, battles between forest moʻo and the Pele clans represent the cycle of forest regeneration.[87]

In summary, there are two standpoints from which to view these forest-related conflicts. A Pele-centric stance perceives moʻo negatively. Moʻo represent old forest growth that strangles rain forests. A moʻo-centric stance perceives moʻo as protectors of freshwater sources and rain forests. Pele is a destructive force that obliterates both, and Hiʻiaka, being her sister, is guilty by association. Both are valid as they each focus on different aspects of their dual natures: they embody the life-giving and death-dealing characteristics of the elements and phenomena with which they are respectively associated.

Postmigration Resentment Born of Perceived Injustices

That moʻo accompanied Pele to Hawaiʻi is clear in Hiʻiaka's encounter with Piliamoʻo and Kuaua. These moʻo live in the Wailuku River and guard the shaky log that people use as a bridge to cross this section of the river, which runs through Hilo. When they see Hiʻiaka, Kuaua tells Piliamoʻo that they should let her pass but Piliamoʻo refuses. She grumbles, "Since all of us in our clan were brought here by Pele, and the two of us were left here to endure the cold, while she and her younger sisters and her brothers dwell in the warmth, then the sacred bridge of Wailuku should not be gained so effortlessly by that cheeky girl who so brazenly requests it." Hiʻiaka overhears them and tells her companions,

"Our elder sister and chiefess placed them here, where food and fish are abundant, and yet they complain about it."[88]

Postmigration Unexplained Clan-Related Enmity

In Kapihenui's version, the mo'o of Wailuku River are Piliamo'o and Nohoamo'o. Their kinship with the Pele clan is clear as they are Hi'iaka's male kūpuna.[89] Piliamo'o tells Nohoamo'o, "E! O ka moopuna o kaua la" (Eh, that's our grandchild). Nohoamo'o says he does not care, and if she refuses to pay the toll to cross the bridge, they should kill her. Kapihenui does not explain their anger, but perhaps their reason mirrors that of Piliamo'o and Kuaua. They are also related to the Pele clan and accompanied them in their migration in Kaili's version, but here they are female.[90]

After Hi'iaka battles Pana'ewa, she encounters another group of mo'o at the outskirts of Pana'ewa forest. They refer to her as their younger relative, yet all but two mo'o detest her. That their hatred arises from a gross injustice a Pele clan member committed is evidenced when one mo'o, Haili, observes, "It seems to be . . . that the innocent one we thrashed still exists, did not die, and is headed this way."[91] As with Pana'ewa, their ill will toward Hi'iaka may stem from the fact that her sister's lava flows are a threat to their forest home.

———————

The roles mo'o deities and members of the Pele clan play in Hawaiian culture encapsulate the depth and breadth of our worldview: spiritual, intellectual, political, economic, societal, and genealogical. There are simply too many instances linking the mo'o and Pele clans in Hawaiian traditions to ignore their familial connection or the similarities of their roles in Hawaiian culture. It is possible that certain traditions highlighting the conflict between the two clans were composed to express the perspectives of competing ideologies. If this is true, it is reasonable to assert that it was accomplished by using the dyads of water and fire, heat and cold, fresh water and ocean water as metaphors. But the elemental division between the mo'o and Pele clans is not as distinct as it may seem, as I have shown.

Mo'o appear in many traditions, and although they are fearsome in these accounts, they do not harass Pele or her near relatives. Yet, in the Pele and Hi'iaka traditions, battles between Hi'iaka and mo'o are a prominent theme. Why? Here, I share ho'omanawanui's insight: "Mo'o are metaphorical representations of obstacles to Hi'iaka's kuleana and journey, thus a different role than moʻo per se in other traditions."[92] The traditions in which the moʻo and Pele clans appear reflect the importance of balance in Hawaiian thought. Moʻo are water deities, and the Pele clan are volcanic entities, yet as I have shown, these boundaries are sometimes blurred. If both families hold mana over fire, water, and land, then how should we interpret their enmity? Although these hoahānau (siblings or near cousins) seem to be in eternal strife, they represent the cosmic circle of nature and life in which destruction and creation go hand in hand. Their complicated natures mirror the dynamic forces that rule our island world.

The symbolism behind their kinship and antagonism is potentially multilayered. They represent dyads that can be oppositional and complementary: female and male mana, contrasting elements and natural phenomena, and competing schools of religious practices. At their best, the moʻo and Pele clans embody passion and physical beauty coupled with intelligence and fearlessness. At their worst, they are capricious and vengeful and reap the negative consequences of their obsessive desires, but even then, they are glorious and their mana immense. Whatever these traditions' symbolism and for whatever reason they were and continue to be told, whether as historical treatises, belief narratives, entertainment, cautionary tales, or political statements, they remain valuable cultural resources for ʻŌiwi and testimonies about our resilience and survival despite the historical challenges we have faced and continue to face.[93]

Chapter 5

Mo'o Roles and Functions Past and Present

During an earlier period in Hawaiian history, mo'o akua held different roles and filled a variety of functions in overlapping sectors—familial, societal, economic, political—but religion was the foundation upon which these roles and functions were established as it was the belief in mo'o akua that engendered them. Previous chapters laid the groundwork for better understanding these roles and functions, which are based on the kinds of powers attributed to mo'o as a class of reptilian deities associated with water and, in some instances, also to their kino lau.

Familial-Societal Role: 'Aumākua Mo'o

A critical familial role that mo'o deities played (and continue to play) is that of 'aumakua (plural, 'aumākua; ancestral guardian). During the course of a *Ka Leo Hawai'i* broadcast, Jonah Kamalani, a kama'āina of North Kohala, Hawai'i, told Kimura that his kupuna wahine could understand mo'o and would often speak with their mo'o 'aumakua. It would give her news, such as if a visitor would arrive the next day or if trouble was coming, which she would then share with the family. If someone in their family killed a mo'o, she would be angry because their 'aumakua was a mo'o.[1] The 'aumakua's primary function is to protect its descendants and lead their souls into the afterlife.[2]

There are three main ways by which a family has an 'aumakua. The first is to belong to a lineage that descends from a union between an akua and a human. That akua becomes an 'aumakua for its descendants.[3] The second is for people to pray to akua with the hopes that at least one of them would recognize them as kin and become their 'aumakua.[4] The third is to entreat an 'aumakua to deify deceased relatives by transforming them into another form such as a shark, a mo'o, etc. This ritual is termed kākū'ai. Kamakau wrote extensively about mo'o-related kākū'ai.

The section below is my translation summary of his treatise, to which I have added supplementary details for today's readers to make more intelligible that which would have been clearer to the readers of Kamakau's time.

Kamakau on Kākūʻai

The kākūʻai was an elaborate ritual that involved several steps. In the case of aliʻi, the first step was to build a special house, a hale moku (house set apart), which was surrounded with a wooden fence. This house was termed a hale puaniu (coconut flower house), and within it, offerings were made with ʻawa (kava, *Piper methysticum*). The mōhai (offering, sacrifice) for the kākūʻai rite in which the dead would be transfigured into moʻo were specific to this class of deities. Kapa was dyed with turmeric and noni bark, which resulted in shades of dark and light yellow, a color to which moʻo were believed to be partial. This kapa was then made into mantles and skirts, which were deposited in the hale moku as offerings. Fires were lit for the imu at waihau (a type of heiau to honor moʻo) and koʻa (a stone altar) of these many-bodied ʻeʻepa (supernatural entities) to bake pigs and dogs. The dogs destined as mōhai were those with colors or patterns of fur considered pleasing to moʻo. These types included ʻīlio makuʻe (dark brown), ʻīlio ʻiʻi ʻulaia (reddish-brown), and ʻīlio moʻo hulu peʻelua ʻulaia (brindled with reddish stripes). The corpse or its bones, which had been wrapped in yellow turmeric-dyed kapa, was carried to the water, along with the pigs and dogs for the moʻo deity to whom the deceased would be dedicated so that the deceased, in turn, would become a moʻo.

The terrifying forms of these moʻo, big and small, lay in the water. While the kahu moʻo (caretaker of the moʻo) prayed, they were all given ʻawa to drink and the baked pig and dogs to eat. The kahu moʻo then took the corpse and placed it before the designated moʻo ʻaumakua who had the power to transform the corpse, which then took it away.

Within two or three days perhaps, the spirit of the deceased would return to speak through or fully possess a loved one and say to the family, "You must continuously drink ʻawa and call my name, and eat food dedicated to my name; your drinking and eating will be our eating and drinking together, which will give me strength. Then, if you want to see me, you will see me." In this way, loved ones saw their transfigured relative, which relieved their uncertainty about whether the transfiguration had been successful.[5]

The first sighting signified the kā'ili, and the haka (medium) through whom the spirit of the deceased had spoken began drinking 'awa from morning to evening, which strengthened the deceased's spirit. Thus did these po'e kino lau 'e'epa (beings with supernatural forms) become incredibly powerful. This is the reason they reward the living by blessing their existence, keeping them safe from trouble and accidents, teaching them about the lā'au lapa'au (medicine) to treat any illnesses in the family, and educate them in the knowledge of kilokilo (seers), kāula (prophets), 'ike akakū (visions), and to ho'āla (awaken—i.e., call upon) the spirits of the po'e kupua, kūpuna, and hoahānau (siblings or close cousins—i.e., near relatives).[6]

Maka'āinana (the nongoverning class, not of royal rank) who wished to transfigure the deceased into a mo'o did not usually erect a hale puaniu. Those who did so built small hale puaniu, and their mōhai were less lavish—an 'īlio 'i'i 'ulaia (reddish-brown dog), small pieces of turmeric-dyed kapa, and 'awa, all of which were acceptable to the mo'o deity in some cases but not in others. Should a mo'o refuse the mōhai, the bundle containing the deceased's remains stayed there, floating in the water.[7]

Considerations about 'Aumakūa as Life-Giving and Death-Dealing Entities

It is essential to remember that mo'o 'aumākua are akua and therefore not to be confused with ordinary lizards. That said, ordinary lizards are sacred to those 'aumākua whose divine form is reptilian. Moreover, just because a family's ancestor was transformed into a mo'o does not signify that all mo'o akua were their 'aumākua. By way of illustration, it would be inaccurate for someone with a mo'o 'aumakua to say, "Geckos and skinks are my 'aumākua," or "All mo'o akua are my 'aumākua because my ancestor was transformed into a mo'o."[8] An accurate phrase would be, "I have a mo'o 'aumakua. Because the lizard is its kino lau, I consider it sacred."

'Aumākua severely punish descendants who break their kapu (prohibition, especially one having to do with the sacred). One of the most grievous infractions against an 'aumakua is to eat or otherwise harm its kino lau. Depending on the severity of the infraction, the 'aumakua might cause the transgressor to become ill and even bring about the person's death.[9]

When an 'aumakua is offended, the family needs to placate it. In 1865, Samuela Ekaula wrote an installment about 'aumākua for the Lahainaluna Seminary series "Hoomana Kahiko" (Ancient Religion).

Ekaula discusses "mohai e oluolu ai na Aumakua" (offerings to appease Ancestral guardians), including mo'o 'aumākua:

> Eia na mohai, ina he moo, a ua inaina i kona Kahu, a i kana hanauna paha, a ke mai nei, a nawaliwali loa paha, penei ka mohai ana, he ilio moo ka ilio, huipu me ka awa, a me ka ia ula, he kumu, he ko ula, he kohekohe, a o ke kapa olena ka wah-i; alaila lawe aku iloko o ka lua o ka moo, hana a paa, alaila oluolu mai ka Aumakua moo, a hoola mai i ka mai.[10]

> Here are the offerings, if a mo'o, and its attendant had angered it, or his descendants perhaps, and were beset with illness, or were extremely weak, this is how the offering was carried out: the dog was a brindled dog, along with 'awa, red fish, a kūmū (goat fish), red sugarcane, and sedge. These were all wrapped up in yellow-turmeric-dyed bark cloth and then brought to the mo'o's pit, and when this was done, then the mo'o 'Aumakua was appeased, and took away the illness.

The brindled dog's fur recalls the lizard kino lau of the mo'o, and such attention to detail is pleasing to akua. The red fish and red sugarcane are exceptions to the use of yellow in mo'o-related rituals. Seeing as this ritual calls upon the mo'o 'aumakua to spare the life of those who have offended it, perhaps these items are appropriate because red recalls blood and thus life. 'Awa is an excellent offering for all akua.[11] The sedge grows in marshy areas, which is perhaps why it is included.

In 1859, H. F. Kaluapihaole listed the proper mōhai for dozens of gods, including two mo'o, Kalamainu'u and Laniwahine. Their mōhai is a black pig.[12] Solid-black pigs (pua'a hiwa) are desirable mōhai for akua.[13] "Hiwa" denotes "entirely black" and thus recalls the deep darkness of the Pō where the akua dwell, which is probably why the pua'a hiwa is a prized mōhai.

Economic-Societal Function: Kia'i Loko I'a

Aquaculture is an economic activity at which 'Ōiwi excel. In their study of fishponds in Hawai'i, Russel Anderson Apple and William Kenji Kikuchi note, "As far as is known, fishponds existed nowhere else in the Pacific in types and numbers as in prehistoric Hawai'i. Only in the Hawaiian Islands was there an intensive effort to utilize practically every body of water, from the seashore to the upland forests, as a

source of food, either agriculturally or aquaculturally."[14] The preva-
lance of kia'i loko i'a (fishpond guardians), whether mo'o, eel, or goby
akua, is unsurprising given the historical importance of fishponds in
the islands. In 1870, Kamakau explained that mo'o akua, like shark
deities, have the mana to attract fish, lead them elsewhere, and help
them to thrive.[15] Because of this mana, 'Ōiwi valued mo'o kia'i whether
they guarded fishponds or coastal areas where fish and shellfish were
plentiful.

Some of the largest fishponds were on O'ahu, and mo'o were kia'i
for many of them.

On O'ahu at Maunalua, the fishpond known as Keahupua o Maunalua, Kuapā, or Maunalua Pond, at 523 acres, was once the largest
walled fishpond in the islands.[16] It was "partially filled in for the
Hawai'i-Kai subdivision; the remnants of the pond are now a marina. It
was once believed that the pond was partly constructed by menehune
people and was connected by a tunnel to Ka-'ele-pulu pond, Kai-lua,
O'ahu."[17] Here, it is helpful to know that menehune are a "legendary
race of small people who worked at night, building fish ponds, roads,
temples; if the work was not finished in one night it remained
unfinished."[18] Laukupu (gender unspecified) is its kia'i.[19] Behind it was a
cliff called Luahine where three other mo'o live: Luahine, for whom the
cliff is named, and her two sons, Kūmauna and Palihala.[20]

Kawainui fishpond, located in the Kawainui-Hāmākua Marsh
Complex, was the second-largest fishpond on O'ahu.[21] Kawainui wet-
lands once reached from far inland to the shore and cover four hundred
hectares (nearly a thousand acres).[22] Hauwahine, according to Kīhei de
Silva, "ensured the wealth of its [Kailua] fish ponds and lo'i kalo [irri-
gated taro patches] and kept watch over the activities of its human
habitants."[23] Many people continue to honor Hauwahine as the tutelary
deity of Kawainui, specifically, and Kailua, generally.

Meheanu is the kia'i of He'eia, which is another sizable fishpond
on O'ahu "enclosing 88 acres of brackish water." Happily, Paepae o
He'eia, a private nonprofit organization, with many helping hands, is in
the process of restoring He'eia.[24] The members of Paepae o He'eia and
many others in the community continue to honor her.

Kaloko fishpond at Honokōhau in Kailua-Kona, Hawai'i, is also being restored. Kaloko kia'i include Kalamainu'unuianoho, Kihawahineikiananea, and 'O'opupo'owainuianiho.[25] The names of the first two kia'i
include "Kalamainu'u" and "Kihawahine." Whether Kalamainu'unuianoho (Great Kalamainu'u to whom belongs the sitting kapu) and

Kihawahineikiananea (Little Kihawahine at repose) are alternative names for Kalamainu'u and Kihawahine or distinct entities remains unknown, but they are undoubtedly mo'o. The third kia'i, 'O'opupo'owainuianiho (Fountain-headed great-toothed goby), is either a mo'o or a goby deity (or both) given its name. The account of the cultural hero Ka-Miki describes Kaloko and its kia'i:

> O Kumakapuu ia, oia ke kiai loko, a he kaulana paa aina ia no ua loko i'a ala, a he unuunu kapu hooulu i'a, hoohanau a hoolaupa'i pua i'a no na ki'o ame na ha a puni ua loko ala. Aole ia he kanaka, he akua ia, a oia ka mea nana e lawe i na mohai apau e kau ia ana no ka mohai ana i na aliiwahine o ua loko ala, oia o Oopu-poowai-nui-a-niho, o Kala-mainuu-nui-a-noho, a o Kihawahine-iki-a-nanea.
>
> O lakou na alii kapu loko i'a o kena loko, a o kela wahi e moku ana iwaena o ka loko la, o ka ipukaia o ka halau alii o lakou o Kapa-kolea ia wahi, a ina e makemake ua poe ala e hele i ka makaikai honua, e huna ana lakou i ka i'a o ka loko, a nele aohe i'a.
>
> Aoe e nalo ka hele, e omaomao ana ka wai o ua loko ala, a ina e hoi mai, aoe e nalo e ula ana ka wai elike me ke koko, alaila, ua hoi mai ua poe ala i ka hale alii o lakou, a pau ka ula ana o ka wai, hoi ae no a ka mau, a oia ka wa e hookui ai ka i'a i ka maka-ha o ka loko.
>
> (O kela mau hoailona a ke kupuna wahine e hoike nei ia Ka-Miki, he mau hoailona oiaio loa ia a hiki i keia la o keia moolelo e puka nei, a ina e ninau i na kamaaina o keia mau wahi, e hooiaio mai no lakou, a o ka mea e kakau nei kekahi i ike pono i keia mau hoike no ke omaomao ame ka ula o ka wai elike me ke koko, a oia mau hoailona eia no ke ikeia nei a hiki i keia manawa.—MEA KAKAU.)[26]

That is Kūmakapu'u, the caretaker and well-known landholder of that fishpond, and there is a stick indicating a fishing prohibition is in effect to increase the number of fish, fish births, and fish fry in the ponds and the sluice gates around that fishpond. He is not human, but a god, and that is who takes all the offerings and deposits them before the high-ranking women of that fishpond, 'O'opu-po'owai-nui-a-niho, Kala-mainu'u-nui-a-noho, and Kihawahine-iki-a-nanea.

They are the sacred, high-ranking women guardians of that fish-pond, and that place bisecting the middle of the fishpond is the en-trance of their royal dwelling called Kapakolea, and if they want to travel about the land, they hide the fish inside, and then there is a lack of fish.

Their departure does not go unnoticed, the fishpond water turns green, and if they return, the water turns red like blood, and then, once they have returned to their royal dwelling, the water ceases to be red. Everything returns to normal, and that is when the fish crowd the fishpond sluice gate.

(Those signs that the female ancestor is revealing to Ka-Miki are actual signs that are still valid today as this moʻolelo is being published, and if you asked the people of these places about them, they would confirm. The writer also saw these signs, the green and blood-red water, and those signs continue to be seen until this time.—WRITER.)

In addition to being a kiaʻi loko iʻa, a moʻo might be a tutelary deity for an area rich in aquacultural resources. Kānekuaʻana was the moʻo guardian of the entire ʻEwa district on Oʻahu, which includes the area and bay called Puʻuloa. Up until the late 1800s, Puʻuloa was full of fishponds and lochs and famed for the quality and quantity of its shellfish. It was especially prized for its pearl oysters, and it was later also known as "Pearl Harbor." An ʻōlelo noʻeau commemorates a belief about oyster harvesting: "E hāmau o makani auaneʻi," which Pukui translates as "Hush, lest the wind arise," and for which she offers this explanation: "Hold your silence or trouble will come to us. When the people went to gather pearl oysters at Puʻuloa, they did so in silence, for they believed that if they spoke, a gust of wind would ripple the water and the oysters would vanish."[27] Kamakau offers this explanation about Kānekuaʻana:

O Kanekuaana ke kiai o Ewa, a ua hilinai ko Ewa poe kamaaina mai Halawa a Honouliuli, aole nae o ko Ewa a pau loa, aia no o kana poe pulapula, a o ka pomaikai e loaa i kana pulapula, ua lilo no ia i pomaikai no na mea a pau loa. Ua hilinai ko na Ewa i ko lakou kiai nana e haawi mai i ko lakou pomaikai.[28]

Kānekuaʻana is the guardian of ʻEwa, and the people of ʻEwa, from Hālawa to Honouliuli, depended on her with trust and confidence. Although not all those of ʻEwa were her descendants, the blessings her descendants received became blessings for everyone. ʻEwa people relied on their guardian who gave them their good fortune. Many of Puʻuloa's fishponds have been filled in and the loch water polluted, and consequently, oysters no longer thrive there.

When there was a scarcity of fish in fishponds, Hawaiians attributed it to someone having offended the kiaʻi. When this happened, Kamakau explains, "Aia no a hoomanao ia ka poe kiai kamaaina o na loko, alaila, e piha no na loko i ka ia, a e piha no i ka momona ka ia" (When the guardians of the fishponds were remembered and shown respect, then, fish filled the fishpond, and the fish were plump). As examples, Kamakau names Hauwahine and the fishponds she guards, Kawainui and Kaʻelepulu, and Laukupu and her fishpond Maunalua.[29]

In the account of Mākālei, Kahinihiniʻula, a young boy who is a descendant of Haumea, joins the community to help remove the limu that is choking up Kawainui and Kaʻelepulu fishponds.[30] Everyone, even the littlest child, is promised a share of fish, but because Kahinihiniʻula runs off to play, he is not there when they hand out fish. This happens twice. His going home empty-handed was an oversight, but nonetheless, Haumea punishes the community. Soon, no one would be able to catch the fish at these ponds. Kahinihiniʻula is taught how to use Mākālei, a piece of kupua wood that has the ability to attract and lead fish. He is told to use Mākālei to lead the fish from these fishponds to the pond near their upland dwelling.[31]

When the community realizes that the fish are suddenly gone, people suspect that Pākuʻi, the fishpond caretaker, has erred in some way.[32] Notably, it is not Hauwahine but Kahinihiniʻula's grandmother, Niula, and his ancestor, Haumea, who decide to remove the fish from Kawainui and Kaʻelepulu. Here it should be pointed out that in some versions of the Hiʻiakaikapoliopele tradition, Hauwahine's name is given as "Haumeawahine," suggesting that she is yet another form of Haumea.[33]

At one point, Pākuʻi decides to take initiative and make an offering to Hauwahine. Unfortunately for Pākuʻi, Hauwahine decides to toy with him. Because this account has never been translated for the public, I offer my translation of this extended passage:

> When Nuhi and the others went back, Pākuʻi remained, and when it was nearly midnight, he grabbed the ti-leaf bundles of lūʻau [cooked taro leaves], unwrapped them in the gourd bowl, and then walked slowly to the fishpond sluice gate. He sat down and scooped up water and poured it into the bowl of lūʻau. He worked it with his hands until it had a smooth consistency, sprinkling it with fine salt and crushed candlenut that he had prepared, and mixed it together. Then he removed his malo [loincloth], set it aside, and stepped into the fishpond with the bowl of lūʻau.

As he walked, he scooped his hand in the bowl and sprinkled its contents here and there where he walked, and when the lūʻau in the bowl was finished, he turned to go back to the sluice gate. He was nearly to the sluice gate when something large slid along the side of his left leg. The water in the fishpond was deep, but there was a thick layer of mud that reached the calves.

Therefore, from the calves past the knees was the size of this slippery thing, and when this slippery thing touched him, he cried out and quickly jumped up, intending to cling to the edge of the sluice gate, but he realized that he had landed right on this huge, slippery-skinned thing. Because this thing he had landed on was slick, his legs were slippery even though they hadn't touched the fishpond mud, and he found himself face up when he fell on the extraordinary thing of the night, soaking his torso completely in the water of ʻUkeke [to shiver with cold], and the gourd bowl flew from his hand, hit the stones of the fishpond walls, and disintegrated.

When he stood up, now truly drenched, he jumped again to grab the border of the fishpond with his left hand, but as he tried to secure his footing, his feet caught in the slippery floor of Captain Nemo's *Nautilus* ship. As fear reigned over him, he stretched his legs up, drawing them up to where his hands grasped the fishpond's stone wall.

He felt with his foot and found a space between the stones of the fishpond's wall. He set his other foot down, feeling around, but didn't find a space between the stones.

Therefore, he pushed his big toe into the mound of dirt and stepped down on it.

While he was worming his body upward with the intention of setting his chest on the edge of the fishpond wall, the dirt mound he had been standing on collapsed, and his foot wobbled again on the deck of the great, broad ship of Hoʻopakika [To cause to slip and slide].

So, drawing up his legs on the fishpond wall, he set his foot down again, and finding purchase between the stones, made an effort to get ahold of it without looking and put his chest on the border of the fishpond wall, feeling around with his hands to find purchase on the stone. Wriggling about, he finally managed to get on the wall.[34]

When Pākuʻi returns home, he continues to dwell upon the fact that he fell upon Hauwahine until sleep overtakes him. Lūʻau (cooked taro leaf) is not on the list of preferred mōhai for moʻo, but it is for Hiʻiaka (she only ate lū'au), which might explain Hauwahine's behavior.[35] Before continuing, I want to draw attention to the terms "'Ukeke" and "Ho'opakika," which are verbs and not actual names for water or a type of ship. "'Ukeke" serves to describe the coldness Pāku'i experienced as he fell in the water, while "Ho'opakiki" is not an actual deck of a ship but describes Hauwahine's slippery body. The contributor of this account, Samuel Keko'owai, uses these terms to transmit the humor of Pāku'i's predicament, a common strategy in Hawaiian writing.

Because Keko'owai passed away, the series ended before it had properly concluded.[36] Given that eventually, Ahiki, the konohiki (a person appointed by a ruling ali'i to manage a district's resources), discovers the cause and takes steps to rectify the fact that Kahinihini'ula had not received his share of fish, we can imagine that the story would have concluded with Haumea restoring the fish to Kawainui and Ka'elepulu.

As for the mo'o Laukupu and the Maunalua fishpond, McAllister's informant Makea Napahi explained in 1930 that her great-grandmother Mahoe began the construction of this fishpond, but the menehune completed it. Mahoe's efforts to appease the kia'i are as follows:

> At times there was a dearth of fish, which Mahoe coped with in this manner. On the nights of Kane, she took a baby pig as it came from the womb of the mother, and had her small grandson carry the squealing animal about the pond. There was a strict tapu until the next night, which was the night of Lono. No fishing was permitted, and no noise was allowed to disturb the praying kahuna. On the night of Lono, seaweed and ilima were gathered and placed on the shrine. After the night of Lono, when this ceremony was apparently completed, there was plenty of fish.[37]

There are several points to explicate in the above passage. To begin, that a kahuna presided over this rite and imposed a kapu signifies that it was a solemn ceremony. 'Ōiwi traditionally calculate the nights according to thirty moon phases, and Kāne and Lono are the twenty-seventh and twenty-eighth nights. It comes naturally to wonder why these nights were chosen to hold the ceremony. There are three overlapping possibilities: first, these nights are auspicious; second, mo'o are akua wai, and these nights are sacred to Kāne, the primary akua wai; and third, they are low-tide nights and thus would have facilitated gathering seaweed for the rite and also performing the rite itself.[38] Pigs, seaweed from the kia'i's pond, and 'ilima are appropriate mōhai for mo'o. Because menstruating women were prohibited from being in the fishpond or on its walls, perhaps this is why Mahoe had her grandson take the piglet about the fishpond.

Last, Kalamainuʻu is credited with having invented the hīnālea fish trap in the Punaʻaikoaʻe tradition. For this reason, according to Kamakau, she is a tutelary deity for hīnālea fishers at Kaʻena Point.[39]

Economic-Political Function: Moʻo, War and Politics, and Aliʻi ʻAi Aupuni

Walinuʻu, Walimānoanoa, Kalamainuʻu, Kihawahine, and Waka are among the moʻo akua wāhine that aliʻi wahine honored.[40] The first four are especially noted for being associated with war and politics.[41] Aliʻi ʻai aupuni worshipped them for their economic-political value. "Aliʻi ʻai aupuni" refers to aliʻi who are supreme rulers. "ʻAi" denotes "to eat" but also "destroy, or consume," and thus its figurative meaning is "to rule, reign, or enjoy the privileges and exercise the responsibilities of rule." "Aupuni" refers to an area independently governed, whether an ahupuaʻa (a district), a moku (district containing several ahupuaʻa), a mokupuni (an island), or several mokupuni. Aliʻi ʻai aupuni believed that these moʻo akua wahine could preserve their reigns, bring prosperity to the land over which they ruled, and help them expand their territories. Aliʻi ʻai aupuni coveted resource-rich areas for their economic and political value. As they took control of such areas, their wealth and power increased. These places could sustain a bigger population, and people are another economic resource. A valley with numerous freshwater sources could contain numerous loʻi kalo (irrigated taro terraces). Coastlines with good fishing grounds meant more and better access to protein. Moreover, farmers and fishers contributed a part of their products to royal households. Access to koa-tree forests meant more war canoes because koa trunks, which were extremely tall and thick, were used to build these long canoes. Aliʻi who controlled resource-rich areas could attract more specialists to their courts, such as experts in prophecy, medicine, canoe construction, heiau construction, and of course, more warriors.

It comes naturally to wonder why moʻo are associated with war and politics, but the ʻŌiwi who discussed them in their treatises never addressed this point. I noted this lacuna early on in my research and mentioned it to Kalei Nuʻuhiwa, who then offered this cogent explanation. Because these moʻo are akua wai, their association with war and politics probably has to do with the fact that they are guardians of freshwater sources. An ahupua'a, she explains, has to have at least one major water source. Mo'o akua have the power to increase water sources or dry them up completely.[42] As my research progressed and I acquired a deeper understanding of mo'o, I thought of another reason, one that builds upon Nu'uhiwa's insight. Mo'o embody and symbolize continuity—"the unbroken and consistent existence or operation of something over a period of time" or "a state of stability and the absence of disruption."[43] This would account for why ruling ali'i believed that these mo'o—Walinu'u, Walimānoanoa, Kalamainu'u, and Kihawahine—who are kumupa'a, or ancestors mai ka pō mai (from the realm of gods—i.e., immemorial) had the power to preserve and maintain their rule. As water deities, mo'o embody the water cycle, without which life as we know it would not continue. Flowing water can also stand as a symbol for the flux of time and thus continuity. As reptilian deities, mo'o embody continuity in the sense of an unbroken lineage. "Mo'o" is the prefix of mo'okū'auhau (genealogy or lineage) and lineage-related terms. As Pukui explains: "*Mo'o* or *kuamo'o* means succession, *mo'okupuna* the succession of ancestors, and *mo'oku'auhau* [sic] the story or telling of genealogy. . . . The imagery of a *mo'o* (lizard, with vertebrae visible) and *kua mo'o* (vertebrate backbone) is apt and obvious as a simile for sequence of descendants in contiguous unbroken articulation."[44] This reasoning can also be applied to the lizard's brindled markings, which also evoke a series or sequence, and thus continuity.

A brindled pattern has uniform darker markings—stripes, lines, spots—that are part of but also stand out against the lighter background of which they are part. This pattern is reversed in two skink species. Like a brindled pattern, the other things that are termed "mo'o" are either part of a longer series or a smaller part of something larger. A mo'o, short for "mo'olelo," is a series of words—a story. A grandchild—a mo'o—is part of a longer lineage; the young of animals such as pigs and dogs are also termed "mo'o"; smaller pieces of kapa—mo'o—will be beaten together to create a larger one; a smaller land division—a mo'o—is part of a larger land section, which is within yet another larger land section; a narrow path or track—a mo'o—is part of and stands out against the land; a raised surface extending lengthwise between irrigation canals—a mo'o—is part of and stands out against the immediate area; a mountain ridge—a mo'o—is the uppermost part of a mountain, which stands out against the sky; a gunwale strake—a mo'o—is the upper edge of a canoe, which stands out against sea and sky.[45]

Moreover, the lizard kino lau of moʻo akua, in this case geckos and skinks, are able to regrow their tails. This ability is a good metaphor for regeneration. Given that the lizard backbone represents an unbroken genealogy, then its tail can stand for new generations. Thus, the lizard's head symbolizes the ancestral source or beginning of the genealogy, the backbone, the genealogy's continuity over countless generations, and the tail, the newest generation. The lizard can also shed its skin, yet another symbol of regeneration.

Moʻoinanea is the ultimate expression of the moʻo as representative of kuamoʻo and moʻokūʻauhau. She is the origin of all moʻo, having either birthed them or created them. And, in the tradition of Haʻinākolo, she allows her moʻopuna, Haʻinākolo, to use her sacred back as a bridge so that she can meet Keanini, the man who will become her kāne.[46] This couple will go on to have children and thus contribute to preserving Moʻoinanea's lineage. Moreover, she sheds her tail, her real form, and gives it to her moʻopuna, ʻAukelenuiaʻīkū and Nāmakaokahaʻi, after which it then becomes weapons that will help them best their enemies and thus survive.

The importance of moʻo wāhine as akua of war and politics cannot be overemphasized. Kamehameha I, who accomplished the unprecedented feat of uniting all the Hawaiian Islands under his rule, worshipped these moʻo wahine for their power to help him in his quest. He honored them in the kapu loulu, in which only akua wāhine were worshipped, which was a concluding rite in the larger complex of luakini ceremonies dedicated to war and politics to divine and petition for a war's positive outcome and to preserve a kingdom.[47] ʻĪʻī describes the kapu loulu in great detail, which includes the origin account about the kiʻi for Kalamainuʻu-Kihawahine and Haumea-Kāmehaʻikana-Walinuʻu. Here is my translation of the rest of his account concerning the rites surrounding the kiʻi of those aforementioned akua wāhine:

> When their kiʻi were brought before the assembly, they looked exactly as the story describes them. This was when the kahuna of Hale o Papa said the appropriate prayer to lift the kapu of the loulu before the assembly. Before he used his fire plough to light a fire, the dogs and pigs intended as sacrifices were killed. At that point, the assembly was still and quiet as nā Wahine Poʻo Aupuni (ruling aliʻi wāhine, the wāhine who headed the kingdom) brought forth their fine white malo, which were destined to clothe the kiʻi. The kahuna leading the malo procession carried a piglet, which squealed in the kahuna's arms. The kahuna held one end of the

malo and carried the piglet while the ali'i wahine to whom that malo and piglet belonged held the other end in her right hand. She said the 'āmama (prayer that lifts a kapu) to end the ceremony in front of the assembly and the ali'i. The kahuna who led this malo procession and rite came from the assembly, and sometimes there were more of them. When the ali'i's malo procession rite was completed, then their pigs were taken for the deities. After the 'āmama, they each returned to the place where they had previously sat, like Keākealani.

After the dogs had been cooked in the imu and then eaten during the feast, the kahuna of Hale o Papa stood and prayed. When the kahuna was done, the ali'i stood to say the 'āmama. The kahuna then replied:

> Let the disgraced one shut the lips and be silent.
> Be—silent—
> Let the godless one who breaks kapu and eats freely be silent.
> Let the wrongdoer shut the lips and be silent.
> Be—silent—

In this way did the kahuna reply to each, and thus did the assembly answer in unison until it was finished. The remainder of the feast and offerings were laid upon the lele altar along with the mai'a pōpō'ulu (roundish yellow banana with pinkish-orange flesh) and mai'a iholena (small yellow banana with pinkish-orange flesh), the things appropriate for that lele altar, which was for akua wahine.[48]

Here, 'Ī'ī notes that these banana species, pōpō'ulu and iholena, are appropriate mōhai for female deities. This point requires further commentary given this ritual's significance—a ritual for ali'i wāhine to honor akua wāhine—but first, I need to provide the context for it.

For countless centuries, the state religion, often referred to as the 'Ai Kapu, permeated and regulated nearly every aspect of 'Ōiwi existence and made religion and politics inseparable. The 'Ai Kapu derived its name from the belief that 'ai (food and food consumption) was kapu (sacred and must therefore be regulated). Its defining features were that men and women could not eat together, and women could not eat certain foods. These foods included pork, whale, shark, ulua (certain *Caranx* species), porpoise, sea turtle, manta, stingray, red fish such as kūmū, most species of coconuts and bananas, and poi made from 'ele'ele and 'ula'ula taro.[49]

The 'Ai Kapu had been in place for so long that it was accorded a mythic origin. A tradition credits Wākea and his kahuna as its devisors, which would situate the 'Ai Kapu's inception at the dawn of Hawaiian history.[50] Wākea and Papa have a daughter, Ho'ohokukalani. Wākea wants to have sex with her and keep it secret from Papa, so the kahuna creates a new religious system. It requires Papa and Wākea to each isolate themselves on certain nights to perform rituals. Papa agrees because Wākea tells her that the akua revealed this new system to the kahuna and commanded him to put it into practice at once. This ploy allows Wākea to have sex with their daughter on the nights he is away to perform his rituals and on the nights Papa is away to perform hers. When Papa discovers he has slept with their daughter, she is furious and they separate. Wākea then establishes what foods Papa may and may not eat and informs her that men and women cannot eat together.[51]

There are two points I want to make about this origin account, which pertain to my commentary on 'Ī'ī's treatise. First, while the story explains why Wākea and his kahuna created the 'Ai Kapu, it does not say why these particular foods were prohibited. The reason for this restriction, according to Pukui and Lilikalā Kame'eleihiwa, is because these foods are the kino lau of primary akua kāne, such as Kanaloa (whale, shark, ulua, possibly sea turtles, manta and stingrays, bananas), Kū (coconuts, kūmū), and Lono (pig, kūmū), which were used in solemn ceremonies, some of which pertained to these akua.[52] Second, as the origin account reveals, the 'Ai Kapu is an arbitrary religious innovation—a scheme two immoral men devised to deceive a wahine so that her kāne could have sex with their daughter. In terms of politics of representation and gender discourse, this point is significant. This origin story, unlike historical treastises on the 'Ai Kapu, does not portray women as inferior to men in some way. The historical premise of the 'Ai Kapu, according to Kamakau, is as follows:

> Ua kapu ka ai pu o ke kane me ka wahine, ma ka hoomana akua keia hookaawale ana i na mea koko a me na mea haumia a ua hookaawale ia na mea paumaele a pau, a o na mea maemae oia ko ke akua makemake.[53]

> It was forbidden for men and women to eat together, which was a religious edict that required segregating those who bleed and who are impure, and thus all those who were polluted were kept separate. The god wanted only those who were pure.

Thus, the 'Ai Kapu is founded on a gender-biased view of women being impure because they menstruate, and consequently, from a ritual-related standpoint, male akua consider women inferior to men. This belief is a cultural construct—there is no biological basis to support the claim that menstruation is haumia. In short, there is more than one way to view menstruation, and, consequently, more than one way to interpret the 'Ai Kapu. Before I continue I should note that scientific explanations are irrelevant here because we are dealing with constructs that are cultural-religious. My aim is to offer a wahine-informed cultural-religious interpretation.

"'Ula" denotes "sacred" but it also means "red," which is considered a sacred color, perhaps because it recalls blood and therefore life.[54] Kame'eleihiwa makes this correlation: "With red being the color of sanctity, as well as the color of menstrual blood, this may have been the time when women were kapu, or sacred; certainly it is the time when we are most sensitive to the suggestions of the ancestors."[55] Notably, wāhine were believed to be at their most fertile just after their menses. From the "menses-as-haumia" viewpoint, this was when wāhine were less impure. From the "menses-as-mana" standpoint, wāhine are at their most powerful spiritually when they are menstruating (i.e., female sexual mana easily overcomes male sexual mana).

Kame'eleihiwa observes that the 'Ai Kapu's purpose is to segregate "the sacred male element from the dangerous female, thus creating order in the world."[56] Her conclusion is based on a detailed argument supported by extensive evidence.[57] This would account for why kino lau of akua kāne were prohibited to women. Here, Kame'eleihiwa offers a cogent explanation, one that no one else has ever given—namely, that four of these kino lau are priapic:

> The pig is a *kinolau* of the fertility *Akua* Lono and is certainly a male symbol because its practice of rooting, in an inherently female earth, is a common Hawaiian sexual metaphor. At the heiau or temple, too, a pig is a substitute for a man. The coconut, on the other hand, is said to be a man whose head is planted in the ground while his penis and testicles dangle above. The coconut tree is also a mystical body of the war *Akua* Kū. The banana, a *kinolau* of Kanaloa, *Akua* of the ocean, has a large purple flower that droops towards the ground in a classically phallic fashion, and the fruit itself has a phallic shape. The banana trunk was also used in spear-throwing practice to symbolize a man. Certain fish, usually those red in color and also *aku* (bonito) were *kapu*

to women because they were used in sacrifices to the *Akua*. Red fish
also represented the fishing Akua Kūʻula (Kū of the red color).

For women to eat these foods would not only allow their mana
to defile the sacrifice to the male Akua, but would also encourage them
to devour male sexual prowess. . . . Given that the word ʻai means "to
eat, to devour" and also "to rule and to control," if women ate the
kinolau of these Akua, they would gain the mana to rule the domains
represented by these Akua; women could then rule male sexual prowess, including war, agriculture, ocean travel, and deep-sea fishing. What
would be left for men to do?[58]

We can apply Kameʻeleihiwa's reasoning about phallic symbols to
the bananas and coconut that Papa was permitted to eat, which are the
pōpōʻulu and iholena bananas, and the niuhiwa. Unlike other bananas,
the pōpōʻulu's roundish-oblong shape does not closely resemble a phallus. The iholena is somewhat phallic, but it is thicker in the middle with
ends that taper into points, which could, for some minds, recall prominent nipples on breasts. Moreover, the flesh of both is a pale pink tinged
with orange. Perhaps pink recalls diluted blood, which may be why
women were allowed to eat these kinds of bananas.

Now that I have provided the context for ʻĪʻī's observation about
appropriate mōhai for akua wāhine, I can return to my examination of
his treatise. As women were deemed haumia, they were prohibited from
entering the luakini compound where akua kāne were worshipped, as
noted in chapter 4. The only exceptions were aliʻi wahine ʻai aupuni,
such as Keākealaniwahine, whom ʻĪʻī mentions. Indeed, the Hale o Papa,
where aliʻi wāhine performed the kapu loulu, was located just outside
the luakini compound. Yet the kapu loulu was the closing rite of the
larger complex of luakini-related ceremonies. As Kameʻeleihiwa observes, "Female sanction was important in every major ceremony, in the
ʻAha and in the Makahiki, so that a women's temple, the Hale o Papa,
was attached to every important male *heiau*."[59] As she also points out,
"The ʻAikapu religion ends only when the women decide that it
should."[60] Here, she is referring to Kamehameha I's wāhine, Keōpūolani
and Kaʻahumanu. After their kāne died in 1819 and their son Liholiho
became Kamehameha II, they convinced him to abolish the ʻAi Kapu.[61]
Kameʻeleihiwa's observation about male and female mana in regard to
balance in the natural and spiritual world, which are one and the same
in Hawaiian thought, is a more persuasive interpretation of the principles grounding the ʻAi Kapu than that of Kamakau, which posits

wāhine-as-haumia as its premise. Historical context is everything. Both Kamakau and Kame'eleihiwa are esteemed historians in their respective periods, but one is a nineteenth-century Hawaiian man who embraced Christianity and wrote during a time of intense Christian indoctrination, while the other is a twenty-first-century Hawaiian woman who proudly proclaims to be "pagan" and writes during a time when Christian- and gender-inflected bias is scrutinized.

Here, I return to my discussion of Walinu'u, Walimānoanoa, Kalamainu'u, and Kihawahine. Not much is known about the first two, who are usually cited as a pair, other than what I have already shared. This lack of commentary suggests they are older akua who, as time passed, were supplanted by other mo'o akua, such as Kihawahine. Here, I return to the topic of the implicit association that 'Ī'ī made between Kalamainu'u and Kihawahine when he presented them as "Kalamainuu (Kihawahine)," as well as their link to an ali'i wahine named Kalā'aiheana.

There are two main competing traditions about Kihawahine's origins. Kihawahine is either Pi'ilani's (a famous ruling ali'i of Maui) daughter by Lā'ielohelohe or Pi'ilani's ancestor. In the first, a version of the Kihapi'ilani tradition published by Abraham Fornander states that Pi'ilani and Lā'ielohelohe had four children: Lonoapi'i, Pi'ikea, Kihawahine, and Kihapi'ilani.[62] As for Kihawahine, the account notes, "Oia ke 'kua moo e olelo ia nei i keia wa, o Kihawahine" (She is the mo'o deity now spoken of as Kihawahine).[63] This is the only data given for her. According to a genealogy that Kamakau presents, Pi'ilani and Lā'ielohelohe also had four children, but their birth order and one of the children's name differ: Lonoapi'ilani, Pi'ikea, Kalā'aiheana, and Kihapi'ilani.[64] The connection between Kalamainu'u, Kihawahine, and Kalā'aiheana becomes clear when Kamakau explains, "Ua kakuai ia kekahi alii wahine o ka mokupuni o Maui o Kihawahine ka inoa, a ua kakuai ia iloko o Kalamainuu a ua lilo i akua kino moo" (An ali'i wahine of Maui Island named Kihawahine underwent the kākū'ai rite, and was transfigured into Kalamainu'u and became a deity with a mo'o form).[65] Another genealogy switches the birth order: Pi'ikea (f), Lonoapi'ilani (m), Kalā'aiheana (f), and Kihapi'ilani (m).[66] While neither of these genealogies show that Kihawahine-Kalā'aiheana had children, it does not necessarily mean she did not have them.

Yet another genealogy reports these same four children, but Kalā'aiheana is reported as Kalaniheana.[67] From Kalaniheana's union with Kamalama is born NihoaKamalama. From NihoaKamalama's union with Kuihewakanaloahano are born Kuwalu, Kahokumaka, and

Maluna.[68] Esther T. Mookini shared a genealogy in which Kalāʻaiheana and Kamalama's child is Nihoa Kamalama, who had three children with Kuihewakanaloahano: Maluna, Kahakumaka, and Kualu.[69] As per this chart, Queen Liliʻuokalani is Kalāʻaiheana-Kihawahine's descendant via her mother, Keohokalole, whose ancestor is Maluna.[70]

Many genealogies appear in the Hawaiian-language newspapers, but nearly all of them fail to mention Kihawahine or Kalāʻaiheana. It comes naturally to wonder why this is so. The reason may have, at least in part, to do with her special status, as Paul Christiaan Klieger reports:

> Famed Hawaiian specialist Mary Kawena Pukui once told historian Dorothy Barrère that the name Kihawahine, referring to Kalāʻaiheana, daughter of Piʻilani, was not mentioned in the genealogies because she was an ʻeʻepa—a human born with some sort of supernatural difference. The distinction could be a special mental or physical ability or disability. As a result, ʻeʻepa were usually not recorded in mundane genealogy. Such people would often become trickster spirits upon death. Pukui also maintained the legend that Kihawahine Kalāʻaiheana was deified and made a moʻo goddess upon her death, with a home at Mauoni pond on Maui.[71]

As for Kihawahine being cited as Piʻilani's ancestor, this is evidenced in a treatise by Pakele, which shows that the worship of Kihawahine can be traced back to at least Loʻe, a ruling aliʻi of West Maui. From Loʻe, "he hoolaha wale no kona mau Akua i na'lii ame ko na kanaka mau Akua pu kekahi" (his Gods spread out to [other] aliʻi and people becoming their Gods too).[72] Loʻe was the direct ancestor of many ruling aliʻi of Maui and, through their unions with others, also of aliʻi from other islands.[73] Between Loʻe and his descendant Piʻilani, there are six generations.[74] Manu's version of the Kihapiʻilani tradition also suggests that Piʻilani's ancestors worshipped Kihawahine:

> O keia moo o Kihawahine, he akua kahiko keia mai na kupuna mai o ua mau alii la, a hiki mai i ko laua mau makua, oia o Piilani a ma ka inoa o keia moo i kapaia iho ai o Kihapiilani.

> This moʻo Kihawahine, this is an ancient god from the ancestors of those aliʻi [Lonoapiʻilani and Kihapiʻilani], to their parents, Piʻilani [and Lāʻielohelohe], and Kihapiʻilani was named after this moʻo.[75]

Even were we to translate "mai nā kūpuna mai" as "from the grandparents" rather than "from the ancestors," the fact remains that here Kihawahine's origin precedes that of Lonoapi'ilani and Kihaapi'ilani. An unsigned version of this tradition, very similar to Manu's, does not note Kihawahine's origin or her connection to Pi'ilani, merely that she was these brothers' akua.[76]

Whether Kihawahine was Pi'ilani's ancestor or his daughter, she was clearly an established deity when Kamehameha I began his quest to conquer the islands. His contemporary, Keaulumoku, a high-ranking ali'i famed for his chant compositions, composed a prophecy-prayer about Kamehameha's rise to power and the fall of Keōua, which invokes Kihawahine.[77] In the following lines, he asks her to aid Kamehameha:

E Kiha, e Kihawahine mana (O Kiha, O Kihawahine divinely powerful),
E Kihawahine mana ia ke poo (O Kihawahine divinely powerful,
   the leader)
I nui ka mana i ko oukou Haku (Increase the mana of your Lord).[78]

Notably, Kamehameha asked for and received permission to take Kihawahine's descendant and the highest-ranking ali'i wahine of her time, Keōpūolani, as his wahine. In doing so, he also strengthened his ties to Kihawahine.[79] His children by Keōpūolani—Liholiho, Kauikeaouli, and Nāhi'ena'ena—secured that connection. Kamakau notes that when Kamehameha decided to take O'ahu, he invoked Kalamainu'u and Kihawahine:

E ai aku oe ia Oahu, ia ku a ka hale o ko akua i ka lai o Waikiki, he hale puaniu no Kala—Kalamainuu no ko akua no Kihawahine.[80]

If you eat [conquer] O'ahu, [I will] build a house for your god in the calm of Waikīkī, a coconut blossom house for Kala—Kalamainu'u, for your deity, for Kihawahine.

Kamehameha then transformed Kihawahine into a national deity when he united the islands and incorporated her into the group of akua who were carried around the island during the Makahiki festival circuit.[81] When her image was carried to a canoe, the kahuna would announce, "Kapu O! Mo–e Kapu O! Moe i ke kapu o Kiha-wahine moe!" (Kapu, Oh! Prostrating Kapu, Oh! Prostrate for the kapu of Kihawahine, prostrate!). Everyone in the vicinity immediately prostrated themselves, even those on canoes. Anyone who failed to do so was killed.[82]

Ki'i of Kihawahine have been variously described. As we have seen, 'Ī'ī says the ki'i in the Hale o Papa was carved to show that she was missing an eye. Kamakau says that sometimes the hair of her ki'i was "pukai ia" (bleached with lime).[83] In 1885, physician Eduard Arning acquired a ki'i of Kihawahine in Hawai'i, which is on display in the Berlin Ethnologisches Museum. In Arning's monographs, according to Adrienne L. Kaeppler, "Arning recounts the occasion when planter Herbert Purvis, with two Hawaiian guides, swam in shark-infested waters on the Hamakua coast to procure sculptures of two Hawaiian gods. The Hawaiians were able to reach the pit which held two sculptures and brought them back for Arning. One of these, a kneeling female figure called '*Kihawahine*,' was so admired by King Kalākaua that he had R. C. Barnfield make a drawing of it . . . before Arning took the sculpture back to Berlin" (figure 5.1).[84] The other ki'i is Kāmeha'ikana according to "knowledgeable Hawaiians."[85]

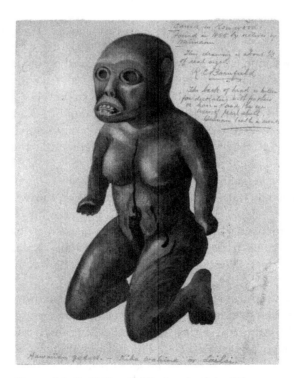

Figure 5.1. R. C. Barnfield's sketch of the Kihawahine ki'i. Courtesy of the Bishop Museum Archive (www.bishopmuseum.org).

Barnfield's drawing and photos of Kihawahine's ki'i from different angles are included in a volume showcasing Arning's research on and collection of artifacts in the Berlin Ethnologisches Museum's collection. Kaeppler, Mark Schindlbeck, and Gisela E. Speidel, who edited this volume, give the following description of this ki'i:

> The sculpture of the goddess . . . is carved with great craftsmanship out of kou wood; it is realistically portrayed and well-proportioned except for the arms, which are too small. The figure is kneeling, a posture unknown otherwise among Hawaiian gods; the upper body is straight; the arms hang down the sides; and the head bends slightly forward. The right foot is missing, as are the eyes, which had been inlaid with mother-of-pearl. When H. Purvis found the sculpture, one of the eyes was still there, but unfortunately it was later lost. Into the protruding mouth, twelve human teeth had been mounted of which six are still there (the other six have been replaced). Some wood between the navel and the well-defined genitals has rotted. The opening at the back of the head, too, has gotten bigger because the wood around the artificial hollow has rotted. Otherwise, the 43-cm-tall [16.9 inches] figure is well-preserved compared with other Hawaiian sculptures of gods. Striking among the facial features are the pronounced prognathism; the very flat forehead; and, for a female, the unnatural, bull-like neck. The ears are only hinted at with shells, elongated at the top and pressed flat against the sides of the head. The nose recedes and the sides of the nostrils are only suggested. These departures from human traits together with the human body give the head an animal-like, ape-like expression. Below the ears and the hole at the back of the head is a row of holes, probably for fastening bundles of hair. The hole near the *Mons Veneris* may have also been originally for fastening hair.[86]

While this entry accurately describes the sculpture's features, it fails to connect them to Kihawahine's status as a mo'o akua. From my perspective, the ki'i captures her reptilian nature and may be intended to depict her in the process of transformation from human to mo'o, which would account for her position and features. As she changes to a reptile, she is brought to her knees and her head moves forward because a lizard's body hugs the ground and its head is horizontal to its body. Her arms are smaller because they are changing to lizard limbs, which are shorter in relation to its body. As her head becomes reptilian, her neck thickens, her jaws begin to project and lengthen, her human nose and ears begin to vanish, and her skull flattens. As for the report that only one mother-of-pearl inlay for her eyes was found, perhaps there had only ever been one, which would match the style of the one-eyed Kihawahine ki'i 'Ī'ī described.

Calling Forth Kihawahine

A detailed and lengthy description of a ritual to summon Kihawahine is found in two versions of the Kihapi'ilani tradition, neither of which have been translated into English for the public. The first version is unsigned (1870), and the second is by Manu (1884). This section has four parts: "Context" (1870 version), "Ritual Protocol" (1870 version), "The Ritual and Its Political Consequences" (Manu's version), and "Conclusion." Due to space constraints, I only offer my translations and translative summaries.

Context. Kihapi'ilani wants to call up Kihawahine to extract revenge upon his older brother, Lonoapi'i. These men are the sons of Pi'ilani, who rules over all of Maui. When their father dies, Lonoapi'i takes his place as ruler of Maui. Lonoapi'i takes every opportunity to humiliate Kihapi'ilani until finally, Kihapi'ilani decides to seek help from the kahuna who cares for Kihawahine, their ancestor. The kahuna tells him that it will be an enterprise of some magnitude to end this abuse but that it will come about through Kihawahine. He warns Kihapi'ilani not to show fear when he sees her: "He akua mana ke akua o olua a'u e malama nei, a oia no ka mea i lilo ai ko kaikuaana i alii hoi o Maui" (Your god whom I attend is a powerful god, and she is the instrument by which your older brother became ruler of Maui). Lonoapi'i also visits the kahuna to ask why the fishermen give Kihawahine the first catch and not him, their ruler. This shows that Lonoapi'i has very little respect for her. Lonoapi'i asks him to call up Kihawahine. The kahuna says that he told his younger brother that their god is not a just god, and were they to see her many different forms, they would understand that she is vicious and dreadful. Lonoapi'i scoffs and denies that he will feel fear when he sees her.[87]

Ritual protocol. A few days after Kihapi'ilani visits the kahuna, Lonoapi'i tells the kahuna that he wants to see Kihawahine. The kahuna informs him that proper protocol must be followed:

> In a single day, the people must go upland to get wood for the house, and all the pillars to finish the house; on that same day the pili grass

must be pulled and thatched to finish the house; and on that very day, a pig must be baked in the imu along with all the other items; only when you have all of these things I have told you readied, then, you will see your god; and you must seek the kapa dyed in turmeric and the cotton plant; and if you obtain all these things within the same day, then, you shall tell me.[88]

The house was built on the islet of Moku'ula, which is where Kihawa-hine lived in an underwater cave. The pigs and dogs were baked in the imu built within the house itself. This next passage shows the care with which everything was done:

This was the process by which preparations for the imu were carried out. The usual covering of ti leaves (*Cordyline fruticosa*) with the stems tied together and spread fanwise was not used. Instead, finely woven mats made of makaloa sedge (*Cyperus laevigatus*) were overlapped so that they covered the imu. Atop this layer two kapa quilts dyed with the ma'o cotton plant (*Gossypium tomentosum*) were laid. The stones used to weigh them down were not normal stones according to what was heard. This account says that it took five people to carry only one stone, and thus was this imu encircled.

When the imu setup was finished, mats were spread out until they covered the floor inside the house. Then, kapa dyed with ma'o and 'ōlena were hung on the walls; the kahuna did these things because these were things associated with that mo'o. When these things were done, the kahuna sent someone to fetch Lonoapi'i and Kihapi'ilani.[89]

The ritual and its political consequences. The kahuna told them that when they saw Kihawahine they were not to show fear and that whoever showed fear and fled would become impoverished, but whoever remained would rule Maui.[90] Lonoapi'i scoffed and told him to get on with the ritual and so he did. The kahuna began the first prayer. When it was finished, he prayed anew, and when the prayer was done, he spoke, "I will begin to pray again, then you should look carefully up at the house rafters to see a white thing like a spider's egg hanging in the middle and when it descends like a spider web until it is above the center of the imu, it will vanish. When you have seen the strange thing, this is your deity, and you must tell me after I am finished praying." Their response was to simply agree. When the kahuna finished speaking, he began to pray.[91]

This prayer was of a very sacred and solemn nature, no movement and no conversing until it was ended. At that very moment they (the two brothers) carefully observed the rafters of the house. Soon afterward, they saw the thing about which the kahuna had spoken. A little spider web released forth, unfolding like a rainbow until it was situated right above the imu. The white thing descended rapidly and settled atop the imu and then immediately disappeared. They listened to the kahuna's prayer. Slowly, the kahuna's voice lessened in volume to just a whisper, and then the whispering ceased, just moving his lips as his eyes bulged from the strain of his efforts, which continued until he finished the prayer.

During the kahuna's prayer, the moʻo ate all the imu's contents, and all the while the kapa covering the imu rose and shifted as if a person were inside, and thus the stones holding down the kapa were pointless. At that very moment, the moʻo made the kapa and mats fly up, which moved like a female hula dancer, but the moʻo's form and actual body could not be seen. Then the kahuna asked the aliʻi what they had seen and they replied, "We saw the things you spoke of earlier, but here is something new, that spider web from the rafters, it was like a rainbow, and as we observed it, it settled upon the imu."[92]

When the kahuna heard this, he told them, "This is the moment that you will see your deity, therefore, if you feel fear, then say so now, beforehand, so it will not be clearly seen." Upon hearing these words, they experienced an initial sense of fear but it soon lessened. Lonoapiʻi spoke, "Whatever indeed is there to flee from, we have come to see the akua." After these words, the kahuna had nothing more to say. At that point, the kahuna grabbed the corner of the kapa with which he had covered the top of the imu and opened it, and there indeed was that moʻo lying inside, its skin like that of an ʻūhā eel but much darker and incomparably shiny.

At that very moment, the moʻo turned its eyes toward them, revealing its full, terrifying nature, and indeed it was incredibly frightening. When Lonoapiʻi witnessed their deity, who was one of their ancestors, he shouted out, "Alas! Alas!! This shall be my death, I thought this was a just god, instead it is monstrous." And then he fled the house. Terrified, he ran to the waters of Mokuhinia and swam with all his might until he reached the shore, where he quickly ran to his house—never to return again to Mokuʻula.

Meanwhile, Kihapiʻilani continued to sit, and with great fortitude, suppressed his fear of the moʻo. Kihawahine revealed all of her eerie forms to him, but he was courageous and persevered so that he could take revenge on his brother. As the mo'o climbed on Kihapi'ilani, the kahuna reminded him, "Be steadfast against the fear so that vengeance may be had, for yours is an akua of power, which is why the ali'i before you honored and cared for her, and this deity, Kihawahine, is a royal akua, a ruling god, which you should take note of, so tolerate your fear." After the mo'o's extraordinary displays, she ran off to the end of the house and disappeared under one of the mats covering the walls. Kihapi'ilani heard water splash, and shortly thereafter, Kihawahine returned in her human form. Kihapi'ilani saw a fine young woman, a true beauty, with a lei 'āpiki on her head. The lei 'āpiki is the 'ilima lei, called such because it was said to attract mischievous spirits. This beautiful apparition was a rather fair-skinned woman and Kihapi'ilani's fear abated.[93]

Conclusion. As foretold, after Kihapi'ilani faces Kihawahine without fear, he supplants his brother as ruler of Maui and rises to greatness while Lonoapi'i, destitute, fades into oblivion.

The Belief in Mo'o Akua Continues

Overwhelming evidence proves that many 'Ōiwi continued to believe in mo'o akua. Reports in Hawaiian- and English-language newspapers of the Hawaiian Kingdom, and after it was dissolved, attest to and criticize this continued belief. Ethnographical research carried out from the 1930s to the 1980s and beyond also provides proof. Among these projects are McAllister's research on archaeological sites of O'ahu in 1930; Handy and Pukui's interviews with kama'āina of Ka'ū, Hawai'i; Pukui's conversations with kūpuna across the islands from the 1930s to the 1970s; Charles Langlas' interviews with kama'āina of Kalapana, Hawai'i, in the 1990s; Kepā and Onaona Maly's conversations with kūpuna in the 2000s; and many others. I have shared information from these different resources throughout this book. To these, I would add my own personal and familial mo'o-related beliefs and experiences and conversations with 'Ōiwi. In this section, I share a few notable examples of commentary from various sources on mo'o-related beliefs and practices, which I have not shared or cited in previous chapters.

On June 12, 1861, forty-one years after the missionaries came to Hawai'i to Christianize Hawaiians, T. W. Kaikuaana wrote to the editors of *Ka Hae Hawaii* to report the near-drowning of a child, which was attributed to a mo'o. Here below is my translation of this lengthy account.

On the evening of the 7th of this month, which was a Friday, two small children were swimming at the Mokuhinia pool in Lahaina near the dock just as the sun was setting.

One child continued swimming, Lono being his name, almost eight years old and four feet tall. Not long after, the child was nowhere to be found, but his parents did not think that he had gone missing in the water.

Another woman, named Paʻahao, saw a long sea creature in the water, shaped like an aʻuaʻu [swordfish], its belly white, and she called out to the mother of the child, "There's a large fish in the water with a white belly." The mother, whose name was Kaʻohe, said, "Perhaps you've just seen a turtle." She spoke again, "Let's go look." When Kaʻohe looked, she saw what Paʻahao had seen. Paʻahao ran to look at the fish from the dock. Meanwhile, Kaʻohe continued watching it, and shortly after, Kaʻohe's eyes were dazzled by the water that had turned white, immediately after which the fish vanished from her sight. As for Paʻahao, when she reached the dock, the fish stirred up the dirt and disappeared completely.

Afterward, they wondered if perhaps Lono had disappeared into the water. The thought occurred to them that this was a moʻo, letting them know about Lono. The two of them searched by looking from the dock, but they could not see him. The child's father, Maalewa, arrived. He searched below the dock, and there he saw the child in the water at the spot where the fish had vanished, his body tangled amid the coral, and only his hair was visible on the water's surface. He pulled him up by his hair and saw that the child was nearly dead; his body was rigid from top to bottom, his eyes sightless, and his skin was slippery, and it was believed that this was due to the moʻo's slime. The parents massaged the child until seven o'clock that evening, until he seemed more comfortable; however, he had yet to speak; and shortly afterward, he did completely recover.

Therefore, this is something astonishing to know about; and our friends from Hawaiʻi to Kauaʻi should be informed about it.[94]

On February 15, 1862, *Ka Nupepa Kuokoa* published an editorial about a fishpond owner who complained that people were feeding the moʻo they believed inhabited it:

We thought that we had abandoned the things from ancient times—the traditional worship, and the devotion to false things with the acceptance of the righteous truth, but no! We have seen by the Prohibition by James Dawson (Kimo) in this paper that it has not ended. He told us that some people have brought dead Dogs, two or three perhaps, and deposited them in the water at the head of the fishpond that belongs to Kimo to feed the mo'o kupua that lives in that fishpond. Our error in judgement has not ended.[95]

On April 7, 1892, Joseph S. Emerson (1843–1930), vice president of the Hawaiian Historical Society (HHS), presented a paper, "The Lesser Hawaiian Gods," to HHS members. After noting the fall of the 'Ai Kapu, Emerson reports:

> But the ancient beliefs of the people, though greatly modified by the changed condition of the country, still continued to exert a powerful influence on their lives. There have always been those who have clung to the faith of their fathers, and who, in secret, have kept up the worship of their ancestral gods. From time to time the outward manifestations of heathen worship have cropped out [sic]. Especially from the year 1863, when Kamehameha V began his reign, up to the death of King Kalakaua in the latter part of the year 1890, has this tendency been more apparent. Under their royal favor and sanction, the heathen party took courage and publicly revived many of their ancient practices. . . . In the mind of the average Hawaiian, the old gods still exist as living and active beings, even though he may defy their power and abhor their worship. In justice to the race, however, we may add that all history shows that the uplifting of an entire people out of a degrading heathenism into the light and liberty of a Christian civilization is not, and in the nature of things cannot be, accomplished in one or two generations.[96]

In a world that often devalues Indigenous testimony, Emerson, a white man, a Christian, and a missionary's son, would be considered an expert witness on the continued belief in akua. His parents were John S. and Ursula Emerson, missionaries in Hawai'i.[97] His statement is important. Not only did some 'Ōiwi continue to believe in akua, but two kings instigated a revival that lasted for three decades. More significant perhaps is the admission that a portion of the population practiced Ho'omana secretly to avoid being ridiculed and punished for their beliefs and that even some 'Ōiwi Christians did not worship akua but believed they existed.

Among the akua J. Emerson discusses is Kihawahine, whom he describes as "the fiercest and most universally dreaded" 'aumakua:

> Everyone who is much acquainted with Hawaiians knows the dread, amounting oftentimes to terror, which the sight of a lizard will produce. "*Auwe ka moo!*" (Oh, the lizard!) as an expression of fear on the part of my Hawaiian associates was familiar to me in my childhood. The introduction of small-pox and leprosy among the Hawaiians is attributed by some of the kahunas to the implacable malice of *Kiha wahine* and her *moos*, who are charged with afflicting people with painful sores such as puha (ulcers) and alaala (scrofolous eruptions), and a general wasting of the system. When a person is taken with a chill on leaving the water it is said to be due to her ill will, expressed by the Hawaiians in these words: *No ke aloha ole o ka moo* [Because the mo'o has no aloha].[98]

Perhaps the link between mo'o akua and skin-related illness can be traced to its lizard kino lau. The lizard's rough skin—scales, brindled markings, and scabrous appearance when it is shedding its skin—may recall these skin afflictions.

Two mo'o are associated with illness in W. H. Rice's version of the Hi'iakaikapoliopele tradition. In their human forms, these mo'o are u'i launa 'ole (incredibly beautiful). When Hi'iaka sees them at a gathering at an ali'i's home in Hilo, they are wearing seaflower lei on their heads. Hi'iaka tells the ali'i, "Auhea oe; aole kela he mau wahine io, aka, he mau wahine akua kela, he moo, a o ka hanalepo no o laua; kaaweawe no la o kau iluna o ke poo, a manao aku nei oukou he lei puakai" (Listen, those are not real woman, but female deities, mo'o, and their dirty work is to disguise the illnesses poised upon their heads, which you all think are seaflower lei).[99] When the mo'o women become aware of Hi'iaka after she chants to get their attention, they flee the gathering: "Ua holo laua a hiki i ka nalowale ana o kekahi o laua ma ke kahawai o Wainanalii, a o kekahi hoi ma kekahi kahawai iho no e pili koke mai ana no" (They ran until one vanished into the Wainānāali'i stream, and the other into a stream near it). On the topic of mo'o and skin, people "on whose skin are patches suggestive of lizard's skin" were believed to be "akin" to mo'o akua.[100] In August of 2018, I asked three former students with whom I had become well acquainted over the years and for whom I felt a deep aloha to be my hānai daughters (informal adoption). At one point, within a year of our new family relationship, we noticed that our hands had begun to peel at the same time. We took this as a sign that my moʻo ʻaumakua was acknowledging their kinship with me and thus with her.

Most notably, less than a month after Queen Liliʻuokalani was deposed on January 17, 1893, by a small group of missionary descendants and white businessmen, the *Hawaiʻi Holomua* published a chant, "He Pule no ke Aliiaimoku" (A Prayer for the Ruling Aliʻi) dedicated to her and the nation she ruled, which first invokes twenty Hawaiian akua to protect the queen and the nation, including Kalamainuʻu and Kihawahine, and then the Christian God.[101] That the composer of this prayer invoked Hawaiian akua for protection is significant. First, it suggests that the composer believed in Hawaiian akua and in the Christian God and would thus be an example of Hawaiians merging two belief systems. Second, Liliʻuokalani was a Christian and stressed this fact in her memoir, *Hawaii's Story by Hawaii's Queen,* published in 1898 before the Hawaiian Islands were annexed to the US.[102] Third, whites in the islands often othered ʻŌiwi as uncivilized, and this prayer, imaginably in their eyes, published at a time when Hoʻomana was vehemently criticized, would have supported their claims. Fourth, for these reasons, although the composer did not sign the pule it was nonetheless a courageous political act. Other nineteenth-century ʻŌiwi, even those who were Christian, honored moʻo in chants, even if as poetic devices. Among the moʻo mentioned in chants in Hawaiian-language newspapers are Laniwahine, Kilioe, Hauwahine, Kalamainuʻu, and Kihawahine.[103]

In 1895 Daniel Kekau and Aola, who spent the night near a gulch upland of Pāhala in Kaʻū, Hawaiʻi, were woken up by a voice saying, "Eia la ke moe nei" (Here they are, sleeping). It was a moʻo, between five and six feet. As it moved to grab Aola, the men attempted to reason with it by claiming kinship: "E, he mau pulapula maua nau, nolaila, e ola maua" (Oh, we are your descendants, therefore, spare our lives). After that, the moʻo left them alone.[104] In 1901 a white man who was touring the "uninhabited southern section of the district of Puna" on Hawaiʻi with a Hawaiian guide claimed to have seen a moʻo one night while camping "in the mouth of a large cave" near the ocean. By the light of the moon, the man could clearly see this moʻo, which was not even fifty feet away. It was between five and six feet long. Frightened, he grabbed his gun to shoot it, but his guide stopped him. The guide explained that although he had never seen one, this creature was clearly a moʻo, and it might be Kihanuilūlūmoku. The guide then chanted to the moʻo as the two men slowly backed away to leave the area.[105] In 1918 J. A. Kahiona wrote to *Ka Nupepa Kuokoa* to complain about moʻo worship at Lāʻie and Waialua, Oʻahu.[106]

Pukui once spoke of her "Hawaiian friend, wealthy, traveled, socially sophisticated, who in the 1970s yet prayed to her *moʻo* (water creature) *ʻaumakua,* and who said with conviction that she had seen *Pele* standing on her land."[107] The subtext here seems to be that we should not equate a belief in moʻo with "backwardness." To do so is an instance of cultural-religious bias. I know many ʻŌiwi—family, friends, and acquaintances from all walks of life—who honor moʻo.

One of the more humorous moʻo-related stories that I have heard belongs to a dear friend, who shall remain unnamed. She was crossing a lava plain near a site where lava was flowing. She was part of a group going to pay their respects to Pele. She and a friend, a well-known kumu hula, were lagging behind the others when they both suddenly realized that they were the perfect mōhai for Pele given that they both honor moʻo akua. I feel the same when I am at Pele's home, Halemaʻumaʻu crater at Kīlauea. When I had to offer ʻawa to Pele at the edge of Halemaʻumaʻu crater as part of a ritual, I was secretly terrified that she'd take me and not the ʻawa I was carrying as a mōhai. I imagined "accidently" falling into the crater (i.e., Pele making that happen). I am sure the rest of the group wondered why I was bent nearly in two with my arms stretched straight out and slightly above my head as I carried the ʻapu (coconut cup) of ʻawa. I was making sure that Pele knew by my abased posture that I was well aware of my dubious position as a descendant of a moʻo and her dislike for them. That I am also kin to the Pele clan did not make me less fearful.

In the summer of 2017, during a community workday to help with Kaloko fishpond's restoration, I witnessed Ruth Aloua offer a chant to the fishpond's kiaʻi, a ritual she performs every time she visits Kaloko. Aloua heads the Hui Kaloko-Honokōhau organization "dedicated to protecting, awakening, and engaging with the Spirit of Kaloko-Honokōhau and all ancestral places through aloha ʻāina."[108] Because I had forgotten water from my land, which I named Moʻo Momona, to offer the kiaʻi moʻo, I chanted in Hawaiian as an offering and asked her to allow us safe passage into her loko iʻa so we could help restore it.

ʻŌiwi, past and present, deem moʻo to be fearsome deities, but they also believe that they can care deeply for their kin and protect them. Examples I have provided of moʻo who harm rather than protect the environment or humans represent the death-dealing powers of water but also the cycle of life and death. It should also be remembered that people transfigured their recently deceased family members into mo'o so they could continue to exist, albeit in another form, and protect the family forevermore as 'aumakua. Moreover, mo'olelo recall the different ways that mo'o who have never led a human existence protected and assisted their descendants, deities and humans alike. While it is true that the Hi'iakaikapoliopele tradition depicts mo'o as evil, it should be remembered that this is the volcano clan's perspective. From the mo'o perspective, Pele destroys their watery abodes and the rain forests in which they make their homes. Mo'o are also beneficent kia'i loko i'a, an important economic resource. Mo'o 'aumākua, kia'i loko i'a, and so forth are examples of the life-giving powers of mo'o. To perceive mo'o only as negative entities without acknowledging their positive aspects stands in opposition to 'Ōiwi understandings about balance in the natural and spiritual world and, furthermore, ignores that 'Ōiwi worshipped them, praised them in chants, that certain mo'o are ancestors of famous and esteemed ali'i, and that these same ali'i worshipped mo'o akua to preserve their reigns.

Epilogue

It is early morning, August 14, 2019. Today is the thirty-third day that a group of kiaʻi, about a hundred people, have been living in and running the puʻuhonua (refuge) at Puʻuhuluhulu (Huluhulu Hill). We are here to protect Mauna a Wākea, our sacred mauna (mountain), from further desecration by blocking the access road to its summit to prevent the construction of the Thirty Meter Telescope (TMT). In many ways our presence on the mauna represents a last stand in a long history of trying to protect the ʻāina—the foundation for our identity as a people, which shaped us physically, intellectually, and spiritually over the centuries. I am one of thirty-eight kūpuna who were arrested on July 17, a consequence of trying to protect the mauna. As I sit in the kūpuna tent, which blocks the access road, I watch as Calvin Hoe, a legendary activist, talented storyteller, and bamboo-nose-flute player and maker extraordinaire pulls out two thin, flat rocks. He taps the point of one rock on the other rock's surface. "Click. Click. Click." He looks at me and asks, "What does that sound like?" I think it sounds like a gecko chirping, but instead of answering, I just smile. "A moʻo," he says. He tells me that he uses these stones to evoke the call of a moʻo before telling moʻolelo but does not explain why because he knows I understand that there is a connection between the moʻo and moʻolelo. He hands the stones to me and tells me that they come from Waiʻololī stream. "Keep ʻem," he says. "You're a storyteller."

The stones' provenance is significant. Waiʻololī and Waiʻololā streams are paired as male and female water sources in a refrain in the Kumulipo. In that moment I have an epiphany, making a connection between moʻo akua, the Kumulipo, and our latest stand to protect the mauna. The first wā begins with a description of the dark, fathomless void as it is undergoing hulihia—a tremendous transformation. This is a time of creation—the earth is hot, the firmament is in turmoil, the sun emerges from the shadows and illuminates the moon, the first constellation (Pleiades) becomes visible, and the earth finally coalesces from the primordial slime. It is during this huliau (time of change) that Pō, the cosmic darkness, gives birth.[1] Out of chaos comes order. Thus begins our collective moʻokūʻauhau as a people. Today, that moʻokūʻauhau risks annihilation. If I had to choose an akua or class of akua who best embody our efforts to preserve that moʻokūʻauhau, it would be moʻo akua because they symbolize continuity, the epitome of which for ʻŌiwi is moʻokūʻauhau. The moʻo backbone stands for a continuous genealogy; its ability to regenerate its skin and regrow its tail represents regeneration. We are fighting to protect the vertebrae that constitute the backbone of who we are as a people—our ʻāina, ways of knowing and being, language, customs, and religious beliefs. Like the first wā in the Kumulipo, we are in the final phase of hulihia after an intellectual and spiritual awakening, cresting a wave of change as we strive to overturn the status quo. For the first time, there is a possibility that order will emerge from chaos—namely, two hundred years of American hegemony.

Mauna a Wākea has been a catalyst for the resurgence of Hoʻomana. Each day, kiaʻi participate in or lead ʻAha (religious ceremonies) four times a day. As a consequence, hundreds of ʻŌiwi have, for the first time in their lives, the opportunity to practice our religion together in public. Because thousands of visitors have witnessed or participated in these ʻAha and because the ʻAha have been videoed and made available to the public on the Puʻuhonua o Puʻuhuluhulu website, there is a growing awareness around the world about Hoʻomana and the fact that it is a living religion. These ʻAha manifest protective mana through prayer chants and hula (in this case, a form of kinetic prayer). Every day, I honor ka poʻe moʻo akua who embody continuity to "mana-fest" their protection for our people so that our moʻokūʻauhau prevails, and because they are water deities, I also ask them to safeguard the major aquifers located beneath Mauna a Wākea, which would be at risk were the construction of the TMT to begin.

"Hopena," like many words in our language, has different meanings, one of which is "conclusion," and this epilogue concludes this book. This work is more than a treatise on moʻo akua. It is a celebration of ʻŌiwi efforts to better understand the intellectual and spiritual thoughts of our ancestors. For nearly two centuries, we ʻŌiwi have been barraged with criticism about the invalidity of our beliefs, including those about moʻo akua. As Pukui, Haertig, and Lee note, "Told their gods were false, their rituals foolish, their dress, dances and manners unacceptable, their skills and talents unimportant, the Hawaiians as a people knew an 'identity crisis' long before the phrase was coined."[2] Beliefs *are* beliefs, and beliefs are often tied to religion, and there is no logical basis for arguing that one religion is more valid or better than another—any attempt to do so is purely a faith-based discourse and an expression of religious bias.

"Hopena" also means "outcome." Our culture informs our identity and studying moʻolelo, including moʻo-related moʻolelo, is an important part of our journey as we reclaim and celebrate being ʻŌiwi. When we become more knowledgeable about our culture, we also strengthen our identity—a critical outcome. Research on moʻolelo has an emotional aspect, and we have to understand that this is a consequence of the historical trauma that we have experienced and from which we are still recovering. Historically, Indigenous peoples' traumatic encounters have largely been with the nonnative other, beginning with early explorers, missionaries, and later, with settlers and their descendants. We ʻŌiwi have experienced demographic collapse from epidemics because of introduced diseases; land dispossession; the destruction of cultural and natural resources; the desecration of sacred sites; the loss of language, culture, and identity from imposed assimilation and blood quantum laws; the effects of being reduced to stereotypes; cultural appropriation; religious discrimination; sexual objectification; marginalization in our own homelands; hate speech; and being othered as uncivilized or even subhuman. Our moʻolelo can help us to heal from these injustices and inform our aloha ʻāina efforts that seek to rectify them.

"Hopena" also means "destiny." Through moʻolelo, our kūpuna speak to us, inspire us, and give us strength so that we can achieve our destiny, as individuals and as a collective. We become acquainted with them, and they teach us many lessons. They remind us that we come from a rich intellectual tradition and culture, that we are a remarkable and resilient people, and that the pursuit of excellence, knowledge, and wisdom is a part of who we are. Our culture has always been dynamic and thus always evolving. Crucially, past, present, and future are tightly woven in ʻŌiwi theory and practice. We adapt to the historical challenges we face so that we can continue to survive and thrive. As we look to the past for knowledge and inspiration on how to face the future, we are aware that we are tomorrow's ancestors, and future generations will look to us for guidance. This is our destiny until the last aloha ʻāina. E ola mau nō ka poʻe ʻŌiwi!

PART II

Catalog of Mo'o

This catalog is the product of more than a decade of extensive and meticulous research. It is by far the most comprehensive catalog of moʻo anywhere—and much more than a list, as I discuss gender and other aspects of moʻo not found in any other single source. I share data on 288 moʻo, which are listed alphabetically. In terms of gender, there are 137 female moʻo, 53 male moʻo, 93 gender unspecified, and 5 who are either male or female depending on the account. In some cases an entry is for a group of moʻo whose names and numbers are not specified. Thus, potentially, this list of moʻo exceeds three hundred examples. Moʻo whose names are not indicated are listed under the heading "Unidentified." These entries are found at the end of the list of identified moʻo. Several moʻo are known by other, often similar, names in different traditions. In a few cases, name variation may be due to a typesetting error (e.g., "Kalamainuʻu" as "Kalimainuʻu" or "Malamainuʻu"). It is important, however, to treat these dual- or even treble-named moʻo as distinct entities so that anyone who knows them by a single name can easily find them in this list. I make an exception for Moʻoinanea because the other names by which she is known clearly refer to her. I also note gender variation and whether gender is unspecified. Because I offer extensive information on certain moʻo thoughout this book, to avoid repetition I do not always include all their details here.

1. **Āhia** (male). This moʻo is a mountain in West Maui. See the introduction.[1]

2. **Ahukini** (female). Ahukini and Kahuku-nui-a-Haleʻa are the parents of Mōlīlele. During Mōlīlele's battle with Ka-Miki, she threw Ahukini into a spring before he could harm her, and there, she became a moʻo. This spring became known as Wai o Ahukini (Water of Ahukini). Mōlīlele became a cliff, and the spring stands at its

base. This cliff and spring are found on the Kona side of Ka Lae, Hawaiʻi.[2]

3. **Aka** (female, a.k.a. Waka). Aka and Kilioe (a.k.a Kilioeikapua) took Lohiʻau, killed him, and took his corpse/spirit to their home at Hāʻena cliff, Kauaʻi. Hiʻiaka killed them.[3]

4. **Akuapehulani** (male, a.k.a. Akuapehuale). A ruling aliʻi of Kona (Hawaiʻi) sent this moʻo, who has a human form, to destroy Puna, which Keāhua ruled.[4]

5. **Alamuki** (gender unspecified). Associated with the moʻo Kamoʻoloa and Kemoʻo, all servants to Laniwahine, the moʻo kiaʻi of ʻUkoʻa fishpond in Waialua, Oʻahu.[5]

6. **Alanapo** (female). See chapter 4. Alanapo and Naulu-o-Weli promise Ka-Miki and Ma-Kaʻiole to no longer harm the people of Keʻei. Alanapo asks that people respect her kapu—namely, to follow proper protocol when gathering the greenery and lehua flowers around her home. As the brothers leave, they look back and see her in her moʻo form on her ridge, "ua hele wale a liliko pua kana-hele i kahinu ia e na kulu wai-naoa a ke kehau" (glistening like a flower in the forest in the chilly water of the dew).[6]

7. **ʻAlekoko** (male). ʻAlekoko and Kalālālehua, brother and sister, each own a fishpond on Kauaʻi—his is called ʻAlekoko. He has human, shark, and moʻo forms.[7]

8. **ʻAlewa** (gender unspecified). Lives in ʻĀlewa, Kapālama ridge, Oʻahu. Termed a "kauā" (outcast) because it has no one to take care of it.[8]

9. **Anahola** (male). Anahola ahupuaʻa is named after this moʻo. He "appeared on land as a man and in the sea as a merman."[9]

10. **ʻAwapuhikeʻokeʻo** (female). Associated with ʻAwapuhimele. See chapter 4.

11. **ʻAwapuhimele** (female). See chapter 3.

12. **Hāʻao** (female or gender unspecified). Linked to Hāʻao, Waikaʻīlio, and Kahoaaliʻi springs in Waiʻōhinu, Kaʻū, Hawaiʻi.[10]

13. **Haapuainanea** (female). Nāmakaokahaʻi's sentry at Kalā-keʻenuiakāne. Instead of killing ʻAukelenuiaʻīkū as Nāmaka-okahaʻi ordered, she played kōnane (a checkers-like game) with him.[11]

14. **Haili** (female). Lives with Pāʻieʻie, Puaʻaloa, Kaʻililahilahi, Puʻumoho, Nāʻū, Maʻū, Kūʻēhoʻopiokalā, Makaliʻi, Kapakapa-kaua, and Honokawailani in Panaʻewa, Hawaiʻi. Hiʻiaka is their pōkiʻi (younger sibling or near cousin), but they try to kill her.[12]

15. **Hailimanu** (female). Lives with Koleana near Honolulu. They hid the aliʻi Kakae upland of Kūkaniloko on Oʻahu.[13]

16. **Haka-aʻano** (male). See Kikipua.

17. **Halekiʻi** (gender unspecified). One of Lāʻieikawai's innumerable moʻo kūpuna who live with her in Paliuli, Hawaiʻi, several of whom are identified by name.[14]

18. **Haui** (gender unspecified). Lives at Kuaihelani with Nāmakaokahaʻi. Haui accompanies Nāmakaokahaʻi as she chases Pele to kill her.[15]

19. **Hauwahine** (female, a.k.a Haumeawahine). See chapters 1, 2, 3, and 5.

20. **Hawaiʻiloa** (male). See chapters 3 and 4.

21. **Heleipaʻewakalani** (gender unspecified). See Halekiʻi.

22. **Hoahoaiku** (female). See chapter 3.

23. **Honokawailani** (male). See Haili.

24. **Hulu** (male). A bird kupua who can change into a moʻo and a human. He lives on Kalalea Hill upland of Anahola in Kawaihau on Kauaʻi.[16] See also Kalalea.

25. **Kaʻauhelemoa** (male). Kiaʻi of Kaʻauhelemoa fishpond, "once located on the Waimea side of Kahuku," who could assume the form of a human or chicken.[17]

26. **Kahalakea** (female). See Hauwahine.

27. **Kahalaopuna** (female). See chapter 1.

28. **Kahanaiki** (female). See chapter 3.

29. **Kaikapu** (female, a.k.a. Luahinekaikapu). A human-eating moʻo whose cave is in Nīnole at Honuʻapo in Kaʻū, Hawaiʻi.[18] See chapter 3.

30. **Kaikapu** (female). This moʻo lurked in the sea near Lāwaʻi (Kauaʻi) hoping to snatch and eat people as they fished along the shoreline. A boy named Liko went fishing there one day to set fish traps for hīnālea. When Kaikapu chased him, Liko "swam into a lava tube that opened onto land from the sea. Kaikapu plunged after him, but she was so large that she became permanently stuck in the tube. The roaring sound one hears as the ocean flows through the tube" belongs to the furious Kaikapu. This blowhole is known as Puhi and Spouting Horn.[19]

31. **Kaʻililahilahi** (female). See Haili.

32. **Kaioʻe** (gender unspecified). See chapter 4.

33. **Kakana** (gender unspecified). See chapter 4.

34. **Kākea** (male). See chapters 1 and 3.

35. **Kakioe** (female). See Kamapiʻi.
36. **Kalālālehua** (female). An aliʻi wahine with a moʻo form (see ʻAlekoko).[20]
37. **Kalalau** (gender unspecified). Associated with a pond at Lāʻiewai, Oʻahu.[21]
38. **Kalalea** (gender unspecified). Lives in Anahola, Kauaʻi.[22] Also a mountain. See Hulu.
39. **Kalamainuʻu** (female). I have discussed her extensively throughout this book. Given the similarity between the names Kalamainuʻu, Kalimianuʻu, Malamainuʻu, Kalanamainuʻu, and Kalamainuʻunuianoho, they may be the same entity called by slightly different names across place or time, or, conversely, they may be distinct entities with similar names.
40. **Kalamainuʻunuianoho** (female). See chapter 5.
41. **Kalamaʻula** (male). See chapter 3.
42. **Kalamaʻula** (female). Grandmother of Maniniholokuaua, a famous thief. She lives in a cave at Kalamaʻula, Molokaʻi.[23]
43. **Kalanamainuʻu** (female). See chapters 1, 3, and 4.
44. **Kalapawai** (gender unspecified). Lives with Olomana in Kailua, Oʻahu. Manu describes these two moʻo as evil because they blocked the road, stole from travelers, and ate humans.[24] Manu mentions Kalapawai elsewhere, and although he does not identify it as a moʻo, he says it is evil for the same reasons.[25]
45. **Kalāwahine** (female). Guardian of water sources in Kalāwahine, Oʻahu.[26]
46. **Kalikoikawao** (female). Daughter of Mahinui (see Kalimainuʻu). Given her kino aka (shadow form) and her connection to Kalimanuʻu, she is either a moʻo or became one.[27]
47. **Kalimainuʻu** (female, either a typesetting error or alternate spelling for Kalamainuʻu). Her elder sister, the moʻo Kilioeikapua, ordered her to live with Mahinui, an aliʻi of Kailua who lived near Kawainui marsh.[28]
48. **Kaluanou** (female). See chapter 3.
49. **Kamakapiʻi** (female). Lives with Kilioeikapua in a cave on Kēʻē cliff, Kauaʻi. She, Kilioe, and Kakioe are "wahine kiai pali o Kaiwikui" (female guardians of Kaiwikui cliff).[29]
50. **Kamākilo** (gender unspecified). This moʻo and its twin, who were raised by a human woman, share the same name. They live in a pond at Waiʻōpai, Kahikinui, Maui. Kamākilo means "the beggar," and that is how these moʻo got their names as they would go about in

their human forms and beg at people's homes. Later, they were transformed into ʻunihipili (spirits trapped in some portion of their human remains and used as errand gods).[30]

51. **Kamākilo** (gender unspecified). See previous entry.
52. **Kamalō** (male or female depending on the account). See chapter 3.
53. **Kamananui** (female). Lives at Waialua, Oʻahu. Hānai mother of Hawaiʻiloa, the woman with whom Waimaikūlani betrays Kahelekūlani. See Kāmehaiʻikana.[31]
54. **Kamaoha** (female). Kiaʻi of "Luakini fishpond, on the summit of Mount Kaala."[32]
55. **Kamawau** (gender unspecified). See Halekiʻi.
56. **Kāmehaʻikana** (female). See chapters 1, 3, 4, and 5.
57. **Kamohoaliʻi** (male). See chapter 4.
58. **Kamōʻiliʻili** (female or male depending on the account). See chapter 3.
59. **Ka-Mōkila-o-Wailua** (male). Lives at Puʻuiki, Wailua, Kauaʻi.[33] The cave that runs through Puʻuiki "from north to south is called Kaluamokila [Mōkila's-cave]." Its "south entrance is under water or near the water and the reptile could leave the cave by one entrance to get into the river [Wailua] and by the other to get on land."[34]
60. **Kamoʻoaliʻi** (male). See chapter 3.
61. **Kamoʻokoa** (gender unspecified). A famous ruling aliʻi who reigned over all of Kauaʻi, Manokalanipō, ordered this moʻo "to open Kīlauea's upper regions for agriculture." The remnants of three long and very ancient irrigation ditches are said to be its "claw marks."[35]
62. **Kamoʻolāliʻi** (gender unspecified). See chapter 1.
63. **Kamoʻoloa** (gender unspecified). See Alamuki.
64. **Kamoʻoloa** (female). See chapter 3.
65. **Kamoʻookamuliwai** (male). Attempted to block Hiʻiaka from crossing a river in Hanalei, Kauaʻi, so she killed him.[36]
66. **Kānekuaʻana** (female). See chapter 5.
67. **Kanenelu** (female). Lives in Kanenelu at Pāhala, Kaʻū, Hawaiʻi. She sits and combs her hair near where people fetch water.[37]
68. **Kanikū** (gender unspecified). See chapter 3.
69. **Kanimoe** (gender unspecified). See chapter 3.
70. **Kaʻōhao** (female). Lives in Laumiha, upland of Maunawili near Kawainui marsh, Oʻahu. The moʻo Kawailoa is her kāne. In her human form, Kaʻōhao is very beautiful. She fights Mahinui (a.k.a. Niuloahiki, a coconut tree kupua). He breaks her ribs as they grapple, so she changes into her "kino alualu o ke ano ilipakalua" (a

thick, rough-skinned body). Their struggles take them into the water of Kawainui, into Kaʻelepulu pond and fishpond, and then back on the dry land of Pelekane. There, Mahinui finally manages to kill Kaʻōhao.[38]

71. **Kapakapakaua** (male). See Haili.

72. **Kapōpanopano** (male, a.k.a. Pōpanopano). In her chant to humiliate Kilioeikapua and Kalanamainuʻu, Pele identifies him and Pōlalowahi as the ancestors of all moʻo.[39]

73. **Kapualei** (female). See chapter 3.

74. **Kaualehu** (female). See chapters 3 and 4.

75. **Kawaiʻiliʻula** (gender unspecified). Guards Mānā and Kekaha on Kauaʻi.[40]

76. **KawailoaikapolioLokoea** (male). See chapters 3 and 4. Termed "ke keiki auau ehukai o Ahualaka, ke keiki e noho ana i ka Uhiwai o ka lewa" (the sea-foam-bathing child of Ahualaka, the child who lives in the heavy mist of the sky).[41]

77. **Kawelolikohau** (gender unspecified). See Halekiʻi.

78. **Kawelopolohinalo** (gender unspecified). See Halekiʻi.

79. **Kawelowai** (female, or gender unspecified). Lives upland of Wailua, Kauaʻi. Female in Laukaʻieʻie: "Ke kaikamahine noho kahawai o Wailua" (stream-dwelling girl of Wailua) of Koʻolau, Kauaʻi. Here, she has a brother named Waiʻehu, also a moʻo.[42]

80. **Kawiliwahine** (female). Human-eating moʻo of Puʻukōlea, Waimea, Hawaiʻi.[43]

81. **Keaolewa** (gender unspecified). Living on Hāʻupu hill, Kauaʻi controls the water of Kemamo and rules over all Kauaʻi moʻo.[44]

82. **Kēʻē** (gender unspecified but probably female). Lives with Kilioe (see Kilioeikapua) at Kēʻē cliff at Hāʻena, Kauaʻi.[45]

83. **Kekamaoleleau** (gender unspecified). See Halekiʻi.

84. **Kemoʻo** (gender unspecified). See Alamuki.

85. **Kiha** (gender unspecified). Served the moʻo Panaʻewa. Hiʻiaka turned it into a stone.[46]

86. **Kihalaninui** (gender unspecified). No available information on this moʻo.[47]

87. **Kihanui** (gender unspecified). A "lizard hula" mentions a "Kihanui" associated with Puʻukamoʻo Hill in Kaunakakai on Molokai.[48] See Puʻukamoʻo.

88. **Kihanuilūlūmoku** (gender unspecified in all traditions in which it appears with one exception, and there it is cited as female). I have discussed this moʻo throughout this book.

89. **Kihawahine** (female). I discuss this mo'o throughout this book.

90. **Kihawahineikiananea** (female). See chapter 5.

91. **Kikipua** (female). She leads a group of mo'o in Hālawa Valley, Moloka'i. The mo'o Haka'a'ano and Oloku'i are her kāne. She stole the latter from the mo'o Papalaua.[49]

92. **Kiki'ula** (gender unspecified). Guards Waioli muliwai in Hanalei, Kaua'i.[50]

93. **Kilikilipua** (gender unspecified). Kia'i of Konahuanui Peak and lives in a cave there.[51]

94. **Kilikilipua** (female). Linked with an underground spring at Mākua, O'ahu.[52]

95. **Kilioe** (female). This Kilioe of O'ahu may be Kilioeikapua of Kaua'i. See Lauhuki.

96. **Kilioeikapua** (female, a.k.a. Kilioe). See chapters 1, 3, and 4.

97. **Kinilau** (female). See chapter 3.

98. **Koe** (gender unspecified). Associated with a cliff at Hā'ena, Kaua'i.[53]

99. **Ko'iahi (female, a.ka. Kūla'ila'i).** Lover of Nanaue. See chapter 4. I grew up near the area with which this mo'o is associated, and I am familiar with her. When I was growing up in the 1970s, she was not named in the stories I heard. In present time, however, some have taken to calling this mo'o "Ko'iahi" after the stream she uses to reach the ocean, or "Kūla'ila'i" after the coral outcropping upon which she sometimes sits.

100. **Koleana** (female). Lived with Kunawai in Moanalua, O'ahu. They are termed "kauā" because no one worshipped them, and thus they eventually faded away. Linked to Hailimanu elsewhere and they are female. They hid the ali'i Kakae upland of Kūkaniloko.[54]

101. **Kūahailo** (male, a.k.a. Kūwahailo). Belongs to the class of Kū gods. See chapter 3.

102. **Kuaua** (female, possibly also Nohoamo'o). See chapters 1, 3, and 4.

103. **Kū'ēho'opiokalā** (male). See Haili.

104. **Kūka'eki** (male). See entry on Piliamo'o of Waimea and 'Ewa, O'ahu (not Wailuku).

105. **Kūmauna** (male). See chapter 5.

106. **Kuna** (male, a.k.a. Kunamo'o). Lived in the Wailuku River at Hilo, Hawai'i.[55]

107. **Kunawai** (gender unspecified). See Koleana.

108. **Kunawai** (gender unspecified). Kia'i of the Kunawai springs at Liliha, O'ahu.[56]

109. **Lanihuli** (male). See chapter 3.
110. **Laniloa** (gender unspecified). A mo'o in one tradition but else-where, he is human with a shark form, and Luhiā, his brother, is a human with a mo'o form.[57] See chapter 3.
111. **Laniwahine** (female). Kia'i of 'Uko'a fishpond in Waialua, O'ahu. Her appearance in her human form is a bad omen because it fore-tells some disaster. She is associated with the saying "pupuhi ka i'a o 'Ukoa" (the fish of 'Uko'a have vanished), which refers to "one who flees." Her brother is Puhi'ula (Red eel). McAllister notes, "Offerings were left for her on a stone, located near Pump Number 4 of the Waialua Agricultural Company. The site of this stone was marked for years by a dead tree which was not removed because of its as-sociation with Laniwahine. Now, neither stone nor tree is to be found."[58]
112. **Lauhuki** (female). She and Kilioe, who both have human forms, control the Kalena water source and the ponds at Makawao on O'ahu. A chant commemorates them: "Ka helena a wahine i ka pali, / I ka luna o Piiholo i Alola, / O Lauhuki ma laua o Kilioe."[59] See Kilioe.
113. **Lauhulu** (gender unspecified). Associated with the mo'o Kamananui and with the Waialua River, O'ahu.[60]
114. **Laukupu** (gender unspecified, possibly female). Kia'i of Maunalua fishpond, most of which was destroyed to build a residential area called Hawai'i Kai.[61]
115. **Laumihi** (female). Member of the Mahiki mo'o horde at Mahiki, Hawai'i.[62]
116. **Lehu** (male). See chapter 3.
117. **Lehuakona** (gender unspecified). Associated with the wai a ka Pāo'o (the water of the Pāo'o) on Lehua Islet near Ni'ihau. The pāo'o is a species of goby.[63]
118. **Lī'aihonua** (female). Lives in Manini pool near Ka'ena Point. Hi'iaka turns her to stone after she lies about the existence of wa-ter sources in that area.[64]
119. **Limaloa** (gender unspecified). Controls the headwater source called Kapuna at Lā'iewai, O'ahu.[65]
120. **Lonokaehu** (male). Lives at Pepe'ekeo, Hawai'i. He nearly killed Māui's mother, Hina.[66]
121. **Lonowahine** (probably female). The "wahine" in this mo'o's name marks her as female. This mo'o is a kumupa'a (ancestral guardian) for her descendants.[67]

122. **Lua'ehu** (female). Lives at Lua'ehu in Lahaina, Maui, which is probably named after her given that she is described as having 'ehu hair.[68]

123. **Luahine** (female). Lives at Luahinewai, a beach and pool named after her, near Kīholo, Kona, Hawai'i.[69] She has red hair.[70] Raymond Keawe Alapa'i says that his grandfather saw her grooming her hair as she sat on a rock but did not see her face, and a female cousin also saw her.[71] A story notes, "It is said there is an opening within this pool by which the old woman enters, and therein are piled the bones of ali'i from long ago. It is said the bones of Kamehameha are also there, but the truth cannot be actually known unless someone goes in her 'cave,' then, the proof that confirms everything about this hidden cave will be found."[72]

124. **Luahine** (female). See Kūmauna.

125. **Luhiā** (male). See chapters 2 and 3.[73]

126. **Luluku** (gender unspecified). Associated with a place and a stream in Kāne'ohe on O'ahu that carry its name. It blocks the road to steal from travelers and eats humans.[74]

127. **Mā'eli'eli** (female). Lives at He'e'ia, O'ahu. She blocks the road to steal from travelers and eats humans.[75] In the tradition of Lauka'ie'ie, she has a female friend, 'Ioleka'a, a rat kupua. Just after the god Makanikeoe passed He'eiauli, he saw two supernatural women descending from upland of Ahulimanu pond who sat in the front of the road and flung dirt on the hill (also named Mā'eli'eli), and Makanikeoe saw the nature of these two women, one woman with very long hair and a tail, and the other with a beard and also a tail.[76]

128. **Mahiki** (male). See chapter 3.

129. **Mahulua** (male). He became a stone at Kailua, O'ahu. His companion is Wai'auia.[77]

130. **Makahuna** (male). See Pōhaku Kīkēkē.

131. **Makali'i** (male). Ma'ū is his wahine (see Haili). Elsewhere, his wāhine are Ulunui and Melemele, and they live between Pu'uonioni in Kīlauea and Pana'ewa in Hilo, Hawai'i.[78]

132. **Makaweli** (gender unspecified). Guards Waiulailiahi in Waimea, Kaua'i.[79]

133. **Mākilo** (female). Lives in Wai'ōpai pond in Kaupō, Maui.[80] See Kamākilo.

134. **Mālama Mo'olelo** (gender unspecified). A mo'o of Nāpo'opo'o, Hawai'i.[81]

135. **Māmala** (female). See chapter 4.
136. **Manaua** (female). See chapter 1.
137. **Ma'ū** (female). Wahine of the mo'o Makali'i (see Haili).
138. **Maulili** (male). See chapter 3.
139. **Maunauna** (gender unspecified). An evil mo'o who lives upland of Līhu'e, O'ahu.[82]
140. **Meheanu** (female). See chapters 1 and 3.
141. **Melemele** (female). See Makali'i.
142. **Miloli'i** (gender unspecified). Associated with a cliff at Hā'ena, Kaua'i.[83]
143. **Mimo** (gender unspecified). See Haleki'i.
144. **Moanaliha** (gender unspecified). See Haleki'i.
145. **Moanalihaikawaokele** (male). See chapter 3.
146. **Moholani** (female). Lives near the sea in an unspecified area in Ka'ū, Hawai'i. Beckwith upholds that Moholani is a mo'o.[84]
147. **Mokoli'i** (gender unspecified). See chapter 3.
148. **Mokuhinia** (gender unspecified, probably female, possibly also Kihawahine). According to Kamakau: "Mokuhinia was seen [in Maui] at Kapunakea in Lahaina, at Paukūkalo and Kanahā at Wailuku, and it showed itself at Kalepolepo [Maui] when Kamehameha Kapuāiwa died, it appeared before hundreds and thousands of people, and around the year 1838 at Mokuhinia, it nearly overturned the ali'i Kekāuluohi as she was on a canoe heading to church from Moku'ula to Waine'e across Mokuhinia pond."[85] In a reminder to readers to renew their subscription to *Ke Au Okoa*, S. W. Nā'ili'ili mentions this mo'o: "Ke maewa nei ka lauoho o ka moo o Mokuhinia" (the hair of the mo'o Mokuhinia is swaying).[86]
149. **Mo'o** (male). Associated with Mauna Pa'upa'u in Lahaina, Maui. This mo'o has a stumped tail, which "is the way the tails of lizards of the present time appear, because of Moo, the great and strong." The ali'i Kamohomoho built a heiau to honor him.[87]
150. **Mo'oalelo** (gender unspecified). Although Mo'oalelo is described as a "gnome," given that its name means "mo'o tongue" it is undoubtedly a mo'o. It was considered evil because it destroyed fishponds, cultivations, coconut trees, and so on.[88]
151. **Mo'oali'i** (gender unspecified). See chapter 1.
152. **Mo'oinanea** (female except in two accounts; a.k.a. Kamo'oinanea, Kamo'oianea, Mo'oianea, Mō'īnānea, Mo'onanea, Mo'omilinanea, Milimilinanea, Ho'okumukahonua, and Holonaeole). I discuss this mo'o throughout this book.

153. **Moʻo Kiko** (male). Molokai family ʻaumakua; "lived near the heiau in Kapualei."[89]
154. **Moʻokini** (female). Lives near the sea of Kapakai at Maliu, Hawaiʻi. She asks and receives a chant of praise from Hiʻiaka. There is a heiau by this name.[90]
155. **Moʻolau** (female, a.k.a. Moʻolauwahine). See chapter 3. Only in N. Emerson's account is this moʻo male.[91]
156. **Moʻomomi** (female). See chapter 2. Geo. Poʻoloa mentions a moʻo who lives in a sea cave at Moʻomomi, which leads to Maui.[92]
157. **Moʻonuiaheahea** (gender unspecified). Kiaʻi of Kawailoa-o-Lau-o-Kamani near Kalepa, Kauaʻi. This moʻo refused a request from some young aliʻi: "The water [descendants] of those aliʻi were lost to Moʻonuiaheahea, to whom the pond Kawailoko-o-Lau-o-Kamani belonged, the heiau, which was upland of Kalepa, and which was the altar of this moʻo to whom the kapu koʻa of Kawailoa fishpond belonged. Moʻonuiaheahea appeared facing its back towards Ahukini, and because of barrenness, those youths combined their voices in chant. The sluice gate of Kawailoa remained unbroken by the young aliʻi."[93]
158. **Nāʻū** (female). See Haili.
159. **Nāwāhineikawai** (female). See chapter 4.
160. **Nohoamoʻo** (male or female, possibly also Kuaua). See chapters 1, 3, and 4.
161. **Nōmilu** (gender unspecified). Lives in the Nōmilu fishpond in Kōloa, Kauaʻi.[94]
162. **Olokuʻi** (male). See Kikipua.
163. **Olomana** (gender unspecified). See Kalapawai.
164. **ʻOloʻolo** (female). At Kalamaʻula near Kaunakakai, Molokai, people often saw a beautiful woman combing her hair as she sat on a little dirt hill near ʻOloʻolo spring, which is probably named after her as "he ololo hoi kona mau waiu" (she had pendulant breasts).[95]
165. **ʻOʻopu-poʻo-wai-nui-a-niho** (female). Possibly a moʻo given that it is a kiaʻi of Kaloko Fishpond (see Kalamainuʻunuianoho). A deity with a similar name, ʻOʻopu-nui-a-niho, is associated with Ka-loko-wai-ʻawaʻawa (The brackish water pool) in North Kona. There are two stones called Kūmakapuʻu in a stream atop the hill called Kauahia, which are termed "hookalakupua" because fishermen came to do rituals at these stones to increase the fish. A woman asked her kāne to bring her to this hill to give birth, but the child slipped out of her without her being aware. The kāne noticed something red trailing

behind the woman. Just then, they noticed a huge ʻoʻopu hue (a poisonous species of puffer fish) with a bloody bundle in its mouth. This ʻoʻopu hue was ʻOʻopunuianiho, who also had a human form. She took this child to raise it. Their child was not human but had two forms: an ʻeʻepa one and a human one. She told them to name the human form, and she would name the ʻeʻepa one, so the girl was called Makai-Wahine-a-Kapohakau and Mahina-hiki-ʻōpulepule.[96] Because some installments are unreadable, I was unable to learn what her kino lau are.

166. **Ouha** (male, also known as Oua). Ouha's parents were a shark and a moʻo. Although he is only noted as being a shark guardian of Waikīkī and the Koko Head area, given his heritage perhaps he could also transform into a moʻo, which is why I include him here.[97]

167. **Paʻe** (female). See chapters 1 and 2.

168. **Pāhoa** (male or female depending on the account). Lives in Kaimukī, Oʻahu.[98]

169. **Pāʻieʻie** (female). See Haili.

170. **Pākole** (gender unspecified). Lives in Kahaluʻu, Oʻahu. An evil moʻo who blocked travelers to steal their belongings and ate people.[99]

171. **Palahemo** (female). See chapter 1.

172. **Palihala** (male). See Kūmauna.

173. **Panaʻewa** (male or gender unspecified). See chapters 1, 3, and 4.

174. **Pāpaʻi** (gender unspecified). Lives in a pili-grass plain of Puʻuopāpaʻi at Hanapēpē in Waimea, Kauaʻi. Pāpaʻi hid the waters of this plain.[100]

175. **Pāpalaua** (female). See Kikipua.

176. **Papalinahoa** (female). Lives in the Papalinahoa swamp in Nāwiliwili, Kauaʻi.[101]

177. **Paukūkalo** (female). Lives in a pond in Wailuku, Maui.[102]

178. **Piʻi** (male, a.k.a. Piʻikalalau). He fought Kauakahialiʻi at the behest of Keliʻikoa, an aliʻi of Kauaʻi. He could transform into a lizard, pygmy, or red-haired giant with tusks.[103]

179. **Piliʻaʻama** (male). A konohiki for the Waimea area on Oʻahu.[104]

180. **Pilialoha** (gender unspecified). Lives in Hulēʻia pond, Kauaʻi.[105]

181. **Piliamoʻo** (male or female depending on the account). See chapters 1, 3, and 4.

182. **Piliamoʻo** (female). Originally from Waimea, Oʻahu. A traveling companion of Awawalei who is leading the mullet to Lāʻie at her brother's request. She takes Kūkaʻeki as her kāne. They enjoyed fishing for

ʻoʻopu with a bow and arrow. They lived as humans until they tired of it and then lived as moʻo in Waiawa stream, ʻEwa, Oʻahu.[106]

183. **Pohakalani** (female). See chapter 3.

184. **Pohakeola** (male). See chapter 3.

185. **Pōhaku Kīkēkē** (female, a.k.a. Ua Līlīlehua, Līlīlehua, Ka-ua-līlī-lehua-o-pālolo). Her brother Makahuna was also her lover.[107] See chapter 3.

186. **Poʻipū** (gender unspecified). Associated with ponds from Wahiawā to Kōloa, Kauaʻi.[108]

187. **Pōlalowehi** (female). See Kapōpanopano.

188. **Poli-o-lehua** (female). A noted "mermaid" of Lāʻauʻōkala, Kauaʻi. For centuries, she would sit on a rock at Lāʻauʻōkala to groom her hair in her human form. Young men tried unsuccessfully to gain her affection, and she often dove into the water to escape them. She finally left the area after an aliʻi followed her beneath the water to her cave.[109]

189. **Pōloahilani** (female). See Halekiʻi.

190. **Poʻo o Moʻo** (gender unspecified). One of two stones said to be moʻo "on either side of the Anahulu Stream above the old Haleiwa Seminary." The other was Wāwae o Moʻo.[110]

191. **Puakoaiʻa** (male). This evil moʻo lives in Panaʻewa, Hilo, Hawaiʻi.[111]

192. **Pūhāwai** (female). This evil moʻo lives in upland Waiʻanae, Oʻahu.[112]

193. **Punahoʻolapa** (gender unspecified). Lives in a deep pool in the seaside plain of Kahuku just after Kahipa point on Oʻahu.[113]

194. **Puʻuʻanuhe** (female). See chapter 1.

195. **Puʻuhele** (male). Kāne of Puʻuokali and father of Puʻuoinaina.[114]

196. **Puʻukamoʻo** (gender unspecified). Lives upland of Līhuʻe on Kauaʻi.[115]

197. **Puʻukamoʻo** (male). Molokai moʻo man. See chapter 3.

198. **Puʻumoho** (male). See Haili.

199. **Puʻuoinaina** (female). See chapters 3 and 4.

200. **Puʻuokali** (female). See Puʻuhele.

201. **Uli-lei-puhi** (gender unspecified). See Halekiʻi.

202. **Uli-papa-eka** (gender unspecified). See Halekiʻi.

203. **Uli-papa-kea** (gender unspecified). See Halekiʻi.

204. **Uli-poha-i-kalani** (female). See Halekiʻi.

205. **Uli-puholo-lau-palula** (gender unspecified). See Halekiʻi.

206. **Ulunui** (female). See Makaliʻi.

207. **Waiākea (female).** See chapters 1 and 3.

208. **Wai'auia** (male). See chapter 3.

209. **Wai'ehu** (male). See Kawelowai.

210. **Wailua** (female). A mo'o who came to Kaua'i from Kahiki. Wailua removed the plank that served as a bridge to cross Wailua River, and when Hi'iaka asked her for it, she refused. After Wailua lost the battle with Hi'iaka, she went to live in the caverns beneath the river.[116]

211. **Wailua-nui-hoano-ka-lani** (gender unspecified). See Haleki'i.

212. **Waka** (female, a.k.a. Waka-ke-aka-i-ka-wai and Aka). I discuss this mo'o throughout this book. Pele turns Waka to stone as she hides in a seaside pond that is named after her, Loko Waka (also Loko Aka), at Keaukaha, Hilo, Hawai'i. This pond is sacred to her.[117]

213. **Walimānoanoa** (female). See chapters 1 and 5.

214. **Walinu'u** (female). See chapters 1, 4, and 5. She appears with Walimānoanoa, Kalamainu'u, and Kilioeikapua in the Kamapua'a tradition. A path along the top of a cliff on Kaua'i on the way to Hā'ena is called the path of death because these four mo'o kill whomever passes their way. When Kamapua'a reached Kalalau cliff, he saw their rumps protruding from a cave and realized they were basking in the sun. He chanted and they turned around to hide their rumps. He chanted again and they responded, "E, auhea wale ana oe, e make aku ana oe ia makou, heaha no la kau o ka mahaoi ana mai nei i ko makou wahi" (Eh, listen up, we will kill you, what the heck is your reason for being insolent at our home). After their voices died down, "o ko ia nei hoomaka aku la no ia lalau i na moo, e kahili ae ana na moo i ko lakou mau huelo, a lilo ae la ka pali he pali ku'i" (he began to grab the mo'o, and twisted the mo'o together by their tails, until the precipice became a row of joined cliffs).[118]

215. **Wāwae o Mo'o** (gender unspecified). See Po'o o Mo'o.

216. **Wewehilani** (gender unspecified). Mo'oinanea chose this mo'o to stay behind and guard Kuaihelani, Kealohilani, Nu'umealani, and the sacred boundaries of Kūkuluokahiki. It gave up an eye, which became a pearl, and this is how pearls were introduced to Hawai'i.[119]

217. **Unidentified** (gender unspecified). This entry is for an unspecified number of mo'o who were disturbed by a person who fished with dynamite in their pond in Wailua, Kaua'i.[120]

218. **Unidentified** (gender unspecified). Group entry for unspecified number of mo'o who serve Pana'ewa.[121]

219. **Unidentified** (female). Entry for two mo'o women whom Hi'iaka killed while they were in their human forms at someone's house at Honoli'i, Hawai'i.[122]

220. **Unidentified** (female). See previous entry.
221. **Unidentified** (gender unspecified). Lives in an upland loʻi, and from there it descends to the sea of Kīpūkai, Kauaʻi. Whenever it does, the shrimp in a nearby river become agitated.[123]
222. **Unidentified** (gender unspecified). The nest of an unspecified number of baby moʻo in Huleʻia river (Kauaʻi) was exposed whenever the river dried up after a run of goby.[124]
223. **Unidentified** (female). Lives in a pool in Hālawa Valley, Molokai. Lahela Naki met her and thought she was a real woman until her facial features suddenly changed rapidly back and forth between human and reptile.[125]
224. **Unidentified** (female). One of two "Peʻe kāua" moʻo. See chapter 2.
225. **Unidentified** (female). See previous entry.
226. **Unidentified** (female). Moʻo of Keālia pond. See chapter 1.
227. **Unidentified** (male). Oʻahu moʻo who took a Kaʻū woman as his lover. See chapter 1.
228. **Unidentified** (female). Took a man named Kaumana as her lover.[126]
229. **Unidentified** (female). Sister to Lehu. See chapter 3.
230. **Unidentified** (female). Sister to Lehu. See chapter 3.
231. **Unidentified** (female). Lives at Konahuanui, Oʻahu. See chapter 2.
232. **Unidentified** (female). Lives in a shrimp-filled pond in Nuʻu, Kaupō, Maui, near a hau grove. Took a boy and then returned him. See chapter 3.
233. **Unidentified** (gender unspecified). An unspecified number of moʻo who live in Alaweo, a small river and waterhole on Kauaʻi.[127]
234. **Unidentified** (female). She brought to life gobies prepped for a meal. See chapter 2.
235. **Unidentified** (female). Moʻo of a Punaluʻu pool destroyed in a lava flow. See chapter 2.
236. **Unidentified** (gender unspecified). Guards the western side of the breadfruit tree Leiwalo in Napehā, Āliamanu, Oʻahu. Souls jump from Leiwalo to get to the afterworld.[128]
237. **Unidentified** (female). Cut the cord of Māui's kite Lupe-nui-a-ka-āiwaiwa.[129]
238. **Unidentified** (female). Moʻo of Kīpū cliff (Kauaʻi) who blocked a stream. See chapter 3.
239. **Unidentified** (gender unspecified). Frequents Sea Life Park at Makapuʻu, Oʻahu.[130]
240. **Unidentified** (gender unspecified). Lives in a cave at Kulaokaiwiʻula. See chapter 1.

241. **Unidentified** (female). Associated with Waiʻākōlea pond, Kalapana, Hawaiʻi. In an interview recorded on June 21, 1959, Gabriel Kalama Pea told Pukui that people still occasionally saw
this Waiʻākōlea moʻo wahine at Kalapana.[131] Charles Langlas
interviewed several people about this moʻo. On March 3, 2011,
Annie Kaʻaukai, wife of Herbert Kaʻaukai, recalled that people
would see her combing her hair and that she had once taken a
boy with ʻehu hair from Kaʻū. This boy had been swimming
with other children in Waiʻākolea pond and had gone missing.
Because no one could find him, they called a woman named
"Lady" Konanui. The reason for calling her is not explained.
After "she called out to him in Hawaiian, he appeared" and
"was already growing scales." Kaʻaukai explains, "They say the
moʻo like those with ʻehu hair." Langlas asked Albert Kaʻaukai
(son of Annie Maluo who is Herbert Kaʻaukai's sister) about her
and related the story about the ʻehu-haired boy. Langlas was
trying to figure out the name of the two ponds where it is said
that a moʻo's head is in one and the tail is in the other. Kaʻaukai
remembered that the tail was in Waiaka, and he and Langlas
supposed that the head was either in Waiʻākōlea, Waipālua, or
Wai ʻōpae.[132]
242. **Unidentified** (male). Lives with a female moʻo at Paukukauwila
stream at Waialua near Waimea, Oʻahu.[133]
243. **Unidentified** (female). See previous entry.
244. **Unidentified** (female). A moʻo twin. See chapter 4.
245. **Unidentified** (female). See previous entry.
246. **Unidentified** (gender unspecified). A huge moʻo who lives at Hanalei, Kauaʻi.[134]
247. **Unidentified** (gender unspecified). Lives at Punaluʻu, Kualoa,
Oʻahu. Turned two children into stones when they neared the
stream it guarded, which was on top of a hill.[135]
248. **Unidentified** (female). Luahine moʻo who uses her eyeballs to fish.
See chapter 2.
249. **Unidentified** (female). A moʻo with a beautiful human form. She
lives in Waialamihi pond, Moanalua, and her name is the name of
the "Bishop's bridge" seaward of Moanalua.[136]
250. **Unidentified** (gender unspecified). Entry for the many moʻo said to
live in Moanalua.[137]
251. **Unidentified** (gender unspecified). Frequents a hidden river beneath Halekiʻi heiau, Pihana, Maui.[138]

252. **Unidentified** (female). Lives at Hi'ilawe waterfall in Waipi'o Valley. See chapter 1.

253. **Unidentified** (female). Julia Naone related an account about this mo'o told by a family who had previously owned her family's house near Ka'apīpā pond in Kīpahulu, Maui. A man who visited this family shot at a rock associated with this mo'o, which may have been her kino lau. He eventually died from an illness, which perhaps can be attributed to defacing this stone. Naone once accompanied her uncle to this pond, and he was "entranced by a strange bubbling in the water which had turned color; the man became sick for three weeks; he craved only water and constantly wanted to visit the pond; he was kept from going there until he was well." Naone also said that a man once saw "a beautiful woman in a hat with feathers and reddish blond hair that tried to get him to go into the cave near the pond; she asked him to buy several cakes and candies and bring them back to her without telling anyone; he procured the items, but told someone what he was doing and died within five weeks; another man who knew of what happened was burned in his house and it is said that the *mo'o* was angry at their talking" about it. There was "a woman who was warned not to wash diapers in the pond, but did so anyway and was cut on the foot by the *mo'o*."[139]

254. **Unidentified** (female). A Maui family had a daughter "who was a beautiful woman on land" but became a mo'o whenever she entered fresh water.[140]

255. **Unidentified** (gender unspecified). This mo'o of Kaua'i (place unspecified) "was angry and burnt down a house."[141]

256. **Unidentified** (gender unspecified). Lives in a pond in 'Alelele just above the road to Kaupō in Hanawī. She "only shows herself to people she likes; many people see only her back while she combs her hair, few ever see her face."[142]

257. **Unidentified** (female). Lives with another mo'o (unidentified) in the Waiakanaloa (Water of Kanaloa) cave pond just below Makana cliff in Hā'ena, Kaua'i. This pond is also known as Waiaka'a'amoo ('A'amo'o water) or Kawai'a'amo'o (The 'a'amo'o water).[143]

258. **Unidentified** (female). See previous entry.

259. **Unidentified** (gender unspecified). Guards Maniniholo cave (a.k.a. Dry Cave), which is "about ten miles from Hanalei," Kaua'i.[144]

260. **Unidentified** (gender unspecified). A group of different-colored mo'o at Kuaihelani.[145]

261. **Unidentified** (female). White-haired moʻo who lives at Hāna, Maui. See chapter 3.
262. **Unidentified** (female). Lives in ʻOheʻo, Kīpahulu, Maui. See chapter 1.
263. **Unidentified** (gender unspecified). Kiaʻi of a fishpond near Kamalō Bay, Molokai.[146]
264. **Unidentified** (female). Lives at Kaluakauwā pond just behind the Hauʻula Fire Station.[147]
265. **Unidentified** (female). One of two old women who are moʻo.[148]
266. **Unidentified** (female). See previous entry.
267. **Unidentified** (gender unspecified). Lives on Puʻu Kawiwi near Mauna Lahilahi, Mākaha, Oʻahu. One of several kupua who guarded the conch-shell trumpet stolen from Keakaokū. A bird kupua, Lūlūkuahiwi, took it back and gave it to Haumea, who then returned it to him.[149]
268. **Unidentified** (female). One of two moʻo sitting in ʻUkoʻa pond who sees Piliamoʻo in her human form accompanying Awawalei but recognizes her as a moʻo.[150] See Piliamoʻo.
269. **Unidentified** (female). See previous entry.
270. **Unidentified** (gender unspecified). A group of moʻo (number unspecified) guarding Ka Wai Ola o Kāne (Kāne's Water of Life).[151]
271. **Unidentified** (gender unspecified). In 1895, Daniel Kekau and Aola encountered this moʻo near a gulch upland of Pāhala in Kaʻū, Hawaiʻi. See chapter 5.
272. **Unidentified** (gender unspecified). Lives in Mokuhinia pool in Maui. See chapter 5.
273. **Unidentified** (gender unspecified). A moʻo of Molokaʻi who tried to take over Kumuʻeli, the territory of Moamoa, a great rooster kupua. They went to battle and Moamoa won, scooping out the moʻo's eyes and then killing it.[152]
274. **Unidentified** (gender unspecified). In 1854, the kamaʻāina of Wailua attributed the drowning of Alfred F. Turner to a moʻo inhabiting the Wailua River.[153]
275. **Unidentified** (male). Kāne of Manaua. See chapter 1.
276. **Unidentified** (gender unspecified). Child of Manaua. See chapter 1.
277. **Unidentified** (gender unspecified). Child of Manaua. See chapter 1.
278. **Unidentified** (female). Described as a "moo, or mermaid." Lived in "a deep place at a turn in the stream" known as "Mermaid Pool," where Kapiʻolani Park now stands in Waikīkī, Oʻahu. Once forty feet deep, the pool's depth was only fifteen feet by 1889.[154]

279. **Unidentified** (gender unspecified). Entry for Kinilau's many children. See chapter 3.
280. **Unidentified** (female). A student at the University of Hawaiʻi at Mānoa, whose name I do not recall, told me this story from her boyfriend, a lifeguard at Keawaʻula, Waiʻanae, Oʻahu. A man who was night fishing was shocked to see a woman in his net, but when he went to help her, she had red eyes, and he realized that she was a moʻo.
281. **Unidentified** (female). During the 1930s, this moʻo terrified Katsumi Ebisu after he caught her in her human form in his fishing net at Mokuleia. She rode him like a horse and, still in her human form, licked him with her three-foot-long tongue.[155]
282. **Unidentified** (female). Lives in Wainānāliʻi stream, Hilo, Hawaiʻi. See chapter 5.
283. **Unidentified** (female). Lives near Wainānāliʻi stream, Hilo, Hawaiʻi. See chapter 5.
284. **Unidentified** (male). Lives in a cave behind a waterfall in Holuamanu above Makaweli in Kauaʻi. When an angry father told his young daughter to go live with that moʻo, she did. The moʻo cared for her for several years until her parents managed to get her back.[156]
285. **Unidentified** (female). This "slim woman with reddish-brown hair" takes a human, Kamanu, as her kāne. They live in her cavern beneath a river (place not specified). A year later, he tells her he is going to visit his family. She warns him to be sure that his father is the first person he kisses. Kamanu's dog kisses (licks) him first. When he returns that evening, she cries and tells him she will never see him again. He soon dies of a broken heart.[157]
286. **Unidentified** (female). ʻAumakua for Jonah Kamalani. See chapter 5.
287. **Unidentified** (gender unspecified). This entry is for a kupua, probably a moʻo, associated with a pond at Halemano upland of Puʻuloa on Oʻahu, which is described as a "kiowai kapu . . . a ke kupua e hunakele ai" (a kapu pond . . . belonging to a kupua who hid there).[158]
288. **Unidentified** (female). ʻAumakua for the author's family.

Notes

Preface
1. Silva, *Aloha Betrayed*, 13.

Hawaiian Terms
1. Kepelino, *Kepelino's Traditions*, 10–11.
2. Malo, *Moʻolelo*, 2:127–137; Kamakau, "Ka Moolelo o Hawaii Nei," August 12, 1865.
3. Pukui and Elbert, *Hawaiian*, s.v. "mana"; Pukui, Haertig, and Lee, *Nānā*, 1:10.
4. *Merriam-Webster Dictionary*, s.v. "entity."
5. Pukui and Elbert, *Hawaiian*, s.v. "mana"; Pukui, Haertig, and Lee, *Nānā*, 1:10.
6. Kamakau, "Ka Moolelo Hawaii," March 24, 1870.
7. Pukui and Elbert, *Hawaiian*, s.v. "hoʻāo."
8. Hooulumahiehie, "Moolelo Hoonaue Puuwai no Kama.A.Ka.Mahiai Ka Hi'apai'ole o ka Ikaika o ke Kai Huki Hee Nehu o Kahului," January 28, February 25, March 25, 1911 (hereafter cited as "Kamaakamahiai"); Kaawa, "Ka Hoomana Kahiko. Helu 16," May 4, 1865.
9. For an extended discussion on the names ʻŌiwi use for themselves, see Brown, *Facing the Spears*, xi–xiii.
10. Papahānaumokuākea, "About."
11. For a treatise on ʻāina akua, see Kikiloi, "Kūkulu."
12. Hooulumahiehie, "Keakaoku," July 27, August 3, 1912.
13. "He Moolelo Hawaii no Laiehau," April 4, 1914.
14. Lokai and Kamoe, "Ka Moolelo Hawaii," August 21, 1886.
15. Kamakau, "Ka Moolelo o Kamehameha," January 5, 1867.
16. "Ka Huakai i na Mokupuni," July 19, 1923.
17. Kaunamano, "Aukelenuiaiku," November 6, 1862.
18. Hooulumahiehie, "Kamaakamahiai," March 3, 1911.

19. Pukui, ʻŌlelo, 57.
20. Hooulumahiehie, Hiʻiakaikapoliopele, 61.

Introduction
1. Birrell, *Chinese Myths*, 22, 28, 42–43, 56.
2. Zecchi, *Sobek of Shedet*, 1, 19; Pinch, *Egyptian Mythology*, 200.
3. Rose, *Giants*, 1.
4. Jones and Ryan, *Encyclopedia of Hinduism*, 300.
5. Darian, "Makara," 29.
6. P. Rice, "Serpents," 866.
7. Imperato, *Legends, Sorcerers, and Enchanted Lizards*, 16.
8. Bacchilega and Brown, *Mermaids*, 273.
9. MacCulloch, "Serpent Worship," 400.
10. Ibid., 400, 401.
11. Sturluson and Gilchrist, *Prose Edda*, 42, 67, 78–80.
12. P. Rice, "Serpents," 866.
13. Taube, *Aztec and Maya Myths*, 37.
14. Baring and Cashford, *Myth of the Goddess*, 187.
15. Bropho, "Indigenous Australian."
16. NFSA, "Rainbow Serpent," n.p.
17. MacCulloch, "Serpent Worship," 401; Fox, *Threshold*, 81–82.
18. Coulter and Turner, *Encyclopedia of Ancient Deities*, 110.
19. Thomson, *Fijians*, 112.
20. Dinu and Balasubramanian, "Practice of Traditional Rituals," 2.
21. Taube, *Major Gods*, 147.
22. Birrell, *Chinese Myths*, 22.
23. MacCulloch, "Serpent Worship," 400.
24. Thomson, *Fijians*, 114.
25. Rose, *Giants*, 1.
26. Russell, *Devil*, 217, 245–246; R. M. Grant, *Early Christians*, 2, 4–5, 51.
27. Singh, Kaptchuk, and Henrich, "Small Gods," 5, 9–11, 14.
28. MacCulloch, "Serpent Worship," 401. No name is given for this deity.
29. MacCulloch, "Serpent Worship," 401; Bacchilega and Brown, *Mermaids*, 282.
30. Tregear, *Maori*, s.v. "The Deluge Legends."
31. Bacchilega and Brown, *Mermaids*, 274.
32. Darian, "Makara," 32, 34.
33. Charlot, "Aspects," 44, 45; Craig, *Dictionary*, s.v. "Pili"; Shultz, "Proverbial Expressions," 223; Turner, *Samoa*, 4–5; Tuvale, "Story of Pili and Sina," 5–8.

34. Charlot, "Aspects," 44.
35. Turner, *Samoa*, 44, 46.
36. Ibid., 44.
37. Ibid., 46–47.
38. Ibid.
39. Wilkes, *Narrative*, 117, 133.
40. Freeman, "Tradition of Sanalālā," 295, 296, 304.
41. Ibid., 304.
42. Gifford, *Tongan Myths*, 19–20.
43. Ibid., 194–195.
44. Ibid., 105.
45. Collocot, "Notes," 152.
46. Ibid., 232–233.
47. Tregear, *Maori*, s.vv. "Mokomoko," "Tutangatakino"; Best, *Maori Mythology*, 1:185, 219, 323.
48. Best, "Notes on the Art of War," 29.
49. Ibid., 30.
50. Ibid.
51. Ibid., 31.
52. Ibid.
53. Ibid., 38.
54. Department of Conservation, "Cultural Values and Tīkanga," n.p.
55. Ibid.
56. Best, "Notes on Maori Mythology," 9; Best, *Maori Mythology*, 1:270; Shortland, *Maori Religion*, 18; Tregear, *Maori*, s.vv. "Punga," "Tutewanana," "Tutewehiwehi."
57. Tregear, *Maori*, s.vv. "Mairangi," "Tuatara," "Tupari," "Mokomoko."
58. Ibid., s.v. "Miru."
59. Tregear, *Maori*, s.v. "Mokotiti"; White, *Ancient*, 96.
60. Craig, *Dictionary*, s.vv. "Hine-hua-rau," "Hotu-Puku," "Koronaki," "Mārongorongo," "Matipou," "Mokomoko," "Mokoroa," "Ngārara-huarau," "Uatai"; Tregear, *Maori*, s.vv. "Paoru," "Paroro-ariki," "Pouatehuri," "Rehu," "Rimurapa," "Rino-o-takaka," "Taungapiki."
61. Tregear, *Maori*, s.v. "Ngarara-Hurarau."
62. Craig, *Dictionary*, s.v. "Te-Rehu-O-Tainui."
63. Best, *Maori Mythology*, 1:219.
64. Ruatapu and Potae, "Three Old Stories," 19.
65. Ibid.
66. Ibid., 20.
67. Ruatapu and Potae, "Three Old Stories," 20.

68. Ibid.
69. Ibid., 20fn2.
70. Pukui and Elbert, *Hawaiian,* s.v. "kiha."
71. Tregear, *Maori,* s.vv. "ika," "ika-whenua," "ika: Te Ika-a-Rangitauria."
72. Te Whetū, "Killing of Te Kaiwhakaruaki," 5.
73. Ibid., 6.
74. Ibid.
75. Ibid.
76. Ibid., 5.
77. Ibid., 7.
78. Ibid., 8.
79. Fowler, "Of Taniwha, 12.
80. Best, *Maori Mythology,* 1:186–187.
81. Fowler, "Of Taniwha," 12, 13.
82. Ibid., 12.
83. Ibid.
84. Ibid., 13.
85. Best, *Maori Mythology,* 2:502–503.
86. "Taniwha of Wanganui River," 3.
87. Ibid.
88. Ibid., 3.
89. Ibid., 4.
90. Ibid., 5.
91. "Tukutuku at Tokomaru Bay," 25.
92. Bird, "Hinepoupou and Te Oriparoa," 11.
93. Best, *Maori Mythology,* 1:188.
94. Ibid., 2:507.
95. Wai Wai, "Waikaremoana," 44.
96. Best, *Maori Mythology,* 2:490.
97. Ibid., 1:191–192.
98. Ibid., 192.
99. Ibid., 193.
100. Ibid., 193.
101. Papamoa Maori School, "Patangata (Patuna)," 43.
102. Ibid.
103. Ibid.
104. Ibid.
105. Ibid., 43–44.
106. Ibid., 44.
107. Ibid., 44.

108. Ibid., 44.
109. Best, *Maori Mythology,* 1:188.
110. Ibid., 1:190.
111. Ibid.
112. Ibid., 1:190–191.
113. Te Reinga Maori School, "Hinekorako Mermaid," 45.
114. Ibid., 45.
115. Ibid., 46.
116. Ibid., 46.
117. Te Reinga Marae, "Our Story," n.p.
118. Cheeseman, "Notes," 452, 453, 455.
119. Ibid., 454, 456.
120. Ibid.
121. "Te Rangihiroa," 34.
122. "Gifts from the Maori People," 65.
123. Best, "Notes on the Occurrence of the Lizard," 325, 326, 330, 331, 332, 333, 334.
124. Ibid., 335.
125. Phillipps, "Incised Designs," 191–196; Barrow, "Maori Decorative Carving," 305.
126. Gill, *Myths and Songs,* 3–5. Vātea appears in other cosmogonies—for example, as Ātea in Tahiti and Pa'umotu and as Wākea in Hawai'i. T. Henry, *Ancient Tahiti,* 349–352, 355–356, 364–368, 374. I discuss Wākea and Papa in chapter 5. Notably, in one Tuamotuan creation chant, Ātea is born female but later exchanges genders with her partner Fa'ahotu because Fa'ahotu insisted on trying to use his nipples to feed their first three newborns, but, receiving no milk, they starved to death. T. Henry, *Ancient Tahiti,* 364–368, 372, 374.
127. Gill, *Myths and Songs,* 8, 10–11.
128. These two gods are known as Kanaloa and Lono in Hawai'i.
129. Gill, *Myths and Songs,* 3–4.
130. Gunson, "Gill, William Wyatt," n.p.; Gill, *Myths and Songs,* xix; Gill, *Life,* 96fn1.
131. Gill, *Myths and Songs,* 4.
132. Gill, *Life,* 96fn1.
133. Ibid., 225.
134. Ibid., 225–235.
135. Ibid., 227–228.
136. Ibid., 229–230.
137. Ibid., 234.

138. Ibid., 235.
139. Ibid., 235–236.
140. Ibid., 233.
141. Raphel Richter-Gravier, who carried out a "comparative study of birds in 300 traditional Polynesian stories," notes that there are no corresponding bird species in the Cook Islands for the *karakerake*. "Manu," 119fn54.
142. Gill, *Myths and Songs,* 20–21, 32, 35.
143. Robineau, *Moorea,* 10.
144. T. Henry, *Ancient Tahiti,* 383.
145. Ibid., 249, 383.
146. Handy, *Polynesian,* 125.
147. "Mo'o, le lézard," n.p.
148. T. Henry, *Ancient Tahiti,* 383.
149. Ibid.
150. Ibid.
151. Ibid., 377.
152. Ibid.
153. Ibid., 383.
154. Ibid., 228, 306. Henry's translation.
155. Walpole, *Four Years,* 135.
156. Ibid., 135–136.
157. Ibid., 136.
158. Ibid.
159. Ibid., 136–137.
160. Ibid., 137.
161. Ibid., 137.
162. T. Henry, *Ancient Tahiti,* 622.
163. Ibid., 622–623.
164. Ibid., 623.
165. "Ana Piro," n.p.
166. "Queue du lézard," n.p.
167. Stimson and Marshall, *Dictionary,* s.v. "moko"; Bacchilega and Brown, *Mermaids,* 5, 13.
168. Stimson and Marshall, *Dictionary,* s.vv. "moku," "mokongārara," "mokotea," "mokouri."
169. Craig, *Dictionary,* 3.
170. Handy, *Polynesian,* 129.
171. Manu-Tahi, *Te Parau,* 60.
172. Ibid., 61.

173. Best, *Maori Mythology*, 1:191.
174. Ibid.
175. Porter, *Journal*, 128.
176. Christian, "Notes," 190.
177. Suggs, *Archeology*, 8, 76, 144; Kjellgren and Ivory, *Adorning*, 88–89, 91.
178. Von den Steinen, "Maui's Fight," 125–126.
179. Handy, "Huuti and Te-Moo-Nieve," in *Marquesan Legends*, 21.
180. Ibid., 22.
181. Ibid., 22–24.
182. Ibid., 24–25.
183. Ibid., 25.
184. Ibid.
185. Ibid., 24, 25.
186. "Légende du tiki," n.p.
187. Candelot, "On the Trail," 95, 102, 103; "Météorite," n.p.
188. A. Akana, "History of Moku'ula."
189. Métraux, *Ethnology*, 18.
190. Candelot, "On the Trail," 95, 96, 100.
191. Routledge, *Mystery*, 243.
192. Geiseler, *Geiseler's Easter Island*, 2, 66, 67, 68, 95, 112, 115, 139, 158; "Lizardman Figure (Moko)," n.p.; "Moko (Lizard Figure)," n.p.
193. Orliac and Orliac, "Wooden Figurines," 627.
194. Métraux, *Ethnology*, 169.
195. Ibid., 170.
196. Ibid.
197. Ibid., 318.
198. Ibid., 370.
199. Ibid.
200. Ibid., 369.
201. Ibid., 369.
202. Ibid.
203. Ibid., 370.
204. Ibid.
205. Craig, *Dictionary*, 319, s.v. "Vie-Moko"; Métraux, *Ethnology*, 316–317, 323.
206. Métraux, *Ethnology*, 323, 367.
207. Ibid., 323.
208. Ibid., 367.
209. Ibid.
210. *Merriam-Webster Dictionary*, s.v. "genre."

211. Examples of genres include mele koʻihonua (genealogical chant cele-
brating the connection between deities, humans, and place); moʻokūʻauhau (genealogy); mele inoa (chants commemorating names); mele maʻi
(chants commemorating the sacred procreative potential of genitals);
kānaenae and kanikau (poetic laments eulogizing deities, people,
places, or things); oli (chants); pule (prayer chants); ʻōlelo noʻeau (poetic sayings that can be didactic and/or commemorative); and inoa
(names).
212. Pukui and Elbert, *Hawaiian,* s.v. "moʻolelo."
213. For a list of genres Pukui includes under "moʻolelo," see Pukui and Elbert, *Hawaiian,* s.v. "moʻolelo."
214. Pukui and Elbert, *Hawaiian,* s.v. "moʻo"; Kamakau, "Ka Moolelo Hawaii," April 28, 1870.
215. Handy and Pukui, *Polynesian Family System,* 197.
216. My decision to spell *Hainakolo* as *Haʻinākolo* is based on Pukui's re-
telling of the story as she heard it from her mother, Mary Paʻahana
Kanakaʻole Wiggin. Pukui related this account to Beckwith, who summarized it in *Hawaiian Mythology:* "She was named Haʻi-na-ko-lo because her mother had followed (hoʻo-ko-lo) and scolded (ko-lo-ko-lo)
her husband" (Beckwith, *Hawaiian Mythology,* 506n1, 506–507). According to Beckwith, this version has never been published (506n1).
The full version is found in Beckwith's personal papers in a document
in which she compares different versions of this account (Beckwith,
"Legend of Hainakolo"). For examples of the Haʻinākolo and
Keaniniʻulaokalani traditions, see Ka-Lama-Ku-I-Ke-Au-Kaahiki, "Hainakolo"; Ka Ohu Haaheo i na kuahiwi, "Hainakolo"; Hooulumahiehie,
"Hainakolo"; Kahoewaa, "Keaniniulaokalani." Westervelt appropriated Kahoewaʻa's account but did not credit him for the story
(Westervelt, "Ke-Au-Nini").
217. Pukui and Elbert, *Hawaiian,* s.v. "kaʻao"; Andrews, *Dictionary,* s.v.
"kaʻao"; Andrews and Parker, *Dictionary,* s.v. "kaao."
218. Haleole, "Laieikawai," November 19–April 4, 1863; Haleole, *Laieikawai,* n.p.
219. "He Moolelo Hawaii Nani no Kekalukaluokewa," April 16, 1910–
November 18, 1911.
220. Kaawa, "Hoomana kahiko. Helu 31," December 23, 1865.
221. Kamakau, "Moolelo o Hawaii nei," September 9, 1865.
222. Bush and Paaluhi, "Hiiakaikapoliopele," January 5, 1893.
223. Charlot, "Aspects," 37. See also Charlot, "Application of Form."
224. Wise and Kihe, "Ka-Miki," January 8, 1914–December 6, 1917.

225. Maly and Maly, *He Wahi Moʻolelo,* 15–16.
226. Perreira, "He Haʻiōlelo Kuʻuna," xiv–xvi.
227. For a discussion on authenticity discourse, see Brown, "Mauna Kea"; hoʻomanawanui, "This Land."
228. Here, I am indebted to Henry Glassie for his work on tradition. See "Tradition."
229. Nogelmeier, *Mai Paʻa,* 1.
230. Mookini, *Hawaiian,* iii, 1–41.
231. Kuwada, "How Blue," 81.
232. Nogelmeier, *Mai Paʻa,* 2.
233. Papakilo Database, "About," n.p.
234. Wise and Kihe, "Ka-Miki," January 8, 1914–December 6, 1917.
235. McMillen and Morris, *Hawaii.*
236. McMillen and Morris, *Hawaii,* 2; Dunn, Haraguchi, and Quirante, "Directory," 4. These papers have since been added to the Papakilo Database.
237. For discussions on the importance of understanding Hawaiian-language newspapers' political and religious orientations, see Silva, *Aloha Betrayed;* Silva, *Power;* Brown, "Politics and Poetics."
238. Pukui, *ʻŌlelo Noʻeau,* 24; Opio, "He Moolelo no Umi," June 1, 1865; unsigned editorial, "No na Kaao," January 16, 1862; K. U., "Hoike Oiaio," May 4, 1878.
239. hoʻomanawanui, "Pele's Appeal," 436–491. See also hoʻomanawanui, *Voices of Fire.*
240. Kimura, *Ka Leo Hawaiʻi.*
241. Pukui and Elbert, *Hawaiian,* 565–572.
242. Kawailiula, "Kawelo," September 26, 1861; hoʻomanawanui, *Voices of Fire.* For a discussion of *Ka Hoku o ka Pakipika* and other Hawaiian-language newspapers, see Silva, *Aloha Betrayed.*
243. Stanford Humanities Center, "What Are the Humanities?," n.p.
244. I will discuss poetic devices and metadiscursive practices more in-depth later on. *Metadiscourse,* in its most basic sense, is the "talk" about a "text" in the text itself.
245. This "visceral aloha for our ʻāina" is one aspect of the term "aloha ʻāina." For discussions on aloha ʻāina, see Silva, *Power,* 4–6.
246. Charlot, *Classical,* 223–247.
247. Ibid., 226.
248. Ibid., 244.
249. Malo, *Moʻolelo,* 2:6.

Chapter 1: Moʻo Akua and Water

1. Eliade, *Patterns,* 188.
2. *Merriam-Webster Dictionary,* s.v. "water."
3. Ibid.
4. Ibid.
5. Eliade, *Patterns,* 189.
6. National Park Service, "Wailuku River," n.p.
7. Hapai, *Legends of the Wailuku,* 2 (hereafter cited as *Legends*).
8. Department of Land and Natural Resources, "Wailuku River State Park," n.p.
9. Hapai, *Legends,* 5.
10. Ibid.
11. Ibid., 6.
12. Ibid.
13. Kelsey, "Kahulihuli," 34.
14. Pukui, Elbert, and Mookini, *Place Names,* s.v. "Kālua-kanaka."
15. Manu, "Keaomelemele," May 9, 1885; Manu, "Laukaieie," *Nupepa Ka Oiaio,* September 14, 1894; Kahoewaa, "Keaniniulaokalani," September 23, 1882.
16. Hooulumahiehie, *Hiʻiakaikapoliopele,* 87.
17. Kelsey, "Kahulihuli," 34.
18. Manu, *Keaomelemele,* 77.
19. Hooulumahiehie, *Hiʻiakaikapoliopele,* 87.
20. Kaili is Emma Nakuina, who is writing under a shortened version of her middle name. Kaili, "Hiiaka," September 15, 1883.
21. David Wallace, personal communication, 2009.
22. Kauhi, *Moʻolelo no Kapaʻahu,* 2, 80.
23. Hawaii Center for Volcanology, "Mauna Kea," n.p.
24. Taylor, "Ku-Kahau-ula and Poliahu," 14–16; Hooulumahiehie, "Hainakolo," January 1–June 20, 1907. In Wiggin's version of Haʻinākolo, Moʻoinanea is a moʻo and Haʻinākolo's kupunawahine (grandmother or female ancestor), but the motif of Moʻoinanea guarding a pool is absent. Beckwith, "Legend of Hainakolo."
25. Taylor, "Ku-Kahau-ula and Poliahu," July 1931.
26. Hooulumahiehie, "Hainakolo," January 31, February 8, March 12, 1907.
27. USGS, "Earth's Largest Active Volcano," n.p.
28. Hooulumahiehie, "Kamaakamahiai," April 29, 1911.
29. Pukui and Elbert, *Hawaiian,* s.v. "lani"; Andrews, *Dictionary,* s.v. "lani"; Andrews and Parker, *Dictionary,* s.v. "lani."

30. Manu, "Keaomelemele," September 6, 1884, April 25, 1885. For an English translation of this story, see Manu, *Keaomelemele*.
31. *Merriam-Webster Dictionary*, s.v. "cloud"; Manu, "Keaomelemele," October 25, 1884.
32. "Kalalau Puna a ka Lawakua," July 15, 1893.
33. Pukui, Elbert, and Mookini, *Place Names*, s.v. "Hiʻilawe."
34. Thomas, "Interview with John Thomas," July 29, 1969, n.p.
35. Akana, "Interview with Dora Akana, Jack Ward and Don Johnson," April 27, 1961, n.p.; Akana, "Interview with Dora Akana and Mary Kawena Pukui," January 19, 1962, n.p.
36. Kahiolo, "Kamapuaa," August 28, 1861.
37. Kaualilinoe, "Kamaakamahiai," August 8, 19, October 7, 1911.
38. Ahiki, "Na hiohiona," October 14, 1871.
39. S. K., "Luahuna," March 26, 1897.
40. Native Plants, "*Metrosideros polymorpha*," n.p.; Native Plants, "*Acacia koa*," n.p.
41. Poepoe, "Ka Moolelo Kaao o Hiiaka-i-ka-Poli-o-Pele," September 25, 1908 (hereafter cited as "Hiiakaikapoliopele"). Poepoe identifies Panaʻewa as male; Hooulumahiehie, "Hiiakaikapoliopele," August 6, 7, 8, 9, 10, 1906. Hoʻoulumāhiehie does not specify Panaʻewa's gender.
42. "Kekalukaluokewa," October 14, 1911.
43. Clark, personal communication, 2009; Clark, *Hawaiʻi Place Names*, s.v. "Pray for Sex"; Leandra Wai, personal communication during a Mākua Valley access.
44. Manu, "Laukaieie," *Nupepa Ka Oiaio*, May 24, 1895.
45. Hapai, *Legends*, 28–33.
46. Wise and Kihe, "Ka-Miki," June 10, 17, 1915.
47. Pukui, Elbert, and Mookini, *Place Names*, s.v. "Palahemo."
48. Kensley and Williams, "New Shrimp," 418.
49. Pukui, *ʻŌlelo*, 136.
50. Kekahuna, Map SP 201869, n.p.
51. Kalakaua, *Legends*, 411.
52. Kekoowai, "Makalei," August 10, 1922. For an English synopsis of this account, see de Silva, "Māpuna," September 1982, n.p.
53. Kawainui is an extensive wetland area that once ran from far inland to the ocean, and it served as a large fishpond. Efforts to restore Kawainui are ongoing. Unfortunately, where Kaʻelepulu fishpond was is now a subdivision known as Enchanted Lakes.
54. Wise and Kihe, "Ka-Miki," April 6, 1914.

55. Handy and Pukui, *Polynesian Family System*, 121.
56. Ii, "Na Hunahuna," September 4, 11, 18, 1869.
57. Ibid., September 4, 1869.
58. Ibid., September 11, 1869.
59. Medeiros, "Interview with Josephine," May 5, 1960, n.p.
60. Handy and Pukui, *Polynesian Family System*, 125.
61. McAllister, *Archaeology*, 157, 186. McAllister was an ethnologist for the Bishop Museum from 1929 to 1931 (Davis and Bramblett, *Report*, n.p.).
62. McAllister, *Archaeology*, 157.
63. Hooulumahiehie, "Hiiakaikapoliopele," January 22, 1906.
64. Kapihenui, "Hiiakaikapoliopele," February 6, 1862.
65. Poepoe, "Hiiakaikapoliopele," July 9, 1909.
66. De Silva, "Māpuna," September 1982, n.p.
67. John Clark, personal communication, 2009. Clark received this information from January Kahana (March 18, 1973) and Kaokai (March 20, 1973).
68. McAllister, *Archaeology*, 73.
69. Punua, "Transcript," n.d.
70. L. L. Henry, *He'eia Fishpond*, n.p.
71. BOSSdancefriends, "3c. Meheanu."
72. Keola, "Ike Hou," September 3, 1892; "Ka Hoolaa Luakini," January 26, 1933.
73. "Ka Ike Hou Ana," January 2, 1914.
74. Pukui, Elbert, and Mookini, *Place Names*, s.v. "'Auwai-o-limu."
75. Naone, "Interview with Julia Naone," May 3, 1960, n.p.
76. Kalei Nu'uhiwa, personal communication.
77. College of Tropical Agriculture, "Rapid 'Ōhi'a Death," n.p.
78. Awana, "Moo Waha," January 27, 1922.
79. Makuakane, "Interview with Elizabeth Makuakane," June 14, 1962, n.p.
80. Farley, "Notes on Maulili," 92.
81. Damon, *Koamalu*, 192–193; Wichman, *Kaua'i*, 40.
82. Wichman, *Kaua'i*, 102.
83. Nakuina, "Punahou Spring," 133–138. For a Hawaiian version of this account, see "Kahi i Loaa," November 26, 1915, which includes other stories about the origins of Punahou Spring.
84. Pua Case, personal communication; Brennan, *Parker Ranch*, 182–183. For an article on Manaua, see Kevin Dayton, "Waimea Water Spirit's Legend Grows," n.p.
85. Poepoe, "Hiiakaikapoliopele," July 16, 1909.
86. Ibid.

87. Ibid.
88. Kamakau, "Ka Moolelo Hawaii," April 28, 1870.
89. McAllister, *Archaeology*, 157.
90. Medeiros, "Interview with Josephine," May 5, 1960, n.p.
91. Ibid.
92. Pukui, Elbert, and Mookini, *Place Names*, s.v. "Ka-moʻo-lā-liʻi."
93. Pukui and Green, *Folktales*, 48.
94. Bacchilega and Brown, *Mermaids*, 273, 276, 277.
95. J. Emerson, "Lesser," 6.

Chapter 2: The Moʻo Akua Form and the Kino Lau Associated with All Moʻo

1. Handy and Pukui, *Polynesian Family System*, 122–123.
2. Ibid., 28, 116.
3. Kanahele, *Ka Honua Ola*, 123.
4. For a bilingual (English-Hawaiian) version of this story, see Fornander, "Legend of Aukelenuiaiku," in Fornander, *Fornander*, 4:32–111.
5. Beckwith, "Legend of Hainakolo," 161.
6. Haleole, *Laieikawai*, 60–86, 99, 104.
7. Ibid., 104–105.
8. Nuʻuhiwa, personal communication, 2019; Allred and Allred, "Development," 67–68.
9. "He Moolelo Nani no Kekalukaluokewa," October 11, 14, 1911.
10. Ibid.
11. Ibid., September 16, 1911.
12. Handy and Pukui, *Polynesian Family System*, 125.
13. Ii, "Na Hunahuna," September 4, 1969; Kamakau, "Ka Moolelo Hawaii," April 28, 1870; "Ka Moolelo no Kihapiilani," November 21, 1870; Manu, "Kihapiilani," February 2, 1884.
14. Wichman, *Kauaʻi*, 38.
15. John Kaimikaua, quoted in Hui Mālama o Moʻomomi, "Moʻomomi," 20.
16. "He Moolelo Hawaii no Laiehau," April 4, 1914.
17. Nipoa and Kuhalaoa, "Keamalu," June 12, July 17, 1862.
18. Olopana-Nui-Akea, "Kila a Moikeha," February 7, 1907.
19. Hooulumahiehie, "Kamaakamahiai," April 20, 1912.
20. Kamakau, "Ka Moolelo Hawaii," January 6, 1870.
21. Mokumaia, "Moanalua," April 7, 1922.
22. Ibid., April 21, 1922.
23. Pukui, *ʻŌlelo*, 225.
24. Ii, "Na Hunahuna," January 15, 1870.

25. Kamakau, "Ka Moolelo Hawaii," April 28, May 4, 1870; Kamakau, *Poʻe Kahiko*, 83.
26. Pukui, Haertig, and Lee, *Nānā*, 1:125.
27. Hooulumahiehie, *Hiʻiakaikapoliopele*, 159–160.
28. Ibid., 269. See also Desha, "He Moolelo Kaao no Hiiaka-i-ka-Poli-o-Pele ka Wahine i ka Hikina a ka La, ao ka Uʻi Palekoki Uwila o Halemaumau," February 22, 1927 (hereafter cited as "Hiiakaikapoliopele"); Bush and Paaluhi, "Hiiakaikapoliopele," May 1, 1893.
29. Hooulumahiehie, "Hainakolo," April 11, 1907.
30. Manu, "He Moolelo Kaao Hawaii no ke Kaua Nui Weliweli mawaena o Pele-Keahiloa me Waka-Keakaikawai," December 9, 1899 (hereafter cited as "Pele and Waka").
31. Pukui and Elbert, *Hawaiian*, s.vv. "moʻo ʻalā," "moʻo kā," "moʻo kaʻalā," moʻo kā lāʻau," "moʻo kāula," "moʻo makāula," "moʻo kiha."
32. Stejneger, "Land Reptiles," 788.
33. Ibid., 783. Because Stejneger neglected to include the common names, I added that information from the Bishop Museum Reptiles and Amphibian Checklist.
34. Ibid., 783–784.
35. Ibid., 784.
36. Makaʻai, "Kaniʻāina." During Makaʻai's conversation with *Ka Leo Hawaiʻi* host Larry Kimura, Makaʻai reiterates the proper pronunciation after Kimura mispronounces it—there is no mistaking that Makaʻai is saying *kīauwahine*, but a search for this term on the Papakilo Database and on Ulukau did not yield results.
37. Pukui and Elbert, *Hawaiian*, s.v. "ʻalā."
38. McKeown, *Field Guide*, 52–53.
39. Holt, "Mottled Snake-Eyed Skink," n.p.
40. "Ka Moolelo no Kihapiilani," November 11, 1870.
41. Pukui and Elbert, *Hawaiian*, s.v. "puhi uha."
42. Manu, "Kihapiilani," February 9, 1884.
43. Ibid.
44. Maciolek, "Taxonomic," 359.
45. Brasher, "Technical Report," 2.
46. Manu, "Ku-ula," 239–240.
47. Pukui and Green, *Folktales*, 48.
48. "Luhi–a," n.d. I could not find more information about Cobb-Adams' address or the location of "Kauwa Bridge."
49. Ahiki, "Na hiohiona," October 14, 1871.

50. Manu, "Pele and Waka," December 9, 1899; Pukui and Elbert, *Hawaiian*, s.v. "hiʻukole." "Hiʻu" means "tail" while "kole" and "ʻula" denote "red."
51. Titcomb, *Native Use of Fish in Hawaii*, 127.
52. Ibid.
53. Pukui and Elbert, *Hawaiian*, s.v. "ʻapowai."
54. Pukui, Haertig, and Lee, *Nānā*, 2:2.
55. Manu, "Kihapiilani," February 23, 1884.
56. Here, I am following Mary Kawena Pukui and Laura C. Green's spelling of "Paʻe" in a publication that preceded the common use of the kahakō (Pukui and Green, *Folktales*, 45–46). The name is likely to be either "paʻē" or "pāʻē" since there is no word "paʻe" and no configuration in which a name would be made up of "pa" (without "kō") and "e" (without "kō").
57. Pukui and Green, *Folktales*, 45–46.
58. Ibid., 44–45.
59. Pooloa, "Na Aui," October 15, 1925.
60. Manu, "Kihapiilani," February 23, 1884; Hooulumahiehie, "Kamaakamahiai," March 30, 1912; Manu, "Pele and Waka," December 9, 1899.
61. Handy and Pukui, *Polynesian Family System*, 125.
62. Simon, "Arachnida," 443–519.
63. Ibid.
64. Prószyñski, "Survey of Havaika," 206.
65. Simon, "Arachnida," 448.
66. Gillespie and Rivera, "Free-Living Spiders," 11.
67. Ibid., 12.
68. Manu, "Pele and Waka," November 18, 1899.
69. Ibid.
70. Ibid., November 4, 1899.
71. Ibid., October 28, 1899.
72. Hooulumahiehie, "Keakaoku," March 15, 23, 30, 1912.

Chapter 3: Moʻo-Specific Kino Lau

1. Westervelt, *Legends of Old Honolulu*, 276.
2. Haleole, "Laieikawai," January 17, February 14, 28, 1863; Kaulainamoku, "Kepakailiula," May 11, 1865; Manu, "Keaomelemele," April 25, May 9, 1885; "He Kaao Hoonaue Puuwai no Puakaohelo," May 5, June 23, July 21, 1894; "He Moolelo Hawaii Nani no Kekalukaluokewa," September 16, October 11, 14, 1911.
3. Pukui, Elbert, and Mookini, *Place Names*, s.v. "Pūʻahuʻula."

4. Desha, "Hiiakaikapoliopele," April 19, 1927. For a similar version of this scene, see Hooulumahiehie, *Hiʻiakaikapoliopele,* 292.
5. Manu, "Keaomelemele," May 9, 1885.
6. Poepoe, "Hiiakaikapoliopele," April 9, 1909. This line is difficult to interpret, and there is insufficient context to know for sure whether Moʻolau's skirt hides something about her body that shows her to be a moʻo, or these little moʻo bodies are her children hiding beneath her skirt, or that her larger moʻo form comprises many tiny moʻo.
7. Ibid.
8. Wise and Kihe, "Ka-Miki," September 17, 1914.
9. Ibid., March 30, 1916.
10. Manu, "Pele and Waka," October 21, November 4, 1899.
11. Beckwith, *Hawaiian Mythology,* 264.
12. Annie Kaʻaukai, interview by Charles Langlas, March 3, 2011, which he kindly shared with me via email on April 20, 2011.
13. Kenui, "Interview with Caroline Kenui," HAW 200.21, August 9, 1968.
14. Sterling and Summers, *Sites,* 208; Pukui, Elbert, and Mookini, *Place Names,* s.v. "Ka-moʻo-aliʻi."
15. Ka Ohu Haaheo i na kuahiwi, "Hainakolo," April 10, 1912.
16. "Kaao no Hoamakeikekula," May 28, June 6, 1935. For a translation of this account, see Fornander, "Legend of Hoamakeikekula," in Fornander, *Fornander,* 4:532–540.
17. Desha, "Hiiakaikapoliopele," October 23, 30, 1924; Poepoe, "Hiiakaikapoliopele," April 3, 17, 1908; this episode is quite similar to one Hoʻoulumāhiehie offers, which is the only epic-length version thus far translated into English. Hooulumahiehie, *Hiʻiakaikapoliopele,* 10–24.
18. Desha, "Hiiakaikapoliopele," October 30, 1924.
19. Hooulumahiehie, *Hiʻiakaikapoliopele,* 146.
20. Poepoe, "Hiiakaikapoliopele," July 9, 1909.
21. Ibid., July 16, 1909.
22. "Ka Moolelo no Kihapiilani," November 28, 1870.
23. Kanepuu, "Hamanalau," March 14, 1861.
24. Manu, "Laukaieie," *Nupepa ka Oiaio,* December 28, 1894.
25. Ibid., January 4, 1894.
26. Ibid., January 5, 1894.
27. Hukilani, "Kumumanao," November 19, 1864.
28. Ibid.
29. Nipoa and Kuhalaoa, "Keamalu," September 18, 1862.
30. Kaulainamoku, "Kepakailiula," April 6, 1865.
31. Beckwith, "Legend of Hainakolo," 161.

32. Hooulumahiehie, "Hainakolo," January 30, 31, 1907.
33. Ibid., February 8, March 12, 19, April 11, 1907.
34. Kaulainamoku, "Hiku i ka Nahele," April 8, 1874.
35. Hooulumahiehie, "Kamaakamahiai," April 20, 1912.
36. Olopana-Nui-Akea, "Kila a Moikeha," November 22, 1913.
37. Hooulumahiehie, "Keakaoku," March 30, 1912.
38. Ibid., January 21, 1882.
39. Ibid., February 18, 1882.
40. W. H. Rice, *Hawaiian Legends*, 110.
41. Ibid.
42. Hooulumahiehie, *Hi'iakaikapoliopele*, 128.
43. Kamakau, "Ka Moolelo Hawaii," December 2, 1869.
44. McAllister, *Archaeology*, 173.
45. Ibid.
46. Punua, "Transcript," n.p.
47. "Novelties," November 21, 1857.
48. Pukui, Elbert, and Mookini, *Place Names*, s.v. "Pū-'ahu'ula."
49. Manu, *Keaomelemele*, 163.
50. Pukui and Elbert, *Hawaiian*, s.v. "puhi."
51. Kamakau, "Ka Moolelo o Hawaii Nei," July 22, 1865.
52. Ibid.
53. Kamakau, *Tales and Traditions*, 28.
54. Kamakau, "Ka Moolelo o Hawaii Nei," September 30, 1865.
55. Kamakau, *Tales and Traditions*, 77.
56. "He Moolelo Hawaii Nani no Kekalukaluokewa," July 23, August 13, 1910.
57. Westervelt, *Legends of Ma-ui*, 153.
58. "Ka Moolelo no Kihapiilani," November 28, 1870; Manu, "Kihapi-ilani," January 19, 1884.
59. Manu, "Pele and Waka," December 16, 1899.
60. Medeiros, "Interview with Josephine," May 5, 1960, n.p.
61. "He Moolelo Hawaii Nani no Kekalukaluokewa," July 23, August 13, 1910.
62. Titcomb, "Native Use of Marine Invertebrates," 337.
63. "He Moolelo Hawaii Nani no Kekalukaluokewa," July 23, August 13, 1910.
64. Manu, "Pele and Waka," December 9, 16, 1899.
65. Kahiolo, "Kamapuaa," July 17, 1861; Fornander, "Kamapuaa," in Fornander, *Fornander*, 5:332.
66. Hooulumahiehie, "Hainakolo," June 27, 28, 1907.

67. Manu, "Pele and Waka," December 16, 1899.
68. Olopana-Nui-Akea, "Kila a Moikeha," May 9, 16, 1914.
69. "Ka Moolelo no Kihapiilani," November 28, 1870; Manu, "Kihapiilani," January 19, 1884.
70. Johnson, *Mo'olelo Hawai'i,* 89.
71. Handy and Pukui, *Polynesian Family System,* 217.
72. Hooulumahiehie, "Kamaakamahiai," March 30, 1912.
73. Hooulumahiehie, *Hi'iakaikapoliopele,* 57; N. Emerson, *Pele and Hiiaka,* 30–46.
74. Handy and Pukui, *Polynesian Family System,* 220–221.
75. Kapihenui, "Hiiakaikapoliopele," January 16, 23, 1862; Bush and Paaluhi, "Hiiakaikapolipele," February 23, 24, 27, 1893; Hooulumahiehie, "Hiiakaikapoliopele," December 15, 16, 1905; Poepoe, "Hiiakaikapoliopele," March 19, 26, 1909; Desha, "Hiiakaikapoliopele," August 18, 20, 1925; N. Emerson, *Pele and Hiiaka,* 49.
76. Hooulumahiehie, "Hiiakaikapoliopele," December 15, 16, 1905; Hooulumahiehie, *Hi'iakaikapoliopele,* 113–115; Desha, "Hiiakaikapoliopele," August 18, 20, 1925.
77. Kapihenui, "Hiiakaikapoliopele," January 16, 23, 1862.
78. N. Emerson, *Pele and Hiiaka,* 49.
79. Manu, "Pele and Waka," December 9, 1899.
80. Ibid., May 20, 1911.
81. Manu, "Keaomelemele," October 25, 1884.
82. Poepoe, "Hiiakaikapoliopele," October 2, 1908.
83. Hooulumahiehie, "Hiiakaikapoliopele," August 22, 1906.
84. Hooulumahiehie, "Kamaakamahiai," May 20, 27, 1911.
85. Ibid., July 1, 1911.
86. *Encyclopedia Britannica,* s.v. "Whirlwind."
87. Kaui, "He Kaao no Pikoiakaalala," February 17, 1866.
88. Ibid., June 24, July 1, 1911.
89. Ibid., July 8, 1911.
90. Pukui and Elbert, *Hawaiian,* s.v. "Kākea."
91. Olopana-Nui-Akea, "Kila a Moikeha," May 2, 9, 16, June 6, 20, 1914.
92. Kanepuu, "Hamanalau," March 14, 1861.
93. Tava and Keale, *Niihau,* 20, 21.
94. W. H. Rice, *Hawaiian Legends,* 112.
95. Ibid. Some of these islands are alternatively known as Mokuālai, Moku'auia, and Kukuiho'olua. Pukui, Elbert, and Mookini, *Place Names,* s.vv. "Mokuālai," "Mokuālai"; Clark, *Hawai'i Place Names,* s.v. "Kukuiho'olua."

96. J. K. Kahele, "He Moolelo no Molokini," July 24, 1930. For a bilingual version of this account, see J. K. Kahele, "Myth Concerning Molokini," in Fornander, *Fornander.*

97. Poepoe, "Hiiakaikapoliopele," July 30, 1909. See also Kapihenui, "Hiiakaikapoliopele," February 13, 1862; Bush and Paaluhi, "Hiiakaikapoliopele," March 20, 1893; N. Emerson, *Pele and Hiiaka,* 91.

98. Olopana-Nui-Akea, "Kila a Moikeha," September 19, 26, 1914.

99. Leandra Wai, personal communication during a Mākua Valley access; Clark, *Hawai'i Place Names,* s.v. "Pray for Sex."

100. McElroy, Eminger, and Elison, "Final," 15–16.

101. Ibid., 16.

102. Ibid.

103. Poole, "Kapualei," n.p.; David Wallace, personal communication, 2009.

104. Hooulumahiehie, *Hi'iakaikapolipele,* 89.

105. Kapihenui, "Hiiakaikapoliopele," May 3, 1862; Desha, "Hiiakaikapoliopele," April 19, 1927; Hooulumahiehie, *Hi'iakaikapoliopele,* 312–316; untitled editorial, June 11, 1897; "Haina Nane," *Ka Nupepa Kuokoa,* October 2, 1908.

106. Hooulumahiehie, *Hi'iakaikapoliopele,* 313, 314; Desha, "Hiiakaikapoliopele," April 19, May 3, 1927. Kamō'ili'ili Church no longer exists. In its place is Kūhiō Elementary School. Pukui, Elbert, and Mookini, *Place Names,* s.v. "Mō-'ili'ili."

107. Kamahele, "Ka Ike Hou," February 6, 1914.

108. Pukui, Elbert, and Mookini, *Place Names,* s.v. "Waināli'i."

109. Sterling and Summers, *Sites,* 277.

Chapter 4: Kinship and Antagonism between the Mo'o and Pele Clans
1. Beckwith, *Hawaiian Mythology,* 127.

2. Pukui and Green, *Folktales,* 49.

3. Beckwith, *Hawaiian Mythology,* 193.

4. Brown, *Facing the Spears,* 5, 9–11.

5. ho'omanawanui, "He Mo'olelo," 139.

6. Ibid., 139–140.

7. Ibid., 140.

8. Ibid.

9. Beckwith, *Kumulipo,* 110, 232; "Moolelo Hawaii," April 14, 1858; Kalimahauna, "O ke kumu," February 13, 1862; Fornander, *Fornander,* 4:13; Kepelino, *Traditions,* 190; Ii, "Na Hunahuna," September 4, 1869; Kamakau, "Ka Moolelo Hawaii," December 2, 1869; Hooulumahiehie, "Kamaakamahiai," February 25, 1911.

10. Bush and Paaluhi, "Hiiakaikapoliopele," January 6, 1893; Kaawa, "Hoomana Kahiko. Helu 5," February 2, 1865; Kaawa, "Hoomana Kahiko. Helu 6," February 9, 1865; Manu, "Pele and Waka," May 13, 1899; W. H. Rice, "He Moolelo no Pele," May 21, 1908; "He Moolelo Hawaii no Laiehau," January 30, 1915; N. Emerson, *Pele and Hiiaka,* ix; Hooulumahiehie, *Hiʻiakaikapoliopele,* 391, 394–395, 397.

11. Bush and Paaluhi, "Hiiakaikapoliopele," January 6, 1893; W. H. Rice, "He Moolelo no Pele," May 21, 1908.

12. Manu, "Pele and Waka," May 13, 1899; Manu, "Keaomelemele," September 6, 1884; Manu, "Laukaieie," *Ka Leo o ka Lahui,* April 26, 1895.

13. Manu, "Keaomelemele," September 4, 1884.

14. Manu, "Pele and Waka," May 13, 1899.

15. Ibid.

16. Ibid.

17. "He Moolelo Hawaii no Laiehau," January 1, 1915.

18. Ibid., April 4, 1914.

19. Ibid.

20. Ibid., February 13, 1915.

21. Kamakau, "Moolelo o Hawaii Nei," June 15, 1865; Fornander, "Legend of Aukelenuiaiku," in Fornander, *Fornander,* 4:32–111; Kaunamano, "Aukelenuiaiku," November 6–December 25, 1862; "He Moolelo no Aukelenuiaiku," *Ka Nupepa Puka ka La Aloha Aina,* October 4–November 17, 1893; Mokumaia, "Aukelenuiaiku," November 17, December 29, 1927; "Ka Moolelo o ka Aina," *Ke Alakai o Hawaii,* April 27–September 28, 1933; "He Moolelo no Aukelenuiaiku," *Hoku o Hawaii,* February 28, 1933; "Moolelo no Aukelenuiaiku," *Hoku o Hawaii,* December 20–January 10, 1939; "Moolelo no Aukelenuiaiku," *Hoku o Hawaii,* September 18, 1939–March 26, 1941. Only the versions offered by Fornander, Kaunamano, and the unsigned versions in *Ke Alakai o Hawaii* and *Hoku o Hawaii* (September 18, 1939–March 26, 1941), which are similar, are complete. With the exception of Fornander and the unsigned version in *Ka Nupepa Puka La Aloha Aina,* the other versions seem to be based on Kaunamano's account. I rely largely on Kaunamano's version because it most closely links Nāmakaokahaʻi to Moʻoinanea.

22. Kaunamano, "Aukelenuiaiku," November 6, 1862.

23. Ibid., November 27, 1862.

24. In Hoʻoulumāhiehie's version, Pele asks their brother Kauilanuimaka-ʻehaikalani to put his lightning into Hiʻiaka's skirt. This "lightning skirt" is mentioned throughout the story, but its origin is explained early on (Hooulumahiehie, *Hiʻiakaikapoliopele,* 33–34, 51, 58, 60, 61). In

Poepoe's version, Pele seems to be the skirt's power (Poepoe, "Hiiakaika-poliopele," June 12, 19, 26, October 9, 1908). In Desha's version, Hiʻiaka also has a lightning skirt, but who embues it with lightning is not explained (Desha, "Hiiakaikapoliopele," April 13, 1926).

25. Handy and Pukui, *Polynesian Family System*, 181.
26. Tangarō Taupōuri, *Wahipana*, n.p.
27. Charlot, "Feather Skirt," 137.
28. Kamakau, "Moolelo o Hawaii Nei," June 15, 1865.
29. Ibid.
30. Kaunamano, "Aukelenuiaiku," November 6, 1862.
31. Ibid., November 27, 1862.
32. Ibid.
33. Poepoe, "Hiiakaikapoliopele," January 17, 1908.
34. Fornander, "Legend of Aukelenuiaiku," in Fornander, *Fornander*, 4:94–96; Kaunamano, "Aukeleniaiku," December 11, 1862.
35. Kaunamano, "Aukelenuiaiku," December 4, 11, 1862.
36. Ibid., December 18, 1862.
37. Kaulainamoku, "Kepakailiula," April 13, 1865.
38. Ibid., June 8, 1865.
39. Ibid., April 13, 1865.
40. Kekahuna, Map SP 201869, March 15, 1952.
41. Kaualilinoe, "Kamaakamahiai," November 26, December 10, 24, 1870, January 14, 1871; Hooulumahiehie, "Kamakamahiai," March 4, 11, April 15, August 5, 19, October 7, 1911; Hooulumahiehie, "Keaka-oku," March 9, 1912.
42. Kaualilinoe, "Kamaakamahiai," January 21, 1871.
43. Fornander, *Fornander*, 4:13.
44. Ibid., 4:12–19.
45. Kamakau, "Ka Moolelo o Kamehameha," December 22, 1866.
46. Kamakau, "Ka Moolelo Hawaii," April 28, 1870.
47. Ii, "Na Hunahuna," September 4, 1869.
48. Kukahi, *He Pule*, 62.
49. Ii, "Na Hunahuna," September 4, 1869.
50. Ibid., September 11, 1869.
51. Ibid.
52. Hooulumahiehie, "Hiiakaikapoliopele," June 4, 1906; Poepoe, "Hiiakaikapoliopele," February 7, 1908.
53. Olopana-Nui-Akea, "Kila a Moikeha," May 9, 16, 1914; Kaiwi, "Story," 115–116; Kapaka, "Interview with Helen Kapaka and Rubellite Kinney," February 4, 1958.

54. Sterling and Summers, *Sites,* 270.
55. Sterling and Summers, *Sites,* 270; Pukui, Elbert, and Mookini, *Place Names,* s.v. "Māmala"; Westervelt, *Legends of Old Honolulu,* 52–54.
56. Nakuina, "Shark-Man, Nanaue," 255–268.
57. Clark, *Hawai'i Place Names,* 160, 297.
58. John Clark credits Caroline Neill as the source of this story, having interviewed her in 1973. When Martha Yent in the Division of State Parks contacted Clark to learn more about Pōhaku Kūla'ila'i, he referred her to Neill. After speaking with Neill, Yent arranged to have the plaque put up (Clark, email communication). Brasher, "Technical Report," 1.
59. Ibid.
60. Macdonald, Abbott, and Peterson, *Volcanoes,* 221, 309.
61. Kaunamano, "Aukelenuiaiku," November 27, 1862.
62. Ii, "Na Hunahuna," September 18, 1869.
63. Beckwith, *Hawaiian Romance,* 340–341.
64. Ibid., 341.
65. Katherine Luomala, foreword to Beckwith, *Kumulipo,* ix.
66. Beckwith, *Kumulipo,* 75.
67. Pukui and Green, *Folktales,* 49n3.
68. Kekahuna, Map SP 201890, July 12, 1951.
69. Hooulumahiehie, *Hi'iakaikapoliopele,* 23.
70. Henry Kaaukai in Charles Langlas, unpublished interview, which Langlas shared with me.
71. "He Moolelo Hawaii no Laiehau," February 13, 1915.
72. Ibid., January 2, 23, 1915.
73. Nakuina, *Hawaii,* 22.
74. Ibid., 23.
75. Ibid.
76. Kaili, "Hiiaka," September 15, 22, 1883.
77. Ibid., September 1, 15, 1883.
78. Poepoe, "Hiiakaikapoliopele," January 10, 1908.
79. Ibid., January 24, 1908.
80. Kaunamano, "Aukelenuiaiku," December 18, 25, 1862.
81. Manu, "Pele and Waka," December 30, 1899.
82. Hooulumahiehie, *Hi'iakaikapoliopele,* 12, 176–184.
83. J. K. Kahele, "Myth Concerning Molokini," in Fornander, *Fornander,* 5:514–518.
84. Hooulumahiehie, *Hi'iakaikapoliopele,* 51.
85. Ibid., 53. I use "it" here because Ho'oulumāhiehie's version does not specify Pana'ewa's gender ("Hiiakaikapoliopele," August 6, 7, 8, 9, 10,

1906). Nogelmeier chose to identify Pana'ewa as male in his translation of Ho'oulumāhiehie's account. Poepoe identifies Pana'ewa as male
and bald in his version ("Hiiakaikapoliopele," September 25, October 2, 1908), as do Bush and Pa'aluhi (January 20, 1893). Kapihenui
does not gender Pana'ewa, but N. Emerson, who appropriated Kapihenui's account, depicts it as male (N. Emerson, *Pele and Hiiaka*, 32).

86. Hooulumahiehie, *Hi'iakaikapoliopele*, 52.
87. Kalei Nu'uhiwa, personal communication.
88. Hooulumahiehie, *Hi'iakaikapoliopele*, 87, 169.
89. Kapihenui, "Hiiakaikapoliopele," January 23, 1862.
90. Kaili, "Hiiaka," September 15, 1883.
91. Hooulumahiehie, *Hi'iakaikapoliopele*, 59, 61.
92. ku'ualoha ho'omanawanui, personal communication.
93. For a treatise on Hawaiian nationalism and Pele and Hi'iaka literature,
    see ho'omanawanui, *Voices of Fire*.

Chapter 5: Mo'o Roles and Functions Past and Present

1. Kamalani, *Ka Leo Hawai'i*, KLH-HV24–053, n.d.
2. Kamakau, "Ka Moolelo Hawaii," April 28, May 5, 1870; Kamakau,
   Po'e Kahiko, 28; Handy and Pukui, *Polynesian Family System*, 141,
   151; Pukui, Haertig, and Lee, *Nānā*, 1:35–40.
3. Kamakau, *Po'e Kahiko*, 28; Pukui, Haertig, and Lee, *Nānā*, 1:36.
4. Ibid.
5. Kamakau, "Ka Moolelo Hawaii," April 28, 1870. That prayers and offerings increased the mo'o 'aumakua's strength is an example of
   ho'omana (to increase mana).
6. Here, to call upon kūpuna seems to imply that our deceased ancestors
   continue to watch over us from the Pō and thus are a type of 'aumākua.
   See Pukui, Haertig, and Lee, *Nānā*, 1:325.
7. Kamakau, "Ka Moolelo Hawaii," May 5, 1870.
8. Pukui stresses this distinction in relation to shark 'aumakua—it "is not
   just 'a shark'; it is a specific, named shark." Pukui, Haertig, and Lee,
   Nānā, 1:41.
9. Handy and Pukui, *Polynesian Family System*, 125, 126, 142–143.
10. Ekaula, "Ka Hoomana Kahiko. Helu 11," March 23, 1865; Ekaula,
    "Ka Hoomana Kahiko. Helu 12," March 30, 1865.
11. Handy and Pukui, *Polynesian Family System*, 150.
12. Kaluapihaole, "Ano Hoomana Kii," March 9, 1859.
13. Pukui and Elbert, *Hawaiian*, s.v. "hiwa"; Andrews, *Dictionary*, s.v.
    "hiwa"; Andrews and Parker, *Dictionary*, s.v. "hiwa."

14. Apple and Kikuchi, *Ancient*, 1–2.
15. Kamakau, "Ka Moolelo Hawaii," April 28, 1870.
16. Pukui, Elbert, and Mookini, *Place Names*, s.v. "Kuapā"; McAllister, *Archaeology*, 69–70; Handy, Handy, and Pukui, *Native Planters*, 483.
17. Pukui, Elbert, and Mookini, *Place Names*, s.v. "Kuapā."
18. Pukui and Elbert, *Hawaiian*, s.v. "menehune."
19. Kamakau, "Ka Moolelo Hawaii," April 28, 1870.
20. Sterling and Summers, *Sites*, 290.
21. Wong, "Windward Y Ulupō Heiau," n.p.
22. "USA Designates Site on Hawaiian Islands."
23. De Silva, "Māpuna," September 1982, n.p.
24. Paepae o He'eia, "Fishpond," n.d.
25. Wise and Kihe, "Ka-Miki," March 26, 1914.
26. Ibid., February 22, 1911.
27. Pukui, *'Ōlelo*, 34.
28. Kamakau, "Ka Moolelo Hawaii," April 28, 1870.
29. Ibid.
30. Kekoowai, "Makalei," January 6, 13, 1922.
31. Ibid., January 13, 20, February 3, 1922.
32. Ibid., February 3, 1922.
33. Bush and Paaluhi, "Hiiakaikapoliopele," March 16, 1893.
34. Kekoowai, "Makalei," February 17, 1922.
35. Kaluapihaole, "Ano Hoomana Kii," March 9, 1859; ho'omanawanui, *Voices of Fire*, 121.
36. Kamoku, Kamoku, and Kekoowai, "He Puolo Waimaka," January 10, 1924.
37. McAllister, *Archaeology*, 69–70.
38. Handy and Pukui, *Polynesian Family System*, 143; Nu'uhiwa, *Kaulana Mahina: 2013–2014*, n.p.
39. Ii, "Na Hunahuna," September 6, 11, 18, 1869; Kamakau, "Ka Moolelo Hawaii," January 6, 1870. For a translation of 'Ī'ī's account, see Brown, "Kalamainu'u." For a translation of Kamakau's account, see Kamakau, *Works of the People*, 79–82.
40. Malo, *Mo'olelo*, 2:165.
41. Kamakau, "Ka Moolelo o Kamehameha," May 25, July 6, 1867; Kamakau, "Ka Moolelo Hawaii," April 28, 1870; Kamakau, *Po'e Kahiko*, 85.
42. Nu'uhiwa, personal communication.
43. *Merriam-Webster Dictionary*, s.v. "continuity."
44. Handy and Pukui, *Polynesian Family System*, 197.
45. Pukui and Elbert, *Hawaiian*, s.v. "mo'o."

46. Manu, "Keaomelemele," September 4, 1884; Manu, "Pele and Waka," May 13, 1899; Beckwith, *Hawaiian Mythology,* 507; Beckwith, "Legend of Hainakolo," 161.

47. Kēlou Kamakau o Kaawaloa, "No Na Oihana," in Fornander, *Fornander,* 6:8–30; Malo, *Mo'olelo,* 2:238–264; Ii, "Na Hunahuna," August 14, 21, 28, September 4, 18, 1869; Ii, *Fragments,* 35–45; Pukui and Elbert, *Hawaiian,* s.v. "luakini."

48. Ii, "Na Hunahuna," September 18, 1869.

49. Malo, *Mo'olelo,* 2:216–220; Kamakau, "Ka Moolelo Hawaii," March 24, 1870; Kukahi, *He Pule,* 86–87; Handy and Pukui, *Polynesian Family System,* 177; Pukui and Elbert, *Hawaiian,* s.v. "ulua."

50. Kukahi, *He Pule,* 86–87; Malo, *Mo'olelo,* 2:98–101; Kamakau, "Ka Moolelo Hawaii," March 24, 1870.

51. Kukahi, *He Pule,* 86–87.

52. Handy and Pukui, *Polynesian Family System,* 177; Kame'eleihiwa, *Nā Wāhine Kapu,* 4–9; Kame'eleihiwa, *Native Land,* 33.

53. Kamakau, "Ka Moolelo Hawaii," March 24, 1870.

54. Pukui and Elbert, *Hawaiian,* s.v. "'ula."

55. Kame'eleihiwa, *Nā Wāhine Kapu,* 6.

56. Kame'eleihiwa, *Native Land,* 25.

57. Ibid., 25, 33–39.

58. Ibid., 33–34.

59. Kame'eleihiwa, *Nā Wāhine Kapu,* 9.

60. Ibid.

61. Kame'eleihiwa, 9, 11; Brown, *Facing the Spears,* 54.

62. Fornander, "Legend of Kihapiilani/He Kaao no Kihapiilani," in Fornander, *Fornander,* 5:176–179

63. Ibid., 5:176–181.

64. Kamakau, "Ka Moolelo o Hawaii Nei," August 26, September 30, 1865.

65. Kamakau, "Ka Moolelo Hawaii," April 28, 1870.

66. Huamuia, "Ka Moolelo kuauhau," December 12, 1874.

67. Adams, *Hawai'i Genealogy #44,* n.p.

68. Ibid. Gender is unspecified for these entries.

69. Mookini, "Keōpuōlani," 5. Gender is unspecified for these entries.

70. Ibid. There are other genealogies, but they are less persuasive. One genealogy shows that Pi'ilani's daughter Kalā'aiheana had a child named Moana by Keākealanikāne but does not mention its gender or progeny (Adams, *Hawai'i Genealogy #44,* 11, 67). Elsewhere, however, a certain Kaleiheana had a son named Moana by Keākealani (Wilcox,

"Mookuauhau Alii," July 27, August 3, 24, 1896). But here, Kaleiheana's parentage is not noted, and Keākealani is the great-grandson of
Umi-a-Līloa, a contemporary of Lonoapiʻilani and Kihapiʻilani who
takes their sister Piʻikea as his wahine, which makes no sense chrono-
logically (Wilcox, "Mookuauhau Alii," July 27, August 3, 24, 1896;
Adams, *Hawaiʻi Genealogy #44*, n.p.). A woman named Kihawahine
appears in a genealogy as the wahine of Keawekūikaʻai, the son of
Keākealanikāne   by   Kaleimakaliʻi.   From   Kihawahine   and
Keawekūikaʻai is born Kaʻaloaikanoa (m), who is the father of the
brothers Palena, Paie, and Luahine (Wilcox, "Mookuauhau Alii," August 31, 1896). But once again, there is a chronological issue, as here
Keākealanikāne is Umi-a-Līloa's great-grandson. Either those women
were named after Kihawahine/Kalāʻaiheana or they are Kihawahine/
Kalāʻaiheana, and they had children with these human partners.

71. Klieger, *Mokuʻula*, 9.
72. Pakele, "Moolelo," November 12, 1864; Kamakau, "Ka Moolelo o
     Kamehameha," May 25, 1867.
73. Wilcox, "Mookuauhau Alii," April 20, 1896.
74. Ibid., April 20, 27, 1896.
75. Manu, "Kihapiilani," January 19, 1884.
76. "Ka Moolelo no Kihapiilani," November 14, 21, 28, December 5, 12,
     1870.
77. Kamakau, "Ka Moolelo o Kamehameha," February 23, 1867; Keaulu-
     moku, "Fallen Is the Chief," in Fornander, *Fornander*, 6:368, 397, 407.
78. Keaulumoku, "Fallen Is the Chief," in Fornander, *Fornander*, 6:407.
79. Kamakau, "Ka Moolelo o Kamehameha," July 6, 1867; Kamakau, "Ka
     Moolelo Hawaii," April 28, 1870; Kamakau, *Poʻe Kahiko*, 85.
80. Kamakau, "Ka Moolelo Hawaii," April 28, 1870; Kamakau, *Poʻe Ka-
     hiko*, 85.
81. Kamakau, "Ka Moolelo Hawaii," February 17, April 28, 1870; Ka-
     makau, *Poʻe Kahiko*, 19–20.
82. "Ka Lahui o Hawaii," May 6, 1899.
83. Kamakau, "Ka Moolelo Hawaii," October 13, 1870; Kamakau, *Poʻe
     Kahiko*, 54.
84. Kaeppler, "Hawaiian Ethnography," 39.
85. Kaeppler, Schindlbeck, and Speidel, *Old Hawaiʻi*, 215.
86. Ibid., 215–216. See Barnfield's drawing at "Kihawahine," https://
     hawaiialive.org/kihawahine/.
87. "Ka Moolelo no Kihapiilani," November 14, 21, 1870.
88. Ibid., November 21, 1870.

89. Ibid.
90. Ibid.
91. Ibid.
92. Ibid.
93. Ibid.
94. Kaikuaana, "Keiki," June 12, 1861.
95. "Pau Ole Ke Kuhi-Hewa," February 15, 1862.
96. J. Emerson, "Lesser," 1.
97. Conchology, "Shellers from the Past," n.p.
98. J. Emerson, "Lesser," 6–7.
99. W. H. Rice, "He Moolelo no Pele," June 18, 1908.
100. Handy and Pukui, *Polynesian Family System*, 125.
101. "He Pule no ke Aliiaimoku," February 7, 11, 1893.
102. Lili'uokalani, *Hawaii's Story*, 1, 188, 293, 314–315, 333, 356, 369.
103. Ii, "Ke ola," June 30, 1866; Kahinawe, "Ka Hope," April 26, 1862; Kaakua, "Keiki," October 3, 1863; M. Kekahuna, "Kanikau," January 19, 1867; I'a, "Ka Wehe," August 23, 1918; Alapuna, "He Mele," April 18, 1902; Kauhi, "He Mele," April 18, 1902; Lepena, Waiolohia, and Holaniku, "No Kamehameha V," August 21, 1865; "Mele Kahiko," December 15, 1866. Manu states the mo'o Laniwahine is mentioned in a line of a name chant for Kamehameha V ("Keaomelemele," April 25, 1885), but the same chant lines are found in an account about Ka'ū shark akua ("He Moolelo Kaao Hawaii no Keliikau o Kau," January 6, 1902). She is a mo'o or a shark depending on the tradition.
104. John, "Mai Pau," May 18, 1895.
105. Hoanoano, "Moo," November 10, 1901; "Ike Hou ia ka Moo," November 23, 1901.
106. Kahiona, "He Puolo," October 4, 1918.
107. Pukui, Haertig, and Lee, *Nānā*, 2:138.
108. Hui Kaloko-Honokōhau FaceBook Group, n.p.

Epilogue

1. Beckwith, *Kumulipo*, 187, 188–199.
2. Pukui, Haertig, and Lee, *Nānā*, 1:85.

Catalog of Mo'o

1. Akana, "History of Moku'ula," 1999.
2. Wise and Kihe, "Ka-Miki," March 25, April 1, 1915; Pukui, Elbert, and Mookini, *Place Names*, s.v. "Wai-'Ahukini."

3. Kapihenui, "Hiiakaikapoliopele," March 6, 1862; Bush and Paaluhi, "Hiiakaikapoliopele," April 12, 1893.
4. Wichman, *Kaua'i*, 81; Westervelt calls this mo'o "Akua-pehu-ale." Westervelt, *Legends of Old Honolulu*, 205, 211–219.
5. Manu, "Keaomelemele," February 2, 1885.
6. Wise and Kihe, "Ka-Miki," September 17, 24, 1914.
7. Kaiwi, "Story," 115–116; Kapaka, "Interview with Helen Kapaka and Rubellite Kinney."
8. Manu, "Keaomelemele," April 25, 1885; Pukui, Elbert, and Mookini, *Place Names*, s.v. "'Ālewa."
9. Wichman, *Kaua'i*, 90.
10. Pukui, Elbert, and Mookini, *Place Names*, s.v. "Hā'ao"; Meinecke, "Interview," July 19, 1959, n.p.
11. Kaunamano, "Aukelenuiaiku," November 20, 1862; Mokumaia, "Aukelenuiaiku," September 29, 1927.
12. Hooulumahiehie, "Hiiakaikapoliopele," August 22, 24, 1906; Hooulumahiehie, *Hi'iakaikapoliopele*, 59, 61.
13. Manu, "Laukaieie," *Ka Leo o ka Lahui*, April 19, 1895.
14. Hooulumahiehie, "He Moolelo Hooni Puuwai no ka Eueu Kapunohuula," December 12, 1912 (hereafter cited as "Kapunohuula").
15. N. Emerson, *Pele and Hiiaka*, xiv–xv.
16. Pukui, Elbert, and Mookini, *Place Names*, s.v. "Kalalea."
17. McAllister, *Archaeology*, 154.
18. Beckwith, *Hawaiian Mythology*, 264; Wise and Kihe, "Ka-Miki," October 1, 1914, July 8, August 10, 1915.
19. Wichman, *Kaua'i*, 38–39.
20. Kaiwi, "Story," 115–116.
21. Manu, "Laukaieie," *Ka Leo o ka Lahui*, May 3, 1895.
22. Manu, "Keaomelemele," April 25, 1885.
23. Fornander, "Legend of Maniniholokuau," in Fornander, *Fornander*, 5:164–167.
24. Manu, "Keaomelemele," April 25, 1885.
25. Manu, "Laukaieie," *Nupepa Ka Oiaio*, January 26, 1894.
26. Pukui, Elbert, and Mookini, *Place Names*, s.v. "Kalāwahine."
27. Hooulumahiehie, "Kapunohuula," March 8, 1912.
28. Ibid.
29. Poepoe, "Hiiakaikapoliopele," September 17, 1909; M. Kahele, "Luahaku," January 7, 1871; W. I. M., "Mele," February 17, 1877; Hooulumahiehie, "Hiiakaikapoliopele," June 14, 1906; Poepoe, "Hiiakaikapoliopele," March 27, 1908; Liokakele, "Kuailo," February 26, 1909.

30. Manu, "Keaomelemele," May 9, 1885.

31. Hooulumahiehie, "Kamaakamahiai," July 8, 1911; Kahiona, "He Puolo," October 4, 1918.

32. McAllister, *Archaeology*, 133.

33. Kapaka, "Interview with Helen Kapaka and Mary Kawena Pukui."

34. Dickey, "Stories," 28–29.

35. Wichman, *Kaua'i*, 102.

36. Ibid., 111.

37. Pukui, Elbert, and Mookini, *Place Names*, s.v. "Ka-nenelu."

38. Olopana-Nui-Akea, "Kila a Moikeha," September 5, 12, 19, 1914.

39. Beckwith, *Kumulipo*, 197, 245; Hooulumahiehie, *Hi'iakaikapoliopele*, 23.

40. Manu, "Keaomelemele," April 25, 1885.

41. Olopana-Nui-Akea, "Kila a Moikeha," May 9, 16, June 20, 1914.

42. Manu, "Keaomelemele," April 25, 1885; Manu, "Laukaieie," *Ka Leo o ka Lahui*, January 25, 1894.

43. Manu, "Pele and Waka," December 9, 1899.

44. Manu, "Keaomelemele," April 25, 1885.

45. Ibid.

46. N. Emerson, *Pele and Hiiaka*, 45.

47. Pukui and Elbert, *Hawaiian*, s.v. "kiha."

48. Kaimikaua, "Kihanui 'o [*sic*] Pu'uamo'o," n.p.

49. N. Emerson, *Pele and Hiiaka*, 84–85.

50. Manu, "Keaomelemele," April 25, 1885; Manu, *Keaomelemele*, 162.

51. Manu, "Keaomelemele," March 28, 1885; Manu, *Keaomelemele*, 150–154.

52. Manu, "Laukaieie," *Nupepa Ka Oiaio*, May 24, 1895.

53. Westervelt, *Legends of Gods*, 258.

54. Manu, "Laukaieie," *Nupepa Ka Oiaio*, April 26, 1895; Manu, "Keaomelemele," April 25, 1885.

55. Westervelt, *Legends of Ma-ui*, 99, 100, 148–153; Hapai, *Legends*, 5.

56. Manu, "Keaomelemele," September 20, 1884; Department of Parks and Recreation, memorial plaque; Pukui, Elbert, and Mookini, *Place Names*, s.v. "Kuna-wai."

57. Manu, "Keaomelemele," April 25, 1885; W. H. Rice, *Hawaiian Legends*, 112; Olopana-Nui-Akea, "Kila a Moikeha," January 31, February 7, 14, 1914.

58. Kamakau, "Ka Moolelo Hawaii," April 28, 1870; Manu, "Laukaieie," *Ka Leo o ka Lahui*, January 23, 26, 1894; Manu, "Keaomelemele," April 25, 1885; Hukilani, "Kumumanao," November 19, 1864; Pukui and Elbert, *Hawaiian*, s.v. "pupuhi"; McAllister, *Archaeology*, 142.

59. "He Moolelo Kaulana no Operia," December 28, 1894.
60. Kahiona, "He Puolo," October 4, 1918.
61. Kamakau, "Ka Moolelo Hawaii," April 28, 1870.
62. N. Emerson, *Pele and Hiiaka,* 52.
63. Manu, "Keaomelemele," April 25, 1885; Tava and Keale, *Niihau,* 20.
64. Poepoe, "Hiiakaikapoliopele," August 27, September 3, 1909.
65. Manu, "Laukaieie," *Ka Leo o ka Lahui,* January 22, 1894.
66. Luomala, "Dynamic," 146.
67. Kamakau, "Ka Moolelo Hawaii," April 28, 1870.
68. Pukui, Elbert, and Mookini, *Place Names,* s.v. "Lua'ehu."
69. Ibid., s.v. "Luahinewai."
70. Maly and Maly, *He Wahi Mo'olelo,* 148–149, 182–183.
71. Ibid., 182–183.
72. "Na Hoonanea o ka Manawa—Luahine Wai," December 6, 1923.
73. "Ka Moolelo no Hauwahine," December 17, 1897; Olopana-Nui-Akea, "Kila a Moikeha," February 7, 1914.
74. Manu, "Keaomelemele," April 25, 1885.
75. Ibid.
76. Manu, "Laukaieie," *Ka Leo o ka Lahui,* January 22, 1894, May 3, 10, 1895. My translation.
77. Olopana-Nui-Akea, "Kila a Moikeha," September 19, 26, 1914.
78. Bush and Paaluhi, "Hiiakaikapoliopele," January 20, 1893.
79. Manu, "Keaomelemele," April 25, 1885.
80. Kenui, "Interview with Caroline Kenui," HAW 200.1.2.
81. Kahaka'ilio, personal communication, May 29, 2019.
82. Manu, "Keaomelemele," April 25, 1885.
83. Ibid.; Westervelt, *Legends of Gods,* 258.
84. Beckwith, *Hawaiian Mythology,* 495.
85. Kamakau, "Ka Moolelo Hawaii," April 28, 1870.
86. Nailiili, "Kunahihi," February 27, 1868.
87. Fornander, *Fornander,* 5:520–523.
88. Kalakaua, *Legends,* 411.
89. McElroy, Eminger, and Elison, "Final," 17.
90. Hooulumahiehie, *Hi'iakaikapoliopele,* 121, 122.
91. Kapihenui, "Hiiakaikapoliopele," January 23, 1862; Manu, "Keaomelemele," May 9, 1885; Kaili, "Hiiaka," September 15, 1883; N. Emerson, *Pele and Hiiaka,* 53–54; Poepoe, "Hiiakaikapoliopele," April 9, 1909; Hooulumahiehie, *Hi'iakaikapoliopele,* 120.
92. Pooloa, "Heoahi," August 19, 1921.
93. Hooulumahiehie, "Kapunohuula," April 26, 1912. I had difficulty

understanding this passage's symbolism, and I am indebted to Kalei Nuʻuhiwa for offering her insights.

94. Kapaka, "Interview with Helen Kapaka and Mary Kawena Pukui."

95. "Ka Waimapuna o Ololo," May 4, 1922.

96. Kapa, "He Hoonanea," October 1, 8, 1909.

97. Sterling and Summers, *Sites*, 270; Pukui, Elbert, and Mookini, *Place Names*, s.v. "Māmala"; Westervelt, *Legends of Old Honolulu*, 52–54.

98. Hooulumahiehie, *Hiʻiakaikapoliopele*, 312–316.

99. Manu, "Keaomelemele," April 25, 1885.

100. Ibid.

101. Handy, Handy, and Pukui, *Native Planters*, 23fn1; Kapaka, "Interview with Helen Kapaka and Mary Kawena Pukui."

102. "Kamapuaa," July 22, 1891.

103. Dickey, "Stories," 28–29; Beckwith, *Hawaiian Mythology*, 127.

104. Kapihenui, "Hiiakaikapoliopele," February 14, 1862; Hooulumahiehie, *Hiʻiakaikapoliopele*, 170, 171.

105. Kapaka, "Interview with Helen Kapaka and Mary Kawena Pukui."

106. "Na Wahi Pana," November 11, 18, December 2, 1899.

107. Desha, "Hiiakaikapoliopele," April 19, 1927; Hooulumahiehie, *Hiʻiakaikapoliopele*, 312–316.

108. Manu, "Keaomelemele," April 25, 1885.

109. Wichman, *Kauaʻi*, 9–11.

110. McAllister, *Archaeology*, 141.

111. Kaili, "Hiiaka," September 1, 1883.

112. Manu, "Keaomelemele," April 25, 1885; Manu, "Laukaieie," *Nupepa Ka Oiaio*, May 18, 1894.

113. Manu, "Keaomelemele," April 25, 1885; Manu, *Keaomelemele*, 75, 161.

114. J. K. Kahele, "Molokini," in Fornander, *Fornander*, 5:515–519.

115. Manu, "Keaomelemele," April 25, 1885.

116. N. Emerson, *Unwritten Literature*, 40.

117. Manu, "Pele and Waka," December 9, 16, 1899; Wise and Kihe, "Ka-Miki," January 6, 1916.

118. "He Moolelo no Kamapuaa," September 8, 9, 1891.

119. Manu, "Keaomelemele," April 25, 1885.

120. Kapaka, "Interview with Helen Kapaka, Eleanor Williamson and Mary Kawena Pukui," July 18, 1963.

121. N. Emerson, *Pele and Hiiaka*, 35, 36.

122. Hooulumahiehie, *Hiʻiakaikapoliopele*, 94–99; Desha, "Hiiakaikapoliopele," July 2, 16, 23, 1925.

123. Kapaka, "Interview with Helen Kapaka and Mary Kawena Pukui."
124. Ibid.
125. Nogelmeier, personal communication, 2009.
126. Pukui and Green, *Folktales,* 50, 51.
127. Lovell, "Interview," August 13, 1959.
128. Kamakau, "Ka Moolelo Hawaii," October 13, 1870.
129. Luomala, "Dynamic," 149.
130. Kevin Won, ex-employee of Sea Life Park, personal communication, 2009.
131. Pea, "Interview," June 21, 1959.
132. Langlas, unpublished interview.
133. Poepoe, "Hiiakaikapoliopele," August 13, 1909.
134. Hinau, "Kailiokalauokekoa," December 5, 1861.
135. Mokumaia, "Holo Kaapuni," June 3, 1921; Mokumaia, "Hooliloia," September 28, 1922.
136. Mokumaia, "Moanalua," May 4, 1922.
137. Ibid.
138. Ashdown, "Interview with Inez Ashdown and Mary Kawena Pukui, 1960, March 30."
139. Naone, "Interview with Julia Naone," May 3, 1960.
140. Ibid.
141. Ibid.
142. Ibid.
143. Manu, "Laukaieie," *Nupepa Ka Oiaio,* June 14, 1895; Kapaka, "Interview with Helen Kapaka and Mary Kawena Pukui."
144. Whitney, *Tourists' Guide,* 131–132; Lauae, "Maikai Kauai," October 22, 1892.
145. "He Moolelo Hawaii no Laiehau," April 4, 1914.
146. David Wallace, personal communication, 2009.
147. John Clark, email communication, 2006.
148. Nipoa and Kuahalaoa, "Keamalu," September 18, 1862.
149. Hooulumahiehie, "Kamaakamahiai," July 22, 29, 1911.
150. "Na Wahi Pana," November 18, 1899.
151. Westervelt, *Legends of Old Honolulu,* 42.
152. "Kumuʻeli," n.p.
153. Damon, *Koamalu,* 371.
154. "Kapiolani Park," June 27, 1889.
155. G. Grant, *Obake,* 28–32.
156. W. H. Rice, *Hawaiian Legends,* 91.
157. Pukui and Green, *Folktales,* 50–51.
158. "Kaao Hooniua Puuwai no Kalelealuaka," July 20, 1910.

Works Cited

Adams, Keith Puhi. Hawai'i State Archives, *Genealogy #44*. Ulukau.

Ahiki. "Na hiohiona o ka aina Waimanalo." *Ka Nupepa Kuokoa*, October 14, 1871. Papakilo Database.

Akana, Akoni. "The History of Moku'ula as Told by Akoni Akana in 1999." Guy Garmont. June 14, 2017. YouTube video.

Akana, Dora. "Interview with Dora Akana and Mary Kawena Pukui." Bishop Museum Archive, Honolulu, January 19, 1962.

———. "Interview with Dora Akana, Jack Ward and Don Johnson, 1961 April 27." Bishop Museum Archive, Honolulu, April 27, 1961.

Alapuna. "He Mele Kanikau no Uilama Olo." *Ka Nupepa Kuokoa*, April 18, 1902. Papakilo Database.

Allred, Kevin, and Carlene Allred. "Development and Morphology of Kazumura Cave, Hawaii." *Journal of Cave and Karst Studies* 59, no. 2 (April 1997): 67–80.

Andrews, Lorrin. *A Dictionary of the Hawaiian Language*. Honolulu: Henry M. Whitney, 1865. Ulukau.

Andrews, Lorrin, and Henry H. Parker. *A Dictionary of the Hawaiian Language*. Revised by Henry H. Parker. Honolulu: Board of Commissioners of Public Archives of the Territory of Hawaii, 1922. Ulukau.

Apple, Russel Anderson, and William Kenji Kikuchi. *Ancient Hawaii Shore Zone Fishponds: An Evaluation of Surviors for Historical Preservation*. Honolulu: Office of the State Director, National Park Service, July 1975.

Ashdown, Inez McPhee. "Interview with Inez Ashdown and Mary Kawena Pukui, 1960, March 30." Bishop Museum Archive, Honolulu, March 30, 1960.

———. "Interview with Inez Ashdown, Mary Kawena Pukui and Winifred Sanborn, 1960, March 30." Bishop Museum Archive, Honolulu, March 30, 1960.

Awana. "Ka Moo Waha Nui o Laiewai." *Ka Nupepa Kuokoa*, January 27, 1922. Papakilo Database.

Bacchilega, Cristina, and Marie Alohalani Brown, eds. *The Penguin Book of Mermaids*. New York: Penguin Classics, 2019.

Baring, Anne, and Jules Cashford. *The Myth of the Goddess: Evolution of an Image*. London: Viking, 1991.

Barnfield, R. C. "Kihawahine." Hawaii Alive. Bishop Museum. https://hawaiialive .org/kihawahine/.

Barrow, T. T. "Maori Decorative Carving—an Outline." *Journal of the Polynesian Society* 65 (1956): 305–331.

Beckwith, Martha Warren. *Hawaiian Mythology*. Honolulu: University of Hawai'i Press, 1976.

———. *The Hawaiian Romance of Laieikawai*. Washington, DC: Government Printing Office, 1918. Internet Archive.

———. *The Kumulipo: A Hawaiian Creation Chant*. Honolulu: University of Hawai'i Press, 1972.

———. "Legend of Hainakolo." Vol. 2, Hawaiian Ethnological Notes. Martha Beckwith Collection. Bishop Museum Archive, Honolulu, 156–178.

Best, Elsdon. *Maori Mythology and Religion*. Vol. 1. 1924. Reprint, Wellington: A. R. Shearer, 1976. New Zealand Electronic Text Collection.

———. *Maori Mythology and Religion*. Vol. 2. 1929. Reprint, Wellington: A. R. Shearer, 1982. New Zealand Electronic Text Collection.

———. "Notes on the Art of War, as Conducted by the Maori of New Zealand, with Accounts of Various Customs, Rites, Superstitions &c., Pertaining to War, as Practiced and Believed by the Ancient Maori. Part 1." *Journal of the Polynesian Society* 11, no. 1 (1902): 11–41.

———. "Notes on Maori Mythology." *Journal of the Polynesian Society* 8, no. 2 (June 1899): 93–121.

———. "Notes on the Occurrence of the Lizard in Maori Carvings, and Various Myths and Superstitions Connected to Lizards." *New Zealand Journal of Science and Technology* (March 1923): 321–335.

Bird, W. W. "Hinepoupou and Te Oriparoa." *Te Au Hou: The New World* 11 (July 1955): 11–12. Te Puna Mātauranga of Aotearoa. http://teaohou .natlib.govt.nz/journals/teaohou/search/results.html?text=taniwha.

Birrell, Anne. *Chinese Myths*. Austin: University of Texas Press, 2000.

Bishop Museum Reptiles and Amphibian Checklist. n.d. http://data.bishop museum.org/HBS/checklist/query.asp?grp=Herp.

BOSSdancefriends. "3c. Meheanu & the Nitrogen Cycle." June 22, 2017. YouTube video. https://www.youtube.com/watch?v=r2m_g6mFrxA.

Brasher, Anne M. *Technical Report 113 Monitoring the Distribution and Abundance of Native Gobies ('o'opu) in Waikolu and Pelekunu Streams on the Island of Moloka'i*. Honolulu: Cooperative National Park Resources

Studies Unit, University of Hawai'i at Mānoa, 1996. ScholarSpace. http://hdl.handle.net/10125/7359.

Brennan, Joseph. *The Parker Ranch of Hawai'i: The Saga of a Ranch and a Dynasty.* Honolulu: Mutual, 1974.

Bropho, Robert. "Indigenous Australian Talk about the Mythical Rainbow Serpent." Cinematography by Daniel Searle. December 6, 2012. YouTube video. https://www.youtube.com/watch?v=QqAwTWn6gE4.

Brown, Marie Alohalani. *Facing the Spears of Change: The Life and Legacy of John Papa 'Ī'ī.* Honolulu: University of Hawai'i Press, 2016.

———, trans. "Kalamainu'u, the Mo'o Who Seduced Puna'aikoa'e." By John Papa Ii. In *The Penguin Book of Mermaids,* edited by Cristina Bacchilega and Marie Alohalani Brown, 116–126. New York: Penguin Classics, 2019.

———. "Mauna Kea: Ho'omana Hawai'i and Protecting the Sacred." In "Indigenous Knowledge, Spiritualities, and Science," edited by Robin M. Wright, special issue, *Journal for the Study of Religion, Nature, and Culture* 10, no. 2 (August 2016): 155–169.

———. "The Politics and Poetics of *Märchen* in Hawaiian-Language Newspapers." In *The Fairy Tale World,* edited by Andrew Teverson, 210–220. London: Routledge, 2019.

Bush, John E., and Simeon Paaluhi. "Ka Moolelo o Hiiakaikapoliopele." *Ka Leo o ka Lahui,* January 5–July 12, 1893. Papakilo Database.

Candelot, J. L. "On the Trail of Lizard-Man in Polynesia." *Rapa Nui Journal* 15, no. 2 (October 2001): 95–104.

Charlot, John. "The Application of Form and Redaction Criticism to Hawaiian Literature." *Journal of the Polynesian Society* 86, no. 4 (December 1977): 479–501.

———. "Aspects of Samoan Literature III: Texts on Historical Subjects and Bodies of Literature." *Anthropos* 87 (1992): 33–48.

———. *Classical Hawaiian Education.* Lā'ie, Hawai'i: Pacific Institute, Brigham Young University, 2005.

———. "The Feather Skirt of Nāhie'ena'ena: An Innovation in Postcontact Hawaiian Art." *Journal of the Polynesian Society* 100, no. 2 (June 1991): 119–165.

Cheeseman, T. F. "Notes on Certain Maori Carved Burial-Chests in the Auckland Museum." In *Transactions and Proceedings of the Royal Society of New Zealand* 39 (1906): 451–456. http://rsnz.natlib.govt.nz/index.html.

Christian, F. W. "Notes on the Marquesans." *Journal of the Polynesian Society* 4, no. 3 (1895): 187–202.

City and County of Honolulu Department of Parks and Recreation. Kunawai Springs memorial plaque. 1966.

Clark, John R. K. *Hawaiʻi Places Names: Shores, Beaches, and Surf Sites.* Honolulu: University of Hawaiʻi Press, 2002. Ulukau.

College of Tropical Agriculture and Human Resources. "Rapid ʻŌhiʻa Death."
n.d. College of Tropical Agriculture and Human Resources, University of
Hawaiʻi at Mānoa. https://cms.ctahr.hawaii.edu/rod/.

Collocot, E. E. V. "Notes on Tongan Religion. Part II." *Journal of the Polynesian
Society* 30, no. 119 (1921): 152–163.

Conchology. "Shellers from the Past and the Present." s.v. "Emerson." n.d.
https://conchology.be/?t=9001&id=17847.

Coulter, Charles Russel, and Patricia Turner. *Encyclopedia of Ancient Deities.*
New York: Routledge, 2000.

Craig, Robert. *Dictionary of Polynesian Mythology.* New York: Greenwood
Press, 1989.

Damon, Ethel M. *Koamalu: A Story of Pioneers on Kauai, and of What They
Built in That Island Garden.* Honolulu: Star-Bulletin Press, 1931.

Darian, Steve. "The Other Face of the Makara." *Artibus Asiae* 38, no. 1 (1976):
29–36.

Davis, E. Mott, and Claud A. Bramblett. *Report of the Memorial Resolution
Committee for J. Gilbert McAllister.* Archived Memorial Resolutions.
University of Texas at Austin. August 31, 1995. https://utexas.app.box
.com/s/emi5y6vqcfzoqsr4uojxq8x44f1yphdc/file/332028272898.

Dayton, Kevin. "Waimea Water Spirit's Legend Grows." *Honolulu Advertiser,*
July 6, 2007.

Department of Conservation, Te Papa Atawhai. "Cultural Values and Tīkanga—
Ngārara, Karara and Mokomoku." https://www.doc.govt.nz/get-involved
/apply-for-permits/interacting-with-wildlife/lizards-cultural-values-and
-tikanga/.

Department of Land and Natural Resources. "Wailuku River State Park." n.d.
https://dlnr.hawaii.gov/dsp/parks/hawaii/wailuku-river-state-park/.

Desha, Stephen. "He Moolelo Kaao no Hiiaka-i-ka-Poli-o-Pele ka Wahine i ka
Hikina a ka La, ao ka Uʻi Palekoki Uwila o Halemaumau." *Hoku o Hawaii,* September 18, 1924–July 17, 1928. Papakilo Database.

de Silva, Kīhei. "Māpuna ka Hala o Kailua." September 1982. http://www.halaumo
halailima.com/HMI/Mapuna_ka_Hala_o_Kailua.html.

Dickey, Lyle A. "Stories of Wailua, Kauai." *Twenty-Fifth Annual Report of the
Hawaiian Historical Society for the Year 1916 with Papers Read during
the Year before the Society.* Honolulu: Paradise of the Pacific Press,
1917, 14–36.

Dinu, Das, and Arumugam Balasubramanian. "The Practice of Traditional Rituals in Naga Aradhana (Snake Worship): A Case Study on Aadimoolam

Vetticode Sree Nagarajaswami Temple in Kerala, India." *SHS Web of Conferences* 33 (2017): 1–7. https://doi.org/10.1051/shsconf/20173300025.

Dunn, Barbara, Mary Louise Haraguchi, and Janel Quirante. "Directory of Historical Records Repositories in Hawai'i." 5th ed. Honolulu: AHA 5th Edition Directory Committee, February 2014. https://hawaiiarchivists.files .wordpress.com/2014/02/5thed_021514.pdf.

Ekaula, Samuela. "Ka Hoomana Kahiko. Helu 11." *Ka Nupepa Kuokoa*, March 23, 1865. Papakilo Database.

———. "Ka Hoomana Kahiko. Helu 12." *Ka Nupepa Kuokoa*, March 30, 1865. Papakilo Database.

Eliade, Mircea. *Patterns in Comparative Religion*. Translated by Rosemary Sheed. London: Sheed and Ward, 1958.

Emerson, Joseph. "The Lesser Hawaiian Gods." Honolulu: Bulletin, 1892, 1–24. Papers of the Hawaiian Historical Society. University of Hawai'i at Mānoa eVols. https://evols.library.manoa.hawaii.edu/handle/10524/963.

Emerson, Nathaniel. *Pele and Hiiaka: A Myth from Hawaii*. Honolulu: Honolulu Star-Bulletin, 1915.

———. *Unwritten Literature of Hawaii: The Sacred Songs of the Hula*. Honolulu: Mutual, 1998. Ulukau.

Encyclopedia Britannica. s.v. "Whirlwind." n.d. https://www.britannica.com/science /whirlwind.

Farley, J. K. "Notes on Maulili Pool, Koloa." In *Hawaiian Almanac and Annual for 1907*, compiled by Thos. G. Thrum, 92–93. Honolulu: Thos. G. Thrum, 1906.

Fornander, Abraham. *Fornander Collection of Hawaian Antiquities and Folk-Lore*. Vols. 4–6. Edited by Thomas G. Thrum. Honolulu: Bishop Museum Press, 1915–1916. Ulukau.

Fowler, Leo. "Of Taniwha, Ngarara and How Paeroa Got Its Name." *Te Au Hou: The New World* 26 (March 1959): 12–14. Te Puna Mātauranga of Aotearoa. http://teaohou.natlib.govt.nz/journals/teaohou/search/results.html ?text=taniwha.

Fox, Charles Elliot. *The Threshold of the Pacific*. London: Alfred A. Knopf, 1924. Google Books.

Freeman, J. D. "The Tradition of Sanalālā." *Journal of the Polynesian Society* 56, no. 3 (1947): 295–317.

Geiseler, Wilhelm. *Geiseler's Easter Island Report: An 1880s Anthropological Account*. Translated by William S. Ayres and Gabriella S. Ayres. Honolulu: University of Hawai'i Press, 1995.

Gifford, Edward Winslow. *Tongan Myths and Tales*. Bernice P. Bishop Museum Bulletin 8. Honolulu: Bishop Museum Press, 1924.

"Gifts from the Maori People." *Te Au Hou: The New World* 69 (1971): 65. Te Puna Mātauranga of Aotearoa. http://teaohou.natlib.govt.nz/journals/teaohou/search/results.html?text=lizard.

Gill, William Wyatt. *Life in the Southern Isles, or Scenes and Incidents in the South Pacific and New Guinea.* London: Religious Tract Society, 1876. Google Books.

———. *Myths and Songs from the South Pacific.* London: Henry S. King, 1876. Google Books.

Gillespie, R. G., and M. A. J. Rivera. "Free-Living Spiders of the Genus Ariamnes (Araneae, Therididdidae) in Hawaii." *Journal of Arachnology* 35 (2007): 11–37.

Glassie, Henry. "Tradition." *Journal of American Folklore* 108, no. 430 (Autumn 1995): 395–412.

Grant, Glen. *Obake: Ghost Stories in Hawaiʻi.* Honolulu: Mutual, 2005.

Grant, Robert M. *Early Christians and Animals.* New York: Routledge, 1999.

Gunson, Niel. "Gill, William Wyatt (1828–1896)." *Australian Dictionary of Biography.* 1972. http://adb.anu.edu.au/biography/gill-william-wyatt-3615.

"Haina Nane." *Ka Nupepa Kuokoa,* October 2, 1908. Papakilo Database.

Haleole, S. N. "Ka Moolelo o Laieikawai." *Ka Nupepa Kuokoa,* November 29, 1862–April 4, 1863. Papakilo Database.

———. *Ke Kaao o Laieikawai ka Hiwahiwa o Paliuli, Kawahineokaliula.* Honolulu: Henry M. Whitney, 1863. Ulukau.

Handy, E. S. Craighill. *Marquesan Legends.* Bernice P. Bishop Museum Bulletin 60. Bayard Dominick Expedition Publication Number 18. Honolulu: Bishop Museum Press, 1930.

———. *Polynesian Religion.* Bernice P. Bishop Museum Bulletin 34. Bayard Dominick Expedition Publication Number 12. Honolulu: Bishop Museum Press, 1927.

Handy, E. S. Craighill, Elizabeth Handy, and Mary Kawena Pukui. *Native Planters in Old Hawaii: Their Life, Lore, and Environment.* Honolulu: Bishop Museum Press, 1991.

Handy, E. S. Craighill, and Mary Kawena Pukui. *The Polynesian Family System of Ka-ʻu, Hawaiʻi.* Honolulu: Tuttle, 2011. Ulukau.

Hapai, Charlotte. *Legends of the Wailuku.* Honolulu: Charles B. Frazer. Internet Archive.

Hawaii Center for Volcanology. "Mauna Kea." May 13, 2013. https://www.soest.hawaii.edu/GG/HCV/maunakea.html.

"He Kaao Hoonaue Puuwai no Puakaohelo ke Kaikamahine Alii. Ka Ui Oi Kelakela o ka Nani a me ka Makani." *Ka Nupepa Kuokoa,* June 23, 1894. Papakilo Database.

"He Moolelo Hawaii Nani no Kekalukaluokewa. Ke Aikane Punahele a Kau-
akahialii. A o ka Mea nana ka Ohe o Kanikawi. A nona ke Kaikaina Ilio
o Kekalukalu.o.Puna A Nona Hoi Ke Kaikuahine o Kahalelehua A O
Kekalukaluokewa Ka Mea Nona ke Kaikaina Ilio Kekalukalu.o.Puna."
Ke Aloha Aina, April 16, 1910–November 18, 1911. Papakilo Database.

"He Moolelo Hawaii no Laiehau a o ka Lua ole hoi ma ka Uʻi." *Ke Aloha Aina*,
February 21, 1914–February 13, 1915. Papakilo Database.

"He Moolelo Kaao Hawaii no Keliikau o Kau." *Home Rula Repubalika*, January 6, 1902. Papakilo Database.

"He Moolelo Kaao no Keaniniulaokalani." *Ke Aloha Aina*, April 16, 1910–November 18, 1911. Papakilo Database.

"He Moolelo Kaulana no Operia. Ka Eueu o Aitiopia a me Aperodite. Ka Mahina Piha o Iopa—Ka Oiwi nona Ka Ui a me Ka Nani, i oi aku i ko
Aliope. Ka Moiwahine o na Iʻa o ke Kai." *Ka Nupepa Kuokoa*, December
28, 1894. Papakilo Database.

"He Moolelo no Aukelenuiaiku." *Hoku o Hawaii*, February 28, 1933. Papakilo
Database.

"He Moolelo no Aukelenuiaiku." *Ka Nupepa Puka ka La Aloha Aina*, October
4–November 17, 1893. Papakilo Database.

"He Moolelo no Kamapuaa." *Ka Leo o ka Lahui*, July 22, 1891. Papakilo
Database.

Henry, Lehman L. *Heʻeia Fishpond: Loko Iʻa Heʻeia: An Interpretive Guide for
the Heʻeia State Park Visitor.* Kāneʻohe: Kealohi Press, 1993.

Henry, Teuira. *Ancient Tahiti.* Bernice P. Bishop Museum Bulletin 48. Honolulu:
Bishop Museum Press, 1928.

"He Pule no ke Aliiaimoku." *Hawaii Holomua*, February 7, 11, 1893. Papakilo
Database.

Hinau. "He Moolelo no Kailiokalauokekoa." *Ka Hoku o ka Pakipika*, December 5, 1861. Papakilo Database.

Hoanoano. "The Moo or Lizard God Said to Have Been Seen on Hawaii." *Hawaiian Star*, November 10, 1901. Chronicling America.

Holt, Owen. "Mottled Snake-Eyed Skink (*Cryptoblepharus poecilopleurus*)."
Herpetological Education and Research Project. http://www.naherp.com
/viewrecord.php?r_id=132230.

hoʻomanawanui, kuʻualoha. "He Moʻolelo mai nā Kūpuna Mai: O Ka We-
hewehe ʻana o ka Moʻolelo ʻO Pelekeahiʻāloa a me Wakakeakaikawaiʻ (A
Story from the Ancestors: An Interpretive Analysis of the ʻPele-of-the-
eternal-fires and Waka-of-the-shadowy-waters' Myth Cycle)." MA thesis,
University of Hawaiʻi at Mānoa, 2007.

—————. "Pele's Appeal: Moʻolelo, Kaona, and Hulihia in 'Pele and Hiʻiaka' Literature (1860–1928)." PhD diss., University of Hawaiʻi at Mānoa, 2007.

—————. "'This Land Is Your Land, This Land Was My Land': Kanaka Maoli versus Settler Representation of ʻĀina in Contemporary Literature of Hawaiʻi." In *Asia Settler Colonialism: From Local Governance to the Habits of Everyday Life in Hawaiʻi*, edited by Candace Fujikane and Jonathan Y. Okamura, 116–149. Honolulu: University of Hawaiʻi Press.

—————. *Voices of Fire: Reweaving the Literary Lei of Pele and Hiʻiaka*. Minneapolis: University of Minnesota Press, 2014.

Hooulumahiehie. *The Epic Tale of Hiʻiakaikapoliopele*. Translated by M. Puakea Nogelmeier. Honolulu: Awaiaulu, 2006.

—————. "He Moolelo Hooni Puuwai no ka Iuiu Kapunohuula. Ke Kama i Hanau ma Keaweula, Waianae—Kona Moolelo Kuauhau Pili Pololei." *Kuokoa Home Rula*, May 6, 1910–December 1912. Papakilo Database.

—————. "Ka Moolelo Hooni Puuwai no Keakaoku ka Moopuna Leo Ole a Kamaakamahiai a o ke Koa Nana i Wehe na Pu Kaula a Makalii." *Ke Aloha Aina*, February 3–September 7, 1912. Papakilo Database.

—————. "Ka Moolelo o Hiiaka-i-ka-poli-o-Pele. Ka Wahine i ka Hikina o ka La, a o ka Ui Palekoki Uwila o Halemaʻumaʻu." *Ka Naʻi Aupuni*, November 30, 1905–December 30, 1906. Papakilo Database.

—————. "Ka Moolelo Walohia o Hainakolo. Ka Ui Pua Ka-Maka-Hala o ka Wailele o Hiilawe." *Ka Nai Aupuni*, January 1–June 20, 1907. Papakilo Database.

—————. "Moolelo Hoonaue Puuwai no Kama.A.Ka.Mahiai Ka Hi'apai'ole o ka Ikaika o ke Kai Huki Hee Nehu o Kahului." *Ke Aloha Aina*, August 7, 1909–September 7, 1912. Papakilo Database.

Huamuia, J. K. "Ka Moolelo kuauhau o na kupuna o ke 'Lii Ekamaekamaeawaia a me Kona mau muli pokii." *Ka Nupepa Kuokoa*, December 12, 1874.

Hui Kaloko-Honokōhau FaceBook Group. FaceBook. https://www.facebook .com/KalokoHonokohauNPS/.

Hui Mālama O Moʻomomi. *Moʻomomi North Coast of Molokaʻi Community-Based Subsistence Fish Area Proposal and Management Plan*. January 2017. https://dlnr.hawaii.gov/dar/files/2017/03/Moomomi_CBSFA_Proposal .rev_.pdf.

Hukilani. "Kumumanao. Na Akua o Koonei Poe i ka Wa Kahiko." *Ka Nupepa Kuokoa*, November 19, 1864. Papakilo Database.

Iʻa, Mrs. W. "Ka Wehe o ka Ua Kukalahale." *Ka Nupepa Kuokoa*, August 23, 1918. Papakilo Database.

Ii, John Papa. *Fragments of Hawaiian History*. Honolulu: Bishop Museum Press, 1959.

———. "Ke ola a me ka make ana iho nei o Victoria K. Kaahumanu." *Ka Nupepa Kuokoa,* June 30, 1866. Papakilo Database.

———. "Na Hunahuna no ka Moolelo Hawaii." *Ka Nupepa Kuokoa,* September 6, 11, 18, 1869. Papakilo Database.

"Ike Hou ia ka Moo Akua." *Ke Aloha Aina,* November 23, 1901. Papakilo Database.

Imperato, Pascal James. *Legends, Sorcerers, and Enchanted Lizards: Door Locks of the Bamana of Mali.* New York: Africana, 2001.

John, J. "Mai Pau i ke Akua." In "Na Hunahuna Mea Hou o Kau." *Ka Nupepa Kuokoa,* May 18, 1895. Papakilo Database.

Johnson, Rubellite K. "Moʻolelo Hawaiʻi" (World of the Hawaiians). Unpublished manuscript, 1993. *Kumu K's Blog.* https://kumuk.wordpress.com/2011/03/23/moolelo/.

Jones, Constance A., and James D. Ryan. *Encyclopedia of Hinduism.* New York: Facts on File, 2006.

K. U. "Hoike Oiaio, Haina Kupono Kuhikuhi Pololei." *Ko Hawaii Pae Aina,* May 4, 1878. Papakilo Database.

Kaakua, H. "Keiki i Make." *Ka Nupepa Kuokoa,* October 3, 1863. Papakilo Database.

"Kaao Hooniua Puuwai no Kalelealuaka, ke Kae'ae'a Ihupani o Keahumoe—ka Pua i Oili mailoko mai o na Ku'e-Maka-Pali o Kaholokuaiwa—ka Hekili Ku'i nei Nakolo iloko o Ikuwa." *Ke Au Hou,* July 20, 1910. Papakilo Database.

"Kaao no Hoamakeikekula." *Ke Alakai o Hawaii,* May 28, June 6, 1935. Papakilo Database.

Kaawa, P. W. "Ka Hoomana Kahiko. Helu 5." *Ka Nupepa Kuokoa,* February 2, 1865. Papakilo Database.

———. "Ka Hoomana Kahiko. Helu 6." *Ka Nupepa Kuokoa,* February 9, 1865. Papakilo Database.

———. "Ka Hoomana Kahiko. Helu 16." *Ka Nupepa Kuokoa,* May 4, 1865. Papakilo Database.

———. Ka Hoomana Kahiko. Helu 31." *Ka Nupepa Kuokoa,* December 23, 1865. Papakilo Database.

Kaeppler, Adrienne, L. "Hawaiian Ethnography and the Study of Hawaiian Collections." In Kaeppler, Schindlbeck, and Speidel, *Old Hawaiʻi* [sic], 2008.

Kaeppler, Adrienne L., Mark Schindlbeck, and Gisela E. Speidel, eds. *Old Hawaiʻi* [sic]: *An Ethnography of Hawaiʻi* [sic] *in the 1880s.* Berlin: Staatliche Museen zu Berlin-Stiftung Preußischer Kulturbesitz, 2008.

Kahele, J. K., Jr. "He Moolelo no Molokini a me Kona Wahi i Loaa mai ai." *Ke Alakai o Hawaii,* July 24, 1930. Papakilo Database.

————. "Myth Concerning Molokini, He Moolelo no Molokini." In Vol. 5, *Fornander Collection of Hawaiian Antiquities and Folk-Lore*, by Abraham Fornander, 515–519. Edited by Thomas G. Thrum. Honolulu: Bishop Museum Press, 1915–1916. Ulukau.

Kahele, Malie. "No Luahaku." *Ka Nupepa Kuokoa*, January 7, 1871. Papakilo Database.

"Kahi i Loaa mai ai ka Inoa Kapunahou." *Ka Nupepa Kuokoa*, November 26, 1915. Papakilo Database.

Kahinawe, H. M. "Ka Hope o ke Kanikau o J. Henry." *Ka Nupepa Kuokoa*, April 26, 1862. Papakilo Database.

Kahiolo, G. W. "He Moolelo no Kamapuaa." *Ka Hae Hawaii*, June 26–September 25, 1861. Ulukau.

Kahiona, J. A. "He Puolo i Loaa e Lana Hele ana i ka Wai." *Ka Nupepa Kuokoa*, October 4, 1918. Papakilo Database.

Kahoewaa, Williama K. "He Moolelo Kaao no Keaniniulaokalani. *Ka Nupepa Kuokoa*, January 14–December 2, 1882. Papakilo Database.

"Ka Hoolaa Luakini ma Kapaa, Kauai." *Ke Alakai o Hawaii*, January 26, 1933. Papakilo Database.

"Ka Huakai i na Mokupuni ma ka Akau-Komohana." *Ka Nupepa Kuokoa*, July 19, 1923. Papakilo Database.

Kaikuaana, T. W. "Keiki puliki ia e ka Moo." *Ka Hae Hawaii*, June 12, 1861. Papakilo Database.

Kaili. "Hiiaka. A Hawaiian Legend by a Hawaiian Native. A Legend of the Goddess Pele, Her Lover Lohiau and Her Sister Hiiakaikapoliopele." *Pacific Commercial Advertiser*, August 25–October 13, 1883. Chronicling America.

Kaimikaua, John, and Hālau Hula o Kukunaokalā. "'Kihanui'o [*sic*] Pu'uamo'o,' Lizard Dance of Moloka'i." *The Hidden*. Produced by Dawn Kaniaupio. Directed by Tremaine Tamayose. Alu Like. Native Hawaiian Library Project. Honolulu: MediaWrite-Alphamedia, 1992.

Kaiwi, J. H. "The Story of the Race of Menehunes of Kauai." In *Hawaiian Almanac and Annual for 1921*, written, translated, and compiled by Thomas G. Thrum, 114–118. Honolulu: Thomas G. Thrum, 1920. Google Books.

"Ka Lahui o Hawaii Nei i ka wa Kahiko." *Ka Loea Kalaiaina*, May 6, 1899. Papakilo Database.

Kalakaua, David. *The Legends and Myths of Hawaii: The Fables and Folk-Lore of a Strange People*. Edited by R. M. Daggett. New York: Charles L. Webster, 1888. Internet Archive.

"Kalalau Puna a ka Lawakua." *Ka Lei Momi*, July 15, 1893. Papakilo Database.

Ka-Lama-Ku-I-Ke-Au-Kaahiki. "Ka Moolelo Walohia o Hainakolo, ka Ui o Waipio ame ka Wai o Hiilawe." *Ka Holomua*, October 4, 1913–November 21, 1914. Papakilo Database.

Kalimahauna, J. M. "O ke kumu mua o ko Hawaii nei kanaka." *Ka Hoku o ka Pakipika*, February 13, 1862. Papakilo Database.

Kaluapihaole. "Ano Hoomana Kii." *Ka Hae Hawaii*, March 9, 1859. Papakilo Database.

Kamahele. "Ka Ike Hou ana o ke Kamahele i ka Mokupuni o Kauai." *Ka Nupepa Kuokoa*, January 2, February 6, 1914. Papakilo Database.

Kamakau, Samuel Manaiakalani. "Ka Moolelo Hawaii." *Ke Au Okoa*, October 14, 1869–February 2, 1871. Papakilo Database.

———. "Ka Moolelo o Hawaii Nei." *Ka Nupepa Kuokoa*, June 15–October 7, 1865. Papakilo Database.

———. "Ka Moolelo o Kamehameha I." *Ka Nupepa Kuokoa*, October 20, 1866–January 5, 1867. Papakilo Database.

———. *Ka Po'e Kahiko: The People of Old*. Edited by Dorothy B. Barrère. Translated by Mary Kawena Pukui. Illustrated by Joseph Feher. Honolulu: Bishop Museum Press, 1964.

———. *Tales and Traditions of the People of Old: Nā Mo'olelo a ka Po'e Kahiko*. Edited by Dorothy B. Barrère. Translated by Mary Kawena Pukui. Honolulu: Bishop Museum Press, 2011.

———. *The Works of the People of Old: Na Hana a Ka Po'e Kahiko*. Edited by Dorothy B. Barrère. Translated by Mary Kawena Pukui. Illustrated by Joseph Feher. Honolulu: Bishop Museum Press, 1976.

Kamakau o Kaawaloa (Kēlou). "No Na Oihana Kahuna Kahiko: Ancient Religious Ceremonies." In Vol. 6, *Fornander Collection of Hawaian Antiquities and Folk-Lore*, by Abraham Fornander, 8–30. Edited by Thomas G. Thrum. Honolulu: Bishop Museum Press, 1915–1916. Ulukau.

Kamalani, Jonah. *Ka Leo Hawai'i*. KLH-HV24–053. "Kani'āina: Voices of the Land." Ulukau.

Kame'eleihiwa, Lilikalā. *Native Land and Foreign Desires: Pehea La E Pono Ai?* Honolulu: Bishop Museum Press, 1992.

———. *Nā Wāhine Kapu: Divine Hawaiian Women*. Honolulu: 'Ai Pōhaku Press, 2002.

Kamoku, Herman K., Lydia K. Kamoku, and Samuel K. Kekoowai. "He Puolo Waimaka no ka Makou Tutu Aloha, Mr. Samuel K. Kekoowai, Ua Hala." *Ka Nupepa Kuokoa*, January 10, 1924. Papakilo Database.

"Ka Moolelo no Hauwahine." *Ka Nupepa Kuokoa*, December 17, 1897. Papakilo Database.

"Ka Moolelo no Kihapiilani a me kona Noho Alii ana ma ka Mokupuni o Maui, a me kana mau Hana Kaulana." *Ka Manawa*, November 14–December 5, 1870. Papakilo Database.

"Ka Moolelo o ka Aina ana ma keia mau Mokupupuni [*sic*] a me ka Laha ana o keia Lahuikanaka. He Moolelo no Aukelenuiaiku." *Ke Alakai o Hawaii*, April 27–September 28, 1933. Papakilo Database.

Kanahele, Pualani Kanaka'ole. *Ka Honua Ola*. *'Eli'eli Kau Mai. Descend, Deepen the Revelation*. Honolulu: Kamehameha Schools Press, 2011.

Kanepuu, Joseph H. "He Moolelo no Hamanalau, Hanai a Hawea. I lawe mailoko mai o na kaao kahiko o Hawaii nei." *Ka Nupepa Kuokoa*, December 28, 1867–August 29, 1868. Papakilo Database.

Ka Ohu Haaheo i na Kuahiwi. "Ka Moolelo Kaili Puuwai no Hainakolo, ka Ui o Waipio ma ka Wai o Hiilawe." *Hawaii Holomua*, April 10, 1912. Papakilo Database.

Kapa, G. K. "He Hoonanea no ka Manawa." *Ka Nupepa Kuokoa*, October 1, 1909–March 8, 1910. Papakilo Database.

Kapaka, Helen Wahineali'i Kapule. "Interview with Helen Kapaka, Eleanor Williamson and Mary Kawena Pukui." Bishop Museum Archive, Honolulu, July 18, 1963.

———. "Interview with Helen Kapaka and Rubellite Kinney, 1958 February 4." Bishop Museum Archive, Honolulu, February 4, 1958.

———. "Interview with Helen Kapaka and Mary Kawena Pukui." Bishop Museum Archive, Honolulu, August 18, 1959.

Kapihenui, M. J. "He Moolelo no Hiiakaikapoliopele." *Ka Hoku o ka Pakipika*, December 26, 1861–July 17, 1862. Papakilo Database.

"Kapiolani Park. Chief Pleasure Ground of Honolulu." *Daily Bulletin*, June 27, 1889. Chronicling America.

Kauaililinoe, J. M. K. "Ka Moolelo no Kamaakamahiai, ka Niuhi Ai Humuhumu o Kahalui i Maui, ke Puhi Nau Okaoka hoi o kona mau La Koa. Kahiluhilu hoi o kona Wa Ui." *Ka Nupepa Kuokoa*, June 18, 1870–January 21, 1871. Papakilo Database.

Kauhi. "He Mele Kanikau no Uilama Olo." *Ka Nupepa Kuokoa*, April 18, 1902. Papakilo Database.

Kauhi, Emma Kapūnohu'ulaokalani. *He Mo'olelo no Kapa'ahu: Story of Kapa'ahu*. Translated by Charles M. Langlas. Hilo: Pili, 1996. Ulukau.

Kaui, S. M. "He Kaao no Pikoiakaalala! Ke Keiki akamai i ka Pana." *Ka Nupepa Kuokoa*, December 16, 1865–March 10, 1866. Papakilo Database.

Kaulainamoku, S. W. Beni. "Hiku i ka Nahele. He Moolelo Hawaii." *Ko Hawaii Ponoi*, April 8, 1874. Papakilo Database.

————. "Ka Moolelo o Kepakailiula." *Ka Nupepa Kuokoa,* April 6, 1865. Papakilo Database.

Kaunamano. "He Moolelo no Aukelenuiaiku," *Ka Hoku o ka Pakipika,* November 6, 1862–December 25, 1862. Papakilo Database.

Kawailiula, S. K. "Moolelo no Kawelo." *Ka Hoku o Ka Pakipika,* September 26, 1861. Papakilo Database.

"Ka Waimapuna o Ololo." *Ka Nupepa Kuokoa,* May 4, 1922. Papakilo Database.

Keaulumoku. "Fallen Is the Chief/Haui ka Lani." In Vol. 6, *Fornander Collection of Hawaian Antiquities and Folk-Lore,* by Abraham Fornander, 368–410. Edited by Thomas G. Thrum. Honolulu: Bishop Museum Press, 1915–1916. Ulukau.

Kekahuna, Henry E. P. Map SP 201869. *Sketch of Kahuluu Beach; Kona, Hawaii; including the residence of Lonoikamakahiki (Umi-Hale), Makole-a-Heiau (formerly a women's heaiu), Keeku or Kueke Heiau, Hapai Alii, Kapuanoni Heiau, Poo Hawaii, and Kuemanu Heiau.* The Maps of Henry E. P. Kekahuna, Bishop Museum, March 15, 1952. http://data.bishop museum.org/Kekahuna/kekahuna.php?b=maps.

————. Map SP 201890. *Pencil Drawing of Punalua Heiau, also known as Kamooinanea (Kamooinanea was the grandmother of Aukeleniaiku); Waiakolea Park, Kalapana, Puna, Hawaii.* The Maps of Henry E. P. Kekahuna, Bishop Museum. http://data.bishopmuseum.org/Kekahuna/kekahuna.php?b=maps.

Kekahuna, Miriama. "Kanikau aloha no Kahananui." *Ka Nupepa Kuokoa,* January 19, 1867. Papakilo Database.

Kekoowai, Samuel. "Makalei, ka Laau Ona a ka I'a o Moa-ula-Nui-Akea i Kaulana, He Moolelo Kahiko no ka Huli Koolau o Kailua ame Waimanalo, ka Nanea o ke Au o ka Manawa." *Ka Nupepa Kuokoa,* January 6, 1922–January 10, 1924. Papakilo Database.

Kensley, Brian, and Dennis Williams. "New Shrimp (Families Procarididae and Atyidae) from a Submerged Lava Tube on Hawaii." *Journal of Crustacean Biology* 6, no. 3 (August 1986): 417–437.

Kenui, Carrie Ka'aelani. "Interview with Caroline Kenui, Caroline Tele Kenui Rost, Eleanor Williamson and Mary Kawena Pukui." HAW 200 1.2. Bishop Museum Archive, Honolulu, August 9, 1968.

————. "Interview with Caroline Kenui, Caroline Tele Kenui Rost, Eleanor Williamson and Mary Kawena Pukui." HAW 200 2.1. Bishop Museum Archive, Honolulu, August 9, 1968.

Keola, J. N. K. "Ike Hou ia Kauai." *Ka Nupepa Kuokoa,* September 3, 1892. Papakilo Database.

Kepelino. *Kepelino's Traditions of Hawaii.* Edited and translated by Martha Beckwith. Honolulu: Bishop Museum Press, 2007.

Kelsey, Theodore. "Kahulihuli ka papa o Wailuku." Mele Collection of Theodore Kelsey. Hilo. Hawaiian Ethnological Notes. MS SC Roberts, Box 4.2. Bishop Museum Archives, Honolulu.

Kikiloi, Kekuewa Scott T. "Kūkulu Manamana: Ritual Power and Religious Expansion in Hawaiʻi. The Ethno-historical and Archaeological Study of Mokumanamana and Nihoa Islands." PhD diss., University of Hawaiʻi at Mānoa, 2012.

Kimura, Larry L. Kauanoe. *Ka Leo Hawaiʻi.* "Kaniʻāina: Voices of the land." Ulukau.

Kjellgren, Eric, and Carol S. Ivory. *Adorning the World: Art of the Marquesas Islands.* New York: Metropolitan Museum of Art; New Haven, CT: Yale University Press, 2005. Exhibition catalog.

Klieger, Paul Christiaan. *Mokuʻula, Maui's Sacred Island.* Honolulu: Bishop Museum Press, 1999.

Kukahi, L. Joseph. *He Pule Hoolaa Alii: He Kumulipo no Ka I-Amamao a ia Alapai Wahine.* Ulukau.

"Kumuʻeli." *23rd Annual Merrie Monarch Festival. 1996, Island of Hawaii.* Event pamphlet. University of Hawaiʻi at at Mānoa eVols.

"Kuwada, Bryan Kamaoli. "How Blue Is His Beard? An Examination of the 1862 Hawaiian-Language Translation of 'Bluebeard.'" *Marvels & Tales* 23, no. 1 (2009): 17–39.

Lauae. "Maikai Kauai. Hemolele i ka Malie. *Ka Nupepa Kuokoa,* October 22, 1892. Papakilo Database.

Lepena, Waiolohia, and Holaniku. "No Kamehameha V." *Ke Au Okoa,* August 21, 1865. Papakilo Database.

Liliʻuokalani. *Hawaii's Story by Hawaii's Queen.* Boston: C. J. Peters & Son, 1898. Google Books.

Liokakele, H. K. "Kuailo." *Ka Nupepa Kuokoa,* February 26, 1909. Papakilo Database.

Lokai, W. S., and J. S. Kamoe. "Ka Moolelo Hawaii." *Ka Nupepa Kuokoa,* August 21, 1886. Papakilo Database.

Lovell, Daisy Valpoon. "Interview with Daisy Lovell and Mary Kawena Pukui." Bishop Museum Archive, Honolulu, August 13, 1959.

"Luhi-a, Maka Apua ke Ola e Napokii" (Luhi–a, or through the Handle of the Ti-Leaf Food Bundle Is Life, Oh Younger Siblings). Hawaiian Ethnological Notes 1:2177. Bishop Museum Archive, Honolulu, n.d.

Luomala, Katharine. "A Dynamic in Oceanic Maui Myths." *Fabula* 4, no. 1 (1961): 137–162. https://doi.org/10.1515/fabl.1961.4.1.137.

———. Foreword to *Hawaiian Mythology,* by Martha Beckwith. Honolulu: University of Hawai'i Press, 1976.

MacCulloch, J. A. "Serpent Worship." In *Sacrifice-Sundra,* edited by James Hastings, John A. Selbie, and Louis H. Gray, 399–410. Vol. 11 of *Encyclopedia of Religion and Ethics.* New York: Charles Scribner's Sons, 1908. Internet Archive.

Macdonald, Gordon Andrew, Agatin Townsend Abbott, and Frank L. Peterson. *Volcanoes in the Sea: The Geology of Hawaii.* Honolulu: University of Hawai'i Press, 1983.

Maciolek, J. A. "Taxonomic Status, Biology, and Distribution of Hawaiian *Lentipes,* a Diadromous Goby." *Pacific Science* 31, no. 4 (October 1977): 355–362.

Maka'ai, Iokepa. *Ka Leo Hawai'i.* HV24–254A, 1981. "Kani'āina: Voices of the Land." Ulukau.

Makuakane, Elizabeth Keaweaheulu Kahoopii. "Interview with Elizabeth Makuakane, Mr. Hoomana and Mary Pukui." Bishop Museum Archive, Honolulu, June 14, 1962.

Malo, Davida. *The Mo'olelo Hawai'i of Davida Malo.* Vol. 2. Edited and translated by Charles Langlas and Jeffrey Lyon. Honolulu: University of Hawai'i Press, 2020.

Maly, Kepā, and Onaona Maly. *He Wahi Mo'olelo no Pu'u Wa'awa'a a me Nāpu'u o nā Kona: A Collection of Cultural and Historical Accounts of Pu'u Wa'awa'a and the Nāpu'u Region—District of Kona, on the Island of Hawai'i.* Hilo: Kumu Pono, 2006. Ulukau.

Manu, Mose. "He Moolelo Kaao Hawaii no ke Kaua Nui Weliweli ma waena o Pele-Keahialoa me Waka-Keakaikawai. He mau kupua Wahine Ka'ea'ae'a [*sic*]." *Ka Loea Kalaiaina,* May 13–December 20, 1899. Papakilo Database.

———. "He Moolelo Kaao Hawaii no Laukaieie. Ke Kino Kamahao Iloko o ka Punohu Ua koko. Ke Kahulileole'a o ke Kuluaumoe o na Pali o Waipio Hawaii." *Ka Leo o ka Lahui,* January 2, 1894–June 28, 1895. Papakilo Database.

———. "He Moolelo Kaao Hawaii no Laukaieie. Ke Kino Kamahao Iloko o ka Punohu Ua-koko. Ke Kahulileole'a o ke Kuluaumoe o na Pali o Waipio Hawaii." *Nupepa Ka Oiaio,* January 5, 1894–September 13, 1895. Papakilo Database.

———. "He Moolelo Kaao no Keaomelemele, ka Pua Nani Iuiu o Kealohilani, Kahiapaiole Nuumealani a me Kuaihelani; ka mea nana i uneune ia Konahuanui a kaawale o Waolani ka aina o ka poe eepa a pau i noho ai." *Ka Nupepa Kuokoa,* September 6, 1884–June 27, 1885. Papakilo Database.

————. "Ka Moolelo o Kihapiilani ka Mea nana Kipapa Kanahele o Oopuloa a me ke Alapupu i Molokai." *Ka Oiaio,* January 12–August 23, 1884. Papakilo Database.

————. *Keaomelemele.* Translated by Mary Kawena Pukui and M. Puakea Nogelmeier. Honolulu: Bishop Museum Press, 2002.

————. "Ku-ula, the Fish God of Hawaii." Translated by M. K. Nakuina. In *Hawaiian Folk Tales: A Collection of Native Legends,* compiled by Thomas G. Thrum, 215–249. Chicago: A. C. McClurge, 1907.

McAllister, J. Gilbert. *Archaeology of Oahu.* Bernice P. Bishop Museum Bulletin 104. Honolulu: Bishop Museum Press, 1933.

McElroy, Windy, Steven Eminger, and Mina Elison. *Final—Archaeological Inventory Survey of TMK: (2) 5–5-001:007 (por.), Keonekūʻino Ahupuaʻa, Kona District, Island of Molokaʻi.* Honolulu: Keala Pono Archaelogical Consulting, September 2013.

McKeown, Sean. *A Field Guide to Reptiles and Amphibians in the Hawaiian Islands.* Honolulu: Diamond Head, 1996.

McMillen, Sophia, and Nancy Morris. *Hawaii Newspapers: A Union List.* Honolulu: Hawaii Newspaper Project, 1987. University of Hawaiʻi at Mānoa eVols. https://evols.library.manoa.hawaii.edu/handle/10524/20.

Medeiros, Josephine. "Interview with Josephine Roback Medeiros, Eleanor Williamson and Mary Kawena Pukui, 1960 May 5." Bishop Museum Archives, Honolulu, May 5, 1960.

Meinecke, William. "Interview with George Kawaha, Pahia, William Meinecke, and Mary Kawena Pukui." Bishop Museum Archive, Honolulu, July 19, 1959.

"Mele Kahiko." *Ka Nupepa Kuokoa,* December 15, 1866. Papakilo Database.

Métraux, Alfred. *Ethnology of Easter Island.* Bernice P. Bishop Museum Bulletin 160. Honolulu: Bishop Museum Press, 1940.

Metropolitan Museum of Art. "Lizardman Figure (Moko)." n.d. https://www.metmuseum.org-/art/collection/search/317746.

Mokumaia, J. K. "Holo Kaapuni o Mr. Ame Mrs. Geo. J. Fern Ia Oahu." *Ka Nupepa Kuokoa,* June 3, 1921. Papakilo Database.

————. "Hooliloia i Kahunapule." *Ka Nupepa Kuokoa,* September 28, 1922. Papakilo Database.

————. "Hoonanea no ka Manawa. He Moolelo no Aukelenuiaiku." *Ka Nupepa Kuokoa,* November 17, December 29, 1927. Papakilo Database.

————. "Moanalua I Kela Au I Hala A O Moanalua I Keia Au." *Ka Nupepa Kuokoa,* February 17–August 31, 1922. Papakilo Database.

Mookini, Esther K. *The Hawaiian Newspapers.* Honolulu: Topgallant, 1974. Ulukau.

———. "Keōpuōlani, Sacred Wife, Queen Mother." *Hawaiian Journal of History* 32 (1998): 1–24.

"Moolelo Hawaii." *Ka Hae Hawaii,* April 14, 1858. Ulukau.

"Moolelo no Aukelenuiaiku." *Hoku o Hawaii,* September 18, 1939–March 26, 1941. Papakilo Database.

"Na Hoonanea no ka Manawa, Ka Loko o Wainanalii." *Hoku o Hawaii,* January 24, 1924. Papakilo Database.

"Na Hoonanea o ka Manawa—Luahine Wai." *Hoku o Hawai'i,* December 6, 1923. Papakilo Database.

Nailiili, S. W. "Kunahihi na Keiki o ke Aupuni Hawaii." *Ke Au Okoa,* February 27, 1868. Papakilo Database.

Nakuina, Emma. *Hawaii. Its People. Their Legends.* Honolulu: T. H., 1904. Internet Archive.

———. "The Punahou Spring." In *Hawaiian Folk Tales: A Collection of Native Legends,* compiled by Thomas G. Thrum, 133–138. Chicago: A. C. McClurge, 1907.

———. "The Shark-Man, Nanaue." In *Hawaiian Folk Tales: A Collection of Native Legends,* compiled by Thomas G. Thrum, 19–32. Chicago: A. C. McClurge, 1907.

Naone, Julia Kaalo. "Interview with Julia Naone, Eleanor Williamson and Mary Kawena Pukui, 1960 May 3." Bishop Museum Archive, Honolulu, May 3, 1960.

National Park Service. "Wailuku River State Park." n.d. https://dlnr.hawaii.gov /dsp/parks/hawaii/wailuku-river-state-park/.

Native Plants Hawai'i. "*Acacia koa.*" 2009. http://nativeplants.hawaii.edu/plant /view/Acacia_koa.

———. "*Metrosideros polymorpha.*" 2009. http://nativeplants.hawaii.edu/plant /view/Metrosideros_polymorpha.

"Na Wahi Pana o Ewa i Nalowale a Hiki Ole ke Ikeia." *Ka Loea Kalaiaina,* June 3, 1899–January 13, 1900. Papakilo Database.

NFSA (National Sound and Film Archive of Australia). "The Rainbow Serpent." NFSA Digital Learning. 2009. https://dl.nfsa.gov.au/module/1565/.

Nipoa, T. W., and John Kuhalaoa. "He Mooolelo no Keamalu." *Ka Hoku o ka Pakipika,* June 12, 1862–April 16, 1863. Papakilo Database.

Nogelmeier, M. Puakea. *Mai Pa'a I Ka Leo: Historical Voice in Hawaiian Primary Materials, Looking Forward and Listening Back.* Honolulu: Bishop Museum Press and Awaiaulu Press, 2010, 1.

"No na Kaao a me na Moolelo." *Ka Hoku o ka Pakipika,* January 16, 1862. Papakilo Database.

"Novelties." *Polynesian,* November 21, 1857. Chronicling America.

Nu'uhiwa, Kalei. *Kaulana Mahina: 2013–2014.* Hilo: Kalei Nu'uhiwa, 2013.

Olopana-Nui-Akea. "He Moolelo no Kila a Moikeha ka Hoolelo Ewe Ku-panaha—A o ke Kama Kapu a Hooipoikamalanai i ka Nalu-kee o Makaiwa." *Ka Holomua,* November 8, 1913–November 21, 1914. Pa-pakilo Database.

Opio, S. F. Napua. "He Moolelo no Umi." *Ka Nupepa Kuokoa,* June 1, 1865. Papakilo Database.

Orliac, Catherine, and Michel Orliac. "Wooden Figurines of Easter Island." In *The Oxford Handbook of Prehistoric Figurines,* edited by Timothy Insoll, 613–634. New York: Oxford University Press, 2017.

Paepae o He'eia. "The Fishpond." paepaeoheeia.org.

Pakele, P. S. K. "Moolelo no ka hoonohonoho ana o na Alii Aiaupuni, a me ko lakou mau Akua o na Alii o ka Wa Kahiko mai Hawaii a Niihau." *Ka Nupepa Kuokoa,* November 12, 1864. Papakilo Database.

Papahānaumokuākea Marine National Monument. "About." https://www.papaha naumokuakea.gov/visit/.

Papakilo Database, Hawaiian Newspapers Collection. "About This Collection." https://www.papakilodatabase.com/pdnupepa/cgi-bin/pdnupepa?a=p&p =home.

Papamoa Maori School. "Patangata (Patuna)." In "Folk Tales from Papamoa." *Te Au Hou: The New World* 19 (August 1957): 43–45. Te Puna Mātauranga of Aotearoa. http://teaohou.natlib.govt.nz/journals/teaohou /search/results.html?text=taniwha.

"Pau Ole Ke Kuhi-Hewa." *Ka Nupepa Kuokoa,* February 15, 1862. Papakilo Database.

Pea, Gabriel Kalama. "Interview with Gabriel Kalama Pea, Andrew Poepoe, George Awai, and Mary Kawena Pukui." Bishop Museum Archive, Hono-lulu, June 21, 1959.

Perreira, Hiapokeikikāne Kitchie. "He Ha'i'ōlelo Ku'una: Nā Hi'ohi'ona me nā Ki'ina Ho'āla Hou i ke Kākā'ōlelo." PhD diss., University of Hawai'i, Hilo, 2011.

Phillipps, W. J. "Incised Designs, Koh Gorge Shelter, Near Waverly." *Journal of the Polynesian Society* 59, no. 2 (1950): 191–196.

Pinch, Geraldine. *Egyptian Mythology: A Guide to the Gods, Goddesses, and Traditions of Anicent Egypt.* Oxford: Oxford University Press, 2004.

Poepoe, Joseph Mokuohai. "Ka Moolelo Kaao o Hiiaka-i-ka-Poli-o-Pele." *Kuo-koa Home Rula,* January 10, 1908–January 20, 1911. Papakilo Database.

Poole, Jason. "Kapualei, the Mo'o of Kamalō (a legend of Molokai)." *Jason Poole* (blog), January 31, 2011. http://www.accidentalhawaiiancrooner .com/?p=3530.

Pooloa, Geo. "Heoahi [*sic*] ua Pohaku ana nei." *Ka Nupepa Kuokoa,* August 19, 1921. Papakilo Database.

————. "Na Aui o ke Au Kahiko," *Ka Nupepa Kuokoa,* October 15, 1925. Papakilo Database.

Porter, David. *Journal of a Cruise Made to the Pacific Ocean.* Vol. 1. New York: Wiley & Halsted, 1822. Internet Archive.

Prószyński, Jerzy. "A Survey of Havaika (Aranei: Salticidae), an Endemic Genus from Hawaii, including Descriptions of New Species." *Arthopoda Selecta* 16 (4): 195–213.

Pukui, Mary Kawena. *'Ōlelo No'eau: Hawaiian Proverbs and Poetical Sayings.* Bernice P. Bishop Special Publication no. 71. Honolulu: Bishop Museum Press, 1983.

Pukui, Mary Kawena, and Samuel H. Elbert. *Hawaiian Dictionary: Hawaiian-English, English-Hawaiian.* Rev. ed. Honolulu: University of Hawai'i Press, 1986. Ulukau.

Pukui, Mary Kawena, Samuel H. Elbert, and Esther Mookini. *Place Names of Hawai'i.* 2nd ed. Honolulu: University of Hawai'i Press, 1974.

Pukui, Mary Kawena, and Laura C. Green. *Folktales of Hawai'i: He Mau Ka'ao Hawai'i.* Honolulu: Bishop Museum Press, 2008.

Pukui, Mary Kawena, E. W. Haertig, and Catherine Lee. *Nānā I Ke Kumu (Look to the Source).* Vol. 1. Honolulu: Hui Hānai, 1972. Ulukau.

————. *Nānā I Ke Kumu (Look to the Source).* Vol. 2. Honolulu: Hui Hānai, 1979. Ulukau.

Punua, Ānuenue. "Transcript. Ānuenue Shares Mo'olelo of Meheanu." He'eia Fishpond, Kamehameha Schools Distance Learning Department. n.d. http://ksdl2.ksbe.edu/heeia/pdf/trans_legend01.pdf.

Ramsar. "USA Designates Site on Hawaiian Islands." ramsar.org.

Rice, Prudence M. "Serpents and Styles in Peten Postclassic Pottery." *American Anthropologist* 85 (1983): 866–880.

Rice, William Hyde. *Hawaiian Legends.* Honolulu: Bishop Museum Press, 1923.

————. "He Moolelo no Pele a me kona Kaikaina Hiiaka I Ka Poli o Pele." *Hoku o Hawaii,* May 21–September 10, 1908.

Richter-Gravier, Raphel. "Manu Narratives of Polynesia: A Comparative Study of Birds in 300 Traditional Polynesian Stories." Vol. 1. PhD diss., University of Otago, New Zealand; l'Université de la Polynésie français, Tahiti, March 2019.

Robineau, Claude. *Moorea.* Paris: Société des Océanistes, 1971.

Rose, Carol. *Giants, Monsters, and Dragons: An Encyclopedia of Folklore, Legend, and Myth.* New York: W. W. Norton, 2000.

Routledge, Katherine. *The Mystery of Easter Island: The Story of an Expedition.* London: Hazell, Watson and Viney, 1920. Internet Archive.

Ruatapu, Mohi, and Henare Potae. "Three Old Stories." Translated by Margaret Orbell. *Te Au Hou: The New World* 56 (September 1966): 18–22. Te
Puna Mātauranga of Aotearoa. http://teaohou.natlib.govt.nz/journals
/teaohou/search/results.html?text=lizards.

Russell, Jeffrey Burton. *The Devil in the New Testament.* Ithaca, NY: Cornell
University Press, 1977.

S. K. "Luahuna ma ke Kulaokaiwiula, Oahu." *Ka Nupepa Kuokoa,* March 26,
1897. Papakilo Database.

Seattle Art Museum. "Moko (Lizard Figure)." http://art.seattleartmuseum.org
/objects/5603/lizardman-figure-moai-moko.

Shortland, Edward. *Maori Religion and Mythology.* London: Longman's, Green,
1882.

Shultz, E. "Proverbial Expressions of the Samoans." *Journal of the Polynesian
Society* 59, no. 3 (1950): 207–231, 223.

Silva, Noenoe K. *Aloha Betrayed.* Durham, NC: Duke University Press, 2004.

———. *The Power of the Steel-Tipped Pen: Reconstructing Native Hawaiian
Intellectual History.* Durham, NC: Duke University Press, 2017.

Simon, Eugène. "Arachnida." Vol. 2, part 5, *Fauna Hawaiiensis or the Zoology
of the Sandwich (Hawaiian) Isles,* 443–519. Honolulu: Bishop Museum
Press, 1900. http://hbs.bishopmuseum.org/pubs-online/fh.html.

Singh, Manvier, Ted J. Kaptchuk, and Joseph Henrich. "Small Gods, Rituals,
and Cooperation: The Mentawai Crocodile Spirit *Sikaoinan.*" September
9, 2019. SocArXiv Papers. https://doi:10.31235/osf.io/npkdy.

Stanford Humanities Center. "What Are the Humanities?" n.d. http://shc.stanford
.edu/what-are-the-humanities.

Stejneger, Leonhard. "The Land Reptiles." In Vol. 21, *Proceedings of the
United States National Museum.* Washington, DC: Smithsonian Institution, 1899.

Sterling, Elspeth P., and Catherine C. Summers. *Sites of Oahu.* Honolulu: Bishop
Museum Press, 2001.

Stimson, John Francis, and Donald Stanley Marshall. *A Dictionary of Some
Tuamotuan Dialects of the Polynesian Language.* Salem: Peabody Museum, 1964.

Sturluson, Snomi, and Arthur Brodeur Gilchrist. *The Prose Edda.* New York:
American-Scandanavian Foundation, 1916. Internet Archive.

Suggs, Robert Carl. *The Archeology of Nuku Hiva, Marquesas Islands, French
Polynesia.* Vol. 49, part 1. New York: Anthropological Papers of the
American Museum of Natural History, 1961.

Tahiti Heritage. "Ana Piro, la grotte qui pue de la vallée de Papenoo." https://
www.tahitiheritage.pf/grotte-ana-piro-papenoo/.

———. "Légende du tiki du Moko (lézard)." n.d. https://www.tahitiheritage .pf/legende-fatutue-hiva-oa/.

———. "Météorite de Pere, Opurei a Pere—Papenoo." n.d. https://www .tahitiheritage.pf/meteorite-pere-papenoo/.

———. "Mo'o, le lézard du supermarché de Papara." n.d. https://www .tahitiheritage.pf/moo-lezard-supermarche-papara/.

———. "Queue du lézard de la Tuauru—Mahina." n.d. https://www .tahitiheritage.pf/queuelezard-tuauru/.

"The Taniwha of Wanganui River." *Te Au Hou: The New World* 39 (June 1962): 3–5. Te Puna Mātauranga of Aotearoa. http://teaohou.natlib.govt.nz/journals /teaohou/search/results.html?text=taniwha.

Taube, Karl Andreas. *Aztec and Maya Myths*. Austin: University of Texas Press, 1993.

———. *The Major Gods of Ancient Yucatan*. Washington, DC: Dumbarton Oaks Research Library and Collection, 1992.

Taupōuri, Tangarō. *Wahipana* (blog). 2011. http://hilo.hawaii.edu/blog/chancellor /files/2011/11/Wahipana.pdf.

Tava, Rerioterai, and Moses Keale Sr. *Niihau: The Traditions of an* [*sic*] *Hawaiian Island*. Honolulu: Mutual, 1990.

Taylor, Emma Ahuena. "Ku-Kahau-ula and Poliahu. The Betrothal of the Pink God and the Snow Goddess. The Pink Snow Is Always Seen upon Mauna Kea." *Paradise of the Pacific,* July 1931, 14–16.

"Te Rangihiroa: His Burial Marks the End of an Epoch." *Te Au Hou: The New World* 39 (Spring 1954): 34–40, 43. Te Puna Mātauranga of Aotearoa. http:// teaohou.natlib.govt.nz/journals/teaohou/search/results.html?text=lizard.

Te Reinga Maori School. "Hinekorako Mermaid of Te Reinga." In "Folk Tales from Papamoa." *Te Au Hou: The New World* 19 (August 1957): 45–46. Te Puna Mātauranga of Aotearoa. http://teaohou.natlib.govt.nz/journals /teaohou/search/results.html?text=taniwha.

Te Reinga Marae. "Our Story." Facebook. n.d. https://www.facebook.com/terein gamarae/.

Teriiteanuanua Manu-Tahi, Charles. *Te Parau Huna o Te Ao Maohi: Le Mystère de l'Univers Maohi*. Papeete, Tahiti: Editions Veia Rai, 1992.

Te Whetū, Karepa. "The Killing of Te Kaiwhakaruaki." Translated by Margaret Orbell. *Te Au Hou: The New World* 61 (December 1967): 5–8. Te Puna Mātauranga of Aotearoa. http://teaohou.natlib.govt.nz/journals/teaohou /search/results.html?text=lizards.

Thomas, John. "Interview with John Thomas, William Mills, Larry Kimura, Eleanor Williamson and Mary Kawena Pukui." Bishop Museum Archives, Honolulu, July 29, 1969.

Thomson, Basil. *The Fijians: The Study of the Decay of Custom.* London: M. Heineman, 1908.

Thrum, Thomas G., comp. *Hawaiian Folktales: A Collection of Native Legends.* Chicago: A. C. McClurge, 1907.

———. "Story of the Race of People Called the Menehune, of Kauai (a Hawaiian Tradition)." *Journal of the Polynesian Society* 29, no. 114 (1920): 70–75.

Titcomb, Margaret. *Native Use of Fish in Hawaii.* With the collaboration of Mary Kawena Pukui. Honolulu: University of Hawai'i Press, 1972, 127.

———. "Native Use of Marine Invertebrates in Old Hawaii." *Pacific Science* 32, no. 4 (1978): 325–386. ScholarSpace. http://hdl.handle.net/10125/1449.

Tregear, Edward. *The Maori-Polynesian Comparative Dictionary.* Wellington: Lyon and Blair, 1891. Internet Archive.

"Tukutuku at Tokomaru Bay." *Te Au Hou: The New World* 39 (September 1961): 24–27. Te Puna Mātauranga of Aotearoa. http://teaohou.natlib .govt.nz/journals/teaohou/search/results.html?text=taniwha.

Turner, George. *Samoa, a Hundred Years Ago and Long Before.* London: Mac-Millan, 1884. Google Books.

Tuvale, Te'o. "The Story of Pili and Sina." *An Account of Samoan History up to 1918.* N.p., 5–8. New Zealand Electronic Text Collection.

Untitled editorial. *Ka Nupepa Kuokoa,* June 11, 1897. Papakilo Database.

USGS (US Geological Survey). "Earth's Largest Active Volcano." https://volcanoes .usgs.gov/volcanoes/mauna_loa/geo_hist_summary.html.

Von den Steinen, Karl. "Maui's Fight with the Nanaa-Lizard." In *Marquesan Myths,* edited by Jennifer Terrell and translated by Marta Langridge. Canberra: Target Oceania/Journal of Pacific History, 1988.

W. I. M. "He Mele Hanau no ke Kama Alii Wohi Victoria Kaiulani Kawekiu o Lunalilo." *Ka Nupepa Kuokoa,* February 17, 24, March 3, 1877. Papakilo Database.

Wai Wai, David. "Waikaremoana." *Te Au Hou: The New World* 17 (December 1956): 44. Te Puna Mātauranga of Aotearoa. http://teaohou.natlib.govt .nz/journals/teaohou/search/results.html?text=taniwha.

Walpole, Frederick. *Four Years in the Pacific in Her Majesty's Ship "Collingwood." From 1844 to 1848.* Vol. 2. London: Richard Bently, 1849.

Westervelt, W. D. "Ke-Au-Nini." In *Legends of Gods and Ghosts.* Boston: Geo H. Ellis, 1915, 163–223. Google Books.

———. *Legends of Ma-ui—a Demi God of Polynesia, and of His Mother Hina.* Honolulu: Hawaiian Gazette, 1920. Google Books.

———. *Legends of Old Honolulu.* Boston: Geo H. Ellis, 1915. Google Books.

White, John. *The Ancient History of the Maori: His Mythology and Traditions.* Vol. 1. Wellington: George Didsbury, 1897.

Whitney, Henry M. *The Tourists' Guide through the Hawaiian Islands, Descriptive of Their Scenes and Scenery.* Honolulu: Henry M. Whitney, 1895. Google Books.

Wichman, Frederick B. *Kauaʻi, Ancient Place-Names and Their Stories.* Honolulu: University of Hawaiʻi Press, 1998.

Wilcox, Robert W. "Mookuauhau Alii, na Iwikuamoo o Hawaii Nei mai Kahiko mai." *Ka Makaainana,* July 27, August 3, 24, 1896. Papakilo Database.

Wilkes, Charles. *Narrative of the United States Exploring Expedition: During the Years of 1838, 1839, 1840, 1841, 1842.* Vol. 2. Philadelphia: Lea and Blanchard, 1842. Google Books.

Wise, John, and J. W. H. I. Kihe. "Kaao Hooniua Puuwai no Ka-Miki." *Ka Hoku o Hawaii,* January 8, 1914–December 6, 1917. Papakilo Database.

Wong, Kaleo. "Windward Y Ulupō Heiau, Loʻi and Kawainui Fishpond Restoration Project (2017 Togetherhood Project)." August 15, 2017. YouTube video.https://www.youtube.com/watch?reload=9&v=RHeGZjjg3Jk.

Zecchi, Marco. *Sobek of Shedet: The Crocodile God in the Fayyum in the Dynastic Period.* Todi, Italy: Tau Editrice, 2010.

Index

Page numbers in boldface refer to illustrations.

About the Author

MARIE ALOHALANI BROWN is associate professor in the Religion Department, specialist in Hawaiian religion, at the University of Hawai'i at Mānoa. She has a BA and MA in Hawaiian language and a PhD in English, specializing in Hawai'i-related literature from the Hawaiian Kingdom and Territorial eras, translation (theory and practice), folklore studies, and Indigenous theories and methodologies. She is an 'Ōiwi (Hawaiian) whose ancestral roots begin in Ho'okena at the foot of Mauna Loa volcano on Hawai'i Island and was raised in Mākaha on O'ahu. She is a world traveler (thirty-plus countries) and multilingual (English, Hawaiian, Italian, and French). Her first book, *Facing the Spears of Change: The Life and Legacy of John Papa 'Ī'ī* (2016), won the Ka Palapala Po'okela Award in 2017 for best book in the categories of Hawaiian language, culture, and history. She is co-editor, along with Cristina Bacchilega, of *The Penguin Book of Mermaids* (2019).